Privatization in Criminal Justice

Past, Present, and Future

David Shichor
California State University at San Bernardino

Michael J. Gilbert
University of Texas at San Antonio

anderson publishing co.
p.o. box 1576
cincinnati, oh 45201-1576
513-421-4142

Privatization in Criminal Justice: Past, Present, and Future

Copyright © 2001
Anderson Publishing Co.
2035 Reading Rd.
Cincinnati, OH 45202

Phone 800.582.7295 or 513.421.4142
Web Site www.andersonpublishing.com

Library of Congress Cataloging-in-Publication Data

Privatization in criminal justice : past, present, and future / David Shichor, Michael J. Gilbert [editors].
    p. cm.
  Includes bibliographical references and index.
  ISBN 1-58360-500-2 (pbk.)
  1. Prisons--United States. 2. Privatization--United States. 3. Corrections--Contracting out--United States. 4. Prisons--United States--Case studies. 5. Privatization--United States--Case studies. 6. Corrections--Contracting out--United States--Case studies. I. Shichor, David. II. Gilbert, Michael J., 1947-

HV9469 .P756 2000
365'.973--dc21

00-036354

Cover digital composition and design by Tin Box Studio, Inc.

EDITOR Gail Eccleston
ACQUISITIONS EDITOR Michael C. Braswell

Acknowledgments

The editors would like to thank each of the contributors for their research, hard work, perseverance, cooperation, and promptness in meeting deadlines. They maintained a positive attitude toward the project in spite of the frequent nagging by the editors. Since the authors of the chapters did most of the work, they are obviously responsible for all the shortcomings of their respective chapters. However, because our editorial suggestions undoubtedly enhanced their final product, we gracefully accept all the credit for the merits of the volume.

Seriously, it was an intellectually stimulating experience to collaborate with our contributors who made our editorial task relatively easy and definitely pleasant.

We also want to acknowledge the support and encouragement provided by our editors at Anderson Publishing Company—Mickey Braswell and Gail Eccleston.

Finally, we hope that the readers of this volume will benefit from the discussions in this book dealing with the important criminal justice policy issue of privatization.

Michael J. Gilbert
David Shichor

Table of Contents

Chapter 3
How Much Is Too Much Privatization in Criminal Justice?   41
Michael J. Gilbert

Part II
Privatization of Justice System Components   81

Chapter 4
Policing and the Private Security Option: Functional Transparency, Re-Privatization, and Implications in Law   83
James D. Calder

Chapter 5
Rent-a-Judge and Hide-a-Crime:
The Dark Potential of Private Adjudication   113
Steve Russell

Introduction

Private participation in the provision of public services including criminal justice is not a new phenomenon. That is especially true for countries having an Anglo-Saxon historical and cultural heritage. During the last two decades since the beginning of the Reagan and Thatcher administrations in the United States and the United Kingdom respectively, this trend has expanded in criminal justice. Currently, private companies not only continue their long-standing practice of supplying goods and services (food, medical care, education programs, etc.) to various components of the criminal justice system, but now they also control offenders. Thus, for-profit private companies and individuals are providing policing, inmate transportation, diversion programs, bail bonds, justice services, and management of confinement facilities—jails and prisons.

Undoubtedly, this wide-scale private participation in such basic government functions as the keeping of peace and rendering of justice, both of which involve life and death decisions (use of deadly force), loss of liberty and punishment of citizens have an impact not only on the criminal justice system, but on society as a whole. The chapters in this volume focus on the nature and extent of this impact on the criminal justice system in the United States.

There are four major parts in the book. Part I reviews the history and the general issues behind the growing use of privatization within criminal justice. Smith and Morn focus on the history of privatization across the justice system. Their discussion makes it clear that privatization in criminal justice has deep roots in the history of western culture. They document the existence of two justice systems, one for those with economic resources and one for those without. Historically, the private exercise of justice—policing, confinement, and prosecution—allowed affluent offenders to benefit from both more lenient treatment and a broader range of services. Stoltz analyzes the potential influence of private actors in the criminal justice system upon justice policymaking. She describes the development of subgovernments in various components of the criminal justice system. These subgovernments involve formal and informal relationships between public and private actors to influence public policy. Depending on the power balances, at different times and on different issues, one side may become more influential than the others in determining policy. The third chapter in this part, by Gilbert— "How Much Is Too Much Privatization in Criminal Justice" frames the boundary issues surrounding the use of privatization in criminal justice. He suggests a set of parameters defining appropriate and inappropriate forms of privatization and provides a model for understanding and managing the risks that come with privatization.

Part II focuses on privatization in various components of the criminal justice system. Calder provides a critical analysis of private policing and security. He shows how the distinction between public and private policing is becoming blurred. Traditional police functions are increasingly performed by corporations, while public police personnel are increasingly involved in providing services for private use. The author examines the legal implications of this blurring between public and private policing. In the chapter titled "Rent-a-Judge and Hide a Crime," Judge Russell describes the increasing trend toward use of private judges in resolving disputes without making them public. This is particularly attractive to corporations that have the ability to use the civil justice system in avoiding criminal procedures for their law and regulatory violations. This strategy, while helping to decrease the pressure on the criminal justice system, at the same time allows influential groups to maintain a positive public image. This manipulation is not open to the typical working-class clients of the criminal justice system.

Sechrest and Robby discuss public and private substance abuse treatment programs. The private sector has been extensively involved in offender treatment programs of all types for a long time. There is a proliferation of programs managed by both for-profit and non-profit (religious, self-help, and other) organizations. When it comes to treatment of offenders, those organizations operate under contract or agreement with government agencies or the courts. This relationship may involve direct public funding or payment by clients who are under court order. The authors' review identifies some differences in the operations of private for-profit, non-profit, and public treatment programs in spite of the fact that there are few direct comparisons available. Furthermore, because of large number of programs using a wide variety of treatment techniques, evaluations are sparse and difficult to conduct. But as the authors point out, evaluations are badly needed.

The chapter by Kiekbusch focuses on the unique character of jail privatization. Jails represent a large market that has been greatly underutilized by the private confinement industry. Kiekbusch documents the nature and scope of the current state of private sector jail operations and distinguishes it from prison privatization. Perhaps the most unique and important aspect of this chapter is Kiekbusch's analysis of the constraining factors that limit private sector involvement in operations. Yet, jails are probably the high dollar market of the future for criminal justice privatization.

Part III is devoted to a series of case studies about different experiences with criminal justice privatization. In "Not a True Partner: Local Politics and Jail Privatization in Frio County," Gilbert examines the political environment that replaced a public monopoly with a private monopoly over jail operations in a small county in Texas. He documents how inappropriate influences were exerted by a politically powerful contractor at the expense of public interests. Mobley and Geis follow the emergence of the flagship prison privatization company—Corrections Corporation of America (CCA)—and its complicated financial practices to maximize profits primarily for its management and major investors. Hallett and Lee describe CCA's political activities on its "home turf" to privatize to the entire Department of Corrections in the state of Tennessee. They reveal the conflicts of interest among influential political figures in the attempt to transfer the state corrections system into CCA's control.

The Cuvelier and Potts chapter is unique because it centers on a different facet of private involvement in justice processes. They describe how bail bond industry in Houston, Texas became concerned about public competition of release-on-recognizance policies and programs. From the perspective of the long-established private bail bond industry, nonmonetary release programs operated by public agencies endangered their market. The chapter documents the bail bond industry's attempt to discredit the public programs and solidify their industry.

Finally, Part IV consists of a chapter dedicated to methodological problems in the evaluation of privatization and an epilogue dealing with theoretical issues underlying the policy of private delivery of criminal justice services. Although Camp and Gaes focus their critique on evaluations of public and private prisons, many of the points raised are applicable to other aspects of the criminal justice system. This chapter may provide useful guidelines for future research in this field. The book concludes with a short epilogue by Shichor that addresses the historical, social, and political conditions that facilitated the movement toward privatization of public services in general, including criminal justice.

Our intention with this collection of selected essays was to ask questions that should be addressed when major policy decisions that may have far-reaching social, political, and economic impacts on society are made. We hope that the issues raised in these chapters will serve as food for thought for policymakers, researchers, and students, as well as the general public when privatization of justice functions are considered.

Part I

History and Development of Criminal Justice Privatization

1

The History
of Privatization
in Criminal Justice

Beverly A. Smith and Frank T. Morn
Illinois State University

Criminal justice today is typically considered to be a governmental matter. Agencies of criminal justice—police, courts, and prisons—are some of the most expensive services provided by local government. Also, these agencies are the strongest manifestations of governmental power in American life. They can deprive people of their liberty, and their very lives. Even if exonerated, those who go through the criminal justice system have considerable stigma attached. Consequently, the collective wisdom dictates that these be matters that transcend private people and vested interests. The symbol of justice remains a blindfolded goddess holding scales.

Furthermore, the operation of criminal justice agencies is expensive. In 1992, for example, federal, state, and local governments spent $94 billion on criminal justice systems. Forty-one billion dollars were spent on policing, with city governments leading the way. Thirty-two billion dollars were spent on corrections with state governments doing the most. The $21 billion spent on judicial and legal services was spread pretty evenly, with county governments slightly ahead. Still, according to public opinion polls, Americans felt that not enough was being spent (Flanagan, 1996:1-15). Moreover, they have been willing to see government pay private companies to do criminal justice functions. However, this is not the first time in American history we have turned to the private sector.

Privatization here means two things. First, it is the interface between private business and official criminal justice. In this context, businesses simply offer services to the people or to the government so as to replace or compliment governmental action. Profit motive inspires such actions. Instead of a government directly offering a service based upon taxation of the citizens, a private business would do so for a fee. This fee-for-service relationship reputedly has allowed for lower taxes and expanded free enterprise.

Second, privatization means the historic intrusion of the citizenry in place of government action. Historically, it was an obligation of good citizens to play significant roles in criminal justice. This obligation developed early in the Anglo-American tradition with, for example, the requirement that subjects of the king respond to a hue and cry to pursue a fleeing suspect. Democracy also expects and demands citizens be involved. Citizen involvement is necessitated by the widespread suspicions about not just the effectiveness of government, but also the opportunities government has to abuse its power. The criminal justice system is like a Frankenstein monster, created for good reasons but always carrying with it the potential for running amok and being a danger to the people. Many police states, past and present, have unbridled criminal justice systems. Restraints—be they principles of due process or citizen checks and balances—are in place for this reason. The founding people of the United States saw this danger and in the Bill of Rights created obstacles to an overly efficient criminal justice system. More than one-half of the Bill of Rights is directly related to governmental power in criminal justice. On the other hand, too much personal intrusion can be dangerous. It can be a narrow, vested interest at work. Both traditions, ideologically intertwined, run deep in American history.

It is the contention here that arguments today about privatization of criminal justice, either implicitly or explicitly, involve ancient and cherished beliefs that form much of the American psyche and much of our past. Examples of private police, prosecutors, and prisons abound. Still, one of the great historical revolutions of the eighteenth and nineteenth centuries was the increased involvement of government in criminal justice. This has been a bottom-up movement with the local governments being most active and the federal government coming on strong only in the twentieth century. Considerable discussion today centers on the rising importance of privatization in criminal justice. Indeed today's discussion seems too often to be couched in terms that imply privatization emerged only at the end of the twentieth century. Yet historically, private participation in criminal justice processes across the breadth of the system was once much more extensive than it is today. Therefore, any current discussions need to be informed by history to discover not only what "worked," but also why so much privatization developed.

First, there was America's place against the backdrop of other countries. Those civil law countries with well-developed and bureaucratic governments were early to develop official criminal justice systems (Merryman, 1985:1-14). For example, very early, France and Russia developed criminal justice systems that were broad and intrusive. Under Joseph Fouche, France became a spy state (Stead, 1983:46-53). Long before the Soviets, the Czars turned Russia into a police state (Monas, 1961:229-282). Often the Church and/or the military were early models upon which those justice systems were patterned. Frequently, these countries were overbearing and authoritarian; the criminal justice system was used to oppress and repress the citizenry. England had some dictatorial monarchs as well, but a tradition going back to the thirteenth century guaranteed some citizen participation and interference in the system. When the American colonies sought their independence, they turned English history on itself and took steps to restrict government even further.

Second, there was the age of the common man in America, a time starting with Andrew Jackson's presidency that enshrined the right, capability, and obligation of the ordinary person to be involved in all aspects of government, including what we would call criminal justice. This was the time when the private police were invented. Ironically, it was the time that modern policing was created as well. While juries were retreating slightly as a popular aspect of the system, the popular election of judges grew, insuring citizen input into justice. Some of the earliest excursions into juvenile justice—the houses of refuge (Smith, 1989) and the Children's Aid Society—were private in nature. In fact, when government failed, it was a moral imperative for ordinary citizens to step forth and see that justice be done (Friedman, 1993:61-82). Private citizens, in the name of good citizenry, could go too far, as in the rise of the regulator and vigilante movements (Ingalls, 1988) or lynch mobs (Brundage, 1993; Wright, 1990).

Third, there was economics. Establishing and maintaining police forces, running court systems, and building prisons have always been costly. In more parsimonious times there was a reluctance to expand government for a larger, more powerful government was seen as draining citizen power and money. When society was divided between the rich and the poor, the wealthy provided their own justice agencies. The poor were largely left to victimization at the hands of a succession of criminals from highway robbers to urban burglars. As the middle class arose, urban clerks and businessmen needed an orderly business environment and were willing, at least to some extent, to pay for that safety. Taxes on expanded business and personal income allowed for the growth of the modern criminal justice system. But there had to be a conjunction between a critical threat—be it real or just perceived—and disposable wealth before that modern criminal justice system was created (Friedman, 1993:107-108).

Fourth, there was America's development of a business ethic in the nineteenth and twentieth centuries (Cochran & Miller, 1961:129-150). As America became more commercial and industrial, it developed an attitude, a faith, in the principles and personalities of business (Hofstader, 1944:51-67). This country's rise to world power status in the last third of the nineteenth century seemed to validate those principles. Challenged during the Progressive era, the power of business regained its strength during the prosperity of the 1920s. The shock of the Great Depression was followed by the military successes of World War II and the post-war prosperity, which gave new life to business. Many felt that other institutions besides business—such as universities and government—could be run more effectively by business people or principles.

Fifth, much of this can be seen against the backdrop of political ideologies, broadly defined here as liberal and conservative. In those times of a more liberal zeitgeist, people tended to favor greater governmental growth in all spheres including criminal justice. It was in the Jacksonian era that the police and penitentiary movements arose. In the post-Civil War period, conservatives who ruled insisted on governmental laissez-faire and privatization. The liberal Progressive era saw the rise of the federal police and a flurry of prison building. During the next 20 years, largely due to the apparent humiliation of the conservative crusade called Prohibition, and the crisis of gangsters in the cities, some back-peddling occurred as many conservatives saw advantages of criminal justice expansion. The real rise of the FBI occurred under J. Edgar Hoover at this time (Theoharis & Cox, 1988). The Federal Bureau of Prisons was created, too (Keve, 1991).

After World War II, the liberals and conservatives both wanted to use criminal justice extensively—liberals, to rehabilitate criminals, and conservatives, to control them. Certainly since the 1980s, however, starting, if not with Reagan's governorship of California, certainly with his presidency, there has been a growing conservatism in America. Even the liberals have moved right. There is a desire to downsize government. While most are reluctant to translate that to criminal justice—witness the growth of federal criminal justice in all areas—the current privatization movement is part of that reaction (Donziger, 1996; Walker, 1980:234-238).

Law Enforcement

English Background

Certainly one of the more powerful manifestations of governmental power is law enforcement. Going back to medieval England, there was a tendency to have a dual system. Ordinary citizens were to monopolize local justice. The monarch was in charge of a limited self-serving national system. The English frankpledge system required groups of 10 families called tithings to uphold the law. The Statute of Winchester, enacted in

1285, set up a constable/night watch system. Locally elected constables supervised citizenry law enforcement during the day. Locally obtained watchmen cared for the town at night when "good people" were supposed to be asleep. If either the constable or watchman needed assistance, he could raise the hue and cry, a principle that required all able-bodied citizens to come to his aid. By law, citizens were required to maintain weapons in their homes so as to be able to assume policing or military duties quickly. The only real government officials representing the "King's Peace" (protection of special places and people such as the highways, forest preserves, and holy spots) were the sheriffs. They, too, could demand citizen participation within the concept of posse comitatus, the right of sheriffs to summon all males more than 15 years of age to assist in keeping the peace or arresting felons. With even this measure of power came the hint of possible corruption. If folklore serves us well, these sheriffs could be hated and the crooks could be seen as folk heroes. Robin Hood's arch enemy after all was the Sheriff of Nottingham (Radzinowicz, 1956:12).

Indeed, by the seventeenth century, criminal heroes—the highwaymen—were such a problem that the central government passed the Highwayman Act of 1692, which offered financial incentives to citizens aiding in the apprehension and conviction of such crooks. The unintended consequence of this Act was the rise of the thief-takers, men who made a living catching criminals just to recover the rewards. One such thief-taker was Jonathan Wild, who amassed a fortune as a private crime fighter. However, to maintain a profit margin, Wild resorted to several practices that would bring him down. First, he encouraged some people to commit crimes just to turn around and capture them for the reward. Second, he acted as an intermediary, negotiating deals for the return of stolen goods and taking part of the money as a fee. Third, he became a receiver of stolen goods at a time when anti-fencing laws had been passed. This made him a head of a criminal syndicate in London. When he was discovered and executed, members of the crowd pelted him with stones and scorn (Pringle, 1958:9, 216; Howson, 1970:34-36).

One of those in that crowd was Henry Fielding, a novelist and magistrate at Bow Street. He saw the dangers of the private thief-taker movement and even wrote a history of Jonathan Wild. As a judge at Bow Street, he needed people to help him keep order in the court, chase down witnesses, and serve legal papers. Fielding created a group of Runners and moved to a more public policing system. The Bow Street Runners, however, were not across the whole of London, much less the country. Besides, they were under judicial direction, really answerable only to Fielding. They were semi-official, the private officers of one judge (Armitage, 1932:58, 61, 64). The jump to a public police force, once controlled by the executive branch, had not yet been made. Of course, the thief-takers and Runners lasted to the nineteenth century, but as society became more urban, the need for controlling the masses called into being Robert Peel's London Metropolitan police in 1829, the prototype of America's modern police.

America

In colonial America much of the policing was informal, generally based upon historic English notions. In New England there were some religious twists added by the more puritanical values. For example, in Massachusetts the legal system was inquisitorial; confession was good for the soul and for one's legal standing. Punishment was almost biblically retributive. A sheriff system existed mainly in the South, but it was in the hands of the planter class. North and South, there were constable-night watch systems based upon citizen participation in the larger communities, but those were generally considered inept (Richardson, 1974:3-19).

One development in the eighteenth-century South is suggestive. In the 1760s, the backcountry of South Carolina was overrun with Indians, rustlers, and vagrants. Petitions sent to Charleston for sheriffs, county courts, and jails went unheeded. Petitions to London were also ignored. Consequently, people of property and standing in the backcountry formed a private criminal justice system called the "Regulators." These Regulators became a self-contained criminal justice system. Packs of men on horseback chased the criminal classes. After capture, the Regulators became a court and, if necessary by their own terms, an execution squad. Once the region was free of crime, the Regulators turned upon the vagrants setting up work camps and forced the inhabitants into enslavement. Authorities in Charleston were angered by such bold extralegal activity; a counter force called the "Moderators" was set up. Then the countryside was threatened with civil war. The emergency was averted when Charleston relented and the backcountry got its sheriffs, courts, and jails. But a valuable lesson was learned on the eve of the American Revolution, and that was when the legally constituted authority was weak or corrupt the citizens could revolt and set up their own systems of justice. Outside of South Carolina, and well into the middle of the nineteenth century, Regulator movements would continue to pop up. Later they took on a new name—"Vigilantes" (Brown, 1975:95-96).

By the mid-nineteenth century, the modern police—starting in the eastern cities but growing westward—had become established. Not everyone accepted the idea of armed, uniformed policing at public expense. Furthermore, there were some crimes—especially those that moved across expansive territories and jurisdictions—that could not be handled by municipal police. One such crime was employee theft in the railroad industry. In Chicago, six railroad owners commissioned Allan Pinkerton, a local deputy in the Cook County sheriff's department, to offer special protection to the railroads. While private people had been "doing justice" to protect their own property, Allan Pinkerton founded an agency to profit by protecting other people's property. Pinkerton's Northwest Police Agency sought out crooked conductors and work-men for the railroads. After the Civil War, Pinkerton's business expand-ed to chasing railroad robbers like the James brothers, the Youngers, and the Daltons—all gangs that had robbed trains, but also terrorized com-munities. Soon, bankers through American Bankers Association and jewelers through the Jewelers Security Alliance had Pinkerton chase bank robbers and jewel thieves. When organized labor began to disrupt industry with demands and strikes, the Pinkertons were hired to protect property, and infiltrate and expose unions. In some cities, Pinkerton pro-vided a watchman service that walked the streets and competed with the municipal police patrolman (Morn, 1982:17-34, 68-90).

The private police were a boon to a country with weak and politi-cized city police and largely non-existent state and federal police. How-ever, the Pinkertons were quickly embroiled in trouble. For example, their pursuit of crooked conductors was interpreted as the beginnings of class warfare—the capitalist vs. the worker. Something seemed un-American about spying on the workers. Also, even the cornerstone of Pinkerton's fame, chasing bank robbers, which had once seemed nec-essary, even objective, turned personal and vengeful when the James gang killed two Pinkerton detectives. Then Allan Pinkerton condoned the raiding and burning of the home of the bandits' mother and, in effect, altered the equation; the James brothers became Robin Hoods of the West and the Pinkertons became villains. Labor work had its own ugliest chapter at Homestead, Pennsylvania, when hundreds of Pinker-ton strike breakers were confronted by rebellious workers. The army had to be called out to quash the riots and rescue the scabs. Congres-sional hearings, the first to analyze the private police in America, result-ed. State legislatures passed a host of so-called "Pinkerton Laws," for-bidding agency use of such armies. It seemed clear that the Pinkertons were successful because they had few legal restraints upon them and their procedures; but that also made them a danger (Morn, 1982:91-109).

As Pinkerton successes, however, far outweighed their notoriety, numerous other detective agencies sprang up. Some had the scope and success of the Pinkertons, but most were small agencies doing divorce work. During the Progressive era, many agencies that had arisen to spe-cialize in labor work precipitated more Congressional investigations and stigma in the 1930s. Private police showed two faces to the public. On one hand, they offered efficient law enforcement at a cheap price to those citizens with at least some property. Those who had the most property to protect paid the greater fees. Furthermore, the agents seemed glamorous and became a part of popular culture. On the other hand, these agencies did little for the masses and in the name of special interests assumed a villainous position in relation to the working poor (Huberman, 1937:32-50).

Certainly, in the frontier regions of the West citizens joined together to fight crime (Ball, 1981:2-10). The Anti-Horse Thief Associations, for example, were formed to seek out horse thieves, or to hire others to do so, and bring them to justice. These organizations lasted to the twentieth century when they reinvented themselves as Anti Automobile Theft Associations. Cattlemen's Associations would hire and retain range detectives to seek out rustlers and trespassers. Some like Tom Horn in Wyoming and William Bonney, otherwise known as Billy the Kid, in New Mexico became more notorious for their criminality than any law enforcement abilities (McGrath, 1972:247-267). One solution to the weak criminal justice systems in the West and the need to confront criminals was the rise and importance of the reward system. Bounties were placed upon the heads of criminals to encourage citizens to take part in law enforcement. As might be expected, a class of bounty hunters developed that traced and chased known criminals, while ignoring the few rules of law that applied to sworn officers (Traub, 1988:300).

Another example in the West was the rise of Committees of Vigilance. In the beginning of the 1850s, San Francisco was inundated with people seeking fortunes in the gold fields. Some Australian criminals, called the Sydney Ducks, settled in a section of San Francisco and threatened to bully the population as a whole. The existing police system was weak and corrupt. Consequently, a group of businessmen created a Committee of Vigilance, very similar to the Regulator movements of earlier times, and chased out the criminal element. Some criminals fled, while others were brought up on charges before a vigilance court and punished. The notion spread throughout the mining regions of the West (Hafen, 1961:441-451).

Other examples abound. Anthony Comstock, angry over the extent of vice and corruption in the cities, formed the Society for the Prevention of Vice, sort of a morals police. He and his agents went into vice districts to spy on brothels, casinos, and back-alley abortionists. Not above conducting his own raids, Comstock also complained to the police and forced them to make arrests. Other organizations arose to wage purity crusades against, for example, opium dens or roadhouses catering to adolescents (Pivar, 1973:109, 116, 161).

In short, in the nineteenth century—a period of time with weak, corrupt, or non-existent law enforcement—private individuals were responsible for much policing. On one hand, forces such as profit and self-interest resulted in much success. Clearly, the Pinkertons were held in high regard by the middle and upper classes. Sons of Allan Pinkerton, William and Robert, became charter members of the International Association of Chiefs of Police. On the other hand, law enforcement was uneven. People got what they paid for, and only the rich could afford the benefits of the private police. Whether it was the Pinkertons, the Vigilance Committees, or Comstock's crowd, the privatization movement was for the special interests. When the lower classes resorted to such means, it was declared a threat, a riot. Furthermore, for much of the nineteenth century these private movements went unchecked and unregulated. Only with the rise of a more regulatory nation in the twentieth century did these organizations come under governmental scrutiny. Many went out of existence. Others—such as the Pinkertons—made substantial changes in the types of services they offered. While the Pinkertons still offered limited policing services, they became much more of a watchman service, leaving most of what they did in the nineteenth century to the official police of the twentieth.

But the concept remained and haunted governmental policing. That the private police and private citizens took policing into their own hands was an indictment of the public police. In short, when the government could not do the job, private citizens would step in and do it for themselves.

Prosecutions

English and Colonial Background

Today, Americans would probably see the term "private prosecutions" as an oxymoron, for they have become accustomed to thinking of prosecutors, under a variety of names, as paid by the state, ensconced in governmental bureaucracies, and often chosen for office in partisan elections. In what is most often described as an adversarial process, prosecutors represent the victims of crimes, and by extension the state or society as a whole. The rhetorical priority given to actual, individual victims, a visible if not real success of the last 20 years of the victims' rights movement, disguises the fact that prosecutors must balance the personal harm inflicted against the financial and bureaucratic interests of the state. Most notably prosecutors juggle their priorities in plea-bargaining and the exercise of prosecutorial discretion. Yet one more role is expected of public prosecutors. That is the tempering of private revenge, which could prove costly to societal peace. Our unwritten social contract has given state's attorneys, district attorneys, county prosecutors, and so on the right and duty to avenge in circumscribed, predetermined ways the criminal wrongs committed against private citizens, who retain the right to seek monetary redress in civil court.

American public prosecutors, at local, state, and federal levels, are like so much else about our system. They are an admixture of our colonial patterns, rather than an exact copy of only one. In the English adversarial system, to which a greater debt is owed, the same barristers act as both prosecutors and defense attorneys. In other words, a Queen's or King's counsel may prosecute in one trial and defend in another. The continental or inquisitorial system, handed down through Dutch and French colonies, features prosecutors who are state bureaucrats with special obligations toward more abstract entities such as justice or fairness. Despite the emphases on fairness or objectivity and even-handed justice rather than bloody revenge, the American system derives from one more, even older model. In colonial and early republican times, private prosecutors appeared in American criminal courts as paid representatives of victims or their families.

But private prosecutions have been much less prominent than certainly private policing, and even private corrections. It appears that "[p]rivate prosecution dominated criminal justice during the colonial period" (Steinberg, 1984:571). Having brought a complaint to a justice of the peace or magistrate, the private prosecutor paid fees, arranged for witnesses, and hired an attorney. Private prosecutors then were an amalgam of police, witness, and prosecutorial roles. While private prosecutions took place in pre-Revolutionary Massachusetts, New York, Connecticut, and Virginia, it is not surprising that its fullest example was in Pennsylvania with its Quaker tradition of arbitration (Steinberg, 1984:571).

Nineteenth-Century and Later Patterns

The practice of private policing continued after the colonial period, in part, out of necessity. "In the absence of an effective or professionalized police force, law enforcement became the responsibility of a community's residents, and the mechanism they used was the one remaining from the eighteenth-century town—the private criminal suit instituted in the office of the neighborhood alderman" (Steinberg, 1984:572). Unsalaried aldermen received a fee for each complaint. Drunkenness, disorderly conduct, lesser assaults, and petty thefts were either dealt with exclusively by the aldermen in summary judgment or passed through their offices. On a less practical level, private prosecutions were exercises of citizen responsibility and examples of direct access to government.

That access came at a price. Only those who could afford the fees could take their cases to the threshold of the system. Dependent on fees, Philadelphia aldermen had few incentives to stop even frivolous cases or cases involving petty personal disagreements (Steinberg, 1989). Public prosecutors, linked to a public police by the mid-nineteenth century, took over first murders, then serious felonies, and still later a greater range of crimes. Private individuals were deemed less capable of dealing with public order in an increasingly complex urban society. And Philadelphia set the standard for the rest of the state. By contrast, public prosecutors were seen as worthy, or at least more worthy, of the public trust and more capable of exercising wide discretion (Steinberg, 1984:585).

A place for private prosecutions did not completely disappear, however, in the nineteenth or even the late twentieth centuries, especially in less urban areas. In a historical study based largely in the Midwest and border states, Robert Ireland (1995) argues that private prosecutors, paid by victims and/or their families, acted as assistant prosecutors and sometimes as sole prosecutors, in part because the law did not specifically bar their participation. But only those who could pay attorneys could afford that extra measure of justice.

Those private attorneys, acting nominally for the state, could determine whether defendants were convicted. In reputation and in fact, public prosecutors were not the best lawyers in the courtrooms. Without salaried assistants, young, inexperienced, and sometimes old, bumbling prosecutors faced alone more competent, much better paid opposing defense teams. Most clearly in murder trials, over other felony cases, public prosecutors were supplemented by private counsel. Fraternal, family, and political ties may have led to some of the support, but money also played a role. For example, in 1850 the Parkman family paid assistants who helped the attorney general prosecute Harvard professor John White Webster for the murder of Dr. George Parkman. And railroad companies hired at least some of the lawyers in the 1883 Missouri trial of the James brothers (Ireland, 1995:46).

After the Civil War, appellate courts took opposing sides over the legality of private prosecutions or privately paid prosecutions. Courts in Massachusetts, Michigan, and Wisconsin saw those lawyers as an intrusion in the process, one which threatened trial impartiality. But North Dakota's supreme court argued that prosecutors were already zealous advocates for their position (Ireland, 1995:49-51). Crime commission reports and academic studies of prosecution offices in the 1920s and 1930s did little to dispel the image of public prosecutors as inexperienced, incompetent, or even corrupt. Accordingly, in this century the courts in only four more states (as of 1991) have specifically invalidated or barred privately funded prosecutions. Unless the courts or state legislatures actually outlaw the practice, privately funded prosecutors can continue in American courtrooms.

Corrections

Introduction

Private policing has both preceded and co-existed with public policing. Private prosecutions have enjoyed a persistent, if rarely noted, longevity. By contrast, the history of private corrections is an interrupted saga. Having flourished in the nineteenth and early twentieth centuries, private adult corrections disappeared under the weight of prisoner abuse scandals, labor union opposition, and job scarcity in the Great Depression. In altered form, the practice has reappeared near the close of this century. But the lessons of 200, 100, even 70 years ago seem to have been lost or, at the very least, remembered selectively. The assumption has too often been that American corrections has followed an innovative, progressive path—from inhumane to humane, from brutal to, if not benign, at least beneficial, and from amateurish to professional. Self-congratulation and self-deception have led each generation to an unwarranted confidence that its ideas are "new" and that any revival of a past practice will inevitably be "better" than was its first incarnation (Pisciotta, 1994).

Those assumptions are not based on historical fact. Prison reform has been piecemeal, uneven, and sometimes detrimental. One of the most vaunted reforms of early nineteenth-century prisons was the implementation of prison industries, which meant the investment of private capital and the daily involvement of private entrepreneurs or their agents in the affairs of prisons. Early crafts and later industries were lauded as a means to occupy otherwise idle, troublesome prisoners; train inmates in skills and industrial discipline; and make prisons less onerous financial burdens on the state. These arguments appeared as early as the end of the eighteenth century when the Philadelphia Society for Alleviating the Miseries of Public Prisons (soon after renamed the Philadelphia Prison Society) saw to it that the Walnut Street Jail instituted prisoner labor for profit, along with other changes (Meranze, 1996:144).[1] The rhetoric of reformers who first praised the educational value of correctional labor was echoed by politicians whose electoral successes were tied to keeping both expenses and taxes low. It is simplistic to see private corrections as solely the dream of reformers, for it was soon to become their nightmare. Nor was it just the ploy of cynical politicians. The first rise and fall of private corrections were also firmly embedded in the social and economic conditions of the time. Racism, nativism, industrialization, urbanization, and labor force changes all played their own intertwined roles (Ayers, 1984; Gardner, 1987).

The rise of the American prison from the Walnut Street Jail (Meranze, 1996) through the Auburn Penitentiary (Colvin, 1997) and the Elmira Reformatory (Pisciotta, 1994) more than just coincided with the rise of the United States as a nineteenth-century industrial power. The two were linked on both philosophical and practical levels. It has been argued at length (Rothman, 1971) that the industrial prison was a disciplinary tool aimed at its own prisoners and the urban working classes as a whole. The prison removed disruptive criminal elements from the working classes, who then, it was argued at the time, would be more obedient, and therefore more productive, workers. In the industrial prison, inmates were to learn job skills, a work ethic, and a lasting discipline which were all to make them productive, law-abiding citizens upon release. In other words, prisoner rehabilitation, institutional control, and recidivism prevention were key reasons for the introduction of industrial production in prisons. Yet that industrial production, or prison labor, was in the hands of private citizens and the pockets of private capital.

Customarily prison labor has been divided into five categories or types: the lease, the contract, the piece-price, the state account, and the state use. All but the last involved production for sale in the open or free market. State use, the dominant type of prison labor or industry for more than the last 50 years, features use of its products in the prisons of origin and/or other state institutions such as mental facilities. State account industries used prisoner labor, were carried out on state property or in state institutions, and were directed or managed solely by state salaried personnel. State account products were sold in the open market, and any money derived was to go into state accounts, as the name implied. Labor union opposition to much cheaper prisoner labor, manufacturers' cries of unfair market competition from prison-made goods, and consumer rejection of low-quality products led to the 1929 Hawes-Cooper Act which banned the interstate shipment of prison made goods (Conley, 1980; Hougen, 1977). Both state use and state account were, as their names indicate, state enterprises. The other three types of prison industry or labor—contract, the related piece price, and leasing—were private corrections.

Private Corrections in the Nineteenth and Early Twentieth Centuries

Contract labor had certain basic elements. As the name implied, it was predicated on "a legal agreement between the state and a private party for the labor of convicts to be performed within the prison walls for a specific price per day per man over a term of years" (Gildemeister, 1987:33-34). Each side brought something to the table. "In most cases, the state provided suitable workshops, building maintenance, food, clothing, medical care, religious instruction, and security. Contractors, in turn, provided raw materials, tools, mechanics, and shop instructors" (Gildemeister, 1987:34). In the piece-price variation on contract labor, private businessmen contracted for monopolies to buy and market prisoner-made goods at a certain price per item or product, rather than "renting" an entire workforce. When businesses went bankrupt, supplies were depleted, prices fell, or more favorable prison contracts were signed by other states, some contractors defaulted on their agreements. Prison administrators were left to contend with even higher levels of inmate idleness, while state officials faced budget shortfalls. But even when the contracts remained in place, there was a subtle power differential in favor of the contractors. Prison personnel from officers to wardens were political appointees who would sometimes even have to leave their institutions to campaign for their patrons. Contractors, whose leases could stretch across more than one gubernatorial term, had their own political power, through friends, business associates, and their own positions as former, prospective, and even present officeholders.

As industries and products changed over time, short-term leases, one or two years, offered the greatest chances for product flexibility; yet those same short leases often presaged instability and tension within the institutions as staffs, inmates, and company representatives were forced to build new, not-always-friendly relationships. Longer-term leases of 7, 8, 10, or more years meant fewer uncertainties, but also a lesser ability to react to market trends. Contract labor over the course of the nineteenth and early twentieth centuries did move from crafts such as hatting, shoemaking, and coopering (i.e., barrel making) to trade industries relying on machinery. Coopering, for example, enjoyed some financial success with the demand from the oil industry and with the need to move food in quantity from rural areas, where many of the prisons had been built, to the cities. Later prisons manufactured bricks, milled lumber, and turned out machine tool parts, for example.

Shoemaking could be broken down into component parts that required little training, but as machinery became increasingly involved in that process, as well as others, the work became more dangerous. Injuries that convicts sustained in the shops engendered some of the criticism leveled against contract labor. Angered by shop and overall prison conditions, inmates sabotaged machinery, engaged in work stoppages, and set arson fires that bankrupted uninsured contractors, broke annual state budgets when replacements had to be undertaken, and left whole prison populations, already unruly, also idle. There was also no way to predict market changes. For example, the Civil War meant higher prices for shoes sold to the military, yet the shoe industry lost markets when sales to slave plantations and Southern prisons were cut off (Walker, 1988:17). The greater the demand, the harder it was for contractors to walk the fine line between incentives, which quickly could turn to contraband bribes, and punishment, in the forms of whippings, torturous cold showers, and solitary, which most state legislatures had allowed only officers and administrative staff to carry out. On a day-to-day basis, however, many prisons left discipline within the shops to the private contractors (Colvin, 1997:97-98; Staples, 1990:386-87).

Extensive punishment to exact productivity, injuries and deaths during production, smuggled contraband, convict bartering with expropriated shop products, arson fires, and other inmate resistance made the contract labor system vulnerable from within. From without, both businesses, competing with contract industries for raw materials or markets, and emerging unions, feeling their demands for shorter workdays and workweeks and for higher wages undercut, saw contract labor and its products as unfair, state-subsidized competition. Yet contract labor represented the status quo and was not easily displaced. By the beginning of the last decade of the nineteenth century, six Northern, largely industrial states had supposedly abolished contract labor, but multi-year leases and paperwork manipulation continued the practice beyond its formal abolition (Colvin, 1997; Pisciotta, 1994).

Contract or inmate leasing, if anything, had more "lives" and cost more lives in the South from the Confederacy's defeat until the heart of the Great Depression (Fierce, 1994). As Martha Myers argues, the public learned, admittedly in bits and pieces, about the cruelty, deadly epidemics, and degradation experienced by leased convicts. "The most egregious rule violations took the forms of unauthorized subleasing, inhumane conditions, and excessive brutality. But most damaging was evidence of nepotism, neglect of duty by prison commissioners, and conflicts of interest involving state employees" (Myers, 1998:20). Prosecutions, sentences, and paroles were all manipulated to ensure a supply of a disproportionately high number of black inmates, in what some have seen as replication of or an economic replacement for slavery without a capital investment in workers. The Thirteenth Amendment, ratified in 1865, had freed the slaves, but penal servitude and peonage were used to keep a ready, cheap supply of black labor in the South, first to rebuild after wartime destruction, then to develop industries and roads. Southern prisoners in county jails and in state custody were leased to private contractors, who were responsible for housing, feeding, disciplining, and guarding them at privately owned sites. Minimal care and safety were to be assured by state-appointed inspectors or commissioners, men who at worst profited monetarily and politically from leasing and at best issued critical reports that fell on ears deafened by political self-interest. Reformers like Julia Tutwiler and muckraking journalists made minor inroads for change, but humanitarian cries had limited impact in a region of lynchings, Jim Crow laws, and intensive child labor (Mancini, 1996:215). Convict leasing had to outlive its usefulness.

Only Virginia, which made capital investments in actual buildings, was able to escape the worst of convict leasing (Keve, 1986). Other Southern states had either not built prisons to house their relatively few white felons or had seen their prisons destroyed during the Civil War. Cash-poor states put rebuilding railroads, building industries, or creating a steady supply of raw materials for those industries ahead of constructing prisons on the Northern model. Matthew J. Mancini (1996:131) has described how "a familiar tale" beginning with decisions "to lease out of desperation" soon became "an institutionalized addiction."

It is impossible here to outline the individual histories of either leasing or its abolition in all the states that used that form of prison industry/labor. Each had its own twists and turns. But certain stories are particularly illustrative. Mancini (1996:153) describes convict leasing in

Tennessee as Hobbesian—"fittingly nasty, brutish, and short." During the quarter of a century, 1871 to 1896, that leasing existed, convicts were sent first sent to rebuild and expand the railroads and to carry out other tasks including mining. After 1883, mining dominated convict leasing, and preeminence in that industry went to the Tennessee Coal and Iron Company, which later became part of United States Steel. Through its subleases TCI convicts were spread across several mining camps where flogging enforced daily quotas and prisoners slept in coal-begrimed clothes until the rags literally dropped off their backs. Yet in Tennessee "humanitarian indignation was almost absent" (Mancini, 1996:153).

If public outcries were absent, why then did convict leasing end in Tennessee after only 25 years, while it lasted into the twentieth century in eight other Southern states (Fierce, 1994:193)? The answer to that question lay in the concentration of convicts in mining, an industry hit hard during the economic depression of the early 1890s. Even more instrumental was the fervent opposition of free miners who saw convict miners as a drain on their wages and as strikebreakers. Miners were, after all, one of the first, most ardent worker groups to unionize nationwide. Angry Tennessee miners took over convict stockades by force. The first stockade taken and its adjacent buildings were spared, and its prisoners were placed in boxcars for shipment to the state capital at Knoxville (Daniel, 1975). As the conflict escalated, stockades were burned and armed battles broke out between free miners and the militia. Both TCI and the state wanted out of their relationship. Leasing was abolished under an 1893 law, but as was so often the case, it did not end until the expiration of the last lease three years later. "Had convict leasing in Tennessee been providing labor to diverse firms engaged in sundry forms of extraction, construction, or farming, as happened elsewhere, the demand for convict labor could have been much more elastic" (Mancini, 1996:166). And convict leasing would have lasted longer, as it did in Alabama or Georgia.

When TCI ended its lease in Tennessee it still had 1,500 coal miners in the north-central Alabama, supplying the iron mills of Birmingham (Mancini, 1996:166). Injuries and explosions punctuated the history of convict leasing in its coal mines. But the most horrific explosion did not take place in a TCI mine. The Pratt Company's Banner coal mine blew up in April, 1911, killing 122 convict and 6 free miners (Ward & Rogers, 1987). Virtually all the dead Banner miners, free and convict, had been black. The deaths of so many African-Americans was not enough to end leasing. It took the 1924 death of a white, out-of-state convict to bring about the 1928 abolition. His death during a cold shower punishment was made doubly powerful because it was first disguised as a suicide by camp authorities. An anti-leasing gubernatorial candidate won his election and once in office moved prisoners 100 at a time from the mines to a state-owned, state-run prison farm (Mancini, 1996:113-116).

Huge prison farms also marked the end of convict leasing in Mississippi (Taylor, 1993), Louisiana (Carleton, 1971), and Arkansas (Ledbetter, 1993). In 1912 the governor of Arkansas, desperate to end leasing, began wholesale paroles to force the legislature's hand. Equally well-meaning men would soon come to see the "cure"—prison farms, just as bad as the "disease"—convict leasing. Only prison farms were the direct and full-time responsibility of the states. Just the names of those state-account, then state-use farms—Parchman, Angola, and Cummins respectively—have come to symbolize torture, barbarity, and corruption. As much as state officials wanted to publicize their changes as humane, honorable reforms, the choice had really been made primarily on fiscal grounds. In Georgia, for example, the last 20 years of convict leasing showed "mounting criticism, deepening institutional entrenchment, ideological defensiveness, worsening conditions, and . . . signs of concerted convict resistance" (Mancini, 1996:93; *see also* Daniel, 1972).

When the national good roads movement reached Georgia, the lessees' coal mines were petering out. It seemed logical to put convict labor to state use in building and maintaining highways where the chain gangs were the public equivalent of private leasing (Myers, 1998:20-21). The "gradual construction of alternative methods of wringing wealth from convicts' muscles" (Mancini, 1996:181), journalistic outcries, and corruption scandals were not enough to bring down leasing. That happened only when the bottom dropped out of the labor market and made low-paid free workers, who could be fired rather than maintained at company expense, a more desirable alternative than leased convicts. In Texas, free workers were doubly attractive when the bottom also dropped out of the labor-intensive sugar cane industry (Walker, 1988).

In North Carolina, convict leasing and chain gangs seemed to have appeared at the county level first. Inmates sentenced to even 20 years were kept at the county level to serve on county farmlands or roadways. As a result, the state felt shortchanged and unable to negotiate favorable leases without a ready labor force (Hawkins, 1983). The heritage of this very open struggle between state prison authorities and county officials has had long-lasting effects. Young people and women, often the most vulnerable in leasing programs, were also less valuable to local officials who were that much more willing to turn them over to the state. Faced with those inmate populations, the state built institutions to house them. The state offered sanctuary, by comparison, from exhausting road work and brutish sheriffs. When North Carolina made the gradual shift to farms, it did so on a smaller scale with scattered institutions. Those farms and camps were the basis for the state's smaller, dispersed prisons, at least into the 1980s, a century after leasing took hold. Farms, unlike roads and rails, could employ youth and women in what was generally considered to be less strenuous work for prisoners accustomed to rural life. The isolation of scattered farms was also assumed to make escape less attractive. North Carolina centralized its administration of those scattered prison farms and camps in 1933, the same year it abolished leases.

Florida is the last case study, one which has some interesting differences. Florida, more than any other state, leased convicts to companies who extracted pine resin and turned it into turpentine. It was very difficult to get free workers to do the dangerous, debilitating, disease-ridden work in Florida's swamps. Convicts, including women, had no choice. The turpentine camps featured two other types of workers. The few free workers were foremen or supervisors, who could leave at will. But working alongside, essentially indistinguishable from the convicts were peons, those working to pay off their debts or fines. Overpriced company stores, gambling encouraged by overseers, and manipulated bookkeeping all kept the debtors with little hope of freedom (Drobney, 1994, 1998; Shofner, 1981a).

Epidemics, murders, accidents, fires, and suicides marked all aspects of Florida's convict leasing; the path of a convict-built railroad was quite literally strewn with bodies. But convict deaths in the turpentine camps were of even lesser consequence to Florida authorities. There were always more misdemeanants who would not be able to pay fines or convicts with sentences extended by obliging judges to take their places. For many, the horrors of the camps were best illustrated by the Martin Tabert case (Lauriault, 1989; Shofner, 1981b, 1981c). Tabert was a white, middle-class youth jailed for that catch-all crime of vagrancy. Unable to pay his fine, he was shipped to an isolated camp where he was flogged to death. More common, less noticed, but even more powerful today were the tragedies of the largely black workforce. In 1905, turpentine workers at an isolated camp in the Florida panhandle had been chained inside their log cabin housing. When fire broke out, the log chains with which they were restrained could not be broken. Their filthy clothing soaked in flammables easily caught fire. Drunken white officers ignored their cries for help (Mancini, 1996:193). Such incidents are surely worth outrage almost a century later. But the greatest lesson of contract labor and convict leasing, both private corrections, is that anger may be a catalyst for change and an impetus toward gaining knowledge. It is not, however, the means to an end. Only by understanding the context for the invention, growth, and abolition of contract labor and convict leasing can we understand why those systems were in place for decades and, more importantly, how those systems may reappear in altered forms.

Conclusion

The history of criminal justice is a mirror that reflects much about our past and about how that past has shaped our lives today. Clearly, as this history shows, the United States has a long tradition of private participation in the criminal justice system. This participation has occurred in two, necessarily linked, ways. Both are suggestive of, though not necessarily flattering about, the American character.

First, there was the interference of private individuals in the criminal justice process. Beyond being a faint echo of medieval times, this intrusion showed a public distrustful of the government. Other than in times like the Civil War when out of necessity the government expanded, most of the nineteenth century was marked by limited, decentralized governmental responsibility. However, in the twentieth century, progressive mayors, governors, and presidents saw a reformed, more democratically elected government as a tool worthy of greater regulatory and policing powers. This acceptance of a larger, more powerful government was, in part, due to the perceived excesses and irresponsible activities of big business in what was called the era of the "robber barons." Social, not just political justice, argued that poor and exploited people needed government to protect their interests, their property, and their health.

Second, there was the role of business in American society. Tycoons were labeled robber barons for the same reason they were so financially successful; it was their ruthless, single-minded quest for profit. But it was hard to deny that they were also efficient. Progressives, New Dealers, and Great Society advocates promised broad social programs administered efficiently, but not ruthlessly. However, their promises about civil rights, health care, and poverty reduction were, at best, unevenly fulfilled. Moreover, it has become a popular cultural cliche that governmental bureaucracy is plagued with red tape, delayed initiatives, inadequate support, incompetent personnel, and wasteful expenditures of taxes. Even in a short era of balanced budgets, only the most unobservant could miss Wall Street advances of historic proportions. A proposal to invest Social Security funds in the market should come as no surprise. That same proposal reflects the cynical view of government that is so common; it is better to risk retirement funds on Wall Street than to risk falling directly into the hands of bureaucrats and politicians. Yet a wary eye has been cast at businesses that in the name of profits close plants, dislodge loyal employees, and go to third world countries for cheap labor. In short, as in the nineteenth century, it is tempting to see the business model as an alternative to the supposedly bankrupt war and medical models so long employed in our criminal justice policies and institutions. Yet the history of business shows shortcomings, failures, and abuse. Should we trust business, any more than government, to police, prosecute, and punish us?

Private policing, now more reassuringly labeled private security, began as the arm of the wealthy to protect their property, their position in society. Given essentially free reign, agencies like the Pinkertons engaged in virtual vendettas against criminals whose reputations increased with the added publicity. Private policing was used to control groups like labor unions, exercising what we would see today as their legitimate use of strength in numbers to organize and strike. Today private security patrols a new kind of private property—property which the public readily, yet incorrectly, sees as its own—namely shopping malls, airports, and even governmental buildings. To the old list of suspects, such as employee thieves, shoplifters, and muggers, have been added terrorists. Again we are leaving, wisely or not, a vital aspect of policing to a great extent in private hands. We should remember that publicity-hungry terrorists feed off mistakes, whoever commits them. Additionally, it may be all too easy for political dissent to be redefined as threatened violence.

Money is also key with private prosecutions. Those most often victimized are the least likely to have legal recourse. Unlike civil suit contingency fees, fines or financial restitutions in criminal cases would be unlikely to entice lawyers to represent most victims of crime. Private criminal prosecutions rest on uncertain legal foundations, ones that might not withstand excessive use. The legal community, much less the public at large, may not be aware that such precedents exist.

Private corrections probably has the darkest historical shadow of all, yet we have largely ignored its record. While public or state administrators have not been free of scandal, private hands in corrections have been particularly unclean. Inmates beaten to increase production and starved to increase profits are the ghosts that haunt private corrections today. Escapes, suicides, beatings, murders, corruption, and extortion all marked the history of private corrections, which took punishment behind the additional wall of private enterprise. In the coal mines of Alabama and the turpentine camps of Florida, the general racism of the Jim Crow South became even more abusive. With private corrections, the state grew complacent, a few got wealthy, and many died. Today, if we count on government to inspect or supervise private corrections, we are hypocritical and self-deluding, if not irresponsible. Is it logical to expect public officials to supervise a task adequately, when we have already judged that they are incapable of carrying out that task themselves?

Endnote

[1]   According to Negley K. Teeters' (1955) detailed history of the Walnut Street Jail, the jail was a hybrid facility—publicly funded and operated but strongly influenced by the private oversight from a Board of Inspectors composed of members of the Philadelphia Society for Alleviating the Miseries of Public Prisons. As Inspectors, the Philadelphia Society members supervised the day-to-day operation of the public keepers determining practices and allocating resources as needed. There was little distinction between public and private roles.

2 The Criminal Justice Policy-Making Arena and Privatization: Subgovernment in Flux?

Barbara Ann Stolz, Ph.D.

Increased demands for criminal justice services in an era of strained public resources have prompted governments at all levels to consider new approaches for delivering those services. Among the alternatives employed by some state, local, and federal governments is partnership with the private sector. The needs of the criminal justice system addressed through such partnerships range from ancillary services, such as transportation, food, and laundry; to building facilities; to privately run, justice-related organizations (e.g., correctional facilities). Corrections systems at all levels of government have made use of the full range of private services. Other components of the criminal justice system—law enforcement and adjudication—have, generally, engaged in such private public partnerships to a lesser extent, but may use such partnerships more often to meet changing resource needs.

Involving private corporations, particularly for-profit corporations, in a traditionally public sphere has implications for policymaking. Who participates and ultimately influences policy; the stakes and goals of the participants; the techniques used to effect policy; and the mechanisms needed to ensure accountability in the public interest may be affected by involvement of private companies in the criminal justice arena. In the context of this chapter, such changes are viewed as neither positive nor negative, but as matters for policymakers to consider in their decisionmaking in order to ensure public safety and the accountability of the criminal justice system. To examine these changes, this chapter develops a model to compare the policy-making systems of traditional criminal justice systems with those that might emerge with the advent of privatization.

One approach used by political scientists and policy analysts to study policy-making arenas employs the concept of subgovernments.[1] A subgovernment is a group of like-minded individuals who represent key parts of the legislature, the executive branch, and the private sector (Patterson, Davidson & Ripley, 1979:621). In this chapter, a subgovernment model will be developed based on a traditional criminal justice system, accounting for variations among the components within the criminal justice system. Using this model, the chapter then suggests changes that might occur in the criminal justice system with the introduction of privatization. The expectation is that this model will facilitate the analysis of such changes and the determination of appropriate mechanisms for monitoring and accountability.

Subgovernment: Framework for Analysis

According to the subgovernment decision-making model, policy decisions are the result of the ongoing relationship among legislative committees that enact the policies, the government agencies that administer these policies, and the interest groups that lobby in a particular policy area (Patterson et al., 1979:336). These relationships may be depicted as stabilizing and facilitating the formal policy-making process by "bridging the gaps" created by the constitutional separation of powers. Or, they may be described as threatening the public interest, when the three components reach agreement on policy content and are able to dominate policy outcomes (Greenwald, 1977:12; Patterson et al., 1979:336).

A vast literature exists on policymaking within and by each of the three components of a subgovernment—legislature, bureaucracy, and interest groups. Particular attention, however, has been paid to the role of interest groups in American politics at all levels of government (e.g., Dahl, 1961; Greenwald, 1977; Hallett & Palumbo, 1993; Key, 1964; Lowi, 1971; Marion, 1995:76-92), because these groups are not constitutionally defined and they are informal actors within the formal processes. The literature also addresses the variation in the roles played by such groups, including to what extent they are able to influence decision-making, in different policy areas (e.g., Dahl, 1961; Fairchild, 1981; Hallett & Palumbo, 1993; Marion, 1995:76-92; Stolz, 1984b, 1985).

The interest group literature examines the diverse goals that groups seek to attain through the policy-making process. One scheme described by Greenwald (1977:52-53) categorizes interest group goals as "material," "solidary," and "purposive." Material goals are concrete, e.g., monetary. "Solidary" (having or showing solidarity) goals are related to personal rewards to the individual; the groups formed around these goals focus on psychological or ideological rewards. "Purposive" goals are altruistic or superpersonal, e.g., civic reform or civil liberties. Understanding the components within a subgovernment enhances the subgovernment model.

In describing subgovernment policymaking, the political science literature demonstrates that subgovernments not only vary among policy fields, but may change within a policy arena over time. Although subgovernments become institutionalized, they can be changed. The introduction of new participants, the formation of new coalitions, and attempts to influence policy and process at different decision points may produce changes in subgovernments, subgovernment politics, and public policy. Using the tobacco subgovernment as a case study, Fritschler and Hoefler (1996:5-7)) examine the issue of policy change and subsystem politics. They assert that those who seek to change a policy controlled by a subsystem often use the policy-making powers of one institution of government to provide a response to further action from another. For example, a different committee or agency in the bureaucracy—in the tobacco case, those concerned with health issues—might be persuaded to involve itself with the issue. The new participants present a challenge to the established subgovernment. Once control begins to pass from the traditional decisionmakers, it is difficult to predict what direction policy will take. Attempts to change subgovernments may, however, fail; the traditional subgovernment maintains the status quo.

The criminal justice literature has generally not focused on criminal justice policy making through subgovernments, although a recent article by this author examined privatization and the corrections subgovernment (Stolz 1997:92-111). Some attention has, however, been paid to the components of criminal justice subgovernments, particularly the role of interest groups[2] in policymaking (e.g., Fairchild, 1981; Hallett & Palumbo, 1993; Marion, 1995:76-92; Ohlin, 1960; Stolz, 1978, 1984b, 1985). Although this literature is somewhat sparse, nonsystematic, and diverse in its findings, some commonalties have been observed, for example, the importance of professional groups. Such commonalties often provide the keys to a meaningful public discourse about criminal justice subgovernments.

While finding inconclusive and even contradictory evidence in the earlier criminal justice interest group literature,[3] Fairchild (1981:188) asserts several conclusions about interest groups in criminal justice. Two of these conclusions are particularly relevant to this discussion. First, criminal justice legislation is generally conceived by small numbers of influential legislators, administrators, and interest group representatives and enacted on a consensual basis by state legislatures. Second, among the interest groups that attempt to influence criminal justice policy, those that are professionally concerned with the outcomes often exert more influence (see Kiekbusch in this text) than those that have social service or public interest concerns.

The first conclusion provides a basic description of a criminal justice subgovernment and its three categories of participants. Fairchild (1981:189) finds that although the policy-making approach carried out within the legislature is generally characterized as consensual, the literature and media also provide evidence to challenge the consensual model. These seemingly contradictory findings may reflect the functioning of subgovernments at different points in time or in different contexts. A subgovernment functioning through consensus may indicate a stable system, while a subgovernment marked by conflict may be a system experiencing change—a system in flux. For example, a comparison of the juvenile justice subgovernment in Massachusetts before, during, and after the reforms of the late 1960s and 1970s shows a subgovernment operating through consensus during times of stability, but operating through conflict during a crisis or challenge (Stolz, 1975, 1978:15).

Fairchild's second conclusion is that criminal justice groups professionally concerned with the outcomes seem to exert more influence than those that have a social service or public interest concerns. This finding may reflect who is influential at a particular time (Ohlin, 1960; Platt, 1969; Stolz, 1984b:102-104). Or, it may reflect the point in the decision-making process studied by researchers or the objective sought (Stolz, 1984b:96-98). For example, if the objective is to enact legislation, different types of interest groups may influence the process than if the objective is to prevent enactment of legislation. In the former situation professional groups may play a key role in determining the substantive provisions of the legislation, while in the latter situation public interest groups may be able to block enactment of legislation. This analysis underscores the need to examine the influence over criminal justice policy exercised by criminal justice groups professionally concerned with the outcomes, e.g., organizations of police or correctional officers, relative to other types of groups.

The criminal justice literature also includes a tradition, which employs a military-industrial-complex model to explain the context of criminal justice decisions. Quinney (1977:118-124)) developed the concept of a correctional-industrial complex, characterized by a scientific, technocratic approach to crime with industry providing the technology. He asserts that criminal justice is one of the last remaining capital-investment industries, growing since the mid-1960s when the state elevated social control to a "war on crime." Using this model, Lilly and Knepper (1993:154) describe the corrections subgovernment emerging with privatization. They suggest that the participants in this corrections subgovernment include (a) private corporations devoted to profiting from imprisonment, (b) government agencies anxious to maintain their continued existence, and (c) professional organizations that sew together an otherwise fragmented group into a powerful alliance. The authors further assert that the national level organizations are in turn linked to corrections subgovernments within states to form a massive policy-making alliance.

Traditional Criminal Justice Subgovernment

Defining subgovernments in criminal justice is complex due to the multi-faceted nature of the criminal justice system. Mirroring other subgovernments, a traditional criminal justice subgovernment may be expected to include legislators, interest groups, and agency bureaucrats. Moreover, those participants can be expected to have certain stakes and goals and to employ a variety of techniques to influence the policy-making process.

Participants in Traditional Criminal Justice Subgovernments

A traditional criminal justice subgovernment would include those legislative committees, bureaucratic agencies, and interest groups, that are regularly involved in criminal justice policy formulation. The legislators and legislative staff would be those involved in subcommittees or committees responsible for criminal justice authorizations and appropriations. Bureaucrats would include middle to upper level administrative staff, who are responsible for overall agency policies and budgets. Criminal justice interest groups might include a wide range of organizations—legal associations, organizations of criminal justice professionals, employee/labor organizations, religious groups, civil and human rights organizations, and business groups.

The criminal justice system is, however, not one system but comprised of several components—at a minimum—law enforcement, corrections, and courts. These components of the criminal justice system may function as subgovernments. Or, the criminal justice system, as a whole, may function as a subgovernment. For example, a criminal justice system subgovernment may support federal criminal justice grants programs or major criminal law reform, such as the efforts to reform the federal criminal code in the 1970s and 1980s. Because of the different interests of each of the components, maintaining a criminal justice system subgovernment is difficult, particularly over time. Such difficulties were reflected in the history of the Law Enforcement Assistance Administration, which reportedly was discontinued because Congress became tired of the disagreements among the various component participants within the subgovernment. Generally, each criminal justice component would have its own subgovernment. In addition to the three major components of law enforcement, courts, corrections, one may find subgovernments for probation, parole, and bail, among others. While each subgovernment would include the same three components—legislative, bureaucratic, and interest groups—the specific participants within each component, particularly the latter two, would differ. Table 2.1 depicts the criminal justice subgovernment model and suggests possible variations in participation.

Table 2.1
Criminal Justice Subgovernments: A Model

Criminal Justice Subgovernments	Components of Federal, State, and Local Criminal Justice Subgovernment			
	Legislative Committees		Bureaucratic Agency	Interest Groups
General Criminal Justice	Authorizing Committee	Appropriations Committee	Departments, agencies, and other government entities with criminal justice jurisdiction	Bar Association; Unions; Professional organizations, e.g., ACA, IACP; Social welfare organizations; civil liberties groups; and the business sector.
Law Enforcement	Authorizing Subcommittee	Appropriations Subcommittee	Law Enforcement Agency(ies)	Unions; Professional organizations, e.g., IACP, NOBLE; Civil Liberties Organizations; and the business sector.
Corrections	Authorizing Subcommittee	Appropriations Subcommittee	Corrections Department	Unions; Professional organizations, e.g., ACA; Civil Liberties Organizations; and the business sector.
Courts	Authorizing Subcommittee	Appropriations Subcommittee	Judiciary	Professional organizations, e.g., ABA, Court Managers; Civil Liberties Organizations; and the business sector.
Probation	Authorizing Subcommittee	Appropriations Subcommittee	Probation Department	Unions; Professional organizations; Social Welfare Organizations; and the business sector.
Parole	Authorizing Subcommittee	Appropriations Subcommittee	Parole Department	Unions; Professional organizations; Social Welfare Organizations; and the business sector.

The legislative participants in the criminal justice subgovernment would include members and staff serving on committees or subcommittees, which authorize or appropriate funds for criminal justice programs. Because a subcommittee generally has more limited jurisdiction (e.g., one subcommittee might consider judiciary and another law enforcement issues), one would expect to observe subcommittee involvement with specific criminal justice issues and committee involvement with more encompassing legislation. At the local government level, legislative committees might be a city council or a county functional equivalent.

The bureaucratic participants in the criminal justice subgovernment would include the agencies that execute criminal justice policy—law enforcement, courts, corrections, parole, probation, etc. In the case of a specific subgovernment, the agency executing these policies and programs would be the participating agency. The regular participants are usually the career bureaucrats. At times, appointed executives, who typically head these agencies for limited terms, may participate. On occasion, elected executive branch officials may become involved. For example, in Massachusetts during the 1970s, the governor became actively involved in both juvenile and adult corrections reforms, appointing Jerome Miller and John Boone as the respective agency heads. Since the objective of these appointments was reform, these examples suggest that elected executive officials may become active in the policy-making process (Stolz, 1975).

A variety of interest groups participate in the criminal justice subgovernment and its component subgovernments. The literature identifies, for example, professional criminal justice organizations; civil liberties groups; unions; social welfare organizations, including religious groups and secular organizations; and business groups. The types of groups participating within the criminal justice component subgovernments should, generally, be similar, although the specific groups can be expected to differ. For example, within a law enforcement subgovernment, one would expect to find police unions, representatives of citizens' groups, and civil rights organizations, and within a corrections subgovernment one would expect to find corrections unions, prisoners' rights groups, and the ACLU Prison Project. The participation of labor unions in criminal justice policymaking has been documented, but union participation varies from state to state. Business organizations, such as the Chamber of Commerce may participate, but participation by business groups may vary according to the issue or location (Stolz, 1984b:97-98).

The Stakes and Goals Within Traditional Criminal Justice Subgovernments

The participants within each component of a criminal justice subgovernment have certain stakes and seek to achieve particular goals. The goals may be "material," "solidary," or "purposive," as well as broad or narrow.

Elected officials are generally oriented toward re-election. Achieving this goal involves the material secondary goal of obtaining campaign funds to support reelection efforts. The opportunity for, or access to, organizations for securing major campaign contributions may exist in the traditional corrections policy-making arena. For example, the corrections union has been involved in electoral politics in California. In 1992, the California Correctional Peace Officer's Association (CCPOA) was the state's second largest giving PAC (Schiraldi, 1994:2).

Agency programs, budgets, salaries, and benefits are among the material rewards sought by some criminal justice subgovernment participants. Agency bureaucrats; organizations representing agency personnel, e.g., unions; and legislative staff may seek these rewards (Lindbloom, 1979; Stolz, 1984a). Although participants cannot always agree on goals, they may be able to reach consensus on a particular program or salary and benefit level.

A traditional criminal justice policy-making subgovernment includes a wide range of interest groups with different stakes and goals. The presence of unions and their involvement in the political process vary among the states and levels of government (Hunzeker, 1991:26). They tend to seek material goals, e.g., salaries and benefits. Fairchild (1981:188) asserts, based on the earlier literature, that criminal justice groups professionally concerned with the outcomes seem to exert more influence than those that have social service or public interest concerns. One would expect social welfare groups to seek "solidary" or "purposive" goals, e.g., psychological rewards or reform, for their organization members rather than material goals. Obtaining "solidary" or "purposive" goals may be more difficult during periods of maintenance of the status quo within the subgovernment. More importantly, the successful achievement of such goals may be more difficult to measure than incremental material/concrete monetary or programmatic changes. Business groups participate in federal criminal justice policy making. For example, during criminal code revision efforts in the 1970s and 1980s, business organizations sought to change federal law in order to broaden federal authority to prosecute during labor disputes (Stolz, 1984b:97).

Techniques of Influence Within Traditional Criminal Justice Subgovernments

Participants within traditional criminal justice subgovernments use a variety of techniques to influence policymaking. Legislative testimony, expert studies, and draft legislation provide informational support for policy decisions. Interest groups may involve members in "grass-roots" mailing campaigns to demonstrate "public" support for or opposition to policy proposals or positions of politicians. Meetings and informal networking among the actors in the subgovernment are a means to provide information and may result in close working relationships among subgovernment participants (Stolz, 1984b:99).

The criminal justice policy-making process and the processes of the criminal justice system components provide a variety of points of access. The legislative process, through which agency-related legislation and general criminal justice legislation that may affect the agency are considered, and the budget/appropriations process are key arenas for participation. The legislative process provides multiple decision-making points and therefore a variety of points of access for criminal justice subgovernment participants. Administrative decisionmaking, e.g., the development of regulations, may provide points of access for subgovernment participants to influence policy.

On the basis of her review of the literature, Fairchild (1981:189) depicts the criminal justice subgovernment as operating on a consensual basis through state legislatures. It seems reasonable to expect that a criminal justice subgovernment, where the parties tend to operate through regularized relationships, would generally seek to meet the stakes and goals of the various participants through consensus. Criminal justice subgovernments, like subgovernments in other policy areas, however, are subject to challenge. Privatization presents the opportunity to examine the criminal justice subgovernment in the process of change.

Privatization and Changes in a Criminal Justice Subgovernment

The introduction of privatization into a criminal justice system or subsystem suggests the possibility of change in that subgovernment. Changes within a particular criminal justice subgovernment may vary depending on the level of government, the component of the criminal justice system, as well as the nature of the contract provisions and services provided privately. For example, the specific changes one might find in a subgovernment where private companies are running facilities may differ from those found in a subgovernment contracting for transportation services. Within the context of the subgovernment model, however, it is possible to posit general areas of change that may come about due to privatization.

Changes in Participants

With respect to participants, it is likely that private corporations providing criminal justice services will become involved in criminal justice subgovernment policy making. One would expect participation by private corporations not only in the contracting process, but at other deci-sion points in the criminal justice policy-making process in order to attempt to influence a variety of legislative and administrative policy choices relevant to privatization (Gilbert, 1996b:67-71). For example, legislative approval, by either the authorization or appropriations com-mittee, may be required to permit an agency to provide a criminal justice service through a private contract. Accordingly, the private company may seek to influence the appropriate legislative committees to ensure the desired outcome.

The new corporate participants in the criminal justice subgovern-ment may also seek access to the policy-making process by involving other new participants. As Fritschler and Hoefler (1996:5-7) suggest, those seeking to change policy often use the policy-making powers of one institution of government to provide a response to further action from another. To support privatization initiatives, private corporations may seek to involve legislative committees, legislators; or elected offi-cials, e.g., governors, who have not traditionally participated in the appropriate criminal justice subgovernment. Or, they may seek to involve other business interests. In response to the participation of pri-vate companies, groups with opposing interests, such as unions, may become more actively involved in policmaking within the criminal jus-tice subgovernment.

Changes in participants and participation in the criminal justice subgovernment are significant not only because who participates changes, but because such changes have further implications for sub-government politics. Changes in participants may affect the goals and stakes sought, techniques used, decision points, and overall subgov-ernment dynamics.

Changes in Stakes and Goals

The involvement of the private corporations introduces profit, through contracts, as a stake and goal within the criminal justice sub-government. By introducing profit, privatization has the potential to change the reward system of the criminal justice subgovernment. Pri-vatization provides more opportunities for material rewards. Changing the reward structure may potentially affect other participants in the sub-government.

Relative to participants in a traditional criminal justice subgovern-ment, corporations may be better able to meet the campaign finance goals of the elected officials. That is, private for-profit organizations have greater opportunities to meet the material goals of elected officials directly through campaign contributions. Other elected officials may observe the opportunities and become involved in the criminal justice subgovernment. In addition, building a correctional facility in one's district or state creates jobs—"material" rewards to distribute to one's constituents—and thereby support the public officials' re-election goal.

Contractors may also be able to help reduce other political risks for elected officials, for example, lend-lease purchase agreements with private contractors, which require no voter approval, provide an alternative to floating bond issues for corrections construction during an election year. Maghan (1998:54) notes that during the late 1970s and early 1980s, citizens were voting down bonding proposals while demanding more prisons. He states that public officials saw lease-purchase agreements as a way out of this dilemma; rent payments can be paid out of government operating budgets.

Private corporation participation in the criminal justice subgovernment may affect the stakes and goals of the bureaucracy as well. Generally, it is assumed that the private sector will pay lower wages and different benefits than the public sector (Lampkin, 1991:46). Accordingly, criminal justice agency administrators, one of whose goals has been to maintain public jobs and wage and benefit packages, may see competition from the private sector as a threat to the level of benefits and wages. At the same time, privatization may present agency officials with opportunities, e.g., a post-retirement job market. Privatization can also be expected to alter the role of the criminal justice bureaucrat. Traditionally, the criminal justice bureaucracy has been responsible for running programs and ensuring support for funding to continue those programs. With privatization, the government role becomes one of grant monitor, instead of or in addition to service provider. Consequently, bureaucratic interest in programmatic goals and stakes may change.

The involvement of private corporations may also change the relationships among the interest groups within the subgovernment, altering the balance of interests among the participants or generating competition among them. For example, in order to maintain its relative position within the subgovernment, a union may attempt to more actively address the electoral goals of officials. Several authors (Lilly & Knepper, 1993:15-16; Shichor, 1995:240; see also chapters by Gilbert; Hallett & Lee; in this text) have suggested the possibility of a close affiliation between the private corporations and professional criminal justice organizations, such as the American Correctional Association (ACA). The stakes and goals of social welfare organizations, participating in the subgovernment, may change, with changes in goals of the other participants. For example, prison reform groups may not only take steps to try to ensure that the responsible public agencies monitor private corrections contracts, but also, themselves, attempt to monitor private corrections programs. The material goals and rewards of the new participants may affect the prospects for influencing the criminal justice policy-making process for those groups seeking "solidary" or purpose goals. Moreover, the interests of those affected by the criminal justice system, who may be represented by advocacy groups such as the ACLU, may be diminished if material, e.g., monetary, goals become more dominant in the criminal justice subgovernment.

Changes in Techniques of Influence

The participation of private corporations in the criminal justice sub-government may introduce new decision points and the use of different or modified traditional techniques for influencing the policy process. Moreover, the dynamics of influence may change.

With the advent of privatization initiatives, access and decision points in the policy-making process change. Criminal justice privatization involves legislative decisions regarding whether or not to privatize. If the decision is made to privatize, questions arise as to what should be privatized, how, and under what conditions (Gilbert, 1996a:13-29). As indicated above, legislatures may have to enact enabling legislation to establish the conditions under which private contracts may be used in criminal justice. Participants in the subgovernment can be expected to seek access to the decision points where these decisions are made in order to influence policies.

With privatization, the contracting process provides access points to influence decisions in the criminal justice subgovernment. Awarding major state contracts may provide other opportunities to influence executive decisionmaking by top-elected officials as well as administrative decisionmaking (Ethridge & Marquart, 1993:38; Shichor, 1995:236; Cody & Bennett, 1987:844-845). Awarding contracts involves a complex RFP (request for proposal) process (Gemignani, 1992:281-287). Participants may be allowed to submit comments while the RFP is being developed, thus allowing them access to the planning and establishment of contract criteria for privatization (see Hallett & Lee in this text). The administrative processes through which challenges to an award can be made by unsuccessful competitors offer other opportunities for access. The literature also suggests private companies may seek to limit competition and circumvent or change regulations in the pursuit of profits (Shichor & Sechrest, 1995:119).

New techniques may emerge or traditional techniques of influence may be modified. Exerting influence through political action committees, campaign contributions, new job opportunities in exchange for action in support of a contract award become possibilities (Folz & Scheb, 1989; Janus, 1989:34-35; Shichor, 1995:240). Rather than expert studies being used to support new program initiatives, interest groups may develop studies on the cost and quality of private versus public services to support or oppose the use of privately contracted services.

The introduction of private corporations, as regular participants in a criminal justice subgovernment, may change the dynamics of the criminal justice policy-making process as well. Rather than consensus, there is a potential for conflict among the interest groups, particularly between employees unions (in states where they exist) and private corporations. Agency bureaucrats may align themselves with the employees unions or perhaps function as mediators among the diverse interests. The American Federation of State, County, and Municipal Employees (AFSCME); the National Sheriff's Association; the American Civil Liberties Union (ACLU); and the American Bar Association have opposed or expressed concerns regarding privatization (Folz & Scheb, 1989:100; Logan, 1990:10).

Private corporations can be expected to compete with each other for contracts, market shares, and public support. Each interest group can be expected to have its respective champions among elected officials. Resolving these conflicting interests may result in policies different from those that would have been reached through consensus decision-making and in a traditional subgovernment.

Summary: Changing Subgovernments in Criminal Justice

In short, involving private corporations as regular participants in a criminal justice subgovernment has the potential to substantially change key aspects of that subgovernment. The changes are not just changes in who participates, but in the stakes and goals, the tools and techniques of influence, as well as the access and decision points and the dynamics of the process of criminal justice policymaking. With such changes, the potential exists for different criminal justice policies. As Fritschler and Hoefler (1996:5-7) suggest, however, once control begins to pass from the traditional decisionmakers, it is difficult to predict what direction policy will take. That is not to say that policy change is beneficial or detrimental; it is different, meeting different interests or meeting interests differently. Changes in, as well as the possibility of changes in, the criminal justice subgovernment, generally, also have implications for the monitoring of the services provided by the private contractor and the accountability of public officials who oversee the providing of those services and speak for the public interest. These issues will be addressed in the next section.

Changes in Criminal Justice Subgovernments Raise Issues Regarding Monitoring and Accountability

The privatization of criminal justice services raises a variety of issues regarding how best to monitor the performance of private companies providing those services and how to ensure accountability in order to protect the public interest. Monitoring issues include (1) what criteria should be used to assess private sector performance, (2) what data and evaluation mechanisms are needed to ensure effective monitoring, (3) what mechanisms should be used to enforce compliance with those criteria, and (4) what sanctions and rewards should be available to respond to performance failures or successes. Issues related to the accountability of public officials include (1) the need to establish necessary and appropriate laws to protect the public's safety, security, and economic interests; (2) ensuring the implementation of appropriate monitoring mechanisms; (3) preventing monopoly of service delivery; and (4) enacting or changing campaign finance laws.

The responsibility for answering these questions falls primarily on the shoulders of public officials, elected and appointed. The private companies, as the service providers and advocates of privatization, bear some responsibility. Other groups in the subgovernment carry some responsibility as well. Since our society has traditionally defined the state as the victim of crime and, therefore, given the state the ultimate authority for punishment, it bears the primary responsibility for overseeing the carrying out of the imposition of punishment. The purpose of this section is not to become embroiled in a philosophical argument over whether the state can delegate this responsibility, but rather, given that criminal justice privatization is a reality, to address the question of what can the state do to see that its delegation of authority is exercised in an acceptable manner.

Monitoring

With the advent of privatization, a government agency takes on the role of service monitor instead of or in addition to its role of service provider. To carry out its monitoring role, the criminal justice agency must establish criteria against which to monitor the private service provider. In today's political environment, defining those criteria will not be simple (Mays, 1996:9-10). The current emphasis is on measuring performance; traditional output measures, which are commonly used to support requests for new criminal justice programs or for additional resources and to defend current programs and their funding levels, do not assess performance. Federal criminal justice agencies are now struggling to determine outcome goals and appropriate measures of those goals in order to assess their performance and to carry out the Government Performance and Results Act of 1993.[4]

Even if these goals and measures are satisfactorily defined for public agencies, some may not be appropriate for private providers because of differences between the two sectors. Which goals and measures are appropriate will have to be determined for each criminal justice area in which private companies provide services, and the necessary adjustments will have to be made. As part of this effort, the appropriateness of existing standards to assess performance, for example those established by the American Correctional Association, should also be reviewed. They may be applied, as deemed appropriate.

Once the criteria are established, the types of data necessary to measure that performance will have to be determined. Different types of information may be required of the contractor. Data necessary to assess the established performance criteria and to allow comparisons between the services provided by the public sector and the private sector will have to be identified. These data requirements should be defined in the contract and the service provider held accountable for the collection of this information.

An additional approach that might be used to assess the performance of private contractors would be for the state to bring in independent evaluators periodically (See Camp & Gaes in this text.). These evaluations could assess both the "equivalent" private and public services to help ensure the comparative or competitive quality of public and private services. Such outside reviews could address broader issues than monitoring for contract compliance. A related alternative is for the public agency to establish a semi-autonomous review board to monitor the efforts of the private contractors. As part of their task, such a board might seek ways to improve the performance of both public and private facilities and provide recommendations on an ongoing basis.

Assessing performance also requires the establishment of a system of sanctions and rewards to hold the private contractor accountable. To respond to failures in performance, sanctions are necessary (Gilbert 1996b:69). Termination of the contract, while a powerful threat, is not, in itself, a satisfactory sanction (Office of the Corrections Trustee, 1998, chapter 2:6). Such an approach offers an all or nothing approach with the probability of no action except in the most heinous situations. Rather, a range of sanctions which "fit" the situation would be most appropriate and more effective as a means to ensure performance. For example, fines might be assessed to pay for damage to property or reimbursement to the private service provider might be refused for medical or food services not meeting the criteria agreed to in the contract. In addressing problems in the contract between Washington, DC and the Corrections Corporation of America, the Office of the Corrections Trustee (1998:16) of the District of

Columbia recommended that penalties should be scaled to account for the number of inmates affected, and repeat violations should be penalized more heavily. What sanctions are appropriate, however, need to be evaluated in the context of the particular private service provided. In addition, incentives, such as direct monitoring rewards, should be established to reward performance that exceeds the contract criteria.

What is evident is that establishing criteria for assessing private efforts in criminal justice is complex. Criteria, data requirements, monitoring mechanisms, and sanctions and incentives need to be determined. That determination must be made in the context of the service provided.

Accountability

Since criminal justice is primarily a public responsibility, public officials—elected and appointed—are responsible for, and accordingly, should be held accountable for, monitoring the performance of private correctional contractors and seeing that that performance meets the public's interest. Proponents and opponents of prison privatization differ in their assessment as to whether privatization increases or decreases accountability (Logan, 1990:47; Gilbert, 1996b:61-73). Whether the combination of political and market factors enhances accountability or whether contracting reduces accountability due to the isolation of private actors from the political controls to which government actors are subject are propositions that will be tested over time. What is important at this time is that public officials consider the issues presented below, when deciding whether or not to privatize criminal justice services.

First and foremost, before privatizing criminal justice services, public officials should consider problems that might arise with the privatizing of these services and determine whether state laws are adequate to protect the public, should such problems occur. Texas provides a case in point in the corrections area. When inmates brought from other states to private contract correctional facilities in Texas escaped, the state was unable to prosecute the perpetrators because they had not committed the offense of escape under Texas law (Thompson, 1996:194). That is, existing laws did not address the problems arising from the new arrangements. A second, related issue to be addressed, in contract or law, is who is responsible for the costs incurred in cases of riots, escapes, or other damage to property in contract facilities. To assert that public officials have a responsibility to address such questions prior to implementing privatization initiatives is not meant to be a criticism of private contractors, but to underscore the responsibility of public officials to protect public safety and security.

Public officials are accountable for the implementation of monitoring mechanisms discussed above. Federal agencies, such as the National Institute of Justice; professional organizations such as the ABA and

ACA; and academic organizations may facilitate these efforts by providing technical assistance and recommendations based on research findings. The ultimate responsibility, however, lies with the legislative and
bureaucratic components of the subgovernment.

Public policymakers also must ensure that a monopoly of service
delivery is prevented. States may have laws prohibiting the awarding of
subcontracts to the same contractor. For example, laws may prohibit the
subcontracting of prison medical services to the contractor running
the correctional facility. Through the use of subsidiaries and other
arrangements, however, these laws may be evaded in some states.
Accordingly, oversight of the complexities of corporate organization
requires public vigilance.

The profit orientation of private contractors raises the issue of the
appropriateness of contributions by private contractors to political campaigns, particularly to those officials who may influence decisions about
privatization. Since this issue is not limited to private corporations or to
criminal justice, the remedies lie outside the criminal justice policy
arena. In the case of contracting, however, what can be done is to
make this process as public, visible, and open to scrutiny as possible.
Contractors may be concerned about revealing proprietary information; however, to protect the public's interests, the process should be
competitive and open. Sole-sourcing should be the exception not the
rule. In general, however, campaign finance laws should be reviewed to
ensure that they are adequate to meet the demands of today's political
environment.

Conclusions

In recent years, private corporations have become regular providers
of services to the criminal justice system. Their activities have ranged
from providing associated services, such as food or transportation; to
building facilities; to running prisons and jails. In some cases, this
involvement has changed the policy-making process within criminal
justice subgovernments; in other cases, it has the potential to do so. Such
changes include involving new participants, altering the stakes and
goals sought by those participants, using different techniques to influence decisionmaking, establishing new access and decision points, and
altering overall subsystem dynamics. Moreover, these changes have
implications for monitoring privatized criminal justice services and for
accountability of private contractors and the government to the public.
The purpose of this chapter is to identify changes in the traditional
criminal justice subgovernment that might occur with the introduction
of privatization and the monitoring and accountability issues that would
need to be addressed, in response to such changes. Although the respon-

sibility for monitoring and accountability privately contracted criminal justice services lies primarily with public officials, research and academic institutions may provide insights, advice, and alternative approaches for addressing the issues. It would appear that privatization in criminal justice is here to stay. How well it works and meets the public's interest will depend on the dynamics of the new subgovernment.

Endnotes

[1]   The terms subsystems, whirlpools, action centers, and iron triangles (see for example, Gilbert this text) have also been used to describe these relationships.

[2]   Fairchild (1981:183) defines criminal justice interest groups as those organizations that are entirely or partially dedicated to influencing the formulation and execution of public policy in the areas of crime and criminal justice administration. They include professional groups such as police officers associations and bar associations. They also include groups that provide a mix of political activity and service to clients of the criminal justice system, but not purely service groups or groups whose interest in criminal justice policy is of an ad hoc nature.

[3]   Fairchild reviews the following studies: Downs, 1976; Berk, Brackman & Lesser, 1977; Berk & Rossi, 1977.

[4]   Government Performance and Results Act of 1993, is more commonly referred to as GPRA. The stated purpose of the act is to provide for the establishment of strategic planning and performance measurement in the federal government.

3 How Much Is Too Much Privatization in Criminal Justice?

Michael J. Gilbert
University of Texas at San Antonio

The title of this chapter poses a difficult question. Is there such a thing as too much privatization in criminal justice? At one level, there is a simple answer to this question: the total transfer of production for any public good or service to a single provider is too much privatization. This would replace a public monopoly with a private monopoly. However, the question also concerns a more subtle issue, assessing the boundary between appropriate and inappropriate uses of privatization within criminal justice. Although privatization typically refers to the transfer of governmental activities to the private sector, a less well understood form of privatization transfers public policy to the private sector. Consequently, the boundaries between appropriate and inappropriate privatization may vary by social norms, the public function involved and the extent to which control of justice policy is privatized. The primary purpose of this chapter is to develop a theoretical foundation for structuring criminal justice privatization so that its use is consistent with short-term and long-term public interests and its growth controlled by informed public policy. This chapter also has a secondary purpose; that is, to provide a basis for assessing and managing the risks to public interests once the decision to privatize has been made.

The development of a theoretically sound basis for structuring criminal justice privatization requires a critical examination of several underlying issues. What are the major segments of the private justice market, and what is their potential to influence criminal justice policy for private purposes? Could gradual increases in private criminal justice capacity

41

capture public policy and limit available policy options? Are there governmental functions that should not be privatized? If so, how would these functions be distinguished from public goods and services that could be privatized? Could criminal justice privatization lead to uncontrolled expansion of formal social control systems? What are the new markets in criminal justice? What is the role of government when justice services are privatized? Such questions concern larger issues than mere avoidance of private monopolies.

How Large Is the Private Sector in Criminal Justice?

The term *"prison industrial complex"* has been used by several authors to suggest that the magnitude of private sector involvement in the confinement market is comparable to that found in the "military industrial complex" (Lilly & Knepper, 1993; Schlosser, 1998). The term "criminal justice industrial complex" could just as easily have been used because of the extensive involvement of the private sector in all aspects of the justice system. One market research firm has produced a detailed analysis of the confinement market. Entrepreneurs can purchase their 235-page market analysis for $495. It covers four major segments of the confinement market—private prison management, corrections food service, telecommunications, and healthcare (FIND/SVP, 1999a). Annual growth rates of 15-30 percent are projected for the private prison management segment of the market. The other three market segments are projected to grow more slowly—10-15 percent per year. The total volume in sales by the confinement market is estimated to be $15-20 billion annually (FIND/SVP, 1999b-e).

Other market analysts have noted the earnings potential of the confinement market. In 1995, Chad Rubel (1995:1,7) wrote an article titled "No Larger Captive Market Than This One" for an issue of *Marketing News*. In the article he states that:

> There's a little known field with great marketing potential that has grown dramatically in the last decade, is expected to grow even larger, and is recession proof. . . . That field is prisons. . . .

As an example of this economic growth, consider Corrections Corporation of America (CCA) (see chapters by Hallett & Lee and Mobley & Geis in this volume). CCA was founded in 1983 in Nashville, TN and received its first three facility management contracts in 1984 (Corrections Corporation of America, 1999a:1). By the end of 1984, CCA managed 888 inmate beds. Between 1983 and 1988 CCA reported annual losses totaling $9,351,600 over five years. CCA became profitable for the first time in 1989 with a net income of $1,606,040 on $36,796,393 in gross revenues from the management of 3,848 confinement beds (Corrections Corporation of America, 1993:36-37). By the end of 1997, CCA reported net income of $53,955,000 on $462,249,000 in revenues with 78 correctional facilities and 52,890 beds under contract. Of these beds, 38,509 were in operating facilities and CCA reported a 93.2 percent occupancy rate that fiscal year (Corrections Corporation of America, 1998a:4). In a "Letter to Our Shareholders" published in the '96 *Annual Report*, Doctor R. Crants, Chairman and CEO dramatically captured the nature of CCA's growth with the following statement:

> CCA is receiving higher per diems for the quality of our service, as well as improving profitability by expanding our existing facilities. Despite the mathematical difficulty of growing from a bigger base, we believe we can sustain a 70 percent compounded annual growth rate in earnings. (Corrections Corporation of America, 1997:2)

CCA began selling its operational facilities to CCA Prison Realty Trust in 1997. That year CCA sold 12 of its profitable facilities for $455,000,000 (Corrections Corporation of America, 1999b:1). Doctor R. Crants was also the Chairman of the Board of CCA Prison Realty Trust at the time of the sale.[1] The lease-rates paid by CCA under its *non-cancelable* lease agreements allowed CCA Prison Realty Trust to repay its debts (Corrections Corporation of America, 1998a). This practice enabled CCA to remove long-term construction debt from its balance sheets, repay its debts as a contractual expense, and recycle funds into new projects including development of speculative prisons and jails (i.e., facilities built in anticipation of demand). A Real Estate Investment Trust (REIT), such as CCA Prison Realty Trust, is exempt from taxes on earnings because it pays 95 percent of its earnings back to investors. However, this allows the REIT to raise money inexpensively and to use the funds to finance new ventures in the private prison industry (Hershey, 1999:C6).[2] Mr. Crants described this business strategy in the *1997 Annual Report* (Corrections Corporation of America, 1998a:3-4).

> Through Prison Realty Trust (NYSE: PZN) CCA has an avenue by which it can sell its properties after they are built and operational and recoup its capital costs. The company then leases the facilities back for ten to twelve years at terms that are essentially on par with the costs of continued ownership, except that CCA can take the recovered capital and develop additional facilities more quickly.
>
> . . . At year end our cash balance alone was greater than current liabilities and even exceeded our long-term debt. We plan to continue to sell facilities to PZN and, with our operating

facilities generate increasing cash flow, we are comfortably positioned to develop business at a healthy pace.

. . . the ability to provide large amounts of capital quickly is an important advantage in getting the large, attractive projects in today's market. We are raising the stakes of the game for everyone in our industry by making it more capital intensive.

. . . Our company's market capitalization is now approximately $3.5 billion, compared to a total market cap of $1 billion for the other three [leading] companies. Revenues for CCA exceed their combined revenues by $135 million. And in the all-important category of profitability, CCA is taking about 12% to the bottom line while the other three together are earning 5%. [added]

CCA's optimistic assessment of their growth potential over the next several years may be realized, but only if the rate of public demand for offender confinement continues to increase at levels comparable to that experienced in the 1990s. Between December 31, 1990 and December 31, 1997 demand for confinement beds increased by 1,843 beds per week for each year—619,369 inmates in all (Maguire & Pastore, 1998:481, 490).

Figure 3.1
Confinement Rate (per 100,000 for State and Federal Inmates by Year (excludes jail inmates)

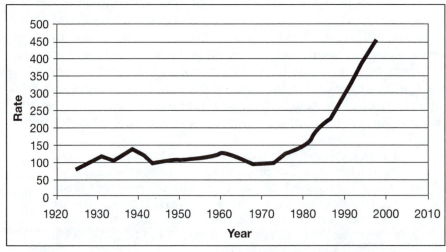

Source: Maguire & Pastore, 1998.

If this increase in the inmate population were housed in medium security facilities, each bed would cost roughly $50,000 per bed to build (Camp & Camp, 1997:69). At that cost, American taxpayers would have spent roughly $4.4 billion each year or $30.8 billion over seven years (December 31, 1990 and December 31, 1997) for prison/jail construction. The construction cost represents only 10 percent or less of the 30-year life cycle costs to operation of a single prison or jail bed (National Institute of Corrections, 1996). Consequently, the public cost of every confinement bed—public or private—is magnified many times during the facility life cycle. The combined operational budgets for correctional services in the United States is between $30 billion and $40 billion annually (Maguire & Pastore, 1998:4). Other market sectors offer a wide array of products and services to public and private confinement operations. These products and services include:

- bed brokerage services for public and private facilities

- prison/jail equipment, furnishings, and finishes

- security systems and equipment

- correctional consulting services

- body armor and weapons (lethal/non-lethal)

- chemical agents and restraint devices

- temporary modular housing units

- security transportation vehicles

- contract inmate transportation service

- computer systems

- security fencing

- inmate and staff uniforms

- drug-testing equipment

- inmate education, vocational and treatment programs

- medical, dental, and psychological healthcare

- prison industry programs and products

The whole cluster of corporate entities involved in selling confinement related products and services to local, state, and federal correctional agencies compose the private sector "prison industrial complex." There are also other market segments for justice-related services within a broader criminal justice market. These market segments include: private security/law enforcement,[3] alternative dispute resolution,[4] community corrections for adult and juvenile offenders,[5] bail bonds and bounty hunters; and ancillary markets.[6]

The combined volume of sales by these segments of the criminal justice market probably exceeds the sales in the confinement market. For example, Wackenhut Corporation (1998:2) is a leading provider of both security/law enforcement and correctional services. However, only 6,300 of its 56,000 employees were employed as correctional workers at the end of 1997. Wackenhut Corporation is also the third largest security services provider in the United States and the leading provider of international security services based in the United States (Wackenhut Corporation, 1998:2, 9-10). In 1997 gross revenues for Wackenhut Corporation were reported to be $1,126,802,000. These revenues were distributed across three business sectors—Security Services, $828,974,000, Correctional Services, $206,930,000, and Staffing Services, $90,898,000 (Wackenhut Corporation, 1998:5). The private security/law enforcement sector composed 73.6 percent of corporate revenues. Two other firms—Borg-Warner Security Company and Pinkerton's, Inc.—exceed Wackenhut Corporation in annual revenues for private security/law enforcement. In 1997 Borg-Warner Security Company reported $1,548,000,000 in revenues for security services (Borg-Warner, 1998:1). These facts suggest that the annual market for private security/law enforcement services alone is valued at more than $3 billion among the top three companies. Given the large number of smaller security/law enforcement companies in this market sector the total annual value of the market is probably $10 billion or more. The term *criminal justice industrial complex* refers to the combined industrial capacity of these market segments.

The criminal justice industrial complex has a direct economic stake in public policy. Schlosser (1998:65) cites a 1997 Prudential Securities report that identified four major threats to the prison industrial complex (and perhaps the criminal justice industrial complex)—falling crime rates, shorter prison sentences, expanded use of alternatives to confinement, and changes in the drug laws. Of these, all but falling crime rates represent changes in justice policy. However, legislation and policies can also influence crime rates by increasing or decreasing crime reporting by citizens. How will criminal justice markets react to public policy shifts that threaten their investments and profitability? Would they lobby against such policy changes? Would they lobby for alternative policies that increase demand for privatization? Would they readily shift to different goods and services in response to policy changes that reduced the need for their current products and services?

The behavior of the military industrial complex provides an instructive example. When the top military and civilian policymakers at the Pentagon rejected or scaled back defense projects, lobbyists for the military industrial complex often worked to continue or expand these projects by seeking political support from members of Congress. The industry clearly saw the members of congress as their customer rather than the Pentagon. In the end, a number of weapon systems were purchased that the Pentagon did not want and perhaps did not need (Kotz, 1988). Hallett and Lee, in Chapter 10 of this book, document a more relevant example—the ongoing efforts by Corrections Corporation of America to privatize the Tennessee prison system. Although CCA's efforts have failed twice, first in 1985-1986 and then in 1997-1998, it is likely that CCA will continue to work politically for privatization of the Department of Corrections in future legislative cycles (Corrections Corporation of America, 1998a; Schlosser, 1998:70). CCA also lobbied Congress and local officials in its efforts to privatize the District of Columbia prison system and use prime economic development land in Ward 8 as the site for a private prison (Charry, 1999; Pyatt, 1999; Redmon, 1999). These examples demonstrate the power of large, well-organized, and well-funded corporate players in any market to protect or advance their economic interests and promote governmental policies that support the industry. Private sector lobbyists representing corporations and industries often seek to influence political officials and thereby influence public policy from initial agenda setting to evaluation and policy termination (Janus, 1993; Lindblom, 1977:123, 178-179, 187-197; Lutrin & Settle, 1992:368; Waldman, 1990).

Figure 3.2
Iron Triangle Relationships

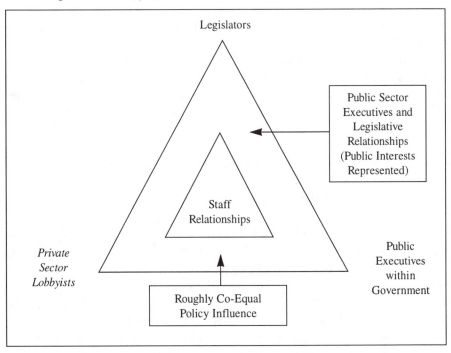

Under these conditions, *"iron triangle"* relationships (i.e., mutually supportive, semi-stable coalitions) between private sector lobbyists, legislators, and bureaucratic officials are likely to form. In Chapter 2 of this book, Stolz refers to these kinds of relationships as subgovernments. These structures may protect or undercut public interests, depending on the issues and industries involved, the economic interests at stake, and the strength of public opinion. Legislators are usually dependent on technocratic experts among the lobbyists and public bureaucracy for information needed to make meaningful policy decisions. This is especially true of complex and vaguely defined policy areas such as crime and justice. The members of an iron triangle usually strive for policy decisions that allow all sides to win (Cayer & Weschler, 1988:25-28; Lutrin & Settle, 1992:53-55). Typically, there is a rough equality in both the power relationships and their influence on policy processes among the three sides (see Figure 3.2). Each side has something the others need or want. However, when win-win-win policies cannot be attained, two sides may overpower the third. It is not unusual for industry lobbyists and legislative officials to overpower bureaucratic and regulatory opposition by government officials as observed in the Pentagon example.

Although public correctional executives tend to oppose privatization, they may resort to it to gain needed capacity when faced with dangerous levels of inmate crowding and the lack of voter support for new facility construction. Privatization buys short-term relief and time for correctional executives. From the politician's perspective, privatization enables them to brag about being "fiscally conservative" and "tough on crime" at the same time. They are "locking up more offenders" and "reducing the cost to taxpayers." These are winning political issues in most jurisdictions. Contractors win with increased business volume and greater market share. Such powerful and mutually supportive interests could make it very difficult to reduce the growth rate of the inmate population even if crime rates dropped and public policy shifted dramatically toward alternatives to confinement.

The modified iron triangle diagram (Figure 3.3) suggests how power relationships and private sector policy influence may change if private sector employees totally replaced public officials within the executive branch.

The diagram shows how total replacement of executive branch officials could sharply erode consideration of non-market public interests and dominate the formation of policy. Under these circumstances short and long-term public interests would be underrepresented in policy discussions and easily ignored. Private interests could be substituted for public interests based on the assumption that market forces and efficiency will adequately protect public interests. However, if that were the case, corporate polluters would have voluntarily cleaned up the pollution they created. Car manufacturers would have voluntarily installed seat belts in their products; and, tobacco companies would have notified the public of the health hazards of their products as soon as the carcinogenic effects of tobacco were known. Unfortunately, none of that happened. Instead, semi-stable coalitions between these industries and legislators were sufficiently strong to protect the industries and overcome bureaucratic opposition and regulatory oversight until adverse public opinion swayed legislative support. In these examples, it is doubtful that non-market public interests in car safety, prevention of tobacco-related cancer, and a clean environment would ever have prevailed if the public bureaucracy attending to public interests had been privatized. It is perhaps wise to remember that public interests and private interests are rarely the same and market forces are unlikely to protect non-market public interests.

Figure 3.3
Modified Iron Triangle—Public Executives Replaced by Private Executives

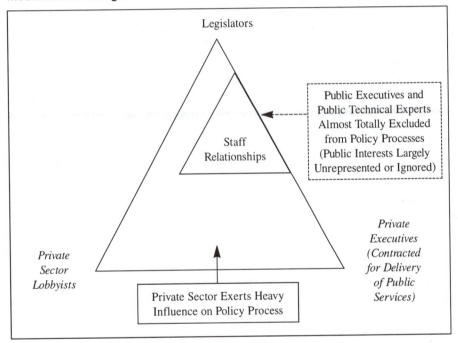

Are There Governmental Functions That Should Not Be Privatized?

Ideally, governments within civil societies govern with the consent of the people, correct for market failures, and serve the common good. Most people would probably agree (at least in principle) that some functions of government should not be privatized, even if they do not agree on which functions should be reserved for government. For example, it is doubtful that many voters would support substantial privatization of the military, the court system, or public law enforcement. It is also unlikely that voters would support contracting out all city management functions, criminal prosecutions, or other services in which control over public policy is delegated to the contractor. It is equally doubtful that voters would support total privatization of education. There is an underlying awareness that public interest requires that some functions be relatively free of private financial bias. The ability to pay should not determine whether a case is heard in court, a criminal prosecution is initiated, a child is educated, or whether the military protects the nation. Stable societies probably require some public production of essential goods and services to define the minimum level of governmental commitment to the welfare of society. Governments must provide a basic array of public goods and services to ensure the common good of society by meeting collective needs for all those who qualify. This is known as the "default level" of public goods and services. Public production is needed to guard against market failure in essential public functions. The concept of a default level is a reasonable place to start our search for boundaries to privatization (Welle, 1996).

Public goods and services combined with democratic policy processes for allocation decisions provide social linkages that help sustain a civil society by connecting its members to one another. When a child does not receive timely vaccinations because his family does not have health insurance or cannot afford the co-payments, the health of the society as a whole is endangered. Societies carry a public and moral obligation to address such basic collective needs, especially when markets fail (Wolfe, 1989). The allocation of default level services in healthcare, education, and justice is based on public interest for the society at large. In this context, *"public interests"* refers to:

> . . . the institutions, practices, and values that promote the well being of every member of society: the common interests and values we share; the public goods and services we provide; and the sacrifices we make for others. The public interest binds a just and civilized society together. (Gilbert, 1996a:17)

At the individual level public interests include civil rights, personal freedoms, opportunities to achieve one's potential, opportunity to satisfy personal goals, and fair play between competing interests. At the societal level, public interests include public safety, national defense, economic security, protection of the economy, protection of the environment, foreign policy, and governmental sovereignty over public policy (Gilbert, 1996b:19). *Public goods* refer to products and services available to all residents within the society without regard to the residents' ability to pay. The combined effects of public goods and services to meet public interests provide a foundation for society by connecting people to form neighborhoods, villages, cities, states, and nations (Wolfe, 1989).

Whether a particular policy is consistent with public interests is a subjective assessment based on a number of factors. These factors include political compromises that must be made, prioritization of competing needs, the nature of the policy problem, the minimum social safety-net needed to address the problem, the likelihood of unintended—but serious—negative consequences and social justice concerns (Welle, 1996:1230-1234). The government has a duty to ameliorate market failures and deficiencies. This is especially important when vulnerable groups or the welfare of the larger society are threatened (e.g., hunger, homelessness, the Chrysler bailout in the 1980s, the Savings & Loan bailout in the 1990s).

From a criminal justice perspective, the appropriateness of any particular form of privatization might be defined by whether a default level of production by government would be retained. This is important if discontinuation of justice services due to market failure is to be avoided. Criminal justice privatization transfers the coercive power of the state to private actors. Criminal justice services also require continuous fulfillment of duty. Total discontinuation of justice services is not a viable policy option because all citizens are eligible for service on demand or at the command of public authorities. Economic status of the client and public cost are largely irrelevant concerns when legitimate needs for justice services are identified. In this sense criminal justice services are public goods. Consequently, public officials must consider what would happen if a service contractor (like Corrections Corporation of America) declared bankruptcy or simply decided to go out of business?[7] What if the contractor sold the contracts to another contractor deemed unqualified by government officials? It is important that government authority be able to resume public service if the vendor is unable or unwilling to perform under the contract. What would be the public price tag when private criminal justice markets fail? Jails still have to be operated; streets still have to be policed; and, courts still have to decide cases.

Public dependency on private delivery of public services could become so extensive that public production could not be resumed in a timely manner or without prohibitive costs. Under these conditions, privatization is probably inappropriate. Public officials cannot rely on assumptions of ethical corporate behavior or continuous service. They also cannot assume that market competition will protect public interests. Consequently, appropriate uses of privatization in criminal justice preserve a default level of public service. In the total absence of public production, privatization would be difficult, perhaps impossible, to reverse. This would be especially true if a private monopoly developed or a contractor gained sufficient political support to block contract modification, block contract termination, or obtain lucrative contract concessions because a strong base of political support protects their interests (Gilbert, 1996b). The case studies included in this book provide clear examples of the ease with which private monopolies in criminal justice privatization could form and abuse public interests.

Although many people probably have an intuitive sense about which governmental functions should or should not be privatized, the U.S. Supreme Court has argued that few inherently governmental functions exist. Consequently, privatization is a legitimate policy option for delivery of public goods and services—including criminal justice services. Beginning in 1974, the U.S. Supreme Court decided a line of cases in which a wide variety of public functions had been privatized without serious criticism (*Jackson v. Metropolitan Edison*, 1974; *Hudgens v. NLRB*, 1976; *Flagg Brothers, Inc. v. Brooks*, 1978; *Procunier v. Navarette*, 1978; *Rendell-Baker v. Kohn*, 1982; *Blum v. Yaretsky*, 1982; *Wyatt v. Cole*, 1992; *Richardson, et al. v. McKnight*, 1997). Quite simply, public officials may privatize public functions, provided that the public purpose can be expressed as an "intelligible principle" (i.e., reducing costs to taxpayers, reducing prison crowding, public safety, etc.) and that private authority is subordinated to public authority (Gillette & Stephan, 1998:501; Ratliff, 1997:382-385).

In *Flagg Brothers, Inc. v. Brooks* (1978:158-164), Justice Rehnquist argued for the majority. He stated that holding public elections was probably the only function exclusively reserved for the government. Although Justice Rehnquist suggested that there might be circumstances in which fire protection, police protection, tax collection, and education could be viewed as reserved for the state, he took no position on these functions. In fact, the opinion explicitly states, "We express no view as to the extent, if any, to which a city or State might be free to delegate to private parties the performance of such functions and thereby avoid the strictures of the Fourteenth [A]mendment." Thus, the Supreme Court held that traditional state functions are not protected from privatization even if federally granted civil rights and federal requirements might be vitiated by privatization (e.g., Americans with Disabilities Act of 1990; Freedom of Information Act of 1974; Title 42 U.S.C. Section 1983; etc.).[8] Despite this ruling, it is unlikely that many voters would be comfortable trusting corporations to voluntarily protect federally granted civil rights, especially when corporate financial interests conflict with their responsibility to protect these rights.

The authority of any public official is delegated from higher authority. Ideally, public rather than private goals and objectives are served. The practice of criminal justice (enforcement of laws, determination of guilt or innocence, sentencing, and the actual imposition of sanctions) clearly involves the application of the coercive power of the state. This is true whether practiced by a public employee or a private contractor.[9] Contractors are empowered to exercise coercive state power because authority to do so has been delegated by public authority. The U.S. Supreme Court's primary argument has been that government responsibilities are politically determined and prescribed by statute; however, the methods used to carry out those responsibilities are not prescribed by statute. In short, public production is not required to satisfy statutorily defined government responsibilities. Some legal scholars argue that when private action substitutes for "state action" it may be considered as the equivalent of state action (Barak-Erez, 1995; Schaffer, 1996; Russell-Einhorn, 1998). Thus, confinement of state inmates in a private prison would be considered state action and civil rights laws would apply equally to public and private organizations that provide equivalent state services. Their views rest largely with the Supreme Court decision in *West v. Atkins* (1988). In this decision the actions of a private physician on contract to a state prison hospital were found to be the equivalent of state action. In recent years, Federal Courts have heard and decided a number of cases filed by inmates under Title 42 U.S.C. § 1983—a civil rights act intended originally to protect citizens from abuse by public agencies and officials—against private prison contractors.[10]

Interestingly, the Supreme Court ruled in *Richardson et al. v. McKnight* (1997) that private correctional officers are not "state actors" for the purposes of extending qualified immunity for public officials to private sector workers. The Court found that private correctional officers did not meet the legal tests required for being recognized as state actors even when state action is involved.[11] For inmates, this meant that punitive damage awards might be more easily attained against private actors since deliberate indifference would not need to be established (Russell-Einhorn, 1998).[12]

There are no guarantees that public interests will be protected simply by the method of production used—public or private. In corrections there is a long history of abuse of public interests by both public and private organizations (Durham, 1989a, 1989b, 1989c; Martin & Ekland-Olsen, 1987; Kentucky Corrections Cabinet, Office of Corrections Training, 1985; Logan, 1990, 1992). However, private criminal justice services introduce private financial interests, market pressures and corporate economic survival as influential factors in both the exercise of coercive state authority and the formation of public policy. Public policy governs both the allocation of resources and the manner in which state authority is exercised. Gradual increases in the proportion of public goods and services delivered by private contractors slowly privatizes public policy (Kolderie, 1986). As private contractors play a larger role in the delivery of public goods and services their influence within the public policy arena increases, and the influence of governmental agencies decrease (see Figure 3.3). The opportunity for private sector abuse of public interests increases dramatically when both production and policy are controlled by the private sector.

There are many examples of corporate abuse of public interests (Shichor, 1993). There were Thalidomide-induced birth defects, the Ford Pinto (exploding gas tank) and Ohio Revco Medicaid Scandals in the 1950s, 1960s, and 1970s. There were the Wall Street Insider Trading/Junk Bond Scandal and the Savings and Loan Crisis of the 1980s and 1990s (Calavita & Pontell, 1991; Friedrichs, 1996, Punch, 1996). These are just a few of the most egregious examples. In each instance, corporate economic interests or the internal culture of competition within an industry prevailed over ethical, prudent, and legally defensible decisionmaking to harm society. Similar abuses by members of the criminal justice industrial complex have occurred and are likely to reoccur in other places. Corporate officials envision ever-increasing demand, expanded markets, greater market share, and greater profits. Yet, such unconstrained growth is probably not in the long-term interest of society. Speculative expansion of private criminal justice capacity could increase formal social controls, restrict individual liberty and erode civil rights in the name of public safety. Incremental expansion of private social control capacity is consistent with business objectives but not long-term public interests.

It is clear that criminal justice privatization approaches some sort of boundary. However, it is not clear where that boundary is or how it might be defined. The U.S. Supreme Court does not recognize the non-delegation doctrine; and, neither tradition nor claims to be an inherent state function can distinguish appropriate from inappropriate forms of privatization. Yet, some elements of a meaningful boundary are beginning to appear. Before criminal justice privatization decisions are made, public officials should consider whether the privatization would:

- Undercut the necessary minimum (default) level of public services and threaten continuous fulfillment of public responsibilities or preclude resumption of public service if market failure occurred (Welle, 1996).

- Overtly transfer public policy processes to the private sector (Kolderie, 1986; Lindblom, 1977:183; Lutrin & Settle, 1992:52-63).

- Present a serious risk to individual liberties and civil rights of the public or clients (Ratliff, 1997; Richardson, 1997)

- Present a conflict of interest inconsistent with long-term public interests (Casarez, 1995; Gillette & Stephan, 1998; Richardson, 1997).

- Shelter the contractor from public accountability under tax law, contract law, or proprietary claims so that the government could not adequately supervise or hold the contractor accountable to public authority (Casarez, 1995; Gilmour & Jensen, 1998).

- Create a private monopoly in the place of a public monopoly—total public dependency represents a loss of sovereignty that may not be easily reversed (Gilbert, 1996a, 1996b; Kolderie, 1986).

Policymakers ought to consider such questions before privatization decisions are made. The answers will help determine whether privatization is appropriate or inappropriate for their particular situation.

Could Privatization Lead to Uncontrolled Expansion of Private Formal Social Control?

To begin to answer this question, it is helpful to look at the private prison and jail management market. Private confinement companies aggressively market their services by claiming they can manage facilities more effectively and at lower cost than public correctional agencies. Some recent research suggests that between 5 percent and 15 percent of the daily costs for inmate care (i.e., unit costs) might be saved through privatization (Archambeault & Deis, 1996b; Logan, 1992; Office of Program Policy Analysis and Government Accountability, 1995, 1997a, 1997b; Texas Sunset Advisory Commission, 1991a). However, an unintended consequence of reduced unit costs could be (and probably will be) increased political pressure to confine more people. Private providers will continue to develop speculative capacity on the presumption that public demand will continue to increase. Finally, the policy influence of industry lobbyists will encourage expansion of the confinement business. Some public officials are surprised to find that total system costs often increase with private confinement, eliminating unit cost savings. Much like the shopper who argues that he saved $100 by buying on sale, jurisdictions that once spent $15.6 million/year to confine 950 inmates (at $45/day) may find $20.6 million/year being spent at $37.55/day to confine 1,500 inmates in privately managed or owned facilities. Lower unit costs only result in lower system costs when the number of clients served remains constant or declines.

Increased system costs for confinement erodes public funding for alternatives to confinement and other important services like education. California has already discovered an inverse relationship between increasing prison costs and decreasing budgets for higher education (Irwin & Austin, 1997:14). From the point of view of the private prison industry, the only boundary to the number of people confined is the point at which politicians or taxpayers refuse to pay for more bed space. However, that point seems a long way off because private confinement capacity is sold like any other commodity—item by item, bed by bed, facility by facility. There are unintended negative consequences to most large-scale human activity. Incremental expansion of private confinement capacity is likely to increase welfare costs for prisoners' families, expand formal social controls over larger and larger segments of society, and produce an entitlement for the confinement industry to public funds. Much like cancer in the human body, unlimited growth of prison and jail capacity is unsustainable to the host (society) over the long-term.

It is clear that market systems exploit every reasonable opportunity for business growth. That is the nature of economic self-interest inherent in a capitalist economy (Lindblom, 1977). Governmental capacity to produce public goods and services is constrained by public budgets, limited by public resources and the policy choices made by governmental leaders. In criminal justice markets, the goods and services produced are purchased directly or indirectly by public agencies supported by tax dollars. Without public sector purchasing, criminal justice markets would whither and die. As long as demand for public justice outstrips public resources, officials will continue to purchase products and services from the private sector. Speculative development of private capacity requires that new products and services be sold in order for businesses to survive. Leasing additional prison capacity—one bed at time—from privately owned prisons will almost always be easier, less controversial, and less expensive (at least initially) than building new facilities with public funds. Private security is now substantially larger than public police, private prison capacity is growing at a faster rate than public capacity, and new business ventures in criminal justice are being explored daily (Find/SVP, 1999a-e; National Center for Policy Analysis, 1996a-f).

Heightened public fears and concerns about street crime lead to public slogans like: "You do the crime, you do the time;" "Three strikes and you're out;" "Zero tolerance;" and, "War on drugs and crime." Many people advocate that we exert as much social control on society as necessary to reduce street crime and fear. Yet, fear of crime is largely the result of vicarious exposure to crime—perceptions of graffiti, neighborhood deterioration, homelessness, economic stress, changes in ethnic distribution in residential areas, and many other social conditions. Often those who express the greatest fear have the lowest risks of street crime victimization (Bohm & Haley, 1999:50-52). Street crime is exploited by politicians to gain votes and by the news and entertainment media for ratings. Fear remains high despite reductions in actual levels of crime (Gilbert, 1996b:62-63; Irwin & Austin, 1997:4-7; Walker, 1998b:8). Each year roughly 15 to 20 million street crimes are reported to police. Victimization studies reveal nearly twice as many street crimes per year (40 million or more) but 50 percent of these crimes are not reported to police (Bohm & Haley, 1999:34-50). Only a small fraction of the reported street crimes result in conviction and confinement. Far more people are harmed each year—deaths, injuries, and property loss—by white-collar and corporate crimes than street crimes. Yet, compared to street crime, fear of white-collar and corporate victimization is low and few offenders are caught, tried, and convicted (Friedrichs, 1996). If the true volume and nature of crime in American society were represented within the justice system it would be functionally, financially, and politically unsustainable. There would simply be too many offenders and a much higher proportion of high status people among the offender population. Criminal justice markets do not recognize these issues.

Predictable increases in demand are essential to continued investment and business success in any market. The criminal justice industry has an economic stake in the continuation and expansion of formal social control policies. As noted earlier, the largest threats to the criminal justice industrial complex are policy shifts that reduce demand. It would be naive to assume that the criminal justice industry would quietly accept shifts in policies that affect their livelihood. Demand for criminal justice services is driven more by public policy responses to crime than actual levels of crime (Irwin & Austin, 1997; Walker, 1998b). The criminal justice industry is capable of aggressive lobbying to kill policies that would hurt its business interests. The industry also is capable of lobbying for laws and policies that are favorable to its interests. The effectiveness of industry to influence public policy has been widely documented (Nader, Green & Seligman, 1976; Lindblom, 1977; Kotz, 1988; Waldman, 1990; Calvita & Pontell, 1991; Friedrichs, 1996; Rosoff, Pontell & Tillman, 1998).

Speculative expansion of private criminal justice capacity cannot be sustained indefinitely without changing the nature of society. Consequently, the appropriate use of privatization in criminal justice requires that government constrain private capacity at some point. Sensible policy boundaries to private sector expansion are needed. In the absence of such boundaries gradual increases in private capacity will go unnoticed. At some point, society could crumble under the combined weight of private law enforcement/security, prisons, probation, parole, prosecution, and judicial proceedings. One likely outcome is a society characterized by ever-heightening concerns for public safety, continued expansion of private social controls systems, reliance on market strategies to deliver criminal justice services, and reduced resources to address other social problems. This society would probably not be the type of society envisioned by the most enthusiastic privatization advocates. Simply stated, excessive formal social control is a plausible outcome of unbounded incremental increases in private criminal justice capacity.

Could the Private Criminal Justice Industry Capture Justice Policy?

Crime and delinquency are complex and vaguely defined social problems that cannot be "solved" in any meaningful sense of that term. No society will ever be crime free. As long as there are impulsive juveniles, there will be delinquency. At best, the harmful nature of street crime and delinquency can be managed to minimize social damage. A variety of policy responses are needed to manage these problems. Of these, only one relies on expanded social controls using the criminal justice system to attack individual offenders—one by one. Such policy responses do nothing to ameliorate factors related to American culture, social structure, and the economic system. Furthermore, criminal justice responses ignore social conditions that impose unearned hardships, afford unearned opportunities, foster the development of learned helplessness and hopelessness among some classes, and overemphasize the meaning of economic success (often by any means necessary) among other classes.[13] These underlying factors have been widely recognized in both theoretical and research literature as being associated with the high levels of crime in American society (street crime, organized crime, white-collar crime, and corporate crime). Political decisionmakers have largely ignored theory and evidence in favor of ideologically based "tough on crime" responses. The underlying factors are ignored when policymakers respond with more laws, tougher sanctions, more police, certification of juveniles as adults, more aggressive prosecution, specialized courts, more prisons, greater use of confinement, fewer due process protections, and restrictions on appeals. Yet, these are precisely the kinds of policy responses that would be most attractive to the criminal justice industrial complex. Over the last two decades punitive policies have steadily increased demand so that more and more private services are needed to augment public capacity. Such conditions present a highly favorable business environment for the criminal justice industrial complex.

This leads to a fundamental question, "How much criminal justice social control capacity can a free society sustain?" How would privatization advocates respond to this question? Would they see the need for boundaries on the speculative expansion of private capacity? How would they view public policy threats to corporate growth and profits? We don't have to guess. All we have to do is read their annual financial reports, examine the writings of privatization advocates and Wall Street market analysts, and look at program materials for privatization conferences. For example, the *Annual Reports* by Corrections Corporation of America (1993, 1997, 1998a-b) concentrate on discussions of occupancy rates, the number of beds under management, projections for future growth, market share, economies of scale, and stock prices. Corporate earnings clearly hold center stage. The World Research Group (1999) has held several annual conferences titled "Privatizing Correctional Facilities" over the last few years. Their brochure on the Fourth Annual Conference for September 23-24, 1999 carried the subtitle "Grow Profits and Maximize Investment Opportunities in this Explosive Industry" and listed the following session titles:

- "Structuring Successful Privatization Projects"
- "Government Agency Perspectives on the Role & Value of Privatization"
- "Bringing Profits to the Bottom Line: Maximizing Facility Savings in a Privatized Environment"
- "Privatization Management Firms: Business Plans, Financial Management and End Results"
- "Measuring and Quantifying Operational Differences Between Public and Private Prisons"
- "REITs Contribution to the Private and Public Sectors"
- "Dynamics and Growth of the Privatization Industry"
- "Managing Cost and Performance Issues Throughout the Corrections Continuum"
- "Public or Private Sector: Who Can Do It Better?"
- "Assessing the Legal Considerations"

These examples demonstrate the extent to which business strategies dominate industry thinking. Concentration on business strategies to promote faster development of speculative projects, more efficient operations and greater profits tends to drive out consideration of the societal implications of such growth in private criminal justice capacity.

Logan (1990) is one of the strongest advocates of correctional privatization today. He employs all the standard arguments for expanded use of private confinement. Privatization will reduce government size and "red tape," eliminate government monopoly, reduce costs to the public through market competition, allow capacity to vary based on crime rates, provide more efficient construction of prisons and jails, and ensure truth in sentencing. Market analysts predict steady growth in the private corrections market. In one article titled "Unappetizing Suggestions for Tasty Stock Profits: Or, How to Clean Up with Grubby-Sounding Companies," published in *Kiplinger's Personal Finance Magazine,* made a direct comparison between CCA and major hotels chains like Hilton and Marriott (Giese, 1991). The author noted that CCA had regularly reported occupancy rates approaching or exceeding 95 percent with strong earnings. As a result, investment in CCA was recommended as long as investors did not mind the "dirty" nature of the business. The industry and its advocates fail to consider the larger implications of privatization for society.

The growth trend for the private prison industry is attractive to profit-seeking investors. Figures 3.4 and 3.5 show the actual (1988-1997) and projected (1998-2002) growth trends in private confinement respectively.

Figure 3.4
Ten-Year Growth Trend in Design Capacity for Secure Private Adult Prisons and Jails

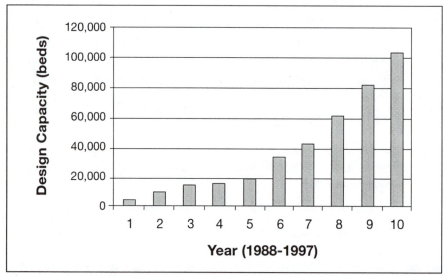

Source: Thomas and Bolinger, 1999a.

This kind of growth was recognized on November 15, 1998 at the Twelfth Annual Ernst & Young Entrepreneur of the Year International Conference in Palm Springs, California. Doctor R. Crants, CEO of Corrections Corporation of America was honored as the 1998 National Entrepreneur of the Year for the service industry. A year later, Crants was fired as part of a reorganization package to bring the company back from the brink of bankruptcy after a series of operational scandals, a failed merger, and roughly $250 million in losses in operational costs and stock valuation (Hershey, 1999; Miller, 1999; West, 2000). But on the night of his award, the citation by the National Director of Entrepreneurial Services for Ernst & Young noted that:

> Entrepreneurs such as Doc Crants . . . ultimately improve the quality of life in America and beyond by proving that exceptional ideas are forever worthy of pursuit. . . .Not only are their

Figure 3.5
Predicted Design Capacity 1998-2002 for Secure Private Adult Prisons and Jails (at year end)

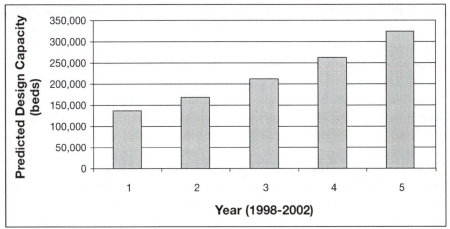

Source: Thomas and Bolinger, 1999a.

products and services generating jobs and pushing their respective industries to the next level of innovation and growth, they are forever changing the way future generations see the world. (Corrections Corporation of America, 1998c:1)

Once again we see that private interests are viewed as synonymous with public interests. With testimonials like this, other segments of the criminal justice industrial complex are likely to strive to be as aggressive in pursuing market expansion as CCA. The privatization industry and its advocates see no outer boundary to the expansion of private capacity. Nor do they have any sense of the destructive potential their industry poses for society. Industry expansion is, from their view, in the interest of American society. As long as there is market demand for private criminal justice services, they intend to meet that demand. Of course the criminal justice industrial complex is unlikely to lobby against tougher criminal sanctions, more funding, expanded private confinement, or greater use of private forms of social control. It is in their interest to keep demand for their goods and services as high as possible. They rarely consider where incremental increase in formal social control by private providers is taking the society.

If Corrections Corporation of America (CCA) were successful in its 1997 efforts to privatize 70 percent of the Tennessee Department of Corrections, the company would almost certainly exert a stronger influence over correctional policy than the residual Department of Corrections. To whom would public policymakers turn for advice on statewide correctional policy? What kind of policy advice would corporate officials provide? Would their policy advice be consistent with continued growth in earnings when long-term public interests would be sacrificed? Would they oppose policy shifts to reduce the use of confinement? Other chapters in this book demonstrate that CCA has exerted strong political influence in Tennessee and other jurisdictions in an effort to influence public policy and advance corporate interests with little regard for long-term public interest. The history of CCA has answered these questions for us. To paraphrase the famous quote by Charles Wilson, an executive at General Motors in 1952 before the Senate Armed Services Committee—"What is good for CCA is good for the country" (Rawson & Miner, 1986:46). In this way, private corporate interests become defined as public interests.

At the most extreme level of privatization, powerful private interests may capture public policy processes that govern the allocation of public resources, operational policies and quality of services provided. The end result could be loss of public control (sovereignty) over both policy and service delivery. In this incremental way, criminal justice policy could be diverted to serve private interests instead of public interests (Kolderie, 1986). Under such circumstances it may be difficult for the government to reassert control over either production or policy. As the case study of Frio County, Texas, later in this book suggests, it may be impossible for some jurisdictions to terminate a contract even when the contractor fails to perform and there is evidence of misfeasance or malfeasance by the contractor. Public dependency on private production erodes public capacity (i.e., professional management, trained and qualified employees, administrative resources, staff expertise, etc.) to resume public service. Furthermore, the jurisdiction may not have the financial resources to buy out the contract, replace lost revenue from the sale of excess capacity to other jurisdictions, pay off the costs of renovations/improvements made by the contractor, or rebuild a trained workforce. Under such conditions, the threat of contract termination may be a hollow one (Gilbert, 1996a, 1996b).

Shichor (1995:74) highlighted the underlying tension between public and private functions. Public functions serve a public purpose, are subjected to public accountability, and to public disclosure. Private functions, on the other hand, serve a private purpose, are subjected to private accountability, and are protected from both public disclosure and public accountability. Private contractors are also afforded considerable protection from liability under property, contract and tax law. For example, many of the operational records generated by a private contractor would be considered proprietary rather than state records. Therefore the federal and state acts requiring public access to government documents (i.e., "freedom of information acts") would not apply (Casarez, 1995). Finally, damage awards against corporations can be treated as tax deductible business expenses (Sabatino, 1997).

Given the protection afforded corporations, it is important to recognize that new private sector opportunities to exploit public-trust and influence public policy will emerge as their involvement in criminal justice expands. The nature of the abuses that occur will vary. But the general intent will probably involve corporate economic interests of some form. One example occurred at the Pahokee Youth Development Center. It is a private juvenile detention center operated by Correctional Services Corporation in Dade County, Florida. In 1996, the facility detained 10 residents nearly three weeks longer than authorized in order to ensure that those residents were available for the next "FTE week." This corporate decision directly increased the education and per diem funds received from the state.[14]

A much more serious example in Louisiana made national news in March 2000. Initial reports by investigators strongly suggested that pressure of reduced per diem costs (i.e., efficiency) within a private juvenile facility operated by Wackenhut Corrections Corporation led to inhuman conditions of confinement and physical abuse of the youths held at that facility (Associated Press, 2000; Butterfield, 2000a, 2000b). Pressures to cut operational costs seem to have resulted in the use of untrained or inadequately trained officers and chronic shortages of food, clothing, educational programming, and medical treatment for youths held at the facility. Many of the 276 boys at the facility were found without shoes, underwear, mattresses, and blankets. During winter months, many of these boys went without shoes or jackets and some refused to attend classes, preferring to stay warm under shared sheets or blankets (Butterfield, 2000a). These shortages caused boys to fight over clean clothes and food. Apparently, some boys ". . . repeatedly mutilated themselves so that they [would] be transferred to the prison's medical unit to avoid being pressured for food or sex by other prisoners" (Associated Press, 2000:2 of 2). The investigators found that 25 percent of the boys had been ". . . traumatically injured in a two-month period, many by untrained guards." These poorly trained officers ". . . routinely threw inmates against walls, twisted their arms or shoved them to the ground because they had not been taught other ways to control the boys." Furthermore, they found that ". . . low pay and poor management . . . led to high turnover in personnel: five wardens since Jena had been opened, and 600 persons have filled its 180 staff positions." Wackenhut apparently failed to conduct background investigations on all applicants and some officers were hired despite having a record of assault. As one investigator succinctly stated ". . . the pervasive lack of shoes, underwear, blankets and mattresses for inmates was 'just cheap'" (Butterfield, 2000a:2-4 of 4). On March 30, 2000 the United States Justice Department filed a lawsuit against Wackenhut Corrections Corporations as a result of the "dangerous and life threatening" conditions and physical abuse by officers at the facility (Butterfield, 2000b). The Acting

Assistant U.S. Attorney General for Civil Rights is quoted as saying that: "We are taking this action on behalf of young people in this facility who cannot help or protect themselves" (Associated Press, 2000:1 of 3).

No doubt there are examples of egregious organizational behavior within public prisons and jails. However, the documented problems at the Pahokee and Jena facilities demonstrate that public and private interests are rarely the same. Different value systems are in operation. The pressure for efficiency in business is often seen as synonymous with effectiveness. The value of what works in the business environment is commonly measured by how much it contributes to the bottom line. However, public policy choices are not driven primarily by efficiency concerns. Instead many non-economic issues often take precedence. One of the first is the primary concern for doing something that actually addresses public needs by meaningfully responding to the social or policy problem at hand. There are also a number of equity principles—individual rights, civil rights, substantive due process, constitutional conditions of confinement, equality, non-discrimination, equal access, transparency in government, etc.—that often take precedence over efficiency concerns. Inefficiencies in government operations may reflect conscious policy choices that maximize equity values or the preference for a certain quality of service. The door-to-door delivery of mail is a prime example. Efficiency becomes a focus of concern after effective policy responses, consistent with non-economic values, have been established. At the Pahokee and Jena facilities, contractors may lose contracts, not because of cost but because the constraints on costs or enhancements to earnings violated individual rights, civil rights, due process, and constitutional standards of care. Put simply, government is not a business.

Corporate executives are unlikely to establish business plans based on whether public or societal interests are served or underlying social problems are ameliorated. In fact, excessive attention to such non-business interests may be contrary to the economic interests of the company, its investors and corporate executives. As noted earlier, the criminal justice industrial complex tends to support social policies that support continuous business growth. Conversely, they are likely to oppose policies that would reduce public demand for their services. Speculative ventures will continue to develop capacity ahead of demand so that the private sector will be able to offer timely responses to public justice needs. Such growth of private capacity will progressively consume public resources and progressively shift the state—inmate by inmate, officer by officer, prison by prison, court by court—toward a private police state. Civil rights, civil liberties, and due process may be gradually eroded in an obsessive search for greater public safety (Amnesty International, 1998).

There are a variety of ways actions by contractors could influence or capture public policy to their advantage. These include:

- Unauthorized changes in practice or quality, which violate contract provisions;

- Bribery of elected officials, government regulators, and contract monitors to overlook violations of the contract, standards, civil rights, or statutory law;

- Encouragement of political officials to influence regulators or contract monitors in ways that discourage vigorous monitoring;

- Lobbying for policies that expand business volume, broaden the scope of services, or increase the severity of criminal sanctions;

- Circumvention of regulatory requirements or procedural controls;

- Substitution of equity based non-market standards of government performance with economic business standards of success;

- Manipulation of public opinion by using the mass media and other strategies to build public support for policies favorable to the industry;

- Erosion of governmental sovereignty over public policy by increasing dependency on private vendors to deliver public goods and services, especially where there is no credible threat of contract termination; and

- Formation of monopolies or stable "iron triangle" coalitions, both of which tend to capture the public policy process so that the private interests are served at public expense (see Figures 3.2 and 3.3).

These kinds of private sector influences over public policy are realistic outcomes. They have been broadly noted in the public administration literature as well as the literature on corporate and governmental crime. It is the responsibility of government to protect public policy processes from misuse or capture by private interests. In the context of criminal justice privatization this implies that governments at all levels must be cautious about when and how they introduce privatization of criminal justice functions into their jurisdictions. The power relationships between the government and private contractors must not be allowed to become so one sided that the government cannot prevent private interest manipulation of criminal justice policy for private economic gains.

What Are the Criminal Justice Markets of the Future?

Over the last two decades there has been increasing advocacy ". . . to expand the role of the private sector to reduced crime and lessen the burden of criminal justice for taxpayers" (National Center for Policy Analysis, 1996a:1). The National Center for Policy Analysis (NCPA) is a Texas based, conservative, think tank with offices in Dallas and Washington, DC. It lobbies federal and state legislators on a variety of policy issues.[15] The NCPA advocates a series of criminal justice reforms to increase private sector involvement in delivery of criminal justice services (National Center for Policy Analysis, 1996a:1-2). When these reforms are considered in the context of non-market core social values some are quite alarming. The criminal justice reforms advocated by NCPA include:

- Shut down pretrial release bureaus and . . . free bonds in favor of competitive, commercial bail bonds.

- Increase the use of private rewards for criminal convictions, including bounties offered by commercial insurance policies.

- Pay bounty hunters for recovering criminals who are wanted on . . . [arrest] warrants.

- . . . [G]reater use of private attorneys to . . . litigate criminal cases at private expense. . . .

- . . . [I]ntegration of criminal prosecution and civil remedies . . . to raise the price of crime to criminals and compensate victims more adequately.

- Require convicts . . . to post a private bond to guarantee good behavior [on probation or parole], thus ensuring supervision by a bondsman, raising the cost of . . . violating the terms of their release and encouraging self control.

- Accelerate private construction and operation of prisons. . . .

- Accelerate the private employment of prison labor and explore private employment of convict labor alongside non-convict labor.

. . . Privatizing the criminal justice system on an incremental basis is a win-win solution: The innovation and productivity of private enterprise can reduce crime, reduce taxes, and improve the protection of civil liberties. [added]

The rationale and details of some of these market oriented policy proposals are spelled out in other NCPA materials (1996b; 1996c:1-2):

> Probation workers have more cases than they can effectively handle, and . . . parole boards are not as selective about whom to parole as they once were. . . . We can put the competitive market mechanism to work on this problem.

> Prisoners eligible for probation and parole should be required to post a financial bond against specified violations of . . . their probation or parole . . . .The amount should be set by the courts or parole boards based on the criminal's history and prospects for a productive, non-criminal life. . . . many criminals would have to seek the help of family and friends . . . to acquire the cosigners and wherewithal to pay the bondsman's fee and receive probation or parole. An important source of funds for parolees could be wages earned while in prison. But if no . . . [one or] any private bondsman cared enough to risk their own money . . . why should the general public risk that person on the streets. Privatizing the probation and parole systems provides a market mechanism for deciding whom to release on probation or parole and whom to continue incarcerating.

> A private bonding system would reduce, if not eliminate, the need for probation and parole officers on the public payroll. . . . with . . . their own money at risk, bondsmen would supervise their charges closely and the fugitive rate would be low.

> . . . bounty hunters have every financial incentive to recover fugitives, and they can go to any jurisdiction and use any means within . . . the law to apprehend a fugitive. Privatizing the entire probation and parole system would not only save taxpayers money but would also result in a far more effective system than we now have. Crime would plummet. [added]

One of the most alarming policy recommendations by the National Center for Policy Analysis is the privatization of criminal prosecution (National Center for Policy Analysis, 1996d:1):

> The law should encourage . . . private preparation of criminal cases. . . .

> Victims should be allowed to hire attorneys and other professionals to prepare cases against the accused and thereby extend public prosecutors' resources. . . .

> . . . A logical extension of private preparation for trial is the complete privatization of the prosecutor's job by contracting out. . . . Private attorneys could be deputized for a single trial or for ongoing prosecutor[ial] work. . . under contract.

> The same remedies are available to finance criminal prosecution as civil litigation. . . . Commercial insurance policies could be expanded or created for this market. Associations and community groups could cover these costs for members and subscribers. [added]

It is clear that some advocates for privatization support total reliance on market systems. This strategy has been called "load shedding"—the complete transfer of a public function to the private sector (Bailey, 1987:139). Load shedding is entirely consistent with the libertarian view of minimalist government. That is, government should have a minimal role within society—ensuring national security, protection of the market system, ensuring equality before the law, and funding major public works projects. In the case of criminal justice services, the government should fund private delivery of justice services and establish the legal environment within which private justice would function. Such views are altogether uninformed by criminal justice history and show little awareness of the threats presented to society.

Justice was once a private matter settled solely between the victim and the offender. When justice consisted of revenge by the victim or compensation by the offender for the victim's losses, justice was attained when the victim was satisfied that offender had suffered an equivalent harm. In the absence of meaningful boundaries, private justice vendettas commonly escalated into blood feuds. It was through the intervention of third party authority—the family patriarch/matriarch, community leaders, clan elders, tribal leaders or the heads of nation states—that boundaries around vendettas were established and the destructive potential of blood feuds was contained (Durham, 1988; Gilbert 1996a; Peters, 1995:10).

The policy positions expressed by the NCPA on criminal justice privatization are also uninformed by more recent history of private sector involvement in criminal justice—law enforcement, confinement, and prosecution. In another chapter of this book Smith and Morn discuss this history. In short, human society has been down the private justice road. Public delivery of justice services became the dominant mode of production largely because the abuse and exploitation of vulnerable people for private interests shocked the conscience of the citizenry (Durham, 1989a, 1989b, 1989c; Kentucky Corrections Cabinet, Office of Corrections Training, 1985; Richardson, 1997; Walker, 1998a).

Although the policy positions advocated by NCPA are at the extreme end of the privatization debate, the ideas presented have attracted support from other market-oriented lobbying groups. The views of these groups often involve libertarian political philosophy, public-choice economic theory (i.e., the power of economic markets to meet public needs), belief in a natural law private justice theory, and a retributive or just deserts orientation to public justice (Gilbert, 1996a). However, such arguments are also likely to be supported by the criminal justice industrial complex. Quite simply, these arguments promise new criminal justice market segments and are consistent with the growth-oriented business plans of the industry. From these perspectives, privatizing as much of the criminal justice system (police, prisons, jails, probation, parole, prosecution and courts) as possible would be a reasonable policy objective. They argue that the private sector could hardly do worse than the government has done.

These views are consistent with those held by a large portion of the electorate. As a result, advocates of broader criminal justice privatization draw on three important societal values as central organizing principals for society—public safety, reduction in the cost to taxpayers, and market competition. Each of these is politically attractive and useful as they seek to wall off criminals and dangerous classes (i.e., the poor, uneducated, unemployed, etc.) from the rest of society. The methods they advocate involve market mechanisms, business principles, and private enterprise to carry out the tasks. Yet, walling off criminals and dangerous classes of people requires restriction of liberty, civil rights, and due process for all citizens. These restrictions cannot be limited to the rights of criminals and those among the dangerous classes.

Advocates of broad criminal justice privatization assume that concern for public safety, public expense, and faith in markets trump all other values. They further assume that their policy prescriptions for public safety are consistent with long-term public interests. Such advocates do not question whether a massive transfer of coercive state power into private hands is a wise or just policy decision. They do not question whether continuous expansion of private justice services is economically or socially sustainable by society. They do not consider whether privatization threatens basic non-market principles of individual liberties, civil rights, and due process. They do not question the transfer of control over public policy to non-elected private interests. They do not recognize that load shedding to the private sector also shifts power relationships weakening public authority and strengthening private authority. They do not consider whether public authority will be able to monitor and control contractor performance. They do not question whether public authority will be able to hold private authority accountable. They do not recognize that private monopoly over public justice exposes public interests to exploitation. They do not see any problem with socially stratified effects of private prosecution or conditional release based on ability to pay. Advocates of criminal justice privatization assume that market approaches will bring only positive outcomes. They argue that government should step back, let them go to work meeting public safety needs and making money.

What Is the Role of Government When Criminal Justice Services Are Privatized?

Perhaps the most fundamental role of government when justice services are privatized is to ask such questions to ensure that public interests are protected from exploitation and abuse by those with private financial interests (Lindblom, 1977:183; Wolfe, 1989). Markets define public interest in terms of efficiency in meeting consumer demand. By this view, efficiency is inherently in the public interest. Although such rationality may be appropriate for privatization of certain public goods and services, it may be less appropriate or totally inappropriate for others. Privatized trash pick-up, emergency ambulance services, or public transportation are not highly controversial policies. In these areas, efficiency may indeed be in the public interest as long as the trash is picked up regularly, ambulances arrive with trained paramedics and the needed equipment, and safe buses run on schedule. Yet, each has been considered a public function in the past. Part of the reason that these are not controversial forms of privatization is that none require the use of coercive state authority. Additionally, the purchaser is the consumer and privatization does not preclude resumption of public production or undercut the minimum default level of essential public services. There is also little risk to personal liberty, civil rights, or public policy in these forms of privatization. Contract termination for non-performance or abuse would be a viable and credible option because genuine markets exist. Private contractors could be monitored and held accountable to public authority as public utilities. In the absence of organized crime, it is unlikely that privatization in these areas would create a stable, destructive, private monopoly. However, controversy would soon appear if the economic calculus of the marketplace threatened core social values such as liberty, equality, civil-rights, open and honest elections, public order and tranquility, due process and democratic policymaking.

The coercive power of the state may be needed to preserve or implement such equity-based social values. State authority was used to preserve core social values in several states when the National Guard forced school desegregation, ensured voting rights, and protected civil rights demonstrators. Other examples include the prosecution of offenders, regulation of financial markets, health inspections of restaurants, protection of worker safety, conservation of public lands, and protection of the environment. In criminal justice, the coercive power of the state is applied daily to exert formal social controls upon individuals. In the process, the criminal justice system directly, immediately, and dramatically affects the lives of those caught up in it. Although, greater private sector efficiency enhances corporate profits, it could be highly destructive to society if efficiency gains are made at the expense of non-market core social values.

Whether genuine criminal justice markets will actually form is questionable. Genuine markets rely on voluntary exchange between customers and sellers. Money is exchanged for the product or service selected from among those available. When criminal justice services are privatized, the consumer of the service is not the customer (Shichor, 1995). Offenders have no ability to make voluntary market choices about criminal justice services. Legislative or administrative officials select vendors to provide services at a designated cost. Private contractors are likely to view elected and appointed public officials as their customers and regard offenders as simply a commodity to be processed. The criminal justice industrial complex operates within an artificial market that is not subject to pressure from the actual consumers of their services who are powerless to boycott the products or services provided (Lindblom, 1977:12, 33-51, 88-89). Additionally, the private prison management market is dominated by a handful of firms who control nearly 100 percent of the market. At the end of 1998, the six largest competitors controlled 98 percent of the United States market and 94 percent of the worldwide market for private prison and jail beds (Thomas & Bolinger, 1999a). In essence, the private confinement industry is a shared monopoly or oligopoly. Similarly, in the private security/law enforcement market a handful of companies control the bulk of the business in the United States and worldwide.

In this context, genuine competitive markets may only exist when initial contracts are offered. Thereafter, major companies within shared monopolies are likely to respect each other's territory. This avoids poaching of established clients unless an incumbent contractor is perceived to be in political trouble. As long as the incumbent appears to "have a lock" on contract renewal, other companies will probably not submit truly competitive bids against the incumbent. When the probability of successfully taking a contract away from the current contractor is low, rational actors are likely to submit "recycled, off-the-shelf" proposals rather than to expend the resources necessary to develop a highly tailored and genuinely competitive proposals. This provides the appearance of a competitive market without the expense required for genuine competition.[16] Such practices would amount to informal "restraint of trade."

Privatization is a legal policy response to criminal justice issues and it is here to stay. The primary question before us now is whether governments will be able to control the criminal justice industry so that privatization serves long-term societal interests. It is possible that criminal justice policy decisions could be manipulated to serve corporate interests rather than public interests. Could capacity control public policy rather than public policy controlling capacity? To prevent this in the criminal justice arena, governments should retain a substantial default level of public production. This strategy has four purposes. First, it helps ensure continuous public services for those arrested, charge and convicted, their families, and crime victims should market failures occur. Second, it ensures that public sector criminal justice professionals are available to provide policy advice to political leaders and other policy-makers. Third, retention of some public capacity makes the resumption of public service a viable policy option and the threat of contract termination credible. Finally, public delivery of criminal justice helps maintain the sense of social obligation and community between governments, citizens, their neighborhoods, cities, and the nation. Total dependency on private production fosters a corporate/franchise identity rather than one based on community and place. For these reasons, total privatization of the public capacity in any area of criminal justice would, in most cases, be an inappropriate form of privatization.

The role of government, however, is to explore the meaning of private criminal justice within a civil society by asking and answering the kinds of questions explored in this chapter. Responsible public officials cannot blithely assume positive outcomes when large segments of the criminal justice system are privatized. These officials have a responsibility to the whole society. They are not responsible for ensuring profitable markets for the criminal justice industrial complex. Public officials must structure criminal justice privatization in such a way that broad public interests are protected from exploitation and insulated (as much as possible) from market failure. This requires active monitoring of market responses and contractor performance. Ineffective performance, unethical behavior, chronic sub-standard quality, violation of contract provisions, or illegal activities by a contractor require corrective action by the state. More than public safety and public funds are at stake with criminal justice privatization—control of public policy, civil rights, non-discrimination, liberty, equal protection, and non-interruption of public services are just a few of the non-market interests at risk. It is the responsibility of government to manage these risks when criminal justice is privatized. Consequently, the government must constrain the private exercise of coercive state authority and the expansionistic impulses that underlie criminal justice markets. The government must retain control over criminal justice policy by limiting contractor involvement in the formation of public policy and making the nature of their involvement as transparent as possible.

A Structure for Understanding and Managing the Risks of Privatization

In order to understand how the risks of privatization are related to correctional services, Gilbert (1996b) synthesized a typology employing three dimensions (see Figure 3.6).

Figure 3.6
Form of Privatization by Risk of Serious Private Sector Abuse

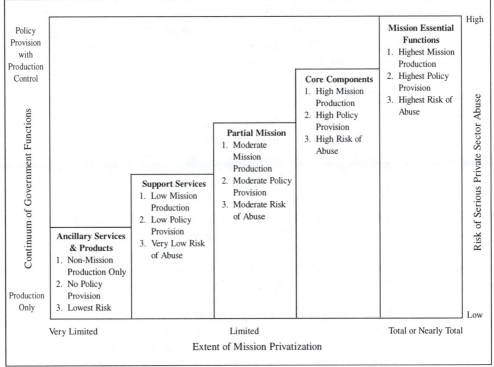

Source: Gilbert, 1996b.

These dimensions are (1) a continuum of government functions (from production only to policy provision with production control); (2) extent of mission privatization (from very limited to total or near total privatization); and (3) the relative risk of serious private sector abuse (from low to high). This typology can be generalized to broader criminal justice privatization. The five general types of privatization apply to any segment of the criminal justice market (adapted from Gilbert, 1996b:67-72). These are:

1. *Ancillary Services/Products* (non-mission-related)
   Lawn maintenance, vehicle maintenance, and janitorial services are examples of ancillary services. Criminal justice equipment and supplies are examples of ancillary products. There is little reason for concern over private sector production of ancillary services or products since they present the lowest risk of serious abuse of public interests and these risks are easily controlled.

2. *Support Services* (marginally mission-related)
   These types of services involve low-level mission-related functions. Inmate commissary services in a jail or prison and clerical or data entry services in a police department are examples. These types of services contribute to mission attainment, but the contractor has very limited involvement in both mission attainment and formation of policy. As a result, these kinds of services present a low risk of serious abuse when privatized, and the risks are also quite easily managed.

3. *Partial Mission* (moderately mission-related)
   These functions include important services needed for attainment of the mission. Some examples are: privatized inmate education, health and food service programs in a prison; contract criminal investigation services at a prosecutor's office; and, contract data analysis services to process crime statistics for a police department. Contractors for such functions are directly involved in the attainment mission and exert influence upon public policy processes related to their areas of expertise. There is a moderate risk of serious abuse when such services are privatized but these risks are easily managed because of fierce competition for these types of contracts.

4. *Core Components* (strongly mission-related)
   These services are strongly related to attainment of the criminal justice mission. For example, contract halfway house services; private management of a public prison; placement of inmates in a private institution; private electronic monitoring services; private patrol services assigned to police public streets; and private security services to operate the 911 emergency responses system. Actual delivery of criminal justice services to citizens directly involves the contractor in mission attainment and public policy processes that affect the allocation of public resources and services. There is a higher risk of serious abuse of public interests and rigorous contract monitoring is essential to the management of these risks.

5. *Mission Essential Functions* (critically related to mission attainment)
   These functions involve privatization of a high proportion of the productive capacity for any public agency to attain its mission. This form of privatization is "load shedding." When a correctional agency privatizes the largest institution within the agency, most of its institutions, or all of its prison beds, it is privatizing mission essen-

tial functions. When lobbyists advocate total privatization of prosecution, probation, parole, and police forces they are advocating
load shedding and possibly the creation of private monopolies.
Load shedding transfers much of the criminal justice policy process
to private providers. It presents the highest risks of serious abuse
and the greatest threat to governmental control over justice policy.
Abuses under this form of privatization are very difficult to control
or correct and present direct threats to civil rights, civil liberties,
equal access to courts, equal protection, public accountability,
and most non-market core social values within a civil society. Contract monitoring is essential to control private sector influences on
and threats to public interests.

When partial mission functions, core components, and mission
essential functions are privatized, special restrictions on the private
contractor's role in policy formation may be needed. The objective is to
ensure that public policy processes are not gradually captured or controlled by the contractor and then publicly implemented.

This typology allows public officials to assess whether privatization
presents high or low risks to the public interests and the community.
Once the risk potential for a particular privatization decision is understood, a more detailed assessment is needed. Policymakers need to
know something about the market segments involved. For example,
the purchase of tangible goods, at least in the criminal justice arena, presents less concern than the production of criminal justice services.
High rates of business growth may indicate speculative development of
criminal justice capacity. Once policymakers understand the market
segment with which they are dealing, they need to consider whether the
function being considered for privatization is appropriate for privatization. Inappropriate privatization would:

- undercut the default level of criminal justice services;

- allow public policy processes to be strongly influenced or controlled by private interests;

- present a serious risk to individual liberties and civil rights;

- protect the contractor from public accountability, or

- replace a public monopoly with a private monopoly.

If a policy decision is made to privatize, the appropriate role of government is to proactively manage the risks of abuse associated with privatization. In this way, long-term public interests may be preserved and
privatization is less likely to expand in ways that threaten either the sus-
tainability of the society or its non-market core social values. Effective

management of these risks is the price of responsible privatization. The following guidelines are intended to help public justice officials control privatization.

Thirteen Guidelines for Controlling Privatization and the Risks to Public Interests

1. Privatization should augment but not replace public capacity to exert formal social controls.

2. Privatization should be understood as a reactive policy response driven by excess demand for justice services. Privatization will increase criminal justice capacity, but do little to reduce street crime.

3. Don't totally privatize core component and mission essential functions. A default level of public capacity must be retained to assure public resumption, should a market failure occur.

4. Don't privatize to a single provider. Whenever possible, use multiple providers to ensure competition and avoid the creation of a private monopoly.

5. Remember that taxpayers always pay for criminal justice production—public or private.

6. Remember that lower unit costs are likely to increase system costs by increasing demand for criminal justice services.

7. Remember that the business logic of criminal justice markets is expansionistic and continuous growth of private capacity is likely to have a destructive, parasitic, relationship to the society.

8. Privatization contracts must be detailed and establish all the necessary standards, monitoring procedures, and restrictions to ensure that public authority can hold contractors accountable. A defective contract is difficult, if not impossible, to correct after it is signed.

9. There must be a formal process for contract monitoring. It is the only independent means to verify contract compliance. Given the risks that criminal justice privatization presents, public officials who fail to establish an effective monitoring program increase public liability, the threat to civil rights, and the potential for abuse of citizens.

10. Contract monitors are targets for co-optation and corruption to hide noncompliance, misfeasance, and malfeasance by the contractor. Consequently, monitors must be insulated, as much as possible, from corruption or political pressure to undercut their effectiveness as monitors.

11. Formal boundaries around the contractor's role in the formation of public policy are needed. Contractor participation and influence in policymaking must be transparent. Public disclosure of contractor involvement in political campaigns, the amounts spent on each lobbying activity; the individuals, parties and campaigns to whom funds were given; and, the use of mass media outlets to sway public opinion would help ensure that criminal justice policy remains publicly controlled.

12. Set the standards necessary to ensure that long-term public interests are preserved. It is the responsibility of government to preserve sovereignty and protect public interests when criminal justice services are privatized. Cost reduction should be a secondary concern.

13. Be prepared to resume public production at any time. The resumption of public production must be a realistic option if monopoly conditions are to be avoided.

Concluding Comments

This analysis makes it clear that some aspects of criminal justice privatization are viable policy options. It is also clear that the criminal justice industrial complex will continue its efforts to expand the size and value of all segments of the market; and, that such expansion could be highly destructive to society. It is entirely possible for criminal justice policy to be captured by the criminal justice industrial complex. Business interests within the criminal justice market are often at odds with public interests. Consequently, sensible boundaries around privatization are needed.

The central role of government is to ensure that: public control over public policy, public accountability of contractors, the welfare of citizens when they are subjected to privatized state power, private interests are subordinate to public interests, and private interests do not exploit public interest for private economic gain. Consequently, governments should impose the controls necessary to ensure that criminal justice privatization serves a constructive role within the society. In this regard, contractors should expect public officials to establish: well-developed requests for proposals, comprehensive contracts, rigorous performance requirements, default level capacity as a hedge against market failure, contracts with multiple providers, and active performance monitoring systems. Contractors who oppose these conditions should not submit bids for these projects.

It is uncertain whether private criminal justice capacity and market pressures will drive public policy; or, public policy will drive criminal justice capacity. Criminal justice privatization has a parasitic relationship to society. Unchecked, it could become highly destructive. The purpose of this chapter has been to provide a theoretical basis for understanding the risks and threats, the appropriateness of criminal justice privatization, and the role of government when justice is privatized so that meaningful boundaries may be established. Such boundaries between appropriate and inappropriate privatization are needed to constrain the growth of the criminal justice industry. Broad criminal justice privatization is becoming a reality; only history will tell whether public interests prevail in an era of privatized delivery of public justice.

Endnotes

[1]   In 1998 and 1999, CCA Prison Realty Trust accumulated sufficient capital to purchase its parent corporation—Corrections Corporation of America. As of January 1, 1999, CCA became a privately held company (West, 2000). It had merged with CCA Prison Realty Trust, its former subsidiary, under the Prison Realty Trust name (NYSE: PZN). During the last week in May 1999, eight lawsuits were filed against Prison Realty Trust by shareholders for understating the fees paid to CCA for its facilities (Flaum, 1999). Shortly after those suits were filed Crants resigned his position as Chairman and CEO of CCA but remained as CEO of Prison Realty Trust. J. Michael Quinlan replaced Crants as the Chief Operating Officer of CCA (Ward, 1999). Quinlan is a former Director of the Federal Bureau of Prisons.

[2]   Initially the REIT structure worked well for Prison Realty Trust/CCA by generating large amounts of low cost capital needed to support new ventures and pay dividends to investors. However, the cash flow requirements needed to maintain its REIT status, repay its debts and support new ventures were simply more than could be sustained. These financial problems were compounded by several lawsuits by shareholders and a number of high-profile operational scandals at its facilities. These factors suppressed its stock prices—losing 75 percent of its value in one year— which made raising new capital more difficult. Huge financial losses ensued (West, 2000). On December 27, 1999 it was announced Prison Realty Trust would be restructured. The restructuring plan would return the company to its original name Corrections Corporation of America, resume its tax paying status, raise $350 million in venture capital, and provide access to new financial instruments totaling $1.2 billion. The financial backers of the reorganization plan required that Doctor R. Crants resign immediately as Chairman of Prison Realty Trust but remain as Chief Executive until the restructuring deal has been finalized. After that Crants would serve solely as *non-executive vice chairman* and *board advisor*. Thomas W. Beasley, the former Chairman and co-founder of CCA assumed the title of Interim Chairman immediately. Once the deal is finalized he would serve as Chief Executive until Corrections Corporation of America has been restored to financial health (Hershey, 1999:C-6; Miller, 1999). It is an open question whether the reorganized company will be able to avoid bankruptcy.

3   The "private security industry" includes the following kinds of law enforcement and protective services—investigative services, executive protection, emergency protection services for commercial properties, residential and building security, crisis management, background investigations, alarm-monitoring, security consulting, and armored car transport.

4   The "alternative dispute resolution market" includes private mediation, private court proceedings with contract judges, and contract prosecution.

5   The "community corrections market" provides services like electronic monitoring, half-way houses, field supervision, and community treatment programs.

6   "Ancillary markets" refers to production and marketing of products and services used in criminal justice activities (weapons, bulletproof vests, riot gear, vehicles, food services, medical services, etc.)

7   The severe financial problems experienced by Prison Realty Trust (the corporate owner of Corrections Corporation of America) in 1999 forced its dissolution. Under the restructuring plan, Corrections Corporation of America resumed its original corporate name and tax status. It also assumed Prison Realty Trust's debts. The financial health of the company will remain uncertain for some time to come. Bankruptcy is a possibility until investor and government confidence has been restored (West, 2000). The potential bankruptcy of CCA raises a number of issues: What would happen to the facilities it owns or operates, the inmates under its supervision, its employees and the communities in which it operates? Could public production be resumed?

8   The Fourteenth Amendment (ratified on March 30, 1870) extends federally established civil rights and federal case law to the states and the citizens of states.

9   The legitimacy of the functions performed or funded by government rests on the participation of the governed, through elected representatives, to determine public policy. Substantive law defines criminal acts and is expressed in penal codes at each level of government. The laws of criminal procedure protect the rights of people accused of crimes and ensure due process. These statutory laws are established in the name of the public, for the public good, by elected public officials. The administrative rules that govern enforcement, arrest, arrest warrants, indictment, prosecution, judicial procedure, and imposition of sanctions were established by public officials—some elected, some appointed. These legal structures protect citizens from abusive use of state authority. In the United States, the exercise of state authority is guided by as The United States Constitution, the *Federalist Papers* (Hamilton, Jay & Madison, 1787), state constitutions, municipal charters, statutory law, legislative intent, case law, and administrative law.

10   See the following cases as examples: *Letcher v. Turner*, 968 F.2d 508 (1992), *Street v. Corrections Corporation of America*, 102 F.3d 810 (1996), *Giron v. Corrections Corporation of America*, 191 F.3d 1281 (1999) and *Moore v. Prison Health Services, Inc.*, 24 F. Supp. 2d 1164 (1999).

11   The majority of the Supreme Court listed four reasons for its decision. First, correctional functions have never been exclusively public. Second, there has been no tradition of immunity for government contractors or their employees. Third, qualified immunity would defeat market pressures that might prevent abuse of inmate

rights by increasing liability exposure. Finally, denial of immunity to private contractors would have no adverse affect the performance of either public or private officials.

[12] One of the ironies of damage awards is that corporations are able to deduct both compensatory and punitive damage awards from their taxable earnings. In the end, the public pays the damages awarded to the plaintiff (Sabatino, 1997).

[13] For analysis of the structural, cultural, and social influences that underlie crime and delinquency in American society and the potential for criminal justice policy responses to reduce crime, see Currie, 1985; Fabelo (1995a, 1995b), Felson (1998), Friedrichs (1996), Heide (1999), Messner & Rosenfeld (1997), Walker, Spohn & DeLone (1996), Zimring & Hawkins (1997) and many other recent research publications in criminology, sociology, and law.

[14] Pahokee Youth Development Center internal facility memorandum to Case Managers dated September 23, 1996 (Copy provided by Judy Greene).

[15] The NCPA operates an Internet Web site (//www.ncpa.org/) with detailed policy statements on each of these issues.

[16] On November 3-4, 1997 while in Oklahoma City, OK for the *First Annual Conference on Public Strategies for Private Prisons* the author had several meetings with executives from major private prison companies. When the author informally asked these executives to consider a scenario in which an incumbent contractor had a high probability (80%+) of the contract being renewed all but one of the executives admitted that they would not submit their most competitive bid. Their bid would be sufficient to allow their company to be "...seen as a player" but they admitted that they probably would not expend significant resources to ensure that their bid was highly competitive because the likelihood of being successful was low. They also admitted that this was not an uncommon scenario.

Part II

Privatization of Justice System Components

_____

4

Policing and the Private Security Option: Functional Transparency, Re-Privatization, and Implications in Law

James D. Calder
University of Texas at San Antonio

After the year 2000, policymakers are expected to debate further the issue of public sector cost containment. It will be impossible to ignore criminal justice agencies in this dialogue because they represent some of the most expensive items in public budgets. Like others, they attract the cost cutter's knife and the private investor's eye (Freeman, 1992; S.L. Mays, 1995; Morgan & England, 1988). In recent years, increasingly, corporate organizations have influenced public decisionmaking, each seeing economic benefits in privatization opportunities. Correctional agencies, for example, have extensive experience with privatization, and civil courts have implemented private mediation to reduce dockets. In contrast to court and police organizations, structural characteristics of correctional facilities sweeten the appeal to business ventures. Simply put, the orderliness of correctional operations is more amenable to unit cost accounting methods. In many cases, arguably rational decisions have been made to transform state-operated institutions into privately operated for-profit prisons.[1] An analytical literature has grown up around important questions concerning real net savings associated with confinement facilities operating under privatization arrangements (Culp, 1998; Farris, 1998; Mays & Gray, 1996). Much of the debate has focused on narrow economic issues. A smaller group of experts has begun to discuss the prospect that private correctional facilities, for example, will eventually be defined under state action principles of law (Dannin,

1998; Juceam, 1997), although it is clear that current conservative inter-pretation of the Constitution has not permitted this development. Should the rationale for a new state action interpretation appear, perhaps through egregious private actions in the performance of criminal justice duties, an entirely new set of rules would apply to actions under priva-tization ranging from police investigations to sentencing.

This chapter is directly concerned with police privatization, partic-ularly as the practice of contracting out certain traditional police services introduces what I call transparency into the public debate about priva-tization in general. In correctional operations, transparency may be more readily understood. For example, when one looks at a private prison, the operational appearance is virtually the same as when one observes a public jail or prison. There is transparency when one image is laid on top of the other image. Now, in the purest sense, I use the term 'transparency' in connection with police privatization to refer to physi-cal attributes, actions, and responsibilities of private police organizations that make them virtually indistinguishable from attributes, actions, and responsibilities of public police. As suggested by the example of priva-tization of correctional facilities, transparency in police work carries sig-nificant implications for justice administration, and the way private police organizations may be expected to conduct themselves in per-forming such actions as arrest, search, seizure of private property, inves-tigations, and handling of criminal information. For purposes of the discussion, the concept of transparency refers mainly to the progressive stages of police development and experimentation with privatization. I assume that each phase of experimentation in terms of re-privatizing police services will lead to an eventual condition in which core and non-core tasks of police are performed regularly by either public or private individuals, thus eclipsing the traditional distinctions between the two types of organizations. Core tasks of police work include patrol and sur-veillance, probable cause stops and searches, arrest and detention for questioning, transportation to lockups, booking, and suspect interro-gations. Non-core tasks are generally considered less threatening to the basic authority of police (Golsby, 1998). A variety of sub-tasks are asso-ciated with each of these main tasks. Core tasks require special grants of authority provided by general or specific elements of constitutional, statutory, or case law.

One of the most interesting features of the privatization debate is that advocacy in one direction or another tends to ignore implications of pub-lic-private transparency. Eventually, debate may depend more on how policymakers resolve transparency issues, particularly in the way private security's actions raise significant implications in law. Economics guides budgetary decisions to find alternatives to public services. Law, on the other hand, creates and obligates consideration of the contradictions aris-ing from transparency that policymakers seem willing to accept and to encourage in criminal justice administration. Law bears ultimate responsibility for resolving these contradictions so that economic self-interest and state authority can be reasonably balanced. These concerns appear in some current debates about corrections privatization, but they are overdue in discussions about police privatization. An even newer topic of concern in this regard is 'third-party policing' (Buerger & Mazerolle, 1998), which refers to civil remedies imposed by police or regulatory units on citizens and obligate more private action to control conditions on private property that authorities believe to be sources of crime, such as, drug dealing, disorderly conduct, and various nuisances. Recently, for example, a court in San Antonio, Texas ordered that gang members could not associate with each other and they were prohibited from using cellular phones and beeper paging systems.

This paper focuses on implications in law that arise when private security and public police become increasingly transparent in their functional operations. Police privatization has not attracted significant formal discussion, despite the fact that successes in policing translate directly into larger workloads and costs for courts and correctional organizations. Incrementally, of course, forms of privatization have been implemented in police agencies for several years. Civilianization[2] has replaced and complemented administrative work in police departments. Agencies have contracted or shed selected non-core tasks. Private security companies have emerged as eligible bidders and participants in the gradual transformation of policing (Boostrom & Draper, 1992; Cunningham, Strauchs & Van Meter, 1990; Jones & Newburn, 1995; Nalla & Newman, 1990; Shearing & Stenning, 1987, 1983, 1980). Some have demonstrated capabilities of delivering comprehensive services in a manner that is comparable to services delivered by police. Factually, however, few comprehensive experiments in police privatization have been implemented, thus limiting both critique and prospectus to a few American examples, such as Starrett City, New York, and Fresno, California, and examples from the international arena (Benyon, 1996; de Waard, 1993; George & Button, 1998; Hesseling, 1995; Johnston, 1993; Oliver, 1998; Tolchin, 1985; Walsh, Donovan & McNicholas, 1992).

Because privatization attracts significant appeal as a logical step in police development, further discussion is required about implications arising from legal principles that distinguish public from private authority. I prefer to use the term 're-privatization' to refer to the evolution of new cooperative ventures in public-private policing. The term observes an evolutionary process and an outcome that includes the return of elements of public policing to private performance, mainly by commercial security organizations. The outcome depends upon deliberations and decisions of political bodies acting in the public interest, presumably on the basis of careful study of the implications. Despite nearly two centuries of institutionalization of the idea of public policing in England, then America (Bayley, 1985; Bittner, 1970; Briggs, Harrison, McInnis & Vincent, 1996; Greenberg, 1976; D. Johnson, 1981; H. Johnson, 1988; Klockars, 1985; Prassel, 1972; Walker, 1998a), the private sector can claim the true historical roots of policing initiatives (Shalloo, 1929, 1933; Bowden, 1977; Nalla & Newman, 1990; Spitzer & Scull, 1977). Originally policing was self-policing, subsequently organized by military and government authorities into bureaucratized functions serving the general interest. As urban areas experienced growth and complexity, the private option became less acceptable in a society in search of rules by which to introduce greater accountability under law over both public and private actions (Bayley, 1994). Public awareness of ineffectiveness and incompetence of private services accounted for substantial commitment to new, publicly supported police departments. Popular support for law, government's role in social order maintenance, and principles of procedural justice called for protection against abuses of public authority in areas such as arrest, search, and seizure.

The main focus of re-privatization in modern times, however, is the actual or potential transparency emergent from nearly 200 years of mirror-imaging between public and private police organizations. As police perform more security and crime prevention functions, and as private companies perform what police organizations have also performed, the marks of functional and legal distinction become less clearly defined. Decades of public usurpation of community crime control and prevention have been matched by continued development of the private sector option in both high-profile uniformed security and private investigative work (Draper, 1978; George & Button, 1995; Ghezzi, 1983; Gill & Hart, 1997). Re-privatization of some police functions has evolved as an outgrowth of similarity of task performance, complementary work relationships (i.e., cooperation and mutual assistance), and new ideas about the distribution of authority and responsibility for crime control (Golsby, 1998; Hesseling, 1995; Hoogenboom, 1991). Not only are some private organizations acting like and looking like public organizations, they are fitting into options under consideration in a range of alternative private sector roles in patrol, investigations, and service aspects of policing (Colletti, 1996; Harvey, 1996: Lee, 1995).

The trend toward re-privatization, specifically private involvement in performing non-core and core elements of police work, magnifies essential differences in respective allocations of legal authority of private and public police. Although police privatization initiatives remain limited at this time, perhaps a result of reduced urban crime rates, reason suggests that further re-privatization will obligate courts and legislative bodies to forthrightly address the distribution of authority embedded in state laws. In this regard, the issue attracting significant attention is 'state action,' an area of law with deep roots in American post-Civil War interpretations of civil rights protection. Privatization, which has already allocated new roles in the operations of state and federal jail and prison management, predictably will creep into many other areas of public-private interaction (Rishikoff & Wohl, 1996; Krotoszynski, 1995; Sullivan, 1987). Logically, the concept of strictly private action is destined to change significantly as private security moves closer to performing duties that police have performed under the exclusive obligations and immunities of state action (Juceam, 1997).

In the following sections, the process and outcomes of the re-privatization issue will be discussed, including some evidence of the creeping transparency of public and private policing functions. Following this outline, I raise a flag of caution about the implications in law for police privatization by referring to the suggestive circumstances in three case decisions. These cases, perhaps more familiar to security professionals than to police experts, set forth certain realities in private security's legal development, thus affording an opportunity to further consider implications of the private security option. In the space available, full representation of leading private security cases bearing on privatization decisions cannot be accommodated. Arguably, more study should be undertaken of the legal implications of police privatization to magnify the likelihood that slow but persistent movement toward transparency will reach advanced stages before significant public policy interest emerges.

Background Issues

The importance of implications in law for public-private transparency suggests that local governments may have been wise in avoiding a leap to adopt privatization experiments. This may change, however, when a mood to slash public costs returns, particularly as private security gains greater familiarity and experience with public operations. Presently, as the concept of police privatization matures at a pace significantly slower than the pace in the corrections field, an opportunity is presented to carefully and critically evaluate initiatives. The policy process should explore contradictions, dilemmas, and implications tied to a closer relationship between police and private organizations that, traditionally, have been held at arm's length.

Priority should be given to developing data to measure the nature of relationships between police and security organizations. Movement toward transparency depends in large measure on how the two protective service providers address their tenuous, and sometimes hostile, working relationships. Police and scholars who study police have questioned the ability of private citizens and private organizations to perform law enforcement tasks in a comprehensive, professional, and lawful manner (Fixler & Poole, 1988; Langworthy & Travis, 1999; Lyman, 1999;

Marx & Archer, 1976; Stenning & Shearing, 1979; Shearing & Stenning, 1981).[3] Negative impressions about the quality of private security work have carried from decade to decade. Some have served to improve image and standards, but others have restricted cooperative relationships (Behar, 1992; Boostrom & Draper, 1992; Dralla, Honig, Port, Power & Simmons, 1975; George & Button, 1998; Marx, 1987; Sarre, 1998; Shearing & Addario, 1985a,b). Research has outlined selective elements of police critiques of private security performance, and of frustrations of private security with the lack of police support and respect, but more data are needed beyond anecdotes (Cunningham, Strauchs & Van Meter, 1990; Hair, 1979; Lipson, 1988; Morley & Fong, 1995). New forms of public-private cooperation will be substantially reinforced when tensions are reduced over issues of competency, organizational territoriality, and law-based regulations on personnel screening, pre- and in-service training, and disciplinary controls.

These challenges are surmountable, because on many occasions police and private security leaders have proven their determination to build constructive relationships, confidence, mutual assistance, respect, and trust (Carr, 1996; Ericson, 1995; Johnston, 1992a,b; Lee, 1995; Loader, 1997b; O'Leary, 1994; Prenzler, Draper & Harrison, 1996; Schneider, 1986; Shearing, 1992). Strong relationships, begun in the mid-1970s, were bonded between the American Society for Industrial Security (ASIS) and the International Association of Chiefs of Police (IACP). Regarding transparency of operations, the resources of each sector should be aimed at the options involved in integrating individual contributions to public safety, and to the direction and pace of transparency. Each is capable of articulating (i.e., expressing and confronting) the hurdles they have in overcoming historical legacies, community acceptance and rejection, support and rejection inside respective organizational cultures, and implications arising from state laws that are essentially geared to maintain separation.

Enduring tensions between public and private police spring mainly from how each sector has presented itself, and has been received by respective client groups. Police have invested heavily in professionalism and accommodation to changing community demands, although change has sometimes occurred grudgingly. Similarly, citizens now expect security personnel and technologies in nearly every aspect of public exposure and vulnerability, such as airports, malls, schools, entertainment parks, stores, and museums. Furthermore, they recognize and accept differences in authority and image between security guards and police patrol officers. Acceptance of the security role also extends to proposals for greater transparency between the two types of organizations, as evidenced by experiments in forms of civilianization and privatization of operations of police. At minimum, then, one may conclude that despite certain tensions between private and public safety organizations, client groups recognize their individual contributions to the overall safety in community life (Stewart, 1985).

But the issue is deeper than impressions of authority and appearance. In fact, the demand for private security services over the past three decades is ubiquitous (Kakalik & Wildhorn 1971, 1977; Institute of Local Self Government, 1974; Brennan, 1975; National Advisory Commission, 1976; Cunningham & Taylor, 1985; Cunningham, Strauchs & Van Meter, 1990). Public authority has insisted upon a large and widely dispersed volume of private security presence, and the number of litigations against business owners for failure to provide adequate security suggests a public mood toward an expected standard of care. Moreover, each of the major investigations into private security's advancement and growth has confirmed, for example, that modern private security delivers human and technological competencies that are not available from police organizations. Private security organizations have expanded, diversified, and strengthened their economic and political postures, and they have learned how to influence public policy decisions to strengthen their bid for a wider role in public safety (Cunningham, Strauchs & Van Meter, 1990; Friedman, Hakim & Spiegel, 1987; Godec, 1987; Johnston, 1993; Loader, 1997a). Accordingly, the important issue now relates to when, and under what conditions, the private security option will attract even more economic and political clout across major thresholds of experimentation to deliver non-core and core police services.

Security services have blended into the fabric of urban society, and they have become increasingly interdependent with public resources. The industry performs tasks that at one time were performed by private citizens, some of which were later absorbed by public police. In some areas of its work, the similarities with police work are clear and unequivocal, such as armed escorts for dignitaries or high-value items and security of nuclear facilities. In other areas, and perhaps in the majority of its work, private security is significantly different from police in methodology, perspective, and measures of success and failure (Kakalik & Wildhorn, 1971; Shearing & Stenning, 1981; Cunningham, Strauchs & Van Meter, 1990). Evidence is in short supply with respect to the aggregate impact of security resources on controlling and preventing crime and other forms of risks to public safety (Hui-Wen & Png, 1994). In fact, proof of the actual net impact on crime by private security is unavailable, thus presenting difficult challenges to the notion that there is inherent added value to overall crime prevention. Private security services are costly, and their measurable impact is largely limited to businesses that can afford them. The security industry has not been stymied by these concerns, however, preferring instead to focus on measures of client perceptions, service delivery, and company profitability. Mission focus emphasizes defensive measures aimed at reducing client fears while implying that a more secure business or residence translates into a safer community.

Security organizations generally maintain the same basic characteristics of appearance, manner, and outlook toward risk and safety concerns as public police. Typically, they are organized in military-style structures similar to police departments. Other similarities include formal practices and routines, uniforms, and, where required, weaponry. Company officials maintain close contacts with police executives, and private security hierarchies employ former members of the police establishment at all levels. Formal and informal communications benefit both organizations. Information usually flows freely through intricate and sometimes elusive channels among thousands of security personnel engaged in investigative or intelligence-gathering functions (Marx, 1987). Police benefit from access to private settings; private security acquires information from inside public bureaucracies closed to ordinary citizens. Naturally, private firms remain interested in opportunities for commercial ventures (Caffuzzi, 1995; Hou & Sheu, 1994; Howe, 1998; Johnston, 1992a; South, 1983, 1984, 1988, 1994).

Police, also, have reorganized in response to community support for closer contacts with grassroots community leaders and organizations. Clearly, the current theme in police management gives priority to the search for opportunities to interact with community groups in ways that were untapped and unrewarded two decades ago (Bayley, 1994; Langworthy & Travis, 1999; Watson, Stone & DeLuca, 1998). As Bayley and Shearing (1996) observe, police reorganization in connection with a community orientation is breaking out in all developed democratic societies. Some efforts are explicitly intended to introduce police to resources available from parallel and complementary organizations where common interests are defined and put to work (Oliver, 1998:123-124). Other initiatives attempt to enrich police participation in community organizations, to increase crime prevention through speedier response to crime and through educational media, to strengthen performance in core tasks, and to redistribute some non-core tasks. Naturally, police organizations resist change in ways that are entirely consistent with other bureaucracies. However, one fact is clear: community expectations about increased access to and accountability of modern police organizations are unlikely to abate in the near future, especially because these trends have introduced pathways to numerous innovations and cooperative ventures. The private security option, although only one contributor to the overall equation of change in public safety management, may assist police in fulfilling expectations of community policing, a concept under perpetual redefinition, evolution, and occasional lukewarm organizational support.

The movement of police departments to reintroduce themselves to their clients is not an unexpected response, particularly as they reflect on the implications of reduced demand for services, resource shortages, and the viability of external competition. Reinvention of a department's mission, focus, and efficiency is, perhaps, a natural consequence of eroded client support and simultaneous availability of competitive organizations. The dialogue about reinvention can include suggestions about shedding functions that produce less value to efficiency, identity, or justification under current demands for service. Some examples here include traffic direction in downtown areas, police station administrative operations, dispatch functions, and prisoner transportation. Similarly, private security organizations, driven mainly by forces of market competition, are engaged in their own form of self-renewal. Part of this effort is directed toward how such companies may add to, compete with, or wholly replace public police services. Naturally, investment costs are associated with security ventures into police privatization, especially where private companies hope to offer service levels on par with police. Both types of public safety organizations, then, face significant challenges in the accommodation of changing public needs and expectations, but creeping transparency of operating services and interests has become an issue of *who* can deliver *which* services at *what* cost and with *what* service quality.

Undoubtedly, community, intellectual, and practitioner debates about police privatization will mature. Narrow dialogues over economic advantages will be replaced with discussions about implications of organizational arrangements where private resources work side-by-side with public resources, or where private resources are given carte blanche to serve the public interest. The design phase of experiments reflecting these allocations of authority and responsibility should focus, first, on isolating the shares of currently defined core and non-core police functions that lend themselves to reallocation, and second, on precise evaluation of private security available resources. Planners and policymakers must advance beyond perceived economic gains to the assessment of dangers associated with private security's new role in policing, such as entanglements at the razor's edge of law, public awareness of potential service limitations, and accountability where private operators do the work of legalized social coercion.

So far, the analysis of police privatization has been limited to a few isolated cases (O'Leary, 1994; Pancake, 1983; Walsh, Donovan & McNicholas, 1992), described only a few internal tasks that may be reallocated to private organizations or to civilian employees (Colletti, 1996; Harvey, 1996), and evaluated the extent of private employment of police in security work (Reiss, 1988; Vardalis, 1992). No textbooks or treatises on policing offer comprehensive discussions of real or imagined outcomes of entirely new organizational designs for public-private interrelationships. Police privatization is largely regarded as an interesting idea with limited operational experience (Lyman, 1999; Windham, 1992). A few discussions have explored implications of an increased volume of private policing services, such as interagency communication and cooperation, accountability, and cost management over time (Dart, 1992; Reiss, 1988; Usher, 1992; Windham, 1992; Walsh, Donovan, & McNicholas, 1992). Discussions of police privatization experimentation appear to be more commonplace in Asian, European, Middle Eastern, and Australian communities (Aydin, 1996; Golsby, 1998; Hesseling, 1995; Hou & Sheu, 1994; Van den Berg, 1995). A limited number of critiques distinguish between the reasonableness of privatization of traditional street policing activities and privatization of essential but, nonetheless, support functions (Fixler & Poole, 1988).

A paucity of literature on police privatization is an odd circumstance, since an extensive body of research has tended to expose significant gaps in police effectiveness regarding crime control and prevention. Numerous studies have questioned overall efficiency of police organizations in such areas as time management in patrol task performance, net impact of police on citizen fear, and time and priorities devoted to investigative work.[4] Bayley's and Shearing's recent analysis (1996) is sharply critical of police ineffectiveness in the prevention of crime, arguing that most departments assign low priority to prevention, allocate few resources to prevention, and provide few incentives to managers and street-level officers to pursue prevention objectives. Across the police literature, in fact, emphasis is placed on developing and maximizing internal resources to strengthen the relationship between police and communities. Typically, however, these concerns are not included in discussions about the private security option. Indeed, as Leo (1996) remarks, the air is filled with the topic of 'community policing,' but so many critical problems and possibilities remain unexplored. For example, privatization of police services is normally not included in this theme. A reasonable assumption is that redistribution of selected functions by means of privatization may enable police organizations to concentrate energies on assignments best performed by them and to release time to reconnect with clients. Currently, no treatises on community policing combine police privatization with the private security option in the context of what police are attempting to achieve by their new community initiatives (Watson, Stone & DeLuca, 1998).

The fundamental concept of community policing, although widely varied in definition and application, includes purposeful and regularized contact between police and community members and groups. Improved communications between the parties are presumed to improve the functional effectiveness of police while inviting the public to contribute to the policing process. Police seek community definition of problems and alternative problem-solving methods. Dialogue relies on discussions and experiments involving a diverse representation of community resources, including the private security option. In theory, the concept depends on active, not passive, involvement in the plan for improving conditions in community life. The private security community, which is only one element in the total complement of resources, is subject to the same commitments to community well-being that is expected of every other citizen group. In any event, the premise of shared responsibility for, and partnership with, community policing is now on the table. These are progressive steps toward fulfillment of the promise of developing organizational arrangements based on constructive and objectively measured assessments of benefits and burdens. Naturally, privatization will continue to travel in different directions, ranging from ideological rhetoric to experimental models. Logically, future debates will consider specific areas of core and non-core task performance. The long-range aim should focus on adjusting the equation of public and private contributions to crime control and prevention, especially with respect to the private security option. Re-privatization of selected public police functions reaches its full potential when the private security community is joined in the overall community policing effort. Decisions in this respect will carry intended and unintended consequences because re-privatization blurs the formerly clear lines of authority and responsibility between public and private policing. Finally, police privatization must be well grounded in community expressions about controls and accountability of the private sector. Questions about the measure of legal authority that the community decides to deliver to private security must take center stage, probably at the level of state legislatures.

The Re-Privatization Phenomenon

It is difficult to imagine a conversation about the future of policing in the year 2000 between two police officers standing on a street corner in 1900. Would they imagine, for example, that in the next 100 years the American police services would employ nearly 625,000 police? Also, would they imagine that nearly 1.6 million people would be employed in the private security sector (Kennedy, 1995). One officer might ask the other officer: What circumstances would cause the private security sector to employ three times as many people as police departments? Speculation would follow, of course, but an even more bizarre extension of this conversation would trade ideas about state authority for crime control and the share of private security responsibility for containment of crime. The essential meaning of this hypothetical conversation is that policing in the late nineteenth century had only just recognized how far it had advanced from the era of private policing before 1845. A conversation like the one offered here would necessarily require a vision that policing would proceed in the direction of re-privatization.

Private security, in fact, has emerged in the past 75 years as an essential element in the total mix of community protective measures (Becker, 1974; Calder, 1980; McCrie, 1988; Scott & McPherson, 1971). A multi-billion dollar industry protects corporations, residential and shopping areas, financial institutions, and all types of commercial buildings (Benyon, 1994; Cunningham, Strauchs & Van Meter, 1990; McCrie, 1988). Protective services range from individuals and small companies providing protection for profit to large multi-location facilities employing thousands of security personnel. Uniformed officers patrol empty parking lots and security perimeters in shopping malls, industrial plants, banks, hotels, and even nuclear weapons facilities. Some are armed and well trained; others are hired off the street with little concern for their backgrounds, character, or ability. Volumes have recorded the growth and relative quality of 'private police' (Shalloo, 1929, 1933; Kakalik & Wildhorn, 1971, 1977; Cunningham & Taylor, 1985; Cunningham, Strauchs & Van Meter, 1990). The term has been widely used to describe the community of private security, but it is rejected by both police and security experts as inaccurate, and perhaps even viewed as an oxymoron.

The term 're-privatization' should be qualified to avoid any misunderstanding that public policing has returned to its roots in private action and voluntary participation. Clearly, this is not the case. For more than 150 years, legal, political, and social commitments have been delivered to public police organizations (Bittner, 1970; Walker, 1998a) and the scope of public responsibility has expanded geometrically throughout most of the twentieth century. From time to time, the Supreme Court has intervened to guard the public-private separation so grounded in American legal tradition. Police have secured dominance over public funding aimed at anti-crime measures, thus allowing them to define the threat and to determine control and prevention methods deployed in the public arena. The private sector retains operational and economic appeal where police cannot or will not perform, and where the risks of loss are most practically reduced by immediate territorial 'guardianship' (Felson, 1994) by non-police individuals or security organizations. Private citizens and protection organizations have hotly pursued interests intended to secure their right to control and direct a sizeable share of personal and property protection. Private actors' insistence on participation in crime control is readily evident in gun control debates and in incidents where the issue of self-defense is raised (Kleck, 1988). Accordingly, an aggressive defense of a private right of action against crime has served to reinforce parallel and competitive work among organizations engaged in crime control and prevention. Occasionally, broader legal entitlement in the private sector has attracted actions by state and local governments to mandate public regulation (Button, 1998; Caffuzzi, 1995; George & Button, 1995; Johnston, 1992b; Murray, 1995). Details aside, it is not unreasonable to suggest, therefore, that the private-public relationship in policing has been cemented in perpetuity. Historical factors and significant popular support have combined to influence public policies making the two sectors virtually interdependent (Bayley & Shearing, 1996; Prassel, 1972; Spitzer & Scull, 1977). Unquestionably, the depth of this interdependence is an important public policy issue. What some fear as the "commercial compromise of the state" (South, 1984) carries unavoidable implications both for expanded constructive cooperation and for danger created by the expansion of private authority (Gagel, 1995; Lee, 1995; Livingston, 1997).

Re-privatization, then, refers to yet another stage in the evolution of protective services, especially in Western nations and their valued legal traditions. As a concept for redistributing services between private and public providers, re-privatization is likely to be successful only where community sentiments are heard with respect to containing public police costs and to efficiencies arising from strengths and weaknesses of each type of organization. Open discussions, informed by experts in private security and public law enforcement, will be required to peel back historical and psychological layers of unchallenged dependence upon police agencies, particularly where such agencies remain wedded to only one model of legal and organizational design. Consideration must be given to expectations held within individual communities regarding police department duties and performance, particularly in connection with territorial coverage, population and structural densities, deployment of technologies, and public recognition of that government responsibility. Crime control is tied directly to circumstances created mainly by private citizens or businesses in their private settings (Cunningham, Strauchs & Van Meter, 1990). Some of these discussions are likely to attract hostile reactions from police organizations, and perhaps from influential community leaders who may believe that dialogues about re-privatization will weaken commitment to public police authority.

One way of opening such discussions is through reconsideration of historical circumstances that reinforced the concept of separate private and public policing functions. For example, there was no inherent reason for public police to usurp responsibility for burglar alarm monitoring and response. Burglar alarm technology was invented and developed entirely within the private sector. In the late nineteenth century, alarm systems were marketed principally to small commercial businesses and to the wealthy (McCrie, 1988). Only much later were police encouraged to have a direct hand in the alarm business, including regulatory practices that imposed police authority over aspects of the alarm response. More broadly considered, however, old and new private security companies responded to new demands for all kinds of protection services where police could not or would not perform (Becker, 1974; Braun & Lee, 1971, Calder, 1980; Lipson, 1988). Increasingly, private security organizations represented a rational method for protecting private interests where a perception might have arisen that police protection favored only private interests to the exclusion of the general interest, such as when a store owner received special police presence at public expense. Furthermore, the specializations in private and public policing often followed trends in criminal sophistication, supported in part by a shifting philosophy to bolster coercive strategies designed to increase capture and control versus passive strategies based on prevention and risk reduction (Hair, 1979; South, 1994; Walsh & Donovan, 1989). Private detectives, for example, evolved side-by-side with police detective bureaus (Gill & Hart, 1997; Klockars, 1985; Morn, 1982; Weiss, 1978, 1981); police crime prevention bureaus evolved along with private security companies (Kakalik & Wildhorn, 1971).

Weighing against closer working relationships in the early years was the public's insistence that police must make their presence known through uniforms and badges, and that police and private security should pursue separate lines of development (Klockars, 1985; S. Walker, 1998a). The distinctive and persistent growth of private security in the twentieth century indicates, if nothing else, that a preference for public responsibility for crime control has also contemplated an option that is privately underwritten. The fact that re-privatization has entered the general debate about police service provisions may open a significant new chapter in police history. Indeed, many major urban communities now have 150 years of policing experience available to challenge earlier assumptions about the distinctive and separate paths of private-public police development. Moreover, a traditional American distrust of full dependence on public protection now can be acknowledged and addressed in light of modern security concepts and capabilities. Only a small leap of insight is needed to accept the proposition that crime risk reduction is most effectively reached through a mix of contributions by different types of police and private organizations (Livingston, 1997).

The trend toward re-privatization was first observed by sociologist Jeremiah Shalloo (1929, 1933) in a study of private security in Pennsylvania in the late 1920s, later published in more detailed format in a special report issued by the American Academy of Political and Social Science. Shalloo investigated the growth of private and special police functions, such as the Coal and Iron Police, the Marine Police, the Railroad Police, in terms of the special circumstances of risk in various areas of the industrial community. At approximately the same time, President Herbert Hoover expressed formal interest in the contributions of private security to commercial crime prevention. Hoover asked the Wickersham Law Observance Commission to measure the growth and contributions of private security to crime prevention (Calder, 1993). It was discovered that industrial police were employed by the thousands in manufacturing organizations in the 1930s to perform ordinary protection, but also to undermine union organizing efforts (Calder, 1985; Couch, 1981; Industrial Policing and Espionage, 1939; Shearing & Stenning, 1987). The violence and property destruction resulting from major industrial riots in this era suggested to corporate employers, legislators, and labor lawyers that private security forces were conducting themselves in a manner that carried public policy implications (U.S. Congress, Senate, 1939). Domestic labor conflict was set aside after 1941 when the focus of security attention turned toward external enemies in wartime. Federal authority and regulation quickly moved to militarize existing industrial security organizations (Calder, 1992). This development, more than any previous experience since the Civil War, provided the means for transforming private security into an activity more analogous to police work.

New interest in private security evolved in the late 1960s, as private providers of protection services diversified and attracted more public attention. Increasingly, private guards and detectives showed up in criminal and civil matters (Scott & McPherson, 1971; Palmer, 1976; Ziff, 1967). The Department of Justice funded Rand Corporation to conduct a broad investigation of private policing in the early 1970s, the first of several large-scale investigations to follow (Kakalik & Wildhorn, 1971; 1977). All such research explored the extent to which private security and police organizations had tightened cooperation and included convincing speculation that private services could be employed in public interest functions. Additionally, studies revealed that police were employed regularly in the private sector, mainly as a source of extra income, but presumably to add qualitatively to the caliber of protection (Reiss, 1988). Related to these matters was a finding that private security had assumed certain duties that police had abandoned or could not accommodate (Bradford & Simonson, 1998; Buerger & Mazerolle, 1998; Cunningham, Strauchs & Van Meter, 1990). Law and regulatory controls imposed upon private security confirmed the struggle of state and local governments to encourage further expansion of private services while carefully reinforcing the notion that private authority must be limited (Dralla et al., 1975; Kakalik & Wildhorn, 1971, 1977; George & Button, 1995).

A frequently overlooked insight of the 1971 Rand report, and subsequent studies of private security's commercial sprawl, is the further advancement of joint operational cooperation between private security and police organizations. Rand researchers acknowledged that if monetary costs were the only criterion for public police, then private forces were less expensive. The report moved on to conclude, however, that the more reasonable interpretation was that private security "could shift the cost-based preference balance by offering more costly and higher-quality services . . .", [and] ". . . public police could depart from their tradition of furnishing only one basic quality of police personnel" (Kakalik & Wildhorn, 1977:87). Local studies, such as Brennan's (1975) investigation of security in Cleveland and the work by the Institute of Local Self-Government (1974) in California, confirmed the largely cooperative relationship between police and security operations. They noted that security organizations had filled many gaps in crime prevention and control that police were unwilling or unprepared to tackle. A study of private security's role in Canadian society (Freedman & Stenning, 1977) resolved that, even though private organizations had not been fully acknowledged in Canadian law, there was every indication that they had surpassed mere complementary assistance to police, and were, therefore, proactively adding to the total efforts of crime prevention and control.

One common feature of these investigations is the detailed accounting of the spread and deepening of the role of private security services. Empirical evidence supported a view that in several Western countries, private security had reached a level of involvement in protection assignments to make distinction between public interest and private service exceptionally difficult (Cunningham, Strauchs & Van Meter, 1990; Draper, 1978; Freedman & Stenning, 1977; Johnston, 1992a; Shearing & Stenning, 1987). By design or default, the two forms of protective services, responsive in most ways to different masters, arrived at a point of potential or actual complementarity (Kilburn & Shrum, 1998), although no study acknowledged full comfort with this outcome. Indeed, private security had achieved accreditation in the social control community.

Advancement beyond this point emerged in the 1980s. New economic reasoning shifted the focus of public policy toward questions about the continued growth of government services, public concern for cost controls, and prospects for expanded private participation in service delivery at lower cost (Fixler & Poole, 1988; Livingston, 1997). In the domain of policing, police chiefs and scholars alike considered the prospects for contracted police services, and the option of shedding services, such as burglar alarm response (Cunningham, Strauchs & Van Meter, 1990:272). Police reached a point of enlightenment about the kinds of services they could jettison, particularly services they had not performed willingly or well in earlier years, driven mainly by their desire to reduce drag on core services in the areas of violent and property crime. Civilianization of services occurred with greater frequency, but gradually the use of private security services evolved as an option where contracting out or special licensing was considered important for department control. The 1990 version of the *Hallcrest Report* concluded that selective examples of comprehensive security services had supplanted police services with at least a reasonable level of success (Cunningham, Strauchs & Van Meter, 1990). Trends in other countries suggest that re-privatization initiatives are in full swing (Johnston, 1992a, 1993; Hou & Sheu, 1994; Walker & Richards, 1996).

The apex of re-privatization is realized in the movement of police and security organizations to perform on each other's traditional territories, partly but not entirely due to the commodification of police services (Johnston, 1993). Police, for example, have been employed privately during off-duty hours at a rapidly increasing rate in fixed-post security assignments where a large private interest is at stake, but also in situations in which events occur on private, quasi-public, or public property. Sporting events, concerts, demonstrations, warehouses and parking lots, and even gated communities are now locations where police are expected to protect both private and public interests in the employ of private businesses. The amount of public expense encountered in these circumstances has not been measured. Unquestionably, the halo of police presence and authority delivers a benefit to the private sector, but all appears to be acceptable to the uninformed observer, since private organizations pay the wages of off-duty officers working in a 'moonlighting' capacity (Reiss, 1988; Vardalis, 1992). Most often, liability for actions, and insurance coverage for injuries, remain public costs. In some ways, these services represent both a natural progression of the re-privatization phenomenon and a lack of clear public policy about acceptable practices for transferring public benefits to private beneficiaries. Where police resources are obligated to protect property under pressure from economically influential individuals or whole communities, the concept of at-large protection by police is stretched. Gated communities in which this type of mandatory climate develops, or in which communities assume full responsibility for policing themselves, raise new questions for courts and legislatures (Stewart, 1996). Important developments in this area are currently unfolding in the matter of extra-territorial jurisdiction of campus police departments (Jacobson, 1995).

Actually, the most important dimensions of re-privatization are less concerned with mere special interest services to businesses or economic elites. Rather, they relate to the development of human and technological resources that can be found in the private sector. These resources introduce possibilities for further relieving public police of duties no longer recognized for their broad public service value, or which can be accomplished more efficiently in the private sector. It will be recalled that at one time private watchmen swept public streets, police directed traffic in downtown Los Angeles, and patrol officers walked beats to shake door handles on commercial and residential property. Modern re-privatization suggests that private security organizations have filled in where public police have redefined their duties, and they have literally crossed into some areas where police have shown less interest in security-type assignments. Aside from the obvious expansion of private security into private property protection, numerous non-state forms of self-help and special police jurisdictions have evolved from earlier ordinary security functions (Livingston, 1997; Ziegenhagen & Brosnan, 1991). Some state constitutions or statutory provisions have introduced bounty hunters (Takacs, 1994) and constables, two groups that continue to serve both public and private interests simultaneously. Campus security organizations were transformed from a watchmen functions to full police jurisdictions on most public and private college campuses in the short span of time from 1960 to 1980 (Calder, 1974; Jacobson, 1995).

The future of re-privatization is likely to include broader involvement in several types of non-core and core activities of patrol, investigative, and crime prevention functions. A significant movement in this direction has already unfolded in other parts of the world (Aydin, 1996; Golsby, 1998; Loader, 1997a; Prenzler, Draper & Harrison, 1996; Walker & Richards, 1996), and private security is now serving in a variety of international contexts, some positive and some negative (Howe, 1998; Private Security, 1997; Zarate, 1998). The scope and direction of American brands of re-privatization will depend on how communities and police articulate complaints and constructive responses to their independent, interactive, and transparent roles in crime control and prevention. Undoubtedly, the perpetually controversial issue of burglar alarm response will resurface as communities address their false alarm rates, including the dangers and public costs associated with conditions that are mainly created or ignored in the private sector (Blackstone & Hakim, 1996). Consider, for example, who should bear the cost of injuries sustained when a private security company responds to an alarm call from a private property owner? Is there a significant difference in responsibility if the alarm call is factually false? This is an important area of patrol duty that private security is fully capable of assuming. The recent sharp decline in the crime rate may reduce the incentive for police managements to curtail alarm response, for police officers and police associations that benefit from the work activity that secures new positions, and for legislators who benefit from the support of all police personnel.

Other possible roles for private security involvement include widespread contracting for services to transport people under arrest from the arrest location to local lockups. Fixed-post human surveillance or camera monitoring are activities destined for dramatic expansion in the near future (Burrows, 1997). If these types of operations can be compartmentalized under contracts that secure public accountability, they are particularly suitable for development as private investigative work. 'Cold case' review and analysis, including some aspects of further investigative 'legwork', could also be privatized in ways that may well contribute a significant public relations benefit to police departments. Many routine investigative leads, file searches, and witness interviews could be privately accomplished. Such proposals will attract heated debate in some circles, but most of these assignments could be organized in ways that neither intrude on core police tasks nor compromise sensitive information. Clearly, experiments instituted in any of these areas, especially those having the greatest exposure to criticism for invasions of privacy or injury to private party interests, must be scrutinized as to the implications of close public-private interaction and information sharing

(Ghezzi, 1983). This will be particularly important where, as Bradford and Simonsen (1998) suggest, new partnerships between police and corporate security investigators offer opportunities to reduce occupational fraud. Public acceptance of private performance in all these possible roles will depend on the clarity of public authorization and limitation, civil liability remedies, personnel screening and background investigations, mandated regular training, close supervision and records audits, and use of sophisticated technologies. Obligatory and intensive discussion must occur in public forums, and in professional organizations representing police and private security, to formulate principles and standards upon which legislatures may craft new law and courts may frame decisions to protect civil rights and public interests.

Hold On! Transparency Has Implications in Law

American and European communities are unlikely to adopt a maximum level of re-privatization of police services for several years. Western democracies have invested heavily in the concept of publicly funded, locally supported, well-trained, and accountable agents of civil law enforcement. But these societies have also supported further privatization of governmental services to cut costs, expand efficiencies, and diversify service capacities. Police privatization, in short, is an idea worthy of attention in the policy community because it holds some hope as a practical solution to meeting these widely discussed objectives. Policing is only one element in the larger context of changing perspectives on the role and effectiveness of government, and it is just as likely that proposals arising from the privatization theme will produce both reasonable and entirely nonsensical initiatives. Each initiative must survive the test of lawfulness, of course, and the one certainty across all proposals is that privatization forces recognition of the implications of transparency of protective services that necessarily results when private agencies take on traditionally public functions.

Addressing only the American prospects for re-privatization, the more private and public policing look alike, the more they need to address implications in law. Legal history has matured and reinforced critical distinctions between these forms of policing, and the key differences find their origins in judicial decisions such as *Boyd v. United States* (1886) and *Weeks v. United States* (1914). *Boyd* was the first case in which the Supreme Court applied the Fourth Amendment to a government agent's invasion of the private home and individual privacy. *Weeks* was the first case to construct an exclusionary rule whereby federal authorities were denied the use of evidence which had been illegally seized. Transparency in law, for purposes of this discussion, refers to the extent to which these policing sectors overlap in terms of their operational characteristics in core task areas of arrest, search and seizure, and off-duty police work (i.e., moonlighting). In the following brief discussion, I revisit two old decisions and one new decision to illustrate the thin wall of distinction that judicial authorities have argued to construct separate authorities for public and private police. Fact patterns and issues in *People v. Zelinski* (1979), *Burdeau v. McDowell* (1921), and *Blackwell et al. v. Harris County, Texas* (1995) raise important implications for police practices and the care that must be exercised in privatizing traditional police functions.

A hypothetical situation may help to focus attention on implications in law. Suppose a private security company, employing armed officers, is contracted by a county police department to *patrol all streets* in a gated community and to *respond to all* burglar alarms. While performing patrol duties, two officers respond to an alarm, and as they arrive at the location they encounter two men who appear to be burglary suspects. The suspects are carrying suitcases as they leave the area and walk on a public street. The officers have the authority and physical ability to catch and detain the suspects, and, if necessary, they are entitled to use weapons in their own defense or in defense of third parties. The suspects are captured, handcuffed, subjected to a search of outer clothing and pockets. After handcuffing them, the suitcases are opened and searched. Inside the suitcases are ski masks, tools, and a box which was also opened. The box contains jewelry and a loaded gun. Several minutes later the county sheriff responds and arrests the suspects on charges of burglary, possession of burglary tools, and possession of a firearm. The private officers take the suspects to jail. Question: Which principles of law (i.e., public or private) should be applied to the field stop, the arrest, the search of the suitcases, and seizure of the mask, tools and box containing the weapon? What reasoning should be employed?

This hypothetical example illustrates a situation in which core policing tasks are performed under private agreement. Authority for actions normally permitted only to sworn police officers has been added to the authority of private persons and organizations, since generally private persons would be prohibited from chasing and subduing a suspect, and from conducting a search as outlined in the example. Under these circumstances, the private officers have been empowered to use the full measure of probable cause generally available only to police, and their arrest and search authorities are indistinguishable from police. In the process, a critical presumption surfaces: that public authorities have considered the implications of these new characteristics of transparency in private police operations. Understandably, this truncated example cannot fully represent all dimensions of the transparency issue, but it provides a rough outline of the types of legal controversies that will continue to appear in civil and criminal litigations in the tricky middle ground of police privatization. Reasonably, police privatization can be expected to expose private security to situations in which actions in performance of core police tasks will raise new legal questions about the existing threshold of public-private authority. Traditionally, for example, persons working in private security positions retain no more arrest authority than the authority granted to ordinary citizens. Generally, in American law a citizen may arrest another person when a crime has been committed in his presence, and provided that the arrest meets the standards of care that individual state court decisions have required. Most states have imposed laws and regulatory standards to circumscribe citizen arrest authority, delivering a greater measure of discretion in decisions to arrest or to detain to business owners and their security personnel. In many states, basic training has been mandated as a prerequisite to exercising private arrest authority. The frequency of citizen or private security arrests is unknown, but there is reason to believe that expansion of private security and police privatization will increase the number of private arrests. The reasoning is simple: there are more eyes and ears focused on formal actions against crime and deviance in combinations with more legal authority to act in formal ways. This outcome cannot be discussed here since this is a complex and unquestionably tangential issue for broader concerns about the scope of social control in democratic societies.

Arrest Authority

Consider the facts and issues raised in the classic California case of *People v. Zelinski* (1979) involving arrest by a private security officer. Virginia Zelinski was detained outside a department store after she was observed with the store's property for which she had not paid. She was taken to the store's security office where a search was made for weapons, followed by another search of her purse. The search of the purse located the store's property, but it also uncovered a pill vial containing a balloon with a white substance. Police were called, and the vial was turned over to them. Zelinski was charged with possession of heroin. Quotes in the following paragraphs are taken from the Court's decision.

The Court, acknowledging special statutory authority granted to merchants to protect their property, observed that private security personnel ". . . instituted a search to recover goods that were not in plain view." The 'goods' given reference by the Court included the drugs. Invoking a criminal law standard applied to public police, the Court determined that the private security actions were not fully in accord with private interests, since drug enforcement is a public policy concern under state law. Moreover, the drug seizure as part of the arrest was unrelated to the original focus of the action aimed at recovering property. Ultimately, the Court suppressed the evidence of heroin possession, charging that ". . . where private security personnel assert the power of the state to make an arrest or detain another person for transfer to custody of the state, the state involvement is sufficient for the court to enforce the proper exercise of that power by excluding the fruits of illegal abuse thereof."

A slight alteration in the facts in this case introduces another relevant hypothetical scenario applying the ruling in *Zelinski*. Let us assume that certain decisions have been made by public officials in a California county to cut police costs by privatizing transportation of prisoners from places where they are arrested by police through the booking process at the county jail. Assume that a private security company has no special police authority under state law, and it has been contracted to pick up, transport, and deliver prisoners to jail. Two men have been placed under arrest by police for assault with a deadly weapon on a third party. At the crime scene, police conduct a typical body search and remove a knife from the pocket of one of the men. The men were charged with aggravated assault with a deadly weapon, as indicated on the police report form. The men were handcuffed by police, then turned over to two private officers who place them in a secured van with instructions to take the men to jail. Along the travel route, one prisoner slips from the handcuffs and strikes the other prisoner repeatedly with the handcuffs. The officers pull off the roadway, open the van, and take physical control of the attacking prisoner. As they take control, they conduct a more thorough body search than was conducted by police, and they find a packet containing a white substance hidden in the lining of a belt which they judge to be cocaine, later confirmed. When the men are booked into jail, they are charged with assault with a deadly weapon, and one is charged with possession of a controlled substance. The information about the nature of the roadway search and the location of the drugs is provided by the private officers. The belt and the white substance are introduced as evidence in a prosecution for both offenses.

The private officers in this situation have secured a suspect after they were given a brief outline of the original assault situation, apart from any information about the search conducted by police. They were hired to carry prisoners, and they were trained to conduct limited searches for weapons. However, they extended their weapon's search authority and training to discovery of drugs. It is reasonable to assume, therefore, that the principle applied in *Zelinski* would find application to the exclusion of the drug evidence, since a court could interpret the actions of the private officers in terms of furtherance of a state policing function. Failure to apply the *Zelinski* test would imply that the private officers retained full authority to search for weapons, and to move beyond this threshold by extending the search to the belt and the drug evidence. As in *Zelinski*, the original action involving a charge of assault, which neither the public nor the private officers observed, is subsequently complicated by the drug possession issue. If *Zelinski* were invoked, a court would exclude any evidence of the drug possession and proceed with the assault issue. As Charles Nemeth (1995:64) questions, "Should private sector justice adhere to the constitutional demands of the public sector when investigating criminality and when criminals are apprehended? Are there occasions when the Fourth Amendment forbids the introduction of tainted evidence or when the exclusionary rule applies in cases involving private sector justice?"

Search and Seizure Authority

The historical progress of both police and private security in the nineteenth and early twentieth centuries failed to attract any significant attention to their distinctive legal foundations. Each sector served different masters. Moreover, the small number of private security companies was engaged principally in investigative work, and police departments asserted control over common aspects of street crime enforcement. In simple terms, neither concern got in the way of the other, and from time to time they shared information. The advent of large private security companies meant that hundreds of guards and detectives would be employed. They were frequently engaged in labor-management conflicts; they used aggressive riot control methods, and over time their relationship with police was permanently altered since police did not wish to be tagged with the image of the lower grade armed security guards. In particular, the close relationship between private security and police afforded opportunities to share information, and eventually situations arose to attract attention by the courts. The 1914 decision in *Weeks v. United States*, and later the 1921 decision in *Burdeau v. McDowell*, addressed the porousness of the divide between strictly private action and state action. So long as private and public actions can be distinguished (e.g., where police merely receive information or other evidence which may be considered fruits of strictly private searches and seizures), they can be used as part of the state's criminal actions against a defendant.

The oft-cited Supreme Court decision in *Burdeau v. McDowell* sets forth the threshold test for private searches in which evidence is subsequently turned over to police for use in prosecution. It is an odd historical fact that these types of searches remained unclarified from the 1886 decision in *Boyd v. United States* until 1921. Thereafter, only government actions in the course and scope of a private search and seizure were governed by constitutional protection to exclude evidence. Justice Arthur R. Day wrote the majority opinion for the Court. McDowell was an employee of an oil and gas company in Pittsburgh, Pennsylvania. In 1920 company executives decided to fire McDowell for "alleged unlawful and fraudulent conduct in the course of the business" (*Bur-*

deau v. McDowell, 1921). A company executive took control of McDowell's office, seized McDowell's records, and "the rooms were placed in charge of detectives." Papers were subsequently turned over to Burdeau, a special assistant to the U.S. Attorney General. A grand jury indictment followed. McDowell argued that his Fourth and Fifth Amendment rights had been violated by the seizure of the documents under the alleged aegis of government direction. The government argued that it should not be prevented from using the evidence.

The decision in *Burdeau*, while challenged in several succeeding litigations, has not been subjected to close examination of the factual record. To do so may raise questions about facts that, if shown, would taint the logic of the government's disclaimer about its direct involvement. The critical importance of the *Burdeau* ruling distinguishes private and public actions in search conduct in a long line of federal and state cases, thus requiring that the facts of the case hold up under scrutiny of possible errors in interpretation. The trial court, for example, supported McDowell by ordering that his books and papers be returned. The appellate court disagreed with the trial court and the issue was taken to the Supreme Court, which supported the appellate decision. Clarification of several essential facts is important to the current issue of privatization: According to the Court's summation, the search of McDowell's office was conducted in the presence of 'detectives.' Were these private detectives who held state licenses? Were they police working off duty as private detectives? Were they local police detectives? Moreover, what did these detectives know, when did they know it, and what did they do in the course of the search?

Clarification of these facts is essential to the Court's leap from the actions of private individuals and ostensible private detectives, neither of whom were presumed to have any connection with government authorities, or to the purported innocent and subsequent acquisition of records by federal postal inspectors. Additionally, it is unclear as to what factual evidence of fraud was uncovered by company officials and subsequently turned over to postal inspectors? Did the private persons take information that was not truly evidence of a crime, and if so, what implications may arise from a private party's mistake of fact in taking the information by force followed by possible complicity in providing bad or inconsequential information to the government? Other questions may be raised about the manner of the search, including the fact that a company safe had been blown open in the presence of 'detectives,' perhaps in violation of state law. The entire situation in *Burdeau* is clouded by the fact that there was no trial jury review of how the private parties were alleged to have acquired evidence of a crime.

The Court's interpretation of the government role is limited to after-the-fact involvement of federal postal inspectors, who ultimately received the seized documents from private persons. The government's appeal from the district court's exclusion of the documents indicated that ". . . the court found . . ." no evidence existed of any government involvement [meaning federal involvement] in the search events, and that federal agents had no knowledge of the evidence for several months after the search. Upheld since 1921 (DeNinno, 1980; Euller, 1980; Gagel, 1995) this decision gives local and federal police the authority to receive evidence of alleged crimes from private persons for use in government prosecutions, so long as that evidence is not seized by the government or at the direction of government agents. In simple terms, government can use information it receives, regardless of the facts of its seizure (i.e., lawful or unlawful) if the seizure involves only private persons. Any number of hypothetical situations could be invented, ranging from slight modifications of the facts in *Burdeau* to whole new fact situations involving private acquisition of information from computer and Internet sources. These concerns take on even more importance as the relationships between public and private police are increasingly institutionalized. There are several other cases that followed the *Burdeau* decision: *Marsh v. Alabama* (1946) [actions by private person who carries out assignments that are normally performed by government must be regarded as performing the duty as the government]; *Lustig v. United States* (1949) [evidence turned over to federal officers by hotel manager]; *Burton v. Wilmington Parking Authority* (1961) [close working relationship between police and private security personnel]; *United States v. Francoeur* (1977) [arrest and search by amusement park security officers produced criminal evidence]; and *Flagg Bros., Inc. v. Brooks* (1978) [raising but not resolving the measure of authority that could be handed over to private persons without carrying implications of state action and the Fourteenth Amendment].

Moonlighting by Public Police

Another implication in law of police privatization involves situations in which police are employed in private sector positions during their off-duty hours. These situations raise questions, some of which include the rules that should apply to the type of authority exercised (i.e., public or private), and to the moment at which a public police officer who is working in a private security assignment is transformed back into the job of police officer. In the latter case, an issue taken up recently has been concerned with liability for injuries sustained by officers serving as private security personnel.

A Texas appellate court considered the facts in a Houston case in which a police officer, working in a private capacity on a funeral escort, died from injuries received when he crashed his motorcycle (*Blackwell et al. v. Harris County, Texas*, 1995). The trial court granted a summary judgment in favor of the Workers' Compensation Commission to bar payment of workers' compensation benefits to the family, but the family appealed on the argument that the officer was within the course and scope of his duties as a police officer when he was performing the private funeral escort protection. As summarized in the *Blackwell* decision, the appellate court reversed the trial court, agreeing with the reasoning in a non-Texas case that the officer was ". . . engaged in the performance of a public duty such as the enforcement of general laws. . . ." The court further instructed that ". . . if the officer observes criminal activity, his status changes from one of a private 'ornament' to a public law enforcement officer" and any injury to him in his effort to effect an arrest falls within the course and scope of his law enforcement position.

Despite the long history of police involvement in off-duty security, a phenomenon labeled several years ago as "moonlighting," litigation by police personnel working in such positions against either their police departments or private employers has only recently unfolded with significant frequency. To a large extent, this litigiousness follows the increasing dependence of private business owners on off-duty police to perform security tasks versus contract security services (Reiss, 1988). In fact, it may be said that the return of public police to territories of private policing has, as was indicated in the *Blackwell* case, further blurred the line between clearly private and clearly public operations. Additional factual scenarios involving public officers in the performance of private security duties are endless. Nearly all such circumstances bring into question the moment at which an officer is transformed from peace officer working under the direction and control of a private organization to police officer in service of the public interest.

From facts and issues considered in *Zelinski, Burdeau,* and *Blackwell,* and in many other similar cases involving a nexus of association between public and private sectors, state and federal courts evaluated the nature and depth of interaction between the litigants. With each new case, exposure of the facts reinforces the significance of the thin line of separation between roles and duties performed by public and private actors. In fact, they are more similar and transparent than dissimilar and under privatization. Accordingly, the "wiggle room" in the interpretation of purely private action, particularly where important civil rights are at stake, is less available.

This author is aware that, to date, the federal courts have not been willing to extend the umbrella of state action to private persons engaged in performing traditional criminal justice functions, particularly in application to police and correctional facilities. So far, the threshold argument in favor of not applying state action to private persons performing criminal justice functions appears to be confined to the reasoning that the Constitution does not specifically require that services be delivered by public officials to the exclusion of private persons.

Summary and Discussion

Dark clouds from several directions hang over the economic arguments in defense of privatization. Philosophical questions, for example, challenge its fit with the fundamental principles of a civil society and the public's expectation of objective measures of justice (Gilbert, 1996a). Social psychologists worry that political decisions to impose privatization where considerable dependence has been placed on public service performance reinforces distrust already present in society with respect to structural solutions and fears of unaccountable private economic decisions (Van Vugt, 1997). Historians and political analysts question the viability of the state and whether or not privatization represents a profound decline in the popular confidence vested in state performance of certain vital functions. Pennell's (1995) study of historical roots of privatization in the Spanish state, concluded that "[p]rivateering has always been a symptom of a state that is politically and economically weak, unable to finance a standing navy to attack the shipping of the enemy." Extending concern to motivations for privatization, Kritsiotis (1998) and Zarate (1998) worry that states are abdicating responsibility for internal and external security at the same time they employ larger numbers of private forces as a means of adding to their overall strengths. Shlapentokh (1996) views this concern in Russian society, proposing that the Russian citizenry is encountering a persistent and subtle removal of public values from their minds. Meanwhile, some feminists have taken aim at police liability for victimization resulting from violent crime, thus further exposing police privatization to concerns about issues of distributive justice (Handsley, 1997). Do these and similar questions indicate that privatization initiatives contain inherent pitfalls associated with abdication of public duty and the need for private accountability, as suggested by the views of Appleby (1997) and Sarre (1998)?

One notion is clear, regardless of the answers to these large questions. Privatization is both a process and an outcome. It causes traditionally public and private functions to become increasingly transparent. Given the philosophical underpinnings of Western democratic societies, overlapping task performance, mainly characterized by significant private involvement in public affairs, cannot overlook implications in law that follow from community interest in public service accountability, equity and fairness, substantive and procedural due process, and duty to provide dependable service (Appleby, 1997; Calder & Mattson, 1990; S.L. Mays, 1995). These expectations are multiplied and taken seriously in the context of public response to crime and emergency situations that threaten life, property, and civil liberties. In essence, the decision to privatize government functions requires assurances of fair treatment, checks on abuses of private action, and conditions under which privatization can be accepted or dismissed for legal, practical, or economic reasons. Democracies have always grappled with the balance between public and private interests. They are currently experiencing a resurgence, indeed a resurrection, of the perceived advantages of private input and control which will encounter all the old, and some new, arguments.

Re-privatization, as I call it, attracts minimal attention from most police organizations, especially in an era in which crime statistics reflect significant across-the-board reductions, thus causing police administrators to rally their natural bureaucratic defenses. For so many years in the twentieth century, informed observers and critics of the police establishment were instructed that the public had delivered entirely too many responsibilities to police departments, and that the trend toward burdensome work in non-core areas of policing distracted from police efficiency in core areas of law enforcement and order maintenance. The legitimacy of this instruction is well supported by evidence of a creeping shift of duties to police organizations, and from the police community a regular stream of objection to added duties that had been frequently expressed through the 1980s. Of course, police organizations are classic bureaucracies that take their cues from what the law orders them to perform, what communities expect them to accomplish, and what they independently absorb over time and experience. Departments have grown larger and more complex because the public has encouraged and permitted such growth, and because they have expertly defended the values of size and diversification of functions. Specialization of functions is a natural consequence of administrative evolution. It magnifies the best and the worst in organizational efficiencies, and, in the long run, sharpens the keen eye of entrepreneurship in areas where parity of existing service performance exists. In contrast to sophisticated studies of corporate merger potentials by financial analysts, no police research has measured the characteristics of police functions that lend themselves to privatization. Thus, it may be concluded that the scientific basis of police privatization, particularly with respect to the private security option, has stalled, and some may argue that re-privatization is little more than an odd concept with severe limitations.

As outlined in the earlier discussion, police privatization is neither a new concept nor a concept without justification. Deep historical roots link public and private engagement in policing. Transparency of administrative and legal functions in connection with the ideas of policing must be viewed from these historical trends, especially in terms of how police services can now be delivered by different forms of resources, and how traditional legal principles that distinguish measures of authority allocated to public and private police create new problems. Each of the three cases demonstrates that significant complications can arise at many points on the thin line of distinction between public and private policing. Furthermore, only slight changes to the fact pattern and judicial interpretations of both facts and law are needed in order to have a

direct and profound impact on public decisions to shift certain responsibilities to the private security option.

I have assumed that an appropriate level of accountability can be
injected into experiments in police privatization, but this assumption is
tied to careful consideration of the implications in law applicable to the
private security option. The verbal haze produced by all the discussions
of alleged economic advantages merely clouds the important legal implications relevant to police and private security transparency. Ultimately,
sufficient experience with privatization of police services in diverse
types of police organizations will serve as the basis for objective analysis. At this point there are few examples from which to draw solid conclusions to guide public policy. Heavy reliance must be placed, therefore,
on reasonable interpretations of logical hypothetical conditions based on
the case law applicable to tests of public and private police authority.

The prognosis here is that every new experiment in privatization of
public police tasks strengthens the argument that private actions in service of public interest bring us closer to actions of state authority. There
is, in my view, sufficient justification for extending the facts and issues
explored in such cases as *Zelinski*, *Burdeau*, *Blackwell*, and others of
similar thrust, in order to address the dilemmas of privatization that
spring from a progression of private security work in core areas of policing. Mainly, these cases contemplate problems tied to permitting private
security personnel to expand their role in actions of arrest, search, and
evidence seizure. Furthermore, case law is only now developing with
respect to police involvement in moonlighting activities, which carry
important implications for public burdens of liability where police appear
to serve strictly private interests during their off-duty hours. In all new situations in which private security personnel conduct themselves in a
manner that reflects transparency with the role of police, such security
actions cross a threshold of legal exception from which they cannot
easily retreat. Further re-privatization of public policing, especially as a
trend continues toward greater involvement of private companies in
core or semi-core responsibilities, virtually guarantees litigations over
questions of authority, and each will carry implications for economic benefits. The worst case scenario is that intended transparency to reduce the
costs of police services will ultimately be self-defeating, since implications
in law will transform private security into public police.

Given inroads and advances that private delivery of police services
have already achieved, no universal agreement has been reached on several issues: Which types of police services can be shed without negative
impact on the community? What standards of care, including personnel
selection and training, will be expected of private policing functions
engaged in work in the public interest? What measures of effectiveness, including professional demeanor, adherence to constitutional procedures, and cost containment, will be laid out in advance of any pro-

grammatic implementation. Perhaps incremental experimentation with privatized police services will be the accepted method of testing the merits of the case, particularly since American policing draws most of its support from local governments, and since states are unlikely to impose more than legal permissibility to allow limited private police authority.

Endnotes

[1] Schlosser (1998) has written the most fully investigative article on this subject, exploring mainly the self-fulfilling nature of the private prison movement which has led to numerous examples of greed and abuse of discretion. He concludes that the public acquiescence to large investments in private prisons represents a modern building boom analogous to the great highway projects of the 1950s and the explosion of the military-industrial complex.

[2] *Civilianization* refers to the transfer of functions previously or currently performed by uniformed personnel or detective personnel to civilian employees with no peace officer authority. *Contracting-out* refers to contractual transfer of some police assignments where the public police organization maintains direction and control. *Functional shedding* of police tasks usually encompasses a total shift of internal tasks or geographic area responsibilities to private security organizations that have assumed operations of street policing or investigative work. The latter type of privatization was demonstrated in Starrett City, a section of Brooklyn, New York, in which a private organization was created principally to perform crime prevention duties and police functions under state law provisions governing on-site special police. Other examples include arrangements by which police departments shed discrete duties, such as parking control, traffic direction, burglar alarm response, airport protection, campus protection, and court security by turning over these duties to private security companies (Cunningham, Strauchs & Van Meter, 1990:275-276). This article is not directly concerned with the civilianization aspect of privatization. Civilianization of police support functions, such as clerical staff, statistical compilation, and dispatch services, lies outside the central concerns of police privatization. These assignments do not pose risks of redefining the lawful authority of enforcement personnel in preventing crimes, making arrests, administering searches, or seizing property.

[3] Police resistance to privatization may also result from legal, logistical, and bureaucratic self-interest, each a natural response to the 150-year legacy of political and social support for public policing. Unquestionably, measurable advances can be counted in the history of public police, particularly with respect to interpersonal demeanor, organizational integrity, accountability, education and training standards, and operational and technological efficiencies.

[4] The literature here is large. Examples include the Kansas City Preventive Patrol Experiment which addressed several myths, among them that private citizens and businesses would likely institute more security measures in areas where crime was perceived to be higher than average (Kelling, Pate, Dieckman & Brown, 1974). The Rand Corporation's study of detectives found that, aside from organizational improvements within police departments, the handling of violent crime cases could be distinguished according to investigative skill levels (Chaiken, Greenwood & Petersilia, 1977).

5

Rent-a-Judge and Hide-a-Crime: The Dark Potential of Private Adjudication

Steve Russell
University of Texas at San Antonio

Whether justice is criminal or civil is often, from the point of view of a victimized person seeking it, a matter of resources. Harms committed upon persons with the means to seek justice in the civil courts can be costly to the perpetrators. For victims without access to civil justice, there is criminal justice or there is no justice. If the justice system is viewed as a means for righting wrongs, criminal justice is public justice and civil justice is private justice. As the policy wave of privatization washes over civil justice, it becomes important to keep criminal justice from getting wet if we are to be a nation of "justice for all."

Privatization of public functions is the major policy movement of post-Cold War American government, mimicking with no visible sense of irony in the West what our erstwhile enemies undertake of necessity in the former Eastern Bloc. Encouraged by the Reagan administration (President's Commission on Privatization, 1988) and debated vigorously in academia (Feigenbaum, 1998; Fitzgerald, 1988; Kent, 1987; Savas, 1987; Yergin & Stanislaw, 1998), privatization is ". . . the most serious conservative effort of our time to formulate a positive alternative to the growth of government" (Starr, 1988:6).

Adjudication is a quintessentially governmental function (Landes & Posner, 1979:235). The monopoly of dispute resolution practically defines government, and the monopoly on adjudication predated professional policing by centuries, if not millennia. Our modern conception of a royal "court" is an aristocratic social circle, but it was at one time a place to petition the government for justice. An absolute monarch may have been chief executive and legislator in one person, but he was also the final authority in adjudicating disputes, an authority diluted in Magna Carta but remaining today in the judicial function of the British House of Lords.

Modern need for dispute resolution has long outstripped both the world's remaining monarchs and the "one supreme Court" created by Article III of the United States Constitution. The "inferior courts" authorized to be created under Article III are both numerous and crowded (Posner, 1985), as are most state court systems. Docket preference generally goes to criminal cases, leaving a waiting list to adjudicate civil disputes that are often measured in years. Shapiro (1990) reported three and one-half years in Bronx County, New York (1990:289) and five years in Los Angeles (1990:275, note 2).

As the process has become slow, it has also become complex, and criminal adjudication has suffered as well:

> The obvious symptoms are . . . delay and high transaction costs; the less obvious indications are erratic patterns of disposition and the dominance of process over substantive coherence (Hazard & Scott, 1988:43).

Privatizing Adjudication

The undeniable shortcomings of public justice have driven the question whether justice in fact needs to be public (Benson, 1990). The privatization answer to crowded dockets is often described in the literature as "rent-a-judge" (Kim, 1994; Litkovitz, 1995) or "alternative dispute resolution" (ADR)(Carbonneau, 1989; Edwards, 1986; Weinstein, 1996), terms that may mask important distinctions in the way private adjudication functions in different jurisdictions, and in different proceedings within the same jurisdiction. Leaving aside forms of ADR conducted by the regular judge, such as mediated settlement conferences (Resnik, 1982) and various forms of mini-trial,[1] there are a number of ways that private actors can come to control public justice, and some of those ways are "subject at no juncture to judicial supervision" (Kronstein, 1944:36).

- Referees or masters are generally appointed by regular judges to find facts with degrees of input from the litigants in selecting the masters that vary among jurisdictions and among judges. The United States Supreme Court is primarily an appellate court, but when its original jurisdiction is invoked, it may find facts by appointing a master. Proceedings before a master are normally recorded and the master's findings are subject to approval by the judge. The cost of the master's services may be taxed against the parties, but usually is not because the process is for the convenience of the court.

- Temporary judges are sometimes practicing lawyers but more often retired judges or sitting judges from jurisdictions with lighter loads. This writer sits as a temporary judge when assigned, paid by the government. Proceedings are recorded and subject to the same appeal process as other judgments but not the approval of the regular judge. Some jurisdictions allow litigants to bring in a temporary judge at their own expense.

- Mediators resolve disputes either by agreement of the litigants or by order of the trial judge. Mediations are usually not recorded and positions taken in mediation are not admissible should the case subsequently go to trial.[2] Appeal is not an issue since a successful mediation results in an agreement, and mediators are usually compensated by the parties (Kovach, 1994).

- Arbitrators may decide existing disputes by ad hoc agreement of the parties or by contractual agreement entered before any dispute has arisen. Proceedings are often not recorded and the only issue in case of an appeal to court is whether the court should enforce the arbitration award. The focus of this question is not the merits of the dispute under arbitration but the validity of the arbitration agreement.

Every state and the Federal Rules of Civil Procedure have provided for referees under some circumstances (Newton & Swenson, 1984:814-815). Referees, masters, and temporary judges work in public, usually on the public payroll, and are subject to supervision by regular courts. The primary criticism of this process in jurisdictions where the parties can fund it themselves for a quicker proceeding is that it creates a two-tiered system of justice, one level for the wealthy and another for ordinary taxpayers (Kim, 1994:167; Newton & Swenson, 1984:816-818; Shapiro, 1990:297-305).

The focus of this chapter is the challenge for criminal justice in the rent-a-judge process: those jurisdictions that allow private funding and adjudication off the record in places other than public courthouses join private mediation and arbitration services in placing dangerous conduct beyond the reach of the regulatory state. A common argument in favor of private adjudication is that "(I)f a defendant is accused of especially damaging or embarrassing business or personal behavior, the evidence can remain hidden" (Shapiro, 1990:291).

Privacy in Litigation

In the cases of public figures like Johnny Carson and John DeLorean, who simply wanted to divorce with as much privacy as possible (Kim, 1994:174), no harm is done. Individual privacy is an important value, but privacy for a corporate enterprise is a closer question, particularly when what is embarrassing for a corporation is often also tortious or criminal. An individual litigant who is not wealthy but has the misfortune to become newsworthy by "embarrassing behavior" is the prey of supermarket tabloids because private adjudication is not an economically viable option.

The other most common use of rent-a-judges is in complex commercial litigation, and it is in the context of corporate behavior that we must remember that private courts do not effectively serve the function of publicly affirming public norms of conduct (Hazard & Scott, 1988:57-58). Even regular judges, if they take ADR behind closed doors, threaten ". . . the uniqueness of the judicial function" (Resnik, 1982:445). The traditional system was, unlike ADR, designed to seek "justice rather than peace" (Fiss, 1984:1085).

Concurrent with the rise of the rent-a-judge, a policy debate has been raging about public access to the materials produced in civil discovery and/or the terms of settlement agreements. Marcus (1991) and Miller (1991) are forceful advocates for privacy of discovery materials and settlements, but they premise their opposition on the courts having authority to weigh the public interest against the privacy interest and order disclosure if necessary.

The policy debate involves potential exposure of trade secrets and other proprietary information, and the use by plaintiffs of publicity as a litigation tool (Burkholder, 1993) weighed against the potential for hiding misconduct and forcing subsequent litigants to reinvent the wheel to bring a case already admitted by a defendant to be meritorious (Doggett & Mucchetti, 1991; Hare, Gilbert & ReMine, 1988). Particularly in products liability and toxic torts,[3] the hidden misconduct could be criminal, with violations ranging from air and water pollution to homicide (Brodeur, 1985; Cherniack, 1986; Mintz, 1985; Schuck, 1986; Stern, 1976).

On February 5, 1993, a Georgia jury assessed General Motors $101 million in exemplary damages as punishment for having intentionally concealed a safety hazard that resulted in death. Fuel tanks placed outside the frame rails had resulted in numerous lawsuits, but those that went badly for GM had been settled under confidentiality agreements that kept crash test results secret (Reed, 1993:308). While this judgment was subsequently reversed, the public policy issue of allowing deadly defects to be hidden remains. The unsuccessful homicide prosecution of Ford Motor Company for the deaths of three young women in a Ford Pinto might not have even gotten to the jury without information obtained from civil discovery (Cullen, Maakestad & Cavender, 1987:258). The evidence that Ford officials were aware of a deadly defect was crucial to the prosecution, and that evidence was only available because of the public character of some civil trials, a public character that depends upon state laws.

The public character of criminal trials is well established (*Press-Enterprise Co. v. Superior Court*, 1986; *Globe Newspaper Co. v. Superior Court*, 1982; *Richmond Newspapers, Inc. v. Virginia*, 1980), but in *Seattle Times Co. v. Rhinehart* (1984) the Supreme Court made it clear that neither common law nor the First Amendment require public access to civil discovery materials. The idea that, as a matter of law, ". . . litigants who use the courts should make a public disclosure of pertinent information as a sort of price tag for admittance" (Marcus, 1991:473) has not prevailed. Even with the legal argument for public access dead, the policy argument lingers on, with most jurisdictions opting for the solution proposed by Marcus (1991) and Miller (1991) to leave confidentiality to the discretion of the trial court (Conlon, 1993).

Several forms of the rent-a-judge phenomenon simply short circuit this policy debate, because nothing is public about the proceeding. In the case of arbitration agreements, there is dispute over whether there should be any discovery at all rather than whether the information discovered should be public (Ho, 1997).

Arbitration Agreements as Substantive Law

Arbitration is also the primary locale of the most disturbing aspect of the ADR movement for criminal justice: the possibility of private parties opting out of substantive law by agreement among themselves (Kronstein, 1944; Ware, 1999). In the case of criminal prohibitions that affect an entire industry, such as pollution regulations that add to operating expenses, or in the case of a potentially criminal choice to market an unsafe product, arbitration agreements can simply keep the activity or the *mens rea* evidence away from public or prosecutorial view. The only other method of uncovering such corporate behavior in advance of a catastrophe—intervention of an employee whistleblower—is problematic because the liability of a whistleblower in the face of an employee confidentiality agreement remains unsettled, leading a prudent employee to remain silent if there is any doubt at all whether the conduct is criminal (Blumberg, 1971; Rützel, 1995; Weinstein, 1997).

If the lips of employees are sealed by confidentiality agreements, the lips of competitors can be sealed by common interest in avoiding regulation, as was the case with the major tobacco companies for so many years. Bob Dylan wrote that "to live outside the law you must be honest,"[4] but he reckoned without interlocking arbitration agreements within an industry. Disputes can be resolved in this manner without publicizing crimes. Therefore, corporate outlaws need not be honest among themselves. Official, but not public, dispute resolution is available, and the potential reach of private arbitration is broad indeed.

The Supreme Court has held that the Federal Arbitration Act[5] (FAA) covers all agreements under the laws of all states co-extensive with Congress' power to regulate under the Commerce Clause (*Allied-Bruce Terminix Cos. v. Dobson*, 1995). This means that any attempts by states to declare some matters inarbitrable for public policy reasons are pre-empted by the FAA (*Perry v. Thomas*, 1987; *Southland Corp. v. Keating*, 1984; Ware, 1994).

Even when there is not agreement within an entire industry, claims under statutes that create crimes can be submitted to private arbitration rather than aired publicly in a courtroom. Early on, the Supreme Court recognized certain claims as inarbitrable as a matter of public policy just as some other types of contracts are declared unenforceable: gambling debts in a jurisdiction where gambling is unlawful, for example. The claims held to be inarbitrable on public policy grounds were generally claims that could include criminal or quasi-criminal activity and therefore were deemed to require a public hearing in a public forum.

The Court held claims under the Securities Act of 1933 to be inarbitrable (*Wilko v. Swan*, 1953) and the lower federal courts similarly excepted antitrust claims, some civil rights claims, and the Racketeer Influenced and Corrupt Organizations[6] statute. This was known as the "public policy defense" to entry of a judgment on an arbitrator's award (Sterk, 1981).

The public policy defense on the federal level took a decisive blow in 1985 when *Mitsubishi Motors Corporation v. Soler Chrysler-Plymouth, Inc.* held antitrust claims to be arbitrable. In a 1991 age discrimination claim, *Gilmer v. Interstate/Johnson Lane Corp.*, the Court made it clear that it meant what it said in *Mitsubishi Motors*. It is particularly disturbing that civil rights discrimination claims can be hidden from public view, since unlawful discrimination by definition affects a class of people in addition to the individual claimant. With the federal public policy defense reversed and state public policy defenses pre-empted, virtually any alleged misconduct has become subject to an arbitration hearing out of public view (Stipanowich, 1997). "Appeal against an award is generally either unavailable or unavailing" (Carbonneau, 1996:1946).

The Supreme Court, in reversing the public policy defense, took the position that if an arbitrator refused to apply substantive law, the court could simply refuse to enter a judgment on the award—not because of the public nature of the claim, but because the claim was wrongly decided.[7] This was surely a figment of the Court's imagination when arbitrators need not be lawyers, need not give reasons for decisions, and typically make no record of testimony. It has been common knowledge for many years that the advantages of arbitration are speed and low cost— not fidelity to the law (Kronstein, 1963).

> Arbitration was not conceived of as a judicial trial. It is priva-
> tized justice, funded exclusively by the arbitrating parties and
> controlled by them, and private arbitral institutions, like the
> American Arbitration Association or the International Chamber
> of Commerce. The arbitral proceeding is not a public hearing,
> and—depending upon the language of the arbitration agree-
> ment—is not governed by the rules of judicial procedure or, in
> many instances, by the substantive rules of law. Arbitrators
> rarely (in domestic practice at least) issue reasons with their
> awards and the prospect of judicial scrutiny of the determina-
> tion is virtually nonexistent . . . Moreover, the determination is
> not intended to serve the public interest, but only that of the
> parties who have paid for the arbitration (Carbonneau,
> 1996:1958).

Landes and Posner (1979) point out that the public justice system serves at least two functions: dispute resolution and rules creation. Privatized justice accomplishes the former at the expense of the latter. A public judicial officer who writes a clearly reasoned opinion applying the law to a particular set of facts has settled the immediate dispute as well as any future disputes that cannot be distinguished in a principled way. Indeed, it is the duty of every public judicial officer, including and particularly Supreme Court justices (Goldstein, 1992) not only to decide but also to explain.

A rent-a-judge who does the same thing has simply rendered herself unemployable in similar cases. However, a rent-a-judge is unlikely to be faced with the task of explaining because private parties are paying for resolution of *their* dispute, not future disputes involving others. Privatized justice assumes that other individuals who may need justice in a similar matter can buy their own. Of course, the ability to purchase justice in this retail fashion varies among individuals, businesses, and cartels.

The advantages to a cartel in staying out of the public court system are self-evident (Kronstein, 1944), but the demise of the public policy exception to arbitrability also has implications for enforcement of deceptive trade practices laws, typically enacted to give public prosecutors authority to protect individual consumers (Schwartz, 1997).

> As a result of these "advances" in the federal law on arbitration,
> it is now possible for a major bank, a car manufacturer or deal-
> ership, a financial broker, or any other economic actor to
> insert a provision for final and binding arbitration in a purchase
> agreement or service contract and make it indispensable to the

transaction. The consumer, if at all aware of the provision and
its meaning, must either accept it as stated or forego doing
business with the actor in question or the entire industry (Carbonneau, 1996:1956).

With the failure of healthcare reform during the first Clinton administration, the instance of binding arbitration that can become, at least,
inconvenient and, at most, deadly for the average citizen is contained in
the contracts of many Health Maintenance Organizations (HMOs). As
Galanter (1974) has so forcefully pointed out, any system of adjudication
tends to favor "repeat players" over "one-shotters," and the one-shotter
patient seeking coverage for a lifesaving medical procedure from a
repeat player HMO is in no position to "forego doing business with the
actor in question or the entire industry." HMOs are often picked by
employers rather than by the individuals covered by the contracts. In the
matter of medical insurance, the crimes of fraud or deceptive trade
practices can quickly turn to homicide.

Conclusion

Privatizing the adjudication process has created a space within
which to hide several kinds of criminal activity. Even if that space is currently vacant, it is unlikely to remain vacant forever, and it is closed tightly enough to require a brave whistleblower and a large scandal to put
inconvenience to the regulatory state on the national agenda.

The regulatory state is, in current political fashion, the enemy, and
may be inconvenienced with impunity. Would-be regulators are on the
political defensive (Rose-Ackerman, 1992; Sunstein, 1990), although
complete termination of public programs remains more problematic
than would be apparent from political rhetoric (Daniels, 1997). Civil
adjudication's public function, its tie to criminal adjudication, is endangered by privatization.

When some major scandal does penetrate the shell of privatized adjudication, many commentators who have pointed out the public character of dispute resolution will be proven correct (Hazard & Scott, 1988;
Lee, 1985; Resnik, 1986). "Where would we be," asks Luban (1995:2629)
in discussing critically Fiss' opposition to settlements, "if *Brown v.
Board of Education* had settled quietly out of court?"[8]

Some civil disputes, such as school integration in *Brown*, involve
public values that deserve public airing. *All* criminal violations involve
public values in a like manner. Adjudication, like policing and corrections, is an element of the justice system that can benefit from some privatization. The problems of cost and delay that created the ADR movement are real. As in policing and corrections, however, we must not

allow public policy to be driven by private interests (Nuzum, 1998). The question of how much privatization and how much corporate privacy are consistent with effectively regulating criminal and tortious activity is one that must remain open for research and analysis, to prevent valid public functions from being privatized out of existence.

In eviscerating the public policy defense, the Supreme Court was not pronouncing constitutional law but merely interpreting a federal statute. Congress retains the power to define potentially criminal conduct as outside the scope of the FAA, and it should explicitly do so rather than relying on the Court to backtrack.

More than 50 years ago, Kronstein (1944:68) charged in the *Yale Law Journal* that "(a)n instrument of cartels and monopolistic trade associations, modern arbitration appears not only to be incompatible with general concepts of positive law, but even to attack in principle the practical mandates of the Constitution." He proposed that the courts apply the due process requirements of the Fifth and Fourteenth Amendments to what we now call ADR. This is impractical because it is the amount of process that is due in public courts that causes expense and delay. We have ADR to avoid expense and delay.

ADR to resolve private matters in private by agreed upon standards is here to stay. Recognizing this, we must still account for ". . . the transformation of arbitration . . . into an institution of social control" (Kronstein, 1963:700). Congress, having preempted the states, must act to bring the construction of penal statutes back within the institution of social control designed for the purpose: the criminal justice system.

Endnotes

[1]   It is possible to hire a rent-a-judge to perform a mini-trial, but the result is normally in the form of advice rather than an order (Lee, 1985:270).

[2]   Rules 408-410, Federal Rules of Evidence. States that have statutory mediation follow similar rules.

[3]   In popular parlance, "toxic torts" are civil actions brought about by the alleged release of dangerous substances into the environment. Depending upon the law of the particular jurisdiction, there may be criminal as well as civil liability. The term is sometimes used in an ironic sense by judges: the complexity of the evidence and the number of victims make such cases "toxic" to the rest of the court's business.

[4]   Absolutely Sweet Marie, (1966; renewed 1994, Dwarf Music).

[5]   9 U.S.C. §§ 1-16.

[6]   18 U.S.C. § 1961.

[7]   "(C)ourts of the United States will have the opportunity at the award-enforcement stage to ensure that the legitimate interest in the enforcement of the antitrust laws has been addressed." 473 U.S. at 638.

[8]   The question is rhetorical in context.

6 Public and Private Substance Abuse Programs in Corrections

Dale K. Sechrest and Matthew A. Robby
California State University,
San Bernardino

Determinate sentencing, "get tough" laws, and increasing penalties for substance abuse have brought many more offenders than before into the criminal justice system, drastically increased the number of people incarcerated, and created significant challenges for treating inmates for substance abuse problems. According to Falkin, Wexler, and Lipton (1992) correctional authorities are using substance abuse treatment programs in an effort to reduce recidivism and control prison crowding. As opposed to the traditional emphasis on security and control, there is a movement toward the use of public and private substance abuse treatment that emphasizes "comprehensive programming, including treatment and rehabilitation" (Markos & Grierson, 1999). Many of these programs emphasize a whole life approach that attempts to improve client life skills, decisionmaking, attitudes, education, motivation, job skills, and overall life chances, thereby reducing drug use, recidivism, and system costs. Substance abuse treatments, both public and private, that appear to be comprehensive often vary in actual scope of programming; at the same time, their effectiveness varies with their intensity or ability to deliver the services they claim to provide. It is often difficult to identify program features that are significantly related to success. This may be especially true for private contract programs that are often not subject to research scrutiny.

The treatment of substance abusers in the correctional system, both public and private, has been a significant problem for many years. Leukefeld and Tims (1993) cite a survey of 1,737 jails indicating that only 28 percent indicated they offered substance abuse treatment (in 1992), with 19 percent indicating they funded drug treatment programs, and only 12 percent reported programs that were isolated from the general jail population. Only 6.7 percent of the average inmate population was enrolled in drug treatment. Two-thirds of the programs focused on white inmates, with an average size of 42 and average age of 26, 80 percent had volunteer staff and three employees.

A 1997 survey of substance abuse and treatment of State and Federal prisoners by the BJS found increases in substance abuse (Mumola, 1999). Overall, 56 percent of state prisoners and one-fourth of the federal inmates indicated they had taken part in some type of substance abuse program in the past. From 1991 to 1997 the percentage of inmates reporting treatment after prison admission declined from one-third to 15 percent. While treatment histories are reported they generally do not identify the origin of treatment for substance abuse for prison or jail inmates or releasees, i.e., whether treatment programs in incarceration or upon release are publicly or privately operated. However, for probationers, various 12-step programs ("Anonymous-type") were common, with little mention of employee assistance programs, methadone programs, emergency rooms, and crisis centers (Mumola, 1999).

Private Sector Programs

According to Shenk (1995:16), "privatization—involving the private sector in public services . . . is the vogue, bipartisan answer to all sorts of governmental problems." Lucken (1997:247) indicates that "In the past decade, private treatment agencies have increasingly taken over the task of rehabilitating offenders." These private programs provide needed intermediate sanctions, which reduces the burden on public corrections personnel (probation, parole, and community service workers), and are more focused on comprehensive models of intervention and treatment. A new partnership has been formed between private treatment agencies and corrections. According to Lucken (1997:248), "This partnership is becoming more formalized through a series of contracts between community corrections and private treatment agencies." These partnerships are occurring at the local, state, and federal levels. Lucken (1997) documents the growth of this profitable enterprise by citing the U.S. Department of Health and Human Services National Drug and Alcoholism and Treatment Survey Unit (1995), which "reports that the number of substance abuse providers alone has grown by 50 percent between 1980 and 1992" (1995:249).

Private substance abuse treatment companies, which are often owned by larger private entities, contract with public agencies to provide services in a variety of settings, both institutional and community. These private companies often benefit when contracts are approved because the public sphere has historically not made sound contract agreements that would protect public interests. If services to be provided are not specified fully in a contract then private substance abuse treatment companies may feel that they are not obligated to provide certain types of services (Hancock, 1998). Such contracts often reflect the interests of the private vendor in reducing overall costs and increasing profits (Shichor & Sechrest, 1995). Liability issues are also a concern, in that both the private and the public agencies are subject to lawsuits when they do not perform as required (Hancock, 1998).

Substance abuse treatment programs operated by private sector entrepreneurs have been a feature of the correctional landscape for many years. They operate both in correctional institutions and in the community for offenders housed in pre-release and halfway house settings. Privately operated programs, such as the therapeutic community programs of Phoenix House, Daytop Village, and Stay'n Out in New York State, often use ex-offenders and ex-addicts in the delivery of treatment services to offenders in institutions and in community settings. These programs claim 22 to 35 percent reductions in rearrest rates for men, and 25 to 40 percent for women (Leukefeld & Tims, 1993). Private substance abuse programs are a source of treatment for inmates in the California Department of Corrections (CDC), such as the Phoenix, Arizona-based Amity RighTurn program.

Several philosophical and operational questions can be raised about the use of private programs for criminal offenders. These range from moral opposition to private agency involvement in treatment to operational problems. Political considerations are a concern when private sector vendors become involved in creating a demand for their services by influencing public agencies. Advertising may also be used to create, sustain, and accelerate the demand for treatment (Lucken, 1997). Such tactics, which may be driven by competition for contracts, may expand the categories of clients to be served. Lucken (1997:257) refers to this as the process of "commodification," the interaction between private vendors and corrections agencies (consumers) to provide treatment services, which involves expanding the definition of illegal behaviors, i.e., the pool of potential clients, and the types of potential services that can be provided. Lucken relies on Ewick (1993) to indicate that commodification also results in controlling offender admission and exit from the programs. "Gradations of deviance and intervention, coupled with thorough and subjective screening mechanisms, ensure that no one is refused [treatment] on the grounds that he or she is well or "normal" (Lucken, 1997:252).

There are additional problems with private substance abuse treatment agencies in corrections. A major concern is the issue of coerced treatment. If participation in a substance abuse program is mandated by the courts, and the service provider is from the private sector, problems may arise. Most often the problem occurs when profit-motivated organizations control definitions of who should be punished and the type or degree of punishment received (Lucken, 1997). Private sector agencies have a financial interest in and may influence the punishment of offenders based on their need to stay in business. As Lucken states:

> One substance abuse agency counselor confided that quotas may be set to ensure a certain percentage of a treatment class will be referred for additional treatment, regardless of need. Accordingly the specification of treatment duration in program orientation material often is open-ended and ambiguous" (Lucken, 1997:254).

This appears to have been the case in Orange County, California, when a private substance abuse program was found to be extending the treatment of court-referred clients (Pfeifer, 1999). The program was for individuals convicted of domestic violence offenses who were required to attend a four-month drug counseling program. Program participation was being extended without the permission of the judge for several patients, and reports of program completion were not being filed. This led the public defender to discontinue the services of the private organization. The problem was further complicated by the fact that staff did not have the necessary qualifications (licensing) to conduct the required therapy. County program managers complain of having too many private programs to monitor to control these types of problems.

An equally important concern for many of the programs discussed in the literature is the effectiveness of the treatment provided, whether public or private. Some substance abuse programs are operated by public agencies, others by private for-profit or non-profit companies. Studies generally focus on recidivism, and reference is seldom made to the public or private operating status of a program. The distinction between private for-profit and non-profit providers of treatment services is seldom made. The reason appears to be that private programs are often attached to a public agency, such as a court-supervised drug program, and the public, for-profit, or non-profit status is not considered important. Also, there are many types of private for-profit and non-profit drug treatment programs that are not connected to public agencies, but serve similar clients. These clients come from various community referral agencies and from the courts, using both informal and formal procedures.

Sometimes studies of program effectiveness do not report the extent of involvement with current or past offenders by the staff, or the public or private nature of the program. For example, Apsler (1994), who was concerned about new federal grants to treat drug users, discussed four types of drug treatment but did not address the public or private aspect of treatment. Moreover, he did not define the populations being treated. He concluded that little is known about the effectiveness of various treatment modalities. At the same time, there are conflicting perspectives on quality, value, and satisfaction for all participants—funders, providers, correctional agencies, and the clients. These factors make it difficult to assess the effectiveness of public and private programs.

Cost Comparisons

It appears that cost savings can be realized through the application of treatment services to the problem of addiction. For example, in California treatment services have been estimated to save more than a billion dollars in crime reductions in excess of the cost of treatment alone (Newton, 1998). It is surprising to know that in this era of greater individual responsibility and fiscal constraint, possible cost savings are not being obtained by providing drug treatment services to many who could benefit from them. With the large numbers of people going to jail or prison for drug-related crimes, and with the large numbers of inmates in need of substance abuse treatment services of some kind, national and local strategies should be redirected or expanded to better address treatment services for incarcerated individuals. Increased use of interventions, such as drug courts, should be considered, rather than merely focusing on law enforcement and prevention concerns.

As always, in comparing public and private service delivery, cost comparisons are difficult due to a host of factors, which include lack of adequate cost estimates for public services and various types of hidden costs that may not be identified by private sector providers, or by persons studying them. A related question is the diversity of treatments in each program, which has been driven by the managed care movement. Many types of treatment are given by each provider. The effectiveness of specific components is difficult to identify because they may simultaneously address mental health, substance abuse, alcoholism, violent behaviors, and educational needs for program participants.

Substance Abuse Programs in Corrections

Leukefeld and Tims (1993) have provided a useful overview of private drug abuse treatment in prisons and jails, based upon findings of a meeting sponsored by the National Institute of Drug Abuse in 1990 (Leukefeld & Tims, 1993). They reviewed the current status of drug abuse treatment in prisons and jails, treatment approaches, evaluation, and special issues, and provided recommendations on the need for treatment, the types of intervention needed, and the best methods for delivery of services. Private programs such as Amity RighTurn and Stay'n Out were described in relation to the value of therapeutic community treatment approaches. Regarding the effectiveness of treatment, the major research finding is that, regardless of type of treatment, the longer an individual remains in treatment (up to 12 months) the greater the chance of success (Leukefeld & Tims, 1993; Meachum, 1998). This finding, discussed below, has implications for the sources of treatment and its funding for both private and public programs.

Leukefeld and Tims (1993) allude to the medical model of treatment in noting that "cures" are often identified as complete abstinence from any type of drug, while criminal justice agencies define a cure as no recidivism. Neither of these goals is easily nor completely achieved. They cite current studies showing very limited availability of treatment in prisons and jails, although most estimates show that more than 50 percent of these populations are convicted of drug law violations and even higher percentages are convicted as drug and alcohol abusers. Treatments for inmates range from drug education to individual and group counseling and therapeutic community approaches.

Leukefeld and Tims (1993) reviewed several private drug treatment programs. They cited the Amity RighTurn program, which is a privately operated program under contract at the R.J. Donovan Correctional Facility of the California Department of Corrections (CDC). California officials found that by 1988, drug offenders were the largest category of commitments to the system and began looking for potential solutions to the recidivism of this population. This increase was driven by determinate sentencing and the 1994 three-strikes law, which have driven the average length of stay up from 41 months in 1991 to 53 months in 1997 (Little Hoover Commission, 1998:17). As stated by the Little Hoover Commission (1998:46), " . . . while the numbers of inmates incarcerated for violent crimes has increased, the numbers of inmates convicted of nonviolent crimes, and drug crimes in particular, has increased even faster." One of the important things California could do is repeal the three-strikes legislation and related public referendum, since most of those sentenced under three-strikes legislation are drug offenders rather than a violent crime.

Amity RighTurn is a private, non-profit substance abuse treatment program at the R.J. Donovan Correctional Facility in San Diego, California. The program is funded by the CDC, and began in late 1990. Program capacity is 200 inmates and 60 parolees, with a significant waiting list (Mullen, Ratelle, Abraham & Boyle, 1996; Mullen, Schuettinger, Arbiter & Conn, 1997; Little Hoover Commission, 1998; Josi & Sechrest, 1998a). The program is based on a therapeutic community model and lasts nine to 12 months. Participants are housed separately at the prison and receive 20 hours of intensive treatment per week, as well as regular institution education and employment programs. An outcome study of 300 volunteers and 200 randomly assigned controls is being completed.

As part of the evaluation of the program, Josi and Sechrest (1998b) were allowed to study the relationship between Amity staff and correctional officers at R.J. Donovan. Open-ended interviews with 15 correctional officers and 12 treatment staff suggested that different goals coupled with problems in communication between the two groups created an adversarial ("we versus them") relationship. While the warden and executive staff supported the program, the adversarial view was held by about one-half of the correctional officers, with some expressing support for the treatment effort. The adversarial position was exacerbated by the use of ex-addicts on the Amity staff, who were used as treaters and role models in order to gain participant trust. Treatment staff felt a majority of the officers wanted the program to fail, and felt they were treated like "second-class citizens." While these problems might have existed had public employees been operating the program, it is likely that the "outside" nature of the program contributed to these attitudes. Recommendations included greater efforts to cross-train staff of both groups. Several of the private treatment programs that operate in correctional settings indicate the need for separation of inmate/clients from the general prison population, and this recommendation is often made for all such programs (Leukefeld & Tims, 1993; Inciardi et al., 1992). Whenever security and treatment personnel work together in correctional or community settings, staff conflicts may be an issue requiring resolution.

Public and Private Treatment

Public and private substance abuse services are organized and financed differently, based largely on the status of those who are being treated. Private sector treatment typically serves persons who have access to health insurance or who can pay for care. Public sector treatment programs often service persons who are uninsured, have exceeded their private health insurance benefits, or are covered by Medicaid (Schydlower & Anglin, 1995).

Schydlower and Anglin (1995) found that private coverage is often more restrictive than public coverage. However, Miller (1992) concluded that substance abuse treatment programs, "particularly in a for-profit healthcare economy, have tended to provide over-sufficient treatment. Residential treatment and other expensive forms of care may be inappropriately given where less intensive interventions would be at least as effective" (1992:99). He was concerned also that the overuse of treatment might mask the impact of more intensive treatment programs.

In their analysis of drug abuse treatment in prisons and jails, Leuke-feld and Tims (1993) described several programs in prisons and jails, few of which had been evaluated. These included Florida's "Tiers" program, which is a graduated release program, the Wisconsin Department of Corrections specialized substance abuse program, which emphasized assessment and coordinated care, and Oregon State Hospital's "Cornerstone Program," a therapeutic community with three other sites. The Oregon program was found to improve client functioning and reduce criminal recidivism, with a very high correlation between time in treatment and decreasing criminal activity. Among other conclusions, Field (1992:153) states that "Addicted offenders who receive little or no treatment show an accelerating pattern of criminal activity over time. [and that] Time in treatment in an intensive program for addicted offenders correlates positively with measured decreases in criminal activity." Although criminal activity did not desist completely for many successfully treated addicts, the extent of criminal involvement was reduced.

The Stay'n Out therapeutic community (TC) program in New York State's correctional system is a private non-profit organization that has been in operation for almost 20 years. The TC design was based in part on the success of Phoenix House in New York City, and the R.J. Donovan Amity program, which is based on the Stay'n Out model. These programs are based on "positive TC treatment environments capable of retaining inmates for optimal treatment durations (2 to 12 months)" (Wexler, Falkin, Lipton & Rosenblum, 1992:157). Wexler et al. (1992:170) concluded that this first large-scale, long-term study:

> provides convincing evidence that prison-based TC treatment can produce significant reductions in recidivism rates . . . [it] was effective in reducing recidivism rates . . . more effective than other prison treatment modalities (e.g., milieu therapy, counseling) in reducing recidivism; and . . . the longer that Stay'n Out clients remained in the prison TC program, the more successful they were after release.

The most curious (or "provocative") finding was that time in this private program was significant and positively related to time until arrest, as hypothesized, but that those who are released after 12 months had higher recidivism rates (Wexler et al., 1992:171). Meachum (1998) cites research that indicates that the effectiveness of a residential treatment program begins to decrease after 12 months. An explanation for this may lie in the fact that the parole board is not releasing these individuals at program completion, resulting in frustration and loss of program gains.

According to Hubbard (1992), several earlier studies support the contention that criminal justice clients do as well or better than other clients in drug abuse programs. This may be due to the ability of the system to keep these clients in treatment, and that additional time in treatment is generally beneficial to these individuals, a finding confirmed by Wexler et al. (1992).

Conclusions and Discussion

Substance abuse in the United States continues to be widespread and represents a societal problem that causes significant social and economic consequences at both the individual and societal levels, especially within the criminal justice system.

A large percentage of incarcerated and paroled offenders at all governmental levels have reported using drugs during or prior to committing offenses for which they were locked up; however, a rather small percentage of all inmates receive any type of drug treatment services. For those who have received treatment, it is sometimes difficult to determine the effectiveness of the treatment modalities because they are not well defined, especially with respect to the organizational entity delivering the services.

When examining the efficiency and effectiveness of substance abuse treatment programs in terms of the delivery of services by public agencies or by private for-profit and non-profit substance abuse treatment programs, many questions remain unanswered, especially for prison-based and community corrections programs. This is because few comparisons have been made across treatment service delivery programs, either for reductions in substance abuse, relapse, recidivism, or cost. These substance abuse treatment issues are multi-faceted, complex, and not readily simplified into singular descriptions or pronouncements. This is the case when considering the topics of substance abuse, substance abusers, treatment approaches, treatment organizations, and the plethora of factors that are known and unknown that influence both the extent and effectiveness of both public and private substance abuse treatment programs.

Comparisons of public and private service delivery are done for substance abuse programs available to all types of individuals, and are often not specific to criminal offenders. Due to recent changes in healthcare funding, these studies are based largely on comparing costs, and they rarely address the quality of services. The provider organization being studied is not often clearly identified as to the source of funds, although funding is related to its ability to continue providing treatment. The focus of most studies is programs operated by public or private organizations, usually in terms of relapse and recidivism, with no comparisons across types of organizations.

As indicated in a survey by *Alcoholism & Drug Abuse Weekly* reported in *Mental Health Weekly* (Early data in SA . . ., 1996), questions are raised about the survival of the substance abuse field as it now exists. Pessimism was expressed by practitioner readers, much of which centered around the merging of substance abuse treatment into "behavioral health" or mental health budgets, coupled with the specter of a managed-care driven system that puts costs first over treatment.

These questions will have to be addressed before the best model for the delivery of substance abuse services in corrections, or for the general population of affected individuals, can be determined. At this time it is unclear whether the public or private sector is the better provider for criminal offenders. Several demonstrations are now being conducted in the United States to determine the best model for the delivery of substance abuse services, although most are highly restricted and not widely replicated. Perhaps the best replications in corrections are those for the Stay'n Out and Amity programs, which are specific to substance abuse. However, these do not address costs.

Lucken (1997:244-245) states the problem in terms that apply to private programs of all types, including substance abuse treatment in prisons and jails:

> Unlike prison privatization, a coherent and comprehensive picture of private offender treatment in community corrections is lacking. National data on privatization in community corrections and/or the use of private sector contracts have not been compiled systematically. The collection of these data has been hampered by two factors in particular, namely the variation in the organizational structures of community corrections programs and varying reporting practices.

Lucken (1997) expresses a concern that the amount of private sector spending is sometimes not well documented in public budget records. She sees the need for reform in the treatment of substance abuse offenders, including better regulation, evaluation, and accountability. The content and outcome of private sector offender treatment programs has yet to be tested.

7 Jail Privatization: The Next Frontier

Richard G. Kiekbusch
University of Texas–Permian Basin

This chapter addresses the private operation of local jails that would ordinarily be operated by a county sheriff. Jail privatization is an important topic in the discourse on criminal justice privatization because local jails will likely replace prisons as the primary target of market development by private correctional operators. Unlike most discussions of correctional privatization which focus heavily on private prisons (Allen & Simonsen, 1998:570-590; Becker, 1997; Houston, 1995:271-289), this chapter focuses exclusively on the operation of adult local detention facilities by for-profit companies. In this context, jail privatization means the total management of a local jail by a for-profit private company. All the functions traditionally and routinely associated with jail operations are managed by a private corporation (American Correctional Association, 1989; American Correctional Association, 1991; Champion, 1990:168-172).[1]

Jail privatization does not mean:

- *Alternative Use of Jail Facilities:* The use of a jail facility by a private company for purposes other than those traditionally served by local jails (i.e., private use of a vacant county jail as a confinement facility for state or federal prisoners, parole violators, or pre-release prisoners) (Mays & Winfree, 1998:121).

133

- *Provision of Selected Inmate Services:* The private provision of such inmate services as meal preparation, medical and mental healthcare, commissary sales, and substance abuse counseling (American Jail Association, 1999a:30-31,46-47,52-53,60-64,78,83,87,101-105; Evancho, 1997; Gallagher, 1998).

- *Financing of Jail Construction:* The private financing of jail construction typically occurs after taxpayers have rejected a jail construction bond issue (Mays & Winfree, 1998:120). The private contractor builds or finances the construction of the facility and then turns it over to the county for operation.

History

During the sixteenth, seventeenth, and eighteenth centuries the county gaols and workhouses of Europe and the Americas were often managed by unpaid or underpaid officials. In England, these confinement facilities were usually under the control of the Sheriff. These institutions were the forerunners of today's jails. During this period, few, if any, rights were afforded to inmates and they were frequently exploited by their overseers for personal gain. Jailers routinely collected fees from inmates for food, clothing, shelter, safety, and even release. They could also withhold services from inmates who were unable to pay (Allen & Simonsen, 1998:20-21; Giever, 1997:419-421; Kerle, 1998:4; Silverman & Vega, 1996:67; Zupan, 1991:9-14). Jailers used inmate labor for their own private purposes and leased the inmates as laborers to business owners. These practices were exported to the American colonies along with the jail (Giever, 1997; Kerle, 1998; Tewksbury, 1997; Zupan, 1991). However, in the American colonies these penal "business" practices were often carried out by public officials, hired by local sheriffs, rather than private entrepreneurs.

Religious denominations, service organizations, and prisoner advocacy groups have long been influential forces in the formulation, implementation, and oversight of correctional laws and policies—including those pertaining to local jails. In 1790, shortly after the Revolution, the Quakers and the Philadelphia Society for the Alleviation of the Miseries of Public Prisons[2] persuaded the Pennsylvania General Assembly to allow a portion of Philadelphia's Walnut Street Jail to be converted into the first rehabilitation-oriented penitentiary in the United States.[3] Although private interest groups have long influenced the administration of jails, the management of American jails was exclusively public until the1980s.

The roots of contemporary jail privatization in the United States can be traced to a contract between Hamilton County, Tennessee, and Nashville-based Corrections Corporation of American (CCA) whereby

CCA assumed managerial responsibilities for that county's Silverdale Facilities in 1984 (Thomas & Bolinger, 1999b). CCA followed-up with additional jail contracts in Bay County, Florida (1985, 1986), Santa Fe County, New Mexico (1986),[4] and Hernando County, Florida (1988). Today, only 15 years after the Silverdale facilities opened, there are seven private companies operating 26 local jail facilities. Their combined bedspace capacity is approximately 8,400 (Thomas & Bolinger, 1999b; personal communication with other sources)

Current Status

The demographics of private jails in the United States are displayed in Table 7.1 below. These data reveal some interesting facts, patterns, and trends that help place jail privatization within the broader contexts of American corrections and the privatization of correctional institutions.

Market Share

Private jail beds represent a minute portion of the total number of jail beds in operation. According to Sawyer (1996:32), there were approximately 487,250 local jail beds in 1994 in the United States. Of these, 8,398 were private jail beds, which represents only 1.7 percent of the total jail capacity. Even after Corrections Corporation of America opened the new Polk County, Florida and Tulsa County, Oklahoma jails in 1999 (see note d in Table 7.1), the private jail capacity was still only around two percent of total jail capacity.

Similarly, private jail beds are only a small percentage of the total number of private correctional beds in use in the United States in 1999. As shown in Table 7.1, the 8,398 private jail beds were less than 10 percent of the 87,204 beds located in private secure adult correctional facilities in this country (Thomas & Bolinger, 1999b). Even with the addition of 2,448 new jail beds in Polk and Tulsa Counties by Corrections Corp. of America, jail bedspace is only about 12 percent of the total private confinement market.

Size

The data in Table 7.1 make it clear that private jails, much like their publicly operated counterparts, are concentrated in the bedspace categories 0-50 and 101-500 (Sawyer, 1996:18-22). Like public sector jails, private jails display a tremendous range of bedspace capacity. The small-

Table 7.1
Private Jails in the United States as of March 5, 1999

CIVIGENICS, INC. (Marlborough, Massachusetts)[a]

Facility	Location	Primary Source(s) of Prisoners	Secondary Source(s) of Prisoners	Capacity	Initial Contract Year
Park County Detention Center	Fairplay, Colorado	Park County, Colorado	None	120	1995
Coloumbiana County Jail	Lisbon, Ohio	Columbiana County, Ohio	Adjoining Counties	190	1998
CORNELL CORRECTIONS, INC. (Houston, Texas)					
Sante Fe County Adult Detention Center	Sante Fe, New Mexico	Sante Fe County, New Mexico	Adjoining counties; Federal Bureau of Prisons; U.S. Marshals Service; U.S. Immigration and Naturalization Service	672	1997
CORRECTIONAL SERVICES CORPORATION (Sarasota, Florida)					
Grenada County Jail	Grenada, Mississippi	Grenada County, Mississippi	Adjoining Counties	160	1997
McKinley County Jail	Gallup, New Mexico	Gallup County, New Mexico	Adjoining counties	368	1997
Frio County Detention Center	Pearsall, Texas	Frio County, Texas	Idaho Dept. of Correction	391	1992
South Fulton Municipal Jail[b]	Union City, Georgia	City of Union City, Georgia; City of Palmetto, Georgia	None	212	1999
CORRECTIONAL SYSTEMS, INC. (San Diego, California)[c]					
Seal Beach Jail	Seal Beach, California	City of Seal Beach, California	City of Garden Grove, California; Federal Bureau of Prisons	40	1994
Baldwin Park City Jail	Baldwin Park, California	City of Baldwin Park, California	None	34	1996
Montebello City Jail	Montebello, California	City of Montebello, California	U.S. Marshals Service	34	1996
Alhambra City Jail	Alhambra, California	City of Alhambra, California	U.S. Immigration and Naturalization Service	75	1997
Downey City Jail	Downey, California	City of Downey, California	None	9	1998
Bell City Jail	Bell, California	City of Bell, California	None	25	1998
Chino City Jail	Chino, California	City of Chino, California	None	25	1998
Hawthorne City Jail	Hawthorne, California	City of Hawthorne, California	None	35	1998
Bay County Jail	Panama City, Florida	Bay County, Florida	U.S. Marshals Service	276	1985

Table 7.1, continued

CORRECTIONS CORPORATION OF AMERICA (Nashville, Tennessee)[d]

Facility	Location	Primary Source(s) of Prisoners	Secondary Source(s) of Prisoners	Capacity	Initial Contract Year
Bay County Jail Annex	Panama City, Florida	Bay County, Florida	U.S. Marshals Service	401	1986
Hernando County Jail	Brooksville, Florida	Hernando County, Florida	U.S. Marshals Service	302	1988
Citrus County Detention Facility	Lecanto, Florida	Citrus County, Florida	None	300	1995
Marion County Jail II	Indianapolis, Indiana	Marion County, Indiana	Indiana Dept. of Correction	670	1997
Metro-Davidson County Detention Facility	Nashville, Tennessee	Davidson County, Tennessee	Tennessee Dept. of Correction	1,092	1992
Silverdale Facilities	Chattanooga, Tennessee	Hamilton County, Tennessee	U.S. Marshals Service	600	1984
Liberty County Jail	Liberty, Texas	Liberty County, Texas	None	382	1995
River City Correctional Center[e]	Louisville, Kentucky	Jefferson County, Kentucky	None	363	1998

GRW CORPORATION (Brentwood, Tennessee)

Facility	Location	Primary Source(s) of Prisoners	Secondary Source(s) of Prisoners	Capacity	Initial Contract Year
Joplin City Jail	Joplin, Missouri	City of Joplin, Missouri	Adjoining counties	60	1997

WACKENHUT CORRECTIONS CORPORATION (Palm Beach Gardens, Florida)

Facility	Location	Primary Source(s) of Prisoners	Secondary Source(s) of Prisoners	Capacity	Initial Contract Year
Delaware County Prison	Thornton, Pennsylvania	Delaware County, Pennsylvania	None	1,562	1992

TOTALS:
- Number of Companies — 7
- Numbers of Facilities — 26
- Number of Beds — 8,398
- Number of States in Which Private Jails Are Located — 13

[a] In addition to its two existing jail operations listed in Table 7.1, Civigenics, Inc. has contracts with Washington County (Akron), Colorado and Lake County (Leadville), Colorado and anticipates opening jail facilities in these two counties in late 1999.

[b] The South Fulton Municipal Jail is the first regional jail in the State of Georgia.

[c] In addition to its eight jail contracts listed in Table 1, Correctional Services, Inc. also contracts with Lincoln County, New Mexico to provide a jail commander for its publicly operated 55-bed facility. This arrangement became effective through a January 5, 1998 memorandum of understanding.

[d] In addition to its nine existing jail operations listed in Table 7.1, Corrections Corp. of America has contracts with Polk County (Lakeland), Florida and Tulsa County, Oklahoma and anticipates opening jail facilities in these two counties in mid 1999 (1,008 beds in Polk County and 1,440 beds in Tulsa County).

[e] The initial private operator of the River City Correctional Center was U.S. Corrections Corp. (1990). In 1998, Corrections Corp. of America purchased U.S. Corrections Corp. and assumed control of the River city Correctional Center.

Sources: Thomas and Bolinger (1999); Personal telephone, fax, and mail communications with various persons associated with the operation of private and public jails.

est private facility is operated by Correctional Systems, Inc. in Downey, California. It has just nine beds. The largest private jail is a Wackenhut facility in Delaware County, Pennsylvania, with 1,562 beds. The Wackenhut facility is located in the heart of the northeast corridor, which is an area that has traditionally resisted the privatization of government services. This resistance has been largely due to the aggressiveness and influence of public employee unions.

Table 7.2
Bedspace Capacities of American Jails

Bedspace	All Jails	Private Jails
0-50	1,750 (53.3%)	7 (26.9%)
51-100	569 (17.3%)	2 (7.7%)
101-500	735 (22.5%)	12 (46.2%)
501-1000	152 (4.6%)	3 (11.5%)
Over 1000	76 (2.3%)	2 (7.7%)
	3,282	26

Sources: Sawyer (1996) for all jails; Thomas and Bolinger (1999b) for private jails.

Private Jail Operators: As of the spring of 1999, there were 12 private for-profit companies operating correctional facilities in the United States. Several of these companies also operate secure and non-secure juvenile correctional facilities and non-secure adult facilities (Thomas & Bolinger, 1999b). Of these, Correctional Systems, Inc. is the only company that operates only jails. Of the rest, five operate only prisons, and six operate both jails and prisons. The bed capacity of the seven private jail operators is summarized in Table 7.3.

Table 7.3
Private Jail Operators and Number of Facilities and Beds Managed by Each

	Number of Institutions	Combined Bedspace
Civigenics, Inc.	2 (7.7%)	310 (3.7%)
Cornell Corrections, Inc.	1 (3.8%)	672 (8.0%)
Correctional Services Corp.	4 (15.4%)	1,131 (13.5%)
Correctional Systems, Inc.	8 (30.8%)	277 (3.3%)
Corrections Corp. of America	9 (34.7%)	4,386 (52.2%)
GRW Corp.	1 (3.8%)	60 (0.7%)
Wackenhut Corrections Corp.	1 (3.8%)	1,562 (18.6%)
	26	8,398

Source: Thomas and Bolinger (1999b).

As of 1999, Corrections Corporation of America was the industry leader with nine jail facilities and 4,386 beds in operation. At that time this represented more than one-half of the nation's private jail capacity. Although Correctional Systems, Inc. was second based on the number of facilities managed, Wackenhut Corrections Corporation was second based on bedspace capacity because it operated the nation's largest private jail—Delaware County, Pennsylvania. However, private jails housed only 9.6 percent of the total bedspace managed by private contractors in the United States.

Contracting Jurisdiction: As shown in Table 7.4, the majority of private jails, in terms of both number of institutions and total bedspace capacity, are county facilities. Eight of the 10 city jails are operated by Correctional Systems, Inc.

Table 7.4
Private Jails By Type of Contracting Jurisdiction

	Number of Institutions	Combined Bedspace
City	10 (38.5%)	549 (6.5%)
County	16 (61.5%)	7,849 (93.5%)
	26 (100.0%)	8,398 (100.0%)

Source: Thomas and Bolinger (1999b).

Geographic Distribution: As shown in Table 7.5, private jails are located in 13 different states, with the highest concentrations in the South and on the West Coast.

Table 7.5
Geographic Distribution

	Number of Institutions	Combined Bedspace
West Coast (CA)	8 (30.8%)	277 (3.3%)
Mountains (CO)	1 (3.8%)	120 (1.4%)
Southwest (NM, TX)	4 (15.4%)	1,813 (21.6%)
South (FL, GA, KY, TN, MS)	9 (34.6%)	3,706 (44.1%)
Northeast (PA)	1 (3.8%)	1,562 (18.6%)
Midwest (IN, MO, OH)	3 (11.6%)	920 (11.0%)
	26 (100.0%)	8,398 (100.0%)

Source: Thomas and Bolinger (1999b).

The large concentration of facilities on the West Coast is due to the operation of eight small city jails in southern California by Correctional Systems, Inc.

Local Role: Twenty of the private institutions shown in Table 7.1 were the sole detention facilities in their jurisdictions and served as either the county or city jail. Two other facilities operated by Corrections Corporation of America in Bay County, Florida composed the entire detention system. The remaining four institutions were operated by CCA and were components of larger public detention systems. These facilities provided overflow housing or confinement for special needs offenders for local detention systems.[5] The local detention roles played by these four private facilities are consistent with the "public-private partnership" arrangements advocated by Cornell Corrections, Inc. (1998), Cox and Osterhoff (1991), the Research and Policy Committee (1982), and Katsampes, Pogrebin, and Winkler (1998). In partnership arrangements, a private operator typically provides supplemental or specialty services for local government (e.g., overflow inmate housing, a facility for substance abusers), or provides facilities that local government leases and operates. With straight privatization, a private operator provides total management of a public service (e.g., operation of the county jail).

Secondary Sources of Prisoners: Each of the 26 private jails shown in Table 7.1 had a primary source of prisoners, typically the city or county government with which its parent company contracted. However, 15 of the 26 private jails also had one or more secondary sources of prisoners. Nine facilities held federal inmates (i.e., Federal Bureau of Prisons, U.S. Immigration and Naturalization Service, and/or U.S. Marshals Service prisoners); six held prisoners for adjoining cities and counties; two held prisoners for the state; and, one jail held prisoners for other states. With respect to prisoners from other jurisdictions, private jails are similar to public facilities that lease excess beds to other jurisdictions—i.e., public-proprietary facilities (Sechrest & Shichor, 1993). These public-proprietary facilities are intended to provide essential detention services, but also turn a profit for the county. Increasingly, local jurisdictions are building jails with excess capacity for the purpose of generating revenue by housing prisoners for other jurisdictions. For example, at the time this chapter was written, there were eight public-proprietary county jails operated in Texas. On February 1, 1999, these jails housed 850 state prisoners from Massachusetts and Wisconsin (Texas Commission on Jail Standards, 1999).

Initial Contract Year: The growth pattern of jail privatization resembles the growth pattern of correctional privatization in general. The privatization of jail operations began slowly in the 1980s, but has accelerated dramatically in the 1990s, particularly in the second half of the decade. Of the 26 private jails shown in Table 7.1, 14 were operated under contracts that had been initiated in 1996 or later. Another seven were operated under contracts initiated between 1990 and 1995.[6] The remaining five institutions had been under contract since the mid 1980s.[7]

American Correctional Association (ACA) Accreditation

ACA accreditation signifies that a jail has undergone a systematic audit and its operations are in compliance with the prevailing performance standards of the detention profession. Of the 26 private jails shown in Table 7.1, five (19.2%) were accredited by ACA on December 31, 1998 (Thomas & Bolinger, 1999b):[8]

- Seal Beach, California Jail (Correctional Systems, Inc.)

- Bay County, Florida Jail (Corrections Corporation of America)

- Bay County, Florida Jail Annex (Corrections Corporation of America)

- Hernando County, Florida Jail (Corrections Corporation Of America)

- Metro-Davidson County, Tennessee Detention Facility (Corrections Corporation of America)

This level of accreditation compares very favorably with America's publicly operated jails. Roughly two percent (64) of the 3,282 facilities identified by Sawyer (1996:18-22) were ACA-accredited in 1999 (Ingley, 1999). However, it is important to recognize that 53.3 percent of America's jails (1,750 facilities) had 50 beds or less (Sawyer, 1996:18) and local officials frequently contend that ACA accreditation is too costly for their cities or counties (Ingley, 1999). Interestingly, of the nine private jails with 60 beds or fewer, only one (Seal Beach, California, City Jail) is ACA-accredited.

While it is risky to generalize about such a diverse population of private jails, some general observations appear appropriate:

(1) Private jails represent a very small percentage of the jails in the United States.

(2) There are many more private prisons than private jails.

(3) Private jails are typically medium-sized facilities with 101-500 beds.

(4) Private jails typically contract with counties.

(5) Private jails are heavily concentrated in the southern states.

(6) Private jails often serve as the only detention facility in the city or county.

(7) Private jails are likely to house prisoners from other jurisdictions.

(8) Most private jail contracts have been in force for three years or less

(9) Only a handful of private jails are ACA accredited.

Limiting Factors

What are the reasons for the lag in jail privatization compared to prison privatization? What political, professional and market forces have influenced the volume and distribution of jail privatization in the United States? Anyone attempting to approach such questions will soon experience frustration because:

- Many of the best works on correctional privatization address issues such as moral propriety, legal authority, and cost-benefit (Chaires & Lentz 1996; Gilbert 1996a, 1996b, 1997; Sechrest & Shichor, 1996). These works have not dealt with the work-a-day particulars of private jail and prison operations.

- The studies that focus on the political and operational practicalities of correctional privatization typically concern private prisons, not jails (Lanza-Kaduce, Parker & Thomas, 1999).

- Much of the professional literature is emotion-laced and anecdotal. This is not surprising, given the line-level experiences and strong opinions of many of the authors. The purpose of these pieces is to persuade rather than to inform. This hinders both objective inquiry and rational explanation.

There are three obvious factors that have constrained jail privatization in the United States: statutory prohibitions, opposition of professional associations, and opposition of sheriffs. There is another more subtle, and perhaps more important, factor: the complexity of both the jail market and jail facilities. The combined effect of these factors has prevented private jails from becoming a common component of the American criminal justice system. The bases for this assertion are discussed below.

Statutory Prohibitions

Is jail privatization legal? As far as the Supreme Court is concerned, jail and prison privatization are legal policy options. The only two caveats are that privatization must serve a clearly articulated public policy objective and the contractor must be subordinate to public authority. States may, of course, restrict correctional privatization under state law (Gilbert, 1999). The staff of the Private Corrections Project at the

University of Florida, Center for Studies in Criminology and Law, have documented the difficulty of constructing and maintaining a clearinghouse for current information on the statutory authority to contract for the operation of jails and prisons (Thomas & Bolinger, 1997, Thomas & Bolinger, 1999b). The primary difficulties are threefold:

- There is considerable statutory variance across the country. This variance precludes generalization and requires careful state-by-state analysis.

- Some states have expressly authorized contracting for correctional services while other states prohibit it. Additionally, there are a few states with statutes that have not been clearly interpreted by the courts.

- Changes in state law occur rapidly as state legislatures introduce, consider, debate, amend, enact, and reject bills. This problem is exacerbated by attorney general's opinions and case law interpretations of existing law.

Statutory prohibition of jail privatization makes it illegal for county and city governments within a state to contract for private jail operations. Typically, such prohibition takes one of two forms: either the statutes expressly prohibit jail privatization, or the state's attorney general or a state or federal court has interpreted existing statutes to mean that the privatization of jail operations is prohibited. Table 7.6 below demonstrates the wide variation in state statutes:

These data reveal an interesting pattern to state-level statutory prohibitions against jail privatization:

- Only 23 of the 50 states permit the privatization of local jail operations: 21 by explicit statutory authority and two by permissive statutory interpretation. In the other 27 states, the statutes are either subject to interpretation (19), have been interpreted as prohibitive (6), or explicitly prohibit jail privatization (2).

- Thirty-eight of the 50 states deliberately permit prison privatization: 27 by explicit statutory authority and 11 by permissive statutory interpretation. The statutes of 10 other states are subject to interpretation regarding the legality of privately operated prisons. The two remaining states (Illinois and New York) expressly prohibit private prisons.

- Hawaii, one of the two states in which statutes have been permissively interpreted to allow privately operated jails, has state-administered jails. The permissive interpretation there applies to state-level contracting in general (i.e., both prisons and jails). The other state is South Carolina.

Table 7.6
State Statutory Provisions Regarding Jail Privatization

Statutory Provisions	Specific States[a]	Number of States	Percent of Total
Statutes allow jail privatization.[b]	AK, AZ,AR, CA, CO, CT, FL, KY, LA, MT, NE, NM, ND, OK, SD, TN, TX, UT, VA, WV, WY	21	42
Statutes are subject to interpretation.[c]	DE, GA, ID, IN KS, MD, MA, MI, MN, NV, NH, NJ, NC, OR, PA, RI, VT, WA, WI	19	38
Statutes have been interpreted as permissive of jail privatization.[d]	HI, SC	2	4
Statutes have been interpreted as prohibitive of jail privatizaiton.[e]	AL, IA, ME, MS, MO, OH	6	12
Statutes prohibit jail privatization.	IL, NY	2	4
	TOTALS	50	100

[a] Thomas and Bolinger (1997) includes separate summaries for local-level and state-level contracting authority. Thomas and Bolinger (1999b) does not similarly address local-level contracting authority in a separate summary. Whenever I was unclear regarding the status of local-level contracting authority in a given state, I used information from Thomas and Bolinger (1997). Additionally, whenever possible, I used updated information on local-level contracting authority from personal communications with state and local officials.

[b] The jails in Connecticut are administered by the state, and Alaska also has an integrated jail/prison system with the exception of five locally operated jails (Kerle, 1998:34). Statutory authorization of state-level contracting in these states includes the state-administered jails.

[c] The jails in Delaware, Rhode Island, and Vermont are administered by the state (Kerle, 1998:34). The statutes in these states are in need of interpretation regarding state-level contracting authority. The subject statutes apply to both jail and prison contracting.

[d] The jails in Hawaii are administered by the state (Kerle, 1998, p.34). The statutory interpretation whereby state-level contracting was deemed permissible applies to jails as well as prisons. The source of the permissive interpretation in Hawaii is not specified, while in south Carolina the permissive interpretation was rendered by the state attorney general.

[e] The unfavorable statutory interpretations in Iowa, Maine, Mississippi, Missouri, and Ohio were rendered by those states' attorneys general. The unfavorable interpretations of the Alabama statutes was rendered by the 11th Circuit U.S. Court of Appeals in *Turquitt v. Jefferson County Alabama*. In *Turquitt,* a case involving a Jefferson County Jail inmate who suffered fatal injuries while incarcerated, the 11th Circuit decided that, in Alabama, sheriffs have full responsibility for the operation of county jails. Most Alabama officials have, in turn, interpreted the *Turquitt* decision to mean that sheriffs may not contract this constitutional and statutory responsibility to a private operator (Haley, 1999).

Sources: Thomas and Bolinger (1997, 1999b); Personal telephone, fax, and mail communications with various persons associated with the operation of private and public jails.

- None of the states that allow jail privatization disallow prison privatization. Conversely, three states disallow jail privatization, but allow prison privatization: Mississippi and Ohio[9] by statutory authority, and Iowa by permissive statutory interpretation. In the two states that expressly prohibit jail privatization (Illinois and New York), the prohibition also applies to prison privatization.

- Of the 40 states that explicitly allow jail privatization or where the statutes are still subject to interpretation, 13 (32.5%) actually have private jails operating in the state. Of the 48 states that explicitly allow prison privatization or where statutes are still subject to interpretation, 24 (50%) have privately operated prisons within the state (Thomas & Bolinger, 1999b).

Against the backdrop of state-by-state legislative variation, there are two generalizations that can be made: (1) state statutes and judicial interpretations are more restrictive for jail privatization than prison privatization; and (2) statutory authority to contract for private jail operations does not necessarily result in actual contracts. Legislative intent to privatize jails at the state capitol does not always transfer to local officials at county courthouses or jails.

Other limiting factors often become important. Two of these are the opposition of professional associations and the opposition of sheriffs.

Opposition of Professional Associations

Ingley (1997) noted the importance of professional associations to the modern practice of corrections. One of the roles played by professional associations is as a persuasive and inspirational opinion leader on important issues. The three largest and most influential professional associations in American corrections are the National Sheriffs' Association (NSA), the American Jail Association (AJA), and the American Correctional Association (ACA) (Thomas, 1996a:2). All three have adopted official policy positions on correctional privatization. Not surprisingly, the two associations that serve the jail community—NSA[10] and AJA—stridently oppose the privatization of jails and prisons. ACA, which serves a broader membership drawn from all segments of corrections, has assumed a more tolerant posture toward correctional privatization (see Appendices 1, 2, and 3).

The NSA has approximately 20,000 members (National Sheriffs' Association, 1999a). The membership is composed mainly of sheriffs, deputies, and other employees of sheriff's departments. NSA's current position on correctional privatization is expressed in a 1994 resolution shown in Appendix 1.[11] There are several reasons for NSA's opposition. First, there are the sheriffs' constitutional and/or legislative mandates to operate local jails. Second, there is the broadly shared perception that the private sector has not demonstrated that it can operate jails more cost-effectively than sheriffs.[12] Third, private operators have not shown that they are willing to manage jails in compliance with the law, professional standards, and the public will. Finally, the NSA contends that sheriffs cannot delegate their liability or accountability for jail management to a private entity.

The AJA has approximately 5,000 members—composed mainly of local jail administrators and employees (Kerle, 1999). Sheriffs are also included in the membership and are regularly represented on AJA's Board of directors. AJA's current position on correctional privatization is expressed in a 1996 resolution shown in Appendix 2.[13] The principal reasons for AJA's opposition to privatization are: that local jails have been traditionally operated by governments; the professionalism and proficiency of local jail officials; the contention that public officials have exclusive responsibility and liability for jail operations; the contention that privatization will not relieve public officials of either their responsibility or liability; and the assertion that private operators will not be held to as high a standard as public officials.

ACA's more tolerant perspective on correctional privatization is expressed in a 1995 policy statement shown as Appendix 3.[14] ACA' s policy statement identifies the private sector as a potentially valuable resource in the delivery of correctional services. ACA is also strongly supported by the private sector.

In addition to NSA and AJA, there are 48 state sheriffs' associations[15] (National Sheriffs' Association, 1999a) and approximately 11 state jail associations[16] (Kerle, 1999). These associations typically align themselves closely with the larger national associations, NSA and AJA, on issues pertaining to local detention. The forceful and persistent opposition of both NSA and AJA to the private operation of local jails has been a factor in restricting the growth of jail privatization in the United States. No opposition has been more telling or had more impact than that presented by elected sheriffs.

Opposition of Sheriffs[17]

To have a sound understanding of the resolute and effective opposition of American sheriffs to jail privatization, it is necessary to understand:

- Why sheriffs object to the private operation of local jails; and

- How their objections are translated into a persistent, potent, and pervasive obstacle to jail privatization.

Smith (1933:39) referred to county government as "the dark-continent of American politics." Illustrative of Smith's observation, the academic literature on the office of sheriff is sparse (Struckhoff, 1994:43-44) and studies of the attitudes of sheriffs have been few (e.g., Ethridge & Liebowitz, 1994[18]). The following discussion presents the sheriffs' objections to privately run jails and explains how these objections have become an effective impediment to the growth of jail privatization.

Many opponents of correctional privatization construct their arguments on legal, economic, and philosophical grounds. They contend that the private operation of jails and prisons is illegal; that it is not cost effective; and that, even if it were legal and cost effective, it is morally wrong. Regarding the morality of correctional privatization, these critics generally assert that it is, at best, morally questionable to dispense involuntary confinement, disciplinary sanctions, and physical force within the context of cost-cutting, profit-generating, and bottom line corporate economics.

Unlike the general opposition to correctional privatization the objections of sheriffs are more focused on the unique role of their office and their piece of American corrections—local jails. Although their objections are consistent with the more general legal, economic, and philosophical arguments, they also voice unique objections. The opposition of sheriffs to jail privatization usually includes one or more of the following five objections: political power and patronage employment; quality of personnel; security; legal, economic, and philosophical concerns; and tradition.

Political Power and Patronage Employment

One of the most valuable currencies of political power a sheriff has is employment. This currency takes one or both of two forms. The first of these is patronage employment—the ability to provide employment in exchange for political support. The other is manpower—the number of employees on one's payroll. Nearly all sheriffs are elected. Consequently, patronage employment is an important political tool for election or re-election. Similarly, there is often a direct relationship between the size of a sheriff's payroll, relative to other county agencies, and the influence the sheriff carries in budget hearings and in other aspects of county government. Unless there is a strong labor union or civil service presence, sheriff's department employees generally work "at the pleasure of" the sheriff. Understandably, few sheriffs are eager to compromise their political strength by giving up a primary source of their political power.

Jail operations account for a substantial proportion of the jobs controlled by American sheriffs. According to the Bureau of Justice Statistics (1998:9), as of June 1996, approximately 30 percent of the 280,124 employees of sheriff's departments were employed in the jails. An examination of the same data for the country's 25 largest sheriff's departments reveals dramatically higher percentages for those agencies (see Table 7.7). With these data it becomes apparent why many sheriffs view the transferring of jobs which they control to private companies as an ill-advised erosion of their political power bases.

Table 7.7

10 Large Sheriff's Departments as of June 1996—Percentage of Sworn Personnel Assigned to Jail Operators

Jurisdiction	Total Personnel	Percent Assigned to Jail Operations
Cook County (Chicago), Illinois	5,309	58
Harris County (Houston), Texas	2,484	60
Bexar County (San Antonio), Texas	1,169	65
Nassau County, New York	1,004	94
Orleans Parish (New Orleans), Louisiana	800	80
Alameda County (Oakland), California	771	53
Suffolk County, New York	764	75
Hamilton County (Cincinnati), Ohio	764	62
Fulton County (Atlanta), Georgia	680	74
Denver City/County, Colorado	645	91

Source: Bureau of Justice Statistics (1998:9).

Quality of Personnel

Many object to jail privatization because they perceive private correctional employees to be a much lower quality workforce. Private sector correctional employees are seen as being poorly paid, "here today-gone tomorrow," untrained or poorly trained, hourly laborers rather than properly compensated, well trained, career-minded, law enforcement/correctional officers. In the eyes of many sheriffs, the private operators get exactly what they pay for—poor quality for low pay. Casey (1997) documents how private operators substitute riskier employee stock ownership plans for traditional and dependable public sector pension plans.[19] The former have value only if the company is solvent at the time of retirement, remains solvent and the value of its stock increases. This illustrates the concerns of many sheriffs regarding staff recruitment, development, and retention practices used by private operators. Some observers do not view this as a legitimate concern on the part of sheriffs because private operators typically hire many of their jailers from the sheriff's department. Many of the privatization contracts require that the contractor offer jobs to the current jail staff before turning to outside recruitment (Hoover, 1999).

Security

Many sheriffs believe that private operators cannot reliably provide the level of institutional security routinely provided by sheriff's departments (Ethridge & Liebowitz, 1994:58). This skepticism is related to their concerns about low quality staff employed by private companies. It is also related to their concerns regarding the efforts of some private operators to reduce staffing levels in order to realize cost savings (Casey, 1996:13-15).

Legal, Economic, and Philosophical Concerns

Of the Texas sheriffs who opposed privatization in Ethridge's and Liebowitz's (1994:58) sample, 31.4 percent said that private companies should not have control of inmates; 28.8 percent asserted that privatization would not relieve their respective counties of liability; and 24.6 percent thought that privatization would be too expensive for their counties. Some expressed the view that public agencies had a superior record of efficiency and effectiveness or that jail management was an inherently public function. Others argued against the exclusive monetary preoccupation of private companies, and the unproven benefits of privatization.

Tradition

The office of sheriff traces its roots back to tenth-century England (Green, 1990; Morris, 1927; Struckhoff, 1994:5-7). No later than the twelfth century, the responsibilities of the office included building jails and employing jailers (Struckhoff, 1994:11). Some modern American sheriffs see jail privatization as a wrongful intrusion into one of their traditional responsibilities—a violation of the very lineage of the office (Billy, 1999).

In summary, the objections of sheriffs to jail privatization expand upon the legal, economic, and philosophical concerns typically presented by those opposed to correctional privatization. Their concerns are typically couched in parochial terms—loss of political power and jobs; poor quality private personnel; weakened institutional security; and erosion of the tradition of the office they hold. Objecting to something, though, is not necessarily the same thing as prevailing against it. This raises another question. How have the concerns and objections of sheriffs served to limit the expansion of jail privatization? What policy-relevant factors have enabled the views of sheriffs to inhibit the growth of jail privatization?

Two socio-political factors, in particular, serve to strengthen the opposition of local sheriffs to jail privatization and make it especially effective:

- The pivotal role played by the jail in the administration of American criminal justice (Kerle, 1998; Kiekbusch, 1998;[20] Mays & Thompson, 1991); and

- The fact that sheriffs are *elected* officials (Kiekbusch, 1999:3).

In short, sheriffs are responsible for an important public institution for which competent management is vitally important to the administration of justice. Furthermore, sheriffs hold a powerful political office, which affords them unique opportunities to influence public opinion and government decisionmaking.

Pivotal Role of the Jail

Unlike other justice agencies, jails have frequent, often daily, working relationship with the rest of the criminal justice system (Kiekbusch, 1998:3). In fact, other justice agencies are highly dependent upon jail management for their own performance. The management of the jail often has a direct bearing on the efficiency of the local criminal justice system. The collaborative relationships that the jail has with various other criminal justice entities include:

- *Police.* The county jail is typically where newly arrested offenders are taken for booking and incarceration. Among those arrested are the mentally ill, mentally retarded, drug addicted, alcoholic, homeless, and those for whom there is no other placement. For many offenders, their criminal violations are due to serious physical, psychological, and social problems (Kiekbusch, 1998:3). The more efficient the jail admission process, the sooner arresting officers are able to return to the streets to continue their enforcement duties. Cooperation between the jail and the police is critical since it must continue during the investigation and trial phases of the case and often involves other inmate-defendants.

- *Prosecutor.* There must be cooperation between the jail and the prosecutor's office throughout the pre-trial phase of jail confinement. Such cooperation typically includes the timely delivery of inmates for interviews, the provision of visitation facilities, and the separate housing and movement of co-defendants.

- *Defense Bar.* The same cooperation and courtesies extended to prosecutors must be extended to defense attorneys. Defense counsel must not be hindered by jail operations as they carry out their constitutional obligations to represent their inmate-clients. Defense attorneys require functional visiting facilities and reasonable accommodations to their work schedules.

- *Courts.* The courts require that jails ensure the timely delivery of prisoners to hearings and trials. They also require local detention facilities and supervision for offenders sentenced to confinement. The courts expect jails to schedule and manage offenders sentenced to weekend confinement and to supervise work-release prisoners.

- *Probation.* Jails must cooperate with the needs of probation staff. This usually requires functional visiting facilities for the interviews needed to conduct pre-sentence investigations. Jails also commonly provide facilities and supervision for those probationers sentenced to shock probation/split sentence, weekend confinement, or work release. Confinement may also be needed for those probationers scheduled for probation revocation hearings.

- *Prisons.* Offenders sentenced to prison are typically held in the local jail until the prison system is ready to admit them and transportation has been arranged. In states where the prison system is seriously crowded, jail confinement of state prisoners can last for months. In some states, substantial numbers of state prisoners do all of their state time in, and are paroled directly from, local jails (Kiekbusch, 1998:3).

- *Parole.* Jails generally provide incarceration for state parolees who are being scheduled for parole revocation hearings. Furthermore, jails often provide hearing rooms in which parole revocation hearings are conducted. In those states where parole hearings examiners are particularly busy, pre-hearing jail confinement of parolees can last for months.

The pivotal role played by the jail in the administration of American criminal justice, as well as the pervasive dependence of other justice agencies upon the jail, contribute to the sheriff's power and influence. So many other agencies are dependent on the cooperation of the sheriff to perform their mission that the sheriff quickly becomes a persuasive opinion leader on criminal justice and corrections policy—including that related to jail privatization. Given these circumstances, it is understandable why many county commissioners, county executives, and other county officials are not inclined to wrest the jail from a sheriff. They know the sheriff personally and understand that they will have to deal with him/her in other political and social settings. They will probably be reluctant to turn the jail over to a faceless and geographically distant corporation. Faced with political opposition from the sheriff, questions about the continuity and efficiency of their justice system, jail-related liability exposure, and the high social, political, and economic stakes, local policymakers are often reluctant to pursue jail privatization.

Sheriffs as Elected Officials

Among the trappings of power that accompany the sheriff's status as an elected official are the following:

- As elected officials, sheriffs are directly accountable to the voters. They do not have to secure the permission of a governor, commissioner, director, or other public bureaucrat before speaking publicly on an issue like jail privatization. They have a highly visible "bully pulpit" from which to voice their opinions and, when so doing, need worry only about their personal credibility in each public appearance. No other correctional official has such unimpeded access to the public and such ready opportunity to shape pubic opinion.

- In most instances, sheriffs already have an established a base of political support among voters. This political support system is broadened by extensive involvement within the community. The voters probably place considerable credence in the sheriff's position on criminal justice issues like jail privatization. Typically, the sheriff has closer and more frequent contact with more citizens than any other elected or appointed official in the county (Struckhoff, 1994:61).

- Because of the ease with which sheriffs can publicly express their views on issues like jail privatization, and the relative intimacy of their relationship with citizens, the sheriff often has "the ear" of other elected officials at local, state, and national levels. When a sheriff speaks out strongly on an issue, other political decision-makers are likely to listen (Kiekbusch, 1999:3).

- Perhaps the most compelling reason for local political officials to accommodate the sheriff's position on the issues is the ability of most sheriffs to strengthen or erode voter support for other candidates simply by the their endorsement or silence. There may be a political price to pay, for example, for the county commissioner who votes to privatize the jail. No other correctional official enjoys such powerful political leverage.

One cannot over-estimate the significance of the sheriff's status as an elected official who is directly accountable to the voters. The broad visibility, political influence, and automatic credibility that accompany this status give the sheriff a powerful voice in the ongoing discourse on jail privatization.

Jail Complexity

Statutory prohibitions, the opposition of important professional associations, and the opposition of sheriffs have been formidable obstacles to the privatization of local jail operations. They are, however obstacles which have not always been effective in the face of a resolute and determined private sector.

In the 1980s and 1990s state legislatures consistently enacted "get tough" anti-crime laws which featured mandatory incarceration, determinate sentencing, and reductions in the amount of discretion enjoyed by paroling authorities. One outgrowth of such legislation has been an increase in the need for jail and prison beds—a need that may have already surpassed many governments' abilities to satisfy. "Get tough" lawmaking, in other words, has created substantial opportunities for private correctional entrepreneurs who propose to assist financially strapped state and local governments by building and operating secure confinement institutions. The private operators have, in turn, very effectively lobbied this window of opportunity—particularly with respect to the construction and management of prisons. Many legislators have been persuaded by the private sector's claim that it can build more quickly and operate less expensively. As the discussion of Table 7.6 indicates, 38 states deliberately permit prison privatization—27 by explicit statutory authority and 11 by permissive statutory interpretation. In no state have the statutes been interpreted as prohibitive of prison privatization. Statutory language is a product of the political process, and that process—as it applies to prison privatization—has been roundly influenced by an aggressive and persuasive private sector (see the chapters by Hallett & Lee; Stolz; and Gilbert in this volume).

The position statements and resolutions passed by professional associations are also the outcomes of political processes and are influenced by persuasive lobbying by corporate and other interest groups (see Appendices 1-3). The NSA and AJA oppose correctional privatization. The ACA supports privatization. These public positions reflect the opinions and preferences of association members, particularly those members who make an effort to organize and shape the association's positions. In recent years, large private institutional operators have assumed a more visible and influential presence within ACA, a presence that undoubtedly has contributed to the Association's favorable posture toward correctional privatization.

Not all sheriffs oppose jail privatization. There are a number of sheriffs who would not be opposed to the private operation of their jails if it would allow them to focus exclusively on their law enforcement responsibilities. The majority of sheriffs come from law enforcement backgrounds. Consequently, most of them are more comfortable in their law enforcement role than they are in their correctional role. Furthermore, they rely heavily upon their law enforcement experience to construct their public crime-fighting images and gain voter support.

Statutory prohibitions, the opposition of professional associations, and the opposition of sheriffs have proven to be troublesome, but not unbeatable, obstacles to the expansion of jail privatization. Why, then, is the private sector so underrepresented in the local jail marketplace? Why do privately operated jails account for only 1.7 percent of America's total local jail bedspace and only 9.6 percent of the total private secure confinement bedspace in the United States (See Table 7.1)? Why has the private sector involved itself so heavily in the prison market, but so cautiously in the jail market?

I suggest that a fourth limiting factor—the complexity of the jail market and the jail institution itself—has had the greatest impact in constraining the growth of jail privatization. Private financial success in the contract delivery of public services requires that management become thoroughly knowledgeable about the nature of the business and the marketplace in which the company will compete. With correctional privatization, corporate executives must establish and maintain a network of personal and political relationships that allow the company to identify opportunities, anticipate problems, influence lawmaking and policy formulation, negotiate contracts with government officials, and ensure the cost-effective delivery of the service. This type of corporation-marketplace collaboration is much more difficult to initiate and maintain in the jail market than in the prison market, and the profits are lower.

In the United States, most prisons are operated by the federal government or one of the 50 states. The American prison market revolves around 51 seats of government—51 centers of prison policy formulation. When the District of Columbia and United States territories are added, the number of governmental entities to which prison corporations must attend remains small and manageable. Contrast that situation with the number of counties that operate jails. The American jail market contains more than 3,000 separate county level seats of government and centers of jail policy formulation (National Association of Counties, 1999).[21] These counties administer approximately 3,200 jail facilities (American

Jail Association, 1999b:2). Thus, the American jail market is considerably more complicated and unwieldy than its more compact and easily defined prison market counterpart.

The complexity of the jail market is attributable to more than the sheer number of counties and jail facilities. Each county is home to its own set of influential elected and appointed officials. Across the country, there are approximately 3,100 sheriffs (National Sheriffs' Association, 1999b[22]) and an untold number of county commissioners, county executives, judges, prosecutors, attorneys, court clerks, and others. Within counties officials are organized in innumerable and shifting political coalitions, professional alliances, business arrangements, and personal friendships. Additionally, the business of county government is strongly influenced by municipalities, the business community, and a variety of citizen groups. Developing a profitable jail privatization business within with this complex mix of people, relationships, and vested interests is considerably more challenging and less predictable than the same kind of involvement in the less complicated, more precisely framed prison market.

Not only are many more public officials involved in the jail market, but local officials have much more direct interest in and influence upon the operation of local jails than their state and federal counterparts have upon prisons. State representatives often have a detached and objective concern focused on two key issues: first, the efficient and secure operation of the state prison system; and, second the total funds needed to support the system. State representatives are not usually held personally accountable for the operation of the prison system or any of its institutions. While a county commissioner has similar concerns about the efficiency, security, and fiscal operation of the jail, there is a big difference in political accountability. County commissioners may be held personally accountable for the operation and management of the jail by the county's voters. Such a high level of personal accountability is a function of the smallness of local legislative bodies as well as the visibility and proximity of their decisionmaking. In many small counties, 3-5 county commissioners literally conduct business in a small room, across a table or countertop from constituents who are also relatives, friends, and neighbors. On a more subtle level, many county commissioners and justice system officials have longstanding personal relationships with the sheriff, jail administrator, and jail employees. Private jail contractors encounter a level of political accountability, self-interest in institutional operations, and personal friendships rarely seen in the prison market.

Jails vary in size to a much greater extent than prisons. Particularly troublesome for the prospective private jail operator is the fact that more than one-half of this nation's jails, approximately 1,750, have bedspace capacities of 50 or less (Sawyer, 1996:18). Another 40 percent, approximately, 1,304 facilities, have bedspace capacities of 51-500 (Sawyer, 1996:19-20). A capacity of 500 represents a large jail, but a small prison.

The limited capacities of many facilities in the jail market may render the per diem return on the investment dollar so small so as to discourage potential private operators and their investors.

Not only is the jail marketplace more complex than the prison marketplace, the jail itself is a more complex institution than the prison. Jail workloads and workload units are more varied than in prisons. The complexity of jail operations is also more difficult to operationally define in contractual language. Some of the ways in which jails are more complex are the following:

- At mid-year 1998, federal and state prisons held an average daily population of approximately 1.2 million prisoners. The jails were holding one-half that number (Bureau of Statistics, 1999). The prisoner turnover rate in the jails, however, is much higher than in the prisons. American jails admit approximately 11 million people, and release another 11 million, each year (O'Toole, 1997). Annually, there are almost 30 times as many admissions to local jails as there are new court commitments to state and federal prisons (Kerle, 1998). Some of the larger jails use specialists who do nothing but admit and release prisoners. O'Toole (1997) depicted a hypothetical prison and a hypothetical jail, each with an average daily population of 1,000 prisoners. The major differences were the greater numbers of admissions and individual inmates handled annually by the jail. The prison admitted 500 offenders and managed a total of 1,500 individual inmates. The jail admitted 23,500 offenders and managed a total of 24,500 different inmates.

- Prisoners admitted to a jail are ordinarily brought in "right off the street" by police officers. They are not transferred from a professionally staffed diagnostic/reception center as are most prison admissions. Relatively little is known about most jail inmates at the time of their admission. When they arrive they are typically less healthy and more likely to have serious physical, mental, and social problems than inmates admitted into a state prison after having been stabilized while in jail custody or in a prison system diagnostic/reception center. Jail employees also do not have access to the extensive case files that usually accompany inmates admitted to prison.

- Jail admissions occur seven days a week, 24 hours a day. Jail admission usually follows a street arrest. There are no scheduled receiving times for new admissions, as in prisons.

- Prisons house only sentenced offenders. Jails house pre-trial and pre-sentence prisoners as well as sentenced offenders.

- Most jails house both male and female inmates. Most prisons house only males or only females. Managing prisoners of both genders often presents problems and challenges to jail staffs with respect to staffing, housing, the delivery of inmate programs and services, and inmate population management in general.

- Many jails house juvenile offenders and incur the responsibility for continuous sight and sound separation of the juvenile and adult offenders. With such cases, jails also have an obligation to provide age-specific programming and must comply with various state and federal standards applicable to juvenile detainees. Prisons do not hold juvenile offenders.

- Unlike their prison counterparts, jail officers routinely prepare prisoners for transport to and from court. This is a daily activity.

- Jails must provide safe, secure, and functional attorney visiting facilities with some monitoring of attorney visitation by jail officers. Attorney visiting is a regular occurrence in jails, particularly with pre-trial prisoners who often compose 50 percent or more of a jail's prisoner population.

- Most jails are located in the middle of cities and towns. They are, quite literally, "next door neighbors" to commercial and residential centers. Because of this, the sheriff or jail administrator needs to develop and nurture an open dialogue with the "neighbors" and remain sensitive to their fears and concerns about personal safety, reduced property values, and declining business volume. The maintenance of constructive community relations is often a more critical and important responsibility for the sheriff or jail administrator than it is for the prison warden.

- Because of crowded conditions in many state prison systems, large numbers of state prisoners are "backed up" in local jails until prison beds become available. In some states, substantial numbers of state prisoners are never transferred to prison (Kiekbusch, 1998:3). Confinement and programming for long-term prisoners in facilities designed for short-term incarceration is a more common problem in jails than in prisons.

- Most jails are located within sheriff's departments where in-house law enforcement operations are often accorded higher priority. Successful jail managers must relate compatibly, yet competitively, with the law enforcement side of the sheriff's department.

Statutory prohibition of jail privatization, the strident opposition of the National Sheriffs' Association and the American Jail Association, the unified opposition of most of the nation's sheriffs, and most importantly, the intimidating complexity of the jail market and jail operations have contributed to the limited involvement of the private sector in local jail management.

The Future

It is difficult, probably impossible, to predict with any semblance of accuracy the future workload or the shape and performance of the criminal justice system. There are simply too many uncontrollable and unanticipated intervening variables at work: crime rates, sentencing and paroling practices, new legislation, politically and media-induced fear mongering about public safety, and more. The same problems apply to predicting trends in jail privatization. Will the number of privately operated local jails in America increase? Will the number of private jails remain roughly the same or even decrease? Will privately operated jails flourish in some geographic areas where it is conducive to privatization, and decline in other regions? Will fluctuations in the private marketplace transcend all other factors in determining the future of jail privatization in the United States?

A re-examination of the four limiting factors discussed above—statutory prohibitions, the opposition of professional associations, the opposition of sheriffs, and the complexity of jails may yield some insights into the near-term future of privately operated jails in America. Discussion of another critical dynamic, the forces of the free enterprise marketplace, may provide the most telling insights of all. Astute private entrepreneurs attempt to shape, anticipate, and profitably respond to marketplace forces. Market forces, more than any other factor, are likely to determine the resolve and effectiveness with which the private operators attempt to involve themselves in the management of local jails.

Statutory Prohibitions

As noted earlier, state statutes and judicial interpretations are more restrictive with jail privatization than with prison privatization. There is no discernible evidence predictive of a change in this pattern. To the contrary, there are some indications that state statutes may become even more restrictive regarding privately operated local jails. At least one state, Missouri, is considering legislation that would prohibit any additional jail or prison privatization (SB0036, 90th General Assembly, State of Missouri). Should this legislation pass, Missouri would join Illinois and New York on the list of states the statutes of which expressly prohibit the private operation of local jails. Given the intensity of their opposition to jail privatization, and the political influence and activism of individual sheriffs and their state associations, it is not inconceivable that similar, sheriff-backed, legislation will be introduced and strongly advocated in other states.

Furthermore, statutes in six states have been judicially interpreted as prohibitive of jail privatization. In only two states have the statutes been interpreted as permissive of privately operated jails. Of these two, Hawaii is only marginally relevant because it has state-administered jails and the permissive interpretation there applies to state-level contracting for both prisons and jails. In the seven states which have traditional, locally administered jails and state statutes that have been judicially interpreted, the interpretations have been unfavorable to privatization in six states. At present, there are 19 other states that have statutes subject to similar interpretation. Given the strident opposition of most sheriffs to jail privatization, it is likely that sheriffs and their professional associations will actively seek statutory interpretations unfavorable toward jail privatization in at least some of these states.[23]

Opposition of Professional Associations

The public opposition of the NSA and the AJA has continued to slow the growth of jail privatization. Both NSA and AJA have passed strongly worded resolutions to this effect (see Appendices 1 and 2), and both organizations enjoy the support of the many state sheriffs' and jail associations on the privatization issue. There are no indications that the organized opposition of either NSA or AJA, or their state-level counterparts, is about to diminish. The AJA actually stiffened its opposition in 1997, one year after the passage of its current resolution, when they voted to disallow private jail operators from advertising in the Association's publications or exhibiting at its conferences (American Jail Association, 1997a, 1997b). The AJA Board of Directors also discontinued its consideration of Tulsa, Oklahoma as a possible site for its 2005 annual training conference following Tulsa County's decision to contract with Corrections Corporation of America for the operation of its jail.

Opposition of Sheriffs

There is no reason to believe that the sheriffs will weaken in their resolve to oppose the private operation of jails. It is relatively safe to assume that they will continue, and perhaps escalate, their opposition to privatization through the power of their office and their influence in state and local politics.

Jail Complexity

There is also no reason to believe that either the jail market or its component institutions will diminish in their complexity. The number of counties and the number of county officials are essentially fixed. Likewise, the boundless network of political, professional, and personal relationships of county officials, as well as their direct interest in the operation of local jails, will remain unaltered. Jails as institutions are also unlikely to change with respect to the complexity of their internal operations, the diversity of their populations, and the sensitivity of their relationships with in-house law enforcement and their adjacent communities. To the extent that jail complexity has been an obstacle to jail privatization to-date, it will remain so in the future.

Market Forces

Viewed in very elementary terms, the American free enterprise marketplace is a playing field regulated by simple rules of demand and supply. The public expresses its demand for certain products (i.e., goods and services), and opportunistic entrepreneurs establish organizations and processes whereby products and services are supplied to meet consumer demand, and the entrepreneurs make a profit along the way. When the nature of the demand changes, alert, proactive, and flexible companies adjust their supply-side endeavors so as to satisfy the revised demand. Particularly astute and aggressive companies conduct targeted marketing and lobbying campaigns to mold public demand and persuade consumers that they need those products that can be supplied most easily and profitably. When a particular sector of the market has been saturated, these companies look elsewhere for income opportunities, or create new opportunity sectors.

The correctional marketplace operates in much the same way. In the 1960s and 1970s, public opinion polls and voter surveys consistently revealed that the majority of the public wanted offenders rehabilitated and reintegrated and that it saw community-based programs as the preferred venue for accomplishing this. The private sector responded with a host of halfway houses, wilderness programs, electronic monitoring systems, and other non-institutional alternatives. As the 1980s emerged, the same polls and surveys depicted a public whose correctional preferences were shifting to retribution, incapacitation, punishment, and a renewed reliance on secure institutions. The private sector responded with an array of selected inmate services (e.g., feeding, healthcare, commissary) that could be contractually provided within public correctional facilities and permit those facilities to be operated less expensively. During the mid to late 1980s and the 1990s the pubic demand for incarceration continued to escalate and challenge government's ability to supply sufficient confinement bedspace. Finite tax revenues and cumbersome public bureaucracies became obstacles to continued public sector delivery of correctional services. The private sector recognized this as an attractive business opportunity and responded with private confinement services as a alternative to public construction and management of jails and prisons. Of concern to some observers is the apparent heightened incentive for private operators to lobby legislatures to enact "get tough" laws which appeal to the voter/consumer and, very importantly, increase the demand for the private sector's primary product—secure correctional institutions (Gilbert, 1996b:64).

For reasons discussed previously, private companies have been much more active in the prison market than the jail market. Arguably, as we enter the third millennium, the prison market is becoming increasingly flooded with privately operated institutions. At some point, there will be few new "big dollar" projects available and the private prison market will reach a saturation point. At that time the private prison industry will probably turn its attention to other related market sectors. Consequently, I suggest that:

- With 3,200 facilities, an average daily population of 600,000, and 22 million annual admissions and releases, the jail market will be seen as their most attractive option by private correctional entrepreneurs as they readjust their market priorities in pursuit of continued growth and profit.

- The private sector will purposefully and aggressively confront the four limiting factors previously discussed—statutory prohibitions, the opposition of professional associations, the opposition of sheriffs, and the complexity of the jail market and its component institutions—and attempt to mitigate their unfavorable impact on jail privatization.

More specifically, I suggest that we might observe the following during the early years of the twenty-first century:

- A concerted lobbying campaign by the private contractors in state legislatures to "open" more of the jail market to privatization.

- A concerted effort by private contractors to involve themselves in influential ways within professional associations that oppose jail privatization—most notably the National Sheriffs' Association and the American Jail Association. The private sector will probably focus their efforts on revenue-generating activities to help financially support the associations—e.g., individual, institutional, and corporate memberships; participation in accreditation and certification programs; advertising in magazines and other publications;

participation in, and sponsorship of, off-site training programs. This is the application of a commonly deployed free market strategy—the exchange of financial support for a more receptive policy position on jail privatization.

- Private operators will probably make more frequent attempts to approach the jail market through county commissioners instead of sheriffs. In most jurisdictions, county commissioners are more receptive to overtures from the private sector than sheriffs. This is due, in part, to the opposition of sheriffs and their associations to jail privatization. But, it is also due to the adversarial professional relationship, which many commissioners have with their sheriffs. Many sheriffs resent having to request their funding from other elected officials and many commissioners are uncomfortable with the limited oversight they have over appropriations to the sheriff. Commissioners often envision having tighter fiscal controls over a private contractor operating the jail than they have over the sheriff. Consequently, they are more likely than sheriffs to be receptive to jail privatization proposals.

- Large mega-jails and their parent county agencies will be courted by private contractors. Presumably discouraged by the large number of small jails with bedspace capacities of 50 or less, contractors will likely concentrate their efforts on large jails with capacities of more than 1,000 (Sawyer, 1996). The per diem return on an investment in such a large local jail facility could be considerable.

- At some point, one or more private contractors will attempt to "bundle" several smaller jails in contiguous jurisdictions with a proposal to operate the entire group as a "package." In this way, the operator could probably realize an acceptable return on his/her investment in small jails and also offer the smaller jurisdictions the benefits of economy of scale through shared facilities (e.g., kitchen, warehouse, hospital) and high volume purchasing. This might be an attractive option to rural or impoverished counties.

- Well known sheriffs or retired sheriffs will be hired, as consultants or full-time staff, by some private operators. The sheriffs will provide contractors with "ready made" experience, credibility, and political or professional contacts that could prove invaluable in lobbying and marketing efforts with state legislatures, local governments, professional associations, individual sheriffs, and other public officials. Corrections Corporation of America, Wackenhut Corrections Corporation, and other private confinement companies have adeptly utilized former commissioners, directors and wardens to strengthen the corporate presence within the prison market.

- There are likely to be proposals by private contractors to assume the management of jail facilities not run by sheriffs. Privatization of these facilities would not receive the initial opposition of a sheriff, and start-up and revenue flow would occur more quickly. Likely targets for this type of private sector attention include regional jails which are typically administered by an independent, multi-jurisdictional board or authority (Halford, 1998) and those jails which are run by the states in which they are located (Alaska, Connecticut, Delaware, Hawaii, Rhode Island, and Vermont).

- The showcasing of large urban jails by their private operators presents an opportunity for the private sector to demonstrate that they can run a large, urban jail with a stable, satisfied, and competent workforce. They will strive to demonstrate their ability to run these facilities in a manner that is secure, safe, cost-effective, efficient, and free of scandal and embarrassment.

In summary, statutory prohibitions of jail privatization, the opposition of large and influential professional associations, the unified opposition of America's sheriffs, and the complexity of the jail market and jail operations will continue to slow the growth of jail privatization. However, as prison markets reach saturation, market forces will probably compel the private sector to begin systematic efforts to overcome these obstacles and pursue continued growth and profit in the large and potentially lucrative jail market.

Endnotes

[1]   This chapter reflects the input of many persons who are associated with the operation of private and public jails.

[2]   The Society's membership included Benjamin Franklin and Dr. Benjamin Rush, an influential Pennsylvania physician considered by many to be the "father" of American Psychiatry (Heitzeg, 1996:219; Mays & Winfree, 1998:4; Schmalleger, 1999:476).

[3]   From 1773-1790, the Walnut Street Jail served as the publicly operated jail for Philadelphia County, Pennsylvania. From 1790-1835, the facility served dual purposes: continued services as Philadelphia county's jail and host to the first penitentiary for the Commonwealth of Pennsylvania. The jail was a publicly run program. See Allen & Simonsen, 1998:30; Champion, 1990:163-164; Giever, 1997:422-423; Mays & Winfree, 1998:44; Silverman & Vega, 1996:74-75; Teeters, 1955:1-2; Zupan, 1991:18-19.

[4]   Initial private operation of the Santa Fe County Adult Detention Center occurred in 1986 through a contract between Santa Fe County and Corrections Corporation of America. In 1997, Sante Fe County transferred the facility to its current private operator, Cornell Corrections, Inc.

[5]   Marion County, Indiana Jail II in Indianapolis; Metro-Davidson County Detention Facility in Nashville, Tennessee; Hamilton County, Tennessee's Silverdale Facilities in Chattanooga; and Jefferson County, Kentucky's River City Correctional Center in Louisville.

[6]   This includes the River City Correctional Center in Louisville, Kentucky. This facility has been managed by its current private operator, Corrections Corporation of America, since 1998. The Center's original private operator, U.S. Corrections Corporation, ran the facility from 1990 to 1998.

[7]   This includes the Santa Fe County, New Mexico Adult Detention Center. This facility has been managed by its current private operator, Cornell Corrections, Inc., since 1997. The Center's original private operator, Corrections Corporation of America, ran the facility form 1986 to 1997.

[8]   Jails of 21 beds or more gain ACA accreditation for their compliance with ACA's *Standards for Adult Local Detention Facilities* (3rd ed.) (1991). Jails of 20 beds or less are accredited in conjunction with ACA's *Standards for Small Jail Facilities* (1989).

[9]   As indicated in Table 7.6, Ohio's disallowance of jail privatization is in the form of an unfavorable attorney general's opinion (Opinion N. 85-008, Office of the Attorney General of Ohio), rather than explicit statutory prohibition. An attorney general's opinion certainly does not carry the force of a state law. Ohio is, nevertheless, identified here as a state that disallows jail privatization because the attorney general's opinion is the most definitive statement, to-date, reflective of the state's official position regarding privately operated jails. Ironically, as shown in Table 1, the Columbiana County, Ohio Jail is currently operated by Civigenics, Inc. The legality of Columbiana County's contract with Civigenics is being challenged in state court (7th District Court of Appeals, *State ex rel. Taylor v. Halleck, et al.,* 98-C0-50), however, and Attorney General's Opinion No. 85-008 is among the authorities being cited by the plaintiffs. Mississippi and Missouri are two other states in which the attorneys general have issued unfavorable statutory interpretations, but which host privately operated jails (i.e., Correctional Services Corporations's Grenada County Mississippi Jail and GRW Corp.'s Joplin, Missouri City Jail).

[10]   The National Sheriffs' Association serves those who provide criminal and civil law enforcement, courtroom security, correctional, and other services through local sheriff's departments. The Association's interest in corrections is almost exclusively the jail, the vast majority of which are operated by sheriff's departments.

[11]   NSA's 1994 resolution was preceded by 1984 and 1987 resolutions and by a 1985 position paper, all of which emphatically opposed correctional privatization.

[12]   Proponents of privatization differ with NSA regarding the cost-effectiveness of private jail operation and cite, for example, Logan and McGriff (1989). At the conclusion of their study, the first cost comparison of public/private jail operations, Logan and McGriff concluded that Hamilton County, Tennessee, saved approximately 5.37 percent annually by contracting with Corrections Corporation of America to operate its 350-bed Penal Farm between 1985 and 1988. The Penal Farm, since then expanded by Corrections Corporation of America, is part of Hamilton County's Silverdale Facilities. For a more current discussion of the cost-effectiveness of private jails, see Gilbert's "How Much Is Too Much Privatization in Criminal Justice?" in this volume.

13   AJA's 1996 resolution is a slightly revised reaffirmation of the Association's original 1985 resolution.

14   ACA's 1995 policy statement is an unrevised rendition of the Association's original 1985 policy statement that had been reviewed and left unchanged once before in 1990.

15   Only Alaska and Hawaii do not have state sheriffs' associations. Several state associations include police chiefs and other criminal justice officials in addition to the state's sheriffs (e.g., Washington Association of Sheriffs and Police Chiefs).

16   The memberships of some state jail associations are limited to jail administrators (e.g., New Jersey, Oregon, Pennsylvania). In some states, there are also associations that serve more specific jail-related constituencies (e.g., Southern California Jail Managers' Association, Virginia Association of Regional Jails).

17   I am not suggesting that *all* sheriffs oppose jail privatization. See, for example, the pro-privatization comments of Bay County, Florida Sheriff Guy Tunnell (Corrections Corporation of America, 1994:13). Also, 25.4 percent of Ethridge's and Liebowitz's (1994:58) sample of Texas sheriffs were in favor of privatization. In general, however, sheriffs are strongly opposed to privately operated jails.

18   Ethridge and Liebowitz surveyed sheriffs in Texas with respect to their attitudes regarding jail privatization. Their data and resulting conclusions are particularly instructive. Texas has 254 counties and more sheriffs than any other state (National Sheriffs' Association, 1998), and houses, by far, the largest concentration of private correctional institutions and beds in the country (Thomas & Bolinger, 1999b). Texas sheriffs, that is, serve in a state in which privatization is a frequently discussed and often-implemented correctional option.

19   Casey's comments flow from his analysis of Wackenhut Corrections Corporation's brief 1990-91 involvement with Monroe County, Florida.

20   *Key Issues* is the newsletter of the Texas Jail Association.

21   There are 3,141 geographically identifiable counties in the United States, but 73 of these do not have functional governments, Connecticut's eight counties, for example as well as its nine jails, are administered by the state (American Jail Association, 1994:57; National Association of Counties, 1999).

22   This number is larger than the number of counties because it also includes city sheriffs (e.g. Alexandria and Richmond, Virginia).

23   In most states, only specified officers of the courts (e.g., Prosecuting Attorneys in Ohio, District Attorneys in Texas) and select others (e.g., state legislators, state agency directors) may request an attorney general's opinion (Collins, 1999). If the attorney general's office is the vehicle of interpretation, then typically sheriffs and their associations must seek interpretation through one of these designated officials.

APPENDIX 1

NATIONAL SHERIFFS' ASSOCIATION

RESOLUTION

OPPOSITION TO THE PRIVATE OPERATION OF JAILS, LOCAL DETENTION, AND CORRECTIONAL FACILITIES

WHEREAS, sheriffs, by reason of their constitutional and or legislative mandate, is charged with the operation of county or city jails and other local detention and correctional facilities in a humane and effective manner for the protection of the local community and those incarcerated; and

WHEREAS, private profit-making organizations have entered into the business of operating local jails, detention, correctional facilities; and

WHEREAS, such profit-making ventures have not demonstrated that they can operate these jails, detention, or correctional facilities at a lower cost or in a more efficient manner than that of the Office of Sheriff, nor that private management will assure the proper operation of local jails, detention or correctional facilities in accordance with law, accepted and proven correctional standards, and/or the pubic will; and

WHEREAS, sheriffs cannot divorce their responsibility to administer such facilities, nor ensure that a non-governmental, profit-making organizations will properly discharge these lawful duties; and

WHEREAS, state and local government officials cannot, through the privatization process on our nation's local jails, detention or correctional facilities absolve themselves of liability and accountability in the proper operation of such facilities in a manner to assure the full protection of the rights of inmates and the safety of the public; and

THEREFORE, BE IT RESOLVED that the National Sheriffs' Association does hereby adopt a policy of opposition to the transfer of the responsibility for the operation and management of county jails and other local detention and correctional facilities to private profit-making organizations.

Adopted at a meeting of the membership

This 15th Day of June, 1994
Pittsburgh, Pennsylvania

APPENDIX 2

AMERICAN JAIL ASSOCIAITON RESOLUTION
PRIVATIZATION OF JAILS

WHEREAS, jails have traditionally been operated by city, county, state, or federal officials, and

WHEREAS, jail officials throughout this country are professional and proficient in discharging their duties, and

WHEREAS, responsibility and constitutional liability of jail operations rest squarely on the shoulders of the officials in charge of the jails and privatization does not relieve jail officials of responsibility or liability of private jail operations, and

WHEREAS, private providers often are not held to the same high standard of public disclosure as is government, thus diminishing the public's ability to know how their jail is operating,

NOW THEREFORE BE IT RESOLVED

by the Board of Directors of the American Jail Association that the Association shall go on record as reaffirming its opposition to the privatization of jails—city, county, state, or federal.

Adopted by the American Jail Association Board of Directors on November 2, 1996, revising and reaffirming the Association's original resolution of 1985.

APPENDIX 3

ACA POLICY STATEMENT

Public Correctional Policy on Private Sector Involvement in Corrections

Introduction:
Although most correctional programs are operated by public agencies there is increasing interest in the use of profit and nonprofit organizations as providers of services, facilities and programs. Profit and nonprofit organizations have resources for the delivery of services that often are unavailable from the pubic correctional agency.

Policy Statement:
Government has the ultimate authority and responsibility for corrections. For its most effective operation, corrections should use all appropriate resources, both public and private. When government considers the use of profit and nonprofit private sector correctional services, such programs must meet professional standards, provide necessary public safety, provide services equal to or better than government, and be cost-effective compared to well-managed governmental operations. While government retains the ultimate responsibility, authority, and accountability for actions of private agencies and individuals under contract, it is consistent with good correctional policy and practice to:

    A. Use in an advisory and voluntary role the expertise and resources available from profit and nonprofit organizations in the development and implementation of correctional programs and policies;

    B. Enhance service delivery systems by considering the concept of contracting with the private sector when justified in terms of cost, quality and ability to meet program objectives;

    C. Consider use of profit and nonprofit organizations to develop, fund, build, operate and/or provide services, programs and facilities when such an approach is cost-effective, safe, and consistent with the public interest and sound correctional practice;

    D. Ensure the appropriate level of service delivery and compliance with recognized standards through professional contract preparation and vendor selection, as well as effective evaluation and monitoring by the responsible government; and

    E. Indicate clearly in any contract for services, facilities, or programs the responsibilities and obligations of both government and contractor, including but not limited to liability of all parties, performance bonding and contractual termination.

This Public Correctional Policy was ratified by the American Correctional Association Delegate Assembly at the Winter Conference in Orlando, FL, January 20, 1985. It was reviewed August 15, 1990, at the Congress of Correction in San Diego, CA, with no change. It was reviewed January 18, 1995, at the Winter Conference in Dallas, TX with no change.

Part III   Case Studies

———————————

8 Not a True Partner: Local Politics and Jail Privatization in Frio County

Michael J. Gilbert
University of Texas at San Antonio

On August 27, 1992, the headline for the weekly *Frio-Nueces Current* read "Jail management changes to save taxpayers money" (Fair, 1992a:1). The article reported a meeting of the Frio County Commissioners Court held on August 24, 1992. The Commissioners had voted 3 to 2 to negotiate a contract with Texas Detention Management (later known as Frio Detention Management) to manage the county Jail. Apparently the margin of victory was insufficient because County Judge Williams reintroduced the same motion at another meeting of the Commissioners Court on the day the newspaper article appeared. This time the vote was 4 to 1 in favor of privatization (Frio County Commissioners Court, 1992a, 1992b).

The newspaper article did not point out that Frio Detention Management was actually Dove Development Corporation (DDC). The owners of Dove Development Corporation also owned Consolidated Financial Resources Incorporated (CFRI)—the same public finance company that had arranged financing to design and build the 166-bed county jail that was about to be privatized. Confinement management was a new business venture based on prior relationships between the owners and county officials. They had no prior correctional experience. After all, how hard could it be to make a buck from housing cons?

At midnight on August 31, 1992, management of the county jail was transferred to Frio Detention Management (FDM). Bobby Ross, a former Texas county sheriff with jail management experience, supervised the initial start-up stages of the operation.[1] With the total transfer of jail operations to FDM, the county replaced a public monopoly with a private monopoly and became totally dependent on a contractor to manage the jail, meet local confinement needs, and protect public interests. A private monopoly over the delivery of any public good or service presents the highest risk of private sector abuse of public interests (Gilbert, 1996b). The decision to privatize the Frio County Jail was to prove irreversible. Subsequent county officials sought to resume public service but they were unable to do so. This chapter concerns the political environment that led to the decision to privatize the county jail, the impacts of that decision on the county over the next several years, the operational and political behavior of the contractor, corruption of local politics, and the political struggle to remove the original contractor.[2]

Frio County and Consolidated Financial Resources Incorporated: The Early Relationship

During the early to mid 1980s the "old" county jail, a small 22-bed facility (later known as the Sanders Unit) became progressively crowded—regularly exceeding its rated capacity. At times, the jail held 30 to 40 inmates. The population increases were largely the result of the enforcement of drug laws along the Interstate highway (I-35) that ran through the county from Laredo to San Antonio. At the same time, local officials were being pressured by the Texas Commission on Jail Standards to make tangible progress toward either reducing the crowding at the jail, renovating the jail to meet state standards, or building a new facility (Sanders, 1996).

As county officials began to take the problems of the jail more seriously they considered various policy responses. They considered building a 40- to 60-bed facility to meet the projected needs of the county, developing a regional facility shared by several counties, and building a large facility so that excess bed space could be leased to other jurisdictions. According to Sheriff Sanders, county officials were first introduced to the idea of jail privatization during this period by a firm from Amarillo, Texas exploring the potential for an 800-bed private jail/prison in Frio County. Although, the privatization plan was initially attractive, it ceased to be a viable option for the county when it was learned that the financing plan relied on funds from a Caribbean bank. The preferred option was rapidly narrowed to the development of a large jail with excess beds that could be leased to offset the costs of jail operations. In short, they would operate a *public-proprietary* jail to produce a revenue stream for the county (Sechrest & Shichor, 1993). It would be a win-win situation for everyone if it worked out as envisioned. It did not work out that way.

Consolidated Financial Resources Incorporated (CFRI), a public finance firm located in Greenville, Texas, had worked with the county in 1986 to help finance an earlier project. They learned of the new project and quickly proposed that the county use a lease-purchase strategy to fund the development of the jail with private funds raised by the sale of certificates of participation to investors (Sanders, 1996). This avoided General Obligation Bonds normally required to fund public construction projects. It also circumvented voter approval. Binding lease-purchase contracts transform long-term capital construction debt into an annual contractual expense. In this way, public construction projects can be initiated quickly, cheaply, with little public input and remain largely hidden from public view (Bunch, 1996a, 1996b). Unfortunately for taxpayers, private financing of public facilities also finances the lessor's costs and profits which increases overall costs to taxpayers over the long term.

On September 1, 1987, County Judge Williams signed a second public finance agreement with CFRI—this time for $3,125,625 with a 15-year payment period (1988-2003). The total value of the contract was $7,681,320 (Consolidated Financial Resources Incorporated, 1987:3, payment schedule). The funds were for design, development and construction of a new jail to meet community needs defined by county officials. Under the lease agreement, financial default by the county would cause the title for the new jail to "revert to the lessor"—CFRI (Consolidated Financial Resources Incorporated, 1987:7). Ten months later, Frio County entered into a third lease-purchase agreement with CFRI for $1,447,000 at 10.5 percent interest. The payment period for the second agreement was 12 years (1988-2000). The total value of the contract was $2,578,325 (Consolidated Financial Resources Incorporated, 1988:3, payment schedule). The purpose was to augment the construction funds so that the sheriff's offices could be completed and computer systems, radios, furniture, medical supplies, kitchen equipment, and dry goods could be purchased for jail operations.

The county was obligated to pay semi-annual lease payments on both lease-purchase contracts. In total, the county had to repay $704,440 each year—$58,703 each month. On August 1, 1988 the new jail opened and Frio County entered the private corrections market as the operator of a public-proprietary facility. Frio County was also heavily in debt to CFRI. As for CFRI, these contracts provided a lucrative and steady revenue stream. The company acted as both lessor and as an informal public finance advisor to the county. If the county defaulted on its lease payments CFRI would gain title to the facility.

The New Jail: Under Public-Proprietary Management

Work on the new jail began almost immediately. When the new jail was completed in June 1988, it provided 166 beds for general population inmates and three isolation beds (Cox, 1988:5). The month of July 1988 was used to finalized policies and procedures and train staff. Inmates moved into the facility early in August 1988 (Sanders, 1996). The new facility had a traditional modified "telephone pole design" with linear cellblocks and open dormitories radiating off a central corridor. The facility design afforded only intermittent or remote supervision of inmates. Because of its design the jail was inefficient and operationally outdated before it opened.

Frio County rarely needed more than 40 jail beds for local offenders before 1987. It certainly did not need 166 jail beds for its own needs. An oversized jail was a deliberate policy decision to make the jail self-supporting. It was much larger than the old 22-bed "Sanders Unit." No one in the county had operated such a large facility. Although the staff had worked in the old jail and had been trained in the new facility, everyone was essentially learning on the job (Sanders, 1996).

Consolidated Financial Resources Incorporated (1987:3; 1988:3) had required that the new facility be occupied and operational before October 1, 1989. However, local officials wanted the facility opened by the end of the summer in 1988. In their haste to design, develop, construct, and open the new jail, no one appears to have carefully evaluated the financial implications of the project. No one assessed whether the size of the facility would provide sufficient excess beds (beyond those needed for Frio County offenders) to support facility operating costs, meet the lease-purchase payments for the facility, and still be competitively priced.[3] Although the facility was over-built for local confinement needs, the capacity (166 beds) was insufficient for it to become self-supporting, let alone generate excess funds for the county.

From August 1988 through January 1989, the facility operated at *less than one-half capacity*. The inability to lease the full number of excess beds in the jail was at least partially due to Sheriff Sanders' failure to be re-elected during the March 1988 primary election.[4] After 24 years in office, Sheriff Sanders had lost to a Hispanic candidate—Gabriel Del Toro. Sheriff Del Toro would become the first Mexican-American Sheriff in Frio County in more than a century. In his "lame duck" capacity Sheriff Sanders did not actively pursue contracts to lease available beds. In the context of ethnic politics in South Texas, the election of a Mexican-American Sheriff represented a direct challenge to the dominant Anglo power structure in Frio County. Sheriff Sanders adopted a passive aggressive response to his defeat in the primary election. He did as little as possible to make the transition easier for his successor (Cubriel, 1996; Waldrum, 1996).

While Sheriff Sanders waited out the rest of his term of office, the number of beds occupied by Frio County inmates ranged from 25 to 35 beds/day. Roughly 40 to 50 beds/day were leased to other local agencies at $30/day or less. Another 90 beds per day were left vacant. Lease revenues barely covered operating costs. The number of beds leased and the daily rates charged were insufficient to cover both operating expenses for inmate care and facility lease-purchase payments (see Table 8.1).

Table 8.1
Frio County Jail: Operational Gains and Losses, Lease Payments and Overall Gains & Losses

Year	Inmate Care Revenues	Inmate Care Disbursements	Gains & Losses (Jail Operations)	Documented Lease Payments	Gains/Losses Less Lease Payment
1988*a	317,799	453,678	(135,879)	(902,425)	(1,038,304)
1989 *	2,069,159	1,909,815	159,344	(704,441)	(545,097)
1990 *	1,745,205	1,951,142	(205,937)	(719,308)	(925,245)
1991 *	2,709,014	2,415,411	293,603	(719,434)	(425,826)
1992■b	2,085,817	2,178,272	(92,455)	(704,440)	(796,895)
1993■	2,938,587	2,764,388	174,199	(704,441)	(530,242)
1994■	5,348,129	4,110,533	1,237,596	(870,765)	366,831
1995■c	1,429,423	1,429,420	3	(940,681)	(940,678)
Total	$18,643,133	$17,212,659	$1,430,474	($6,265,935)	(4,835,456)

a　Jail operational in August 1988　　　* Public-Proprietary Operation
b　Privatized Sept. 1, 1992　　　■ Private Operation
c　Data Collection Stopped September 30, 1995

Sheriff Del Toro took office in January 1989. In less than one month, Frio County officials signed a contract with Washington, DC to house long-term sentenced inmates from the overcrowded prison facilities in Lorton, VA. The contract allowed the county to charge $30/inmate day and to be reimbursed for most medical expenses. By mid-February the first shipment of 73 "DC" inmates arrived. Over the next several months the number of occupied beds under lease gradually increased. By July, nearly 130 beds/day were occupied by DC inmates. The remaining 30 to 40 beds/day were filled with inmates from Frio County. The average daily population over the next four years fluctuated between 150 and 165/month. Then in February 1992 the average daily population of DC inmates declined to less than 100 and stayed at these reduced levels until the middle of August. Then a number of DC inmates set fire to law books in the jail law library. This was the last straw for Frio County officials. They immediately asked that the District of Columbia remove its inmates. Within 10 days, all DC inmates had been transferred to other facilities. Although this emptied the jail of contract inmates, Judge Williams and the Commissioners knew that the jail would be privatized by the end of the month. The return of DC inmates served several purposes. It got rid of troublesome inmates, ended a contract tied to a

$30/day reimbursement rate, and would allow a contractor to exercise a free hand in developing new business, perhaps at higher negotiated lease rates.

In the four years that Frio County operated the jail as a public-proprietary facility it had been marginally profitable—at least operationally. Inmate care revenues had exceeded inmate care expenditures by $1.4 million. However, jail lease revenues had been erratic and the county had been unable to pay both operational costs and lease-purchase costs from jail revenues. This forced the county to use other funds to make the scheduled lease-payments on time (see Figures 8.1 and 8.2). In short, Frio County was going further in debt as it used up its capital reserves to pay the facility lease costs. The facility had become a liability rather than an asset.

Figure 8.1
Frio County Jail—Operational Gains & Losses vs. Facility Lease Purchase Payments

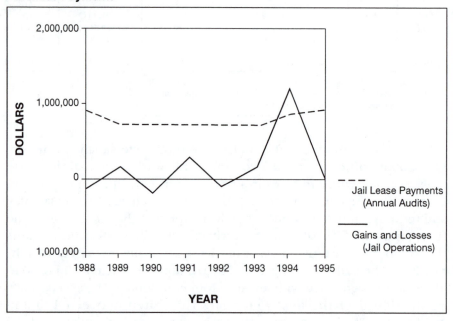

Local Politics and the Privatization Decision

The history of Frio County, TX has been much like that of a feudal state. The County Judge served as the "patron" with the help of politically influential ranch families and business leaders in Pearsall, TX. The County Judge is the county's chief administrative officer. Sid Williams had been County Judge since January 1, 1979. He succeeded Judge Fitch who had served as County Judge for more than 30 years. In this political and social context, the County Judge represented the interests of the most influential members of the community and exerted considerable authority over other Commissioners. Individual Commissioners represent one of four districts. The County Judge has the power to direct resources away from the district of a Commissioner who would not "cooperate." The Commissioners generally voted the way Judge Williams wanted them to vote. As one Commissioner explained ". . . most Commissioners think alike and look up to Sid Williams" (Berrones, 1998). Interestingly, the minutes of Commissioners Court meetings from 1982 to 1994 revealed little or no public disagreement and debate between Commissioners at these meetings. Nearly 100 percent of the votes had been unanimous votes supporting the County Judge.

Figure 8.2
Frio County Jail—Annual Revenues and Disbursements by Year (Inmate Care)

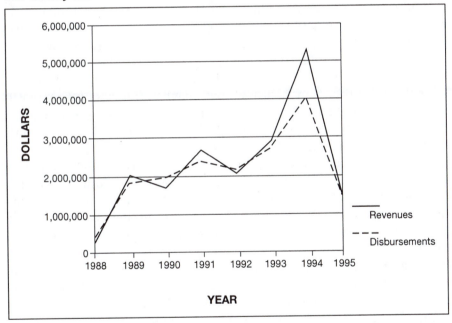

Extensive interviews with many people revealed an independent but shared perception that the County Engineer and the Roads and Bridges Department had been used to intimidate and coerce Commissioners to vote with Judge Williams rather than against him. Those Commissioners who voted the way he wanted got new roads, improved sewer systems, pothole repairs, and other services in their districts. Those Commissioners who didn't vote the way he wanted received fewer and fewer services from the Roads and Bridges Department. Stubborn Commissioners either "came around" or they became increasingly unable to deliver public services to their constituents. The County Engineer, Mark Sorenson, was commonly referred to as the "Enforcer" or the "sixth Commissioner."

Ethnic politics had divided Frio County and the City of Pearsall since its formation in the 1880s. In Pearsall, the railroad tracks literally separated the Anglo and Mexican-American sides of town. The tracks represented a South Texas form of apartheid—economic, social, and political advantage on one side, disadvantage on the other (Foley, Mota, Post & Lozano, 1988). In this social context the election of Sheriff Del Toro threatened the established Anglo power structure. The Sheriff's Office had always been a source of patronage employment of deputies and jailers. For many Mexican-American voters the new jail represented an opportunity to establish a toe hold on political power. After 24 years in office, both Sheriff Sanders and the Anglo power structure were surprised and concerned when solidarity among Mexican-American voters led to Sheriff Sanders defeat in the primary election (Cubriel, 1996; Del Toro, 1996).

Although the county needed a new jail, the construction of a large new jail had a secondary purpose—solidifying and expanding the base of support for the Anglo dominated power structure. Sheriff Sanders was a key player in the political life of the county. Part of the reason the jail had been overbuilt was to allow Sheriff Sanders to influence future voting patterns in the county through patronage employment. The unexpected election of Sheriff Del Toro meant that any new patronage positions would serve to solidify Sheriff Del Toro's political influence among Mexican-American residents and voters.

The election result seems to have led to an effort by county officials to discredit the newly elected Sheriff early in his term of office. The first indication of this effort is that the "lame duck" Sheriff (Sanders) made little or no effort to fill the excess capacity of the jail. Between March and August 1988 Sheriff Sanders did not actively pursue contracts for inmates to fill the new facility. Consequently, the jail operated at or below one-half its rated capacity from its opening in August until January 1989—when Sheriff Del Toro took office. During this period, the jail did not earn enough to cover its operating costs, let alone the lease-purchase payments. Neither Judge Williams nor the Commissioners appear to have pressured Sheriff Sanders to fill the jail so that it would cover its expenses. Each month they needed $58,703 in excess revenues to cover the lease-payments. County officials knew that Sheriff Sanders' inaction during this period would leave Sheriff Del Toro with serious financial management problems at the jail when he took office. They also knew that such financial management problems might provide a campaign issue to use against Sheriff Del Toro's in the 1992 elections (Berrones, 1998).

The second indication of an effort to discredit Sheriff Del Toro was that the real sources of the economic problems experienced by the jail were kept hidden from the public. The original policy decision to build an oversized facility without having fully studied either the needs of the community or the capacity needed to generate the revenues needed was the fundamental problem. The County Judge, the Commissioners Court and the former Sheriff created this problem, not Sheriff Del Toro. The facility had been poorly designed and did not provide enough beds to cover both operating costs and lease-purchase payments. Yet, there was a drumbeat of subtle accusation from the Commissioners Court that the reason the jail was not self supporting was the inability of Sheriff Del Toro and the jail staff to manage the jail in an efficient manner (Cubriel, 1996; Del Toro, 1996; Roberts, 1996). As Table 8.1 and Figures 8.1 and 8.2 reveal, the problem was not operational inefficiency so much as the burden of high lease-purchase payments. There were inefficiencies in the jail operations; however, the most costly were due to decisions by the Commissioners Court. It was the Commissioners Court that accepted contracts for services without knowing the minimum daily rate needed to cover operational and lease costs. It was the Commissioners Court that repeatedly denied the exterior fencing around the jail and other security equipment requested by the Sheriff. It was the Commissioners Court that required that jailers be scheduled for 171 work hours on a 28-day basis. Finally, it was the Commissioners Court that ordered the use of compensatory time (paid time off work) in lieu of overtime pay to compensate jailers for hours worked in excess of 40 hours per week (Frio County Commissioners Court, 1989a-1989f).

The combined effect of the last two decisions (taken on the same day) was that hourly jailers were treated as salaried workers. An analysis of the time cards and payroll records from 1988 to 1992 revealed that jailers were regularly paid for 171 hours whether they worked it or not. The reason for this is that most jailers had accumulated a substantial balance of unpaid overtime hours. They were supposed to gradually work off these balances by taking paid time off. Of course, an officer's absence due to compensatory leave also meant that the jail was short handed. This forced other officers to accumulate new overtime hours. In short, the county paid at least twice and perhaps as much as three times the hourly rate for a large proportion of the work hours delivered by jailers. This problem was exacerbated when officers who had fully depleted their compensatory time balances did not return to an hourly payment rate. As a result, many officers began to accumulate negative balances. They were paid for 171 hours when they actually worked less. This was clearly a good deal for the jailers since in most cases the lost work hours were not made up at a later time. There was no way for the county to recoup its losses once it had paid the employee. Although, these inefficiencies made it more difficult for the jail to become self-sustaining they were not the primary reason that the jail could not generate enough revenues to cover all jail-related costs.

The third indication of a strategy to undermine Sheriff Del Toro's power base came on September 14, 1989. Consolidated Financial Resources Incorporated (CFRI), leaseholder for the jail, made a presentation to the County Commissioners. Representatives of CFRI ". . . proposed to the Commissioners' Court that the county could seek pr(i)vate vendors to manage and operate the county jail in lieu of the County Sheriff and that the Sheriff could then handle the law enforcement duties of the county as he was elected to do" (Frio County Commissioners Court, 1989g). Later at the same meeting, the Commissioners decided to publish a request for proposals for private jail management. A month later Wackenhut Corrections Corporation (WCC) submitted a proposal to manage the jail and a representative of WCC made a formal presentation to the Commissioners Court on this matter (Frio County Commissioners Court, 1989h). No other formal proposals could be found and none are listed in the minutes of the Commissioners Court meetings. The Commissioners took no further action on Wackenhut's proposal but the reason why the Commissioners turned away from privatization at this time is unclear—especially, when privatization was so strongly embraced in 1992.

The final indication of a strategy to undermine Sheriff Del Toro occurred on August 26, 1991. The Commissioners Court voted 4 to 1 to use the "Sheriff's House" for office space (Frio County Commissioners Court, 1991a). Commissioner Alvarez was absent. He was a strong supporter of Sheriff Del Toro and was often at odds with Judge Williams. At that time the Sheriff was paid only $26,500/year and the Sheriff's House traditionally had been considered as part of the Sheriff's salary package. The house was directly behind the County Courthouse and a block from the new jail. This enabled the Sheriff to be on 24-hour/day call. For several months there was a rough standoff on this matter. However, on December 23, 1991—two days before Christmas and less than three months before the 1992 primary election—the Commissioners voted to order Sheriff Del Toro out of the Sheriff's House. Once again they voted in the absence of Commissioner Alvarez. The vote was 3 for the motion, zero against, and one abstention. Judge Williams and two Commissioners strongly tied to the dominant Anglo power structure voted to strip Sheriff Del Toro of the primary symbol of political status and power in county politics (Frio County Commissioners Court, 1991b).[5]

Carl Burris had been Chief of Police of Dilley, TX for 16 months when he announced that he would run for Sheriff in the March 1992 primary election. Dilley, TX is a small town with a 4- to 6-officer police force 17 miles south of Pearsall, TX—the county seat. Almost immediately, support from the Anglo power structure began to gravitate toward his campaign (Berrones, 1998; Burris, 1996). During the campaign Sheriff Del Toro was accused of mismanagement at the jail. It was suggested by some that this mismanagement might bankrupt the county and that it could cause tax increases (Burris, 1996). On March 10, 1992, the campaign against Sheriff Del Toro bore fruit. He was defeated. Another

Anglo—Carl Burris—recaptured the Sheriff's Office. He would take office in January 1993. Few voters realized that the financial problems at the jail stemmed more from the decisions of the Commissioners Court than it did from the Sheriff's Office.

It is unclear exactly when the next movement toward privatization of the jail began but four to five months after the primary election—in late July and early August 1992—it became publicly known. Gradually, Judge Williams and the Commissioners began to introduce the idea to the public—first as rumor and later as a policy decision (Cubriel, 1996). Sheriff Del Toro and the jail staff opposed the privatization of the jail. He requested that the privatization be delayed until he left office but the Commissioners refused (Casanova, 1992; Fair, 1992a). Judge Williams and the others in the voting majority argued that the high operational costs of the jail had pushed the county toward an economic crisis and immediate action was needed. Privatization, they claimed, would reduce the drain on public funds. However, underlying this argument was the political desire to make sure no other Mexican-American Sheriff could use the Sheriff's department to challenge the dominant power structure in the county. Most of the economic problems associated with the jail were directly or indirectly the result of poor policy decisionmaking by Judge Williams and the Commissioners Court. They wanted to distance themselves from the financial problems at the jail as much as possible. Privatization was a way to do this.

Thus, the political pressures to privatize the jail were driven more by ethnic politics and self-defensive political tactics than by the financial condition of the county. Ethnic politics, political animosity and the need to deflect political responsibility for poor decisionmaking were the primary reasons why the Frio County Jail was privatized in 1992. Financial pressures, blamed on Sheriff Del Toro, provided "cover" for the actual reasons, all of which pointed to the existing power structure rather than the first Mexican-American Sheriff.

In Texas, a Sheriff must consent to privatization of a County Jail before it can be privatized (Local Government Code, Section 351.102:50). The former Sheriff, Gabriel Del Toro, claims that he never consented to the privatization of the jail. Yet, the jail was privatized. This scenario suggests that someone intruded into the politics of the community and persuaded the Sheriff to quietly drop his opposition to privatization. If he did not publicly oppose privatization, the jail could be privatized under the authority of Judge Williams and the majority on the Commissioners Court. The Sheriff's signature would not be needed if he did not insist on it and Del Toro could maintain the public posture of not knowing how the jail happened to be privatized without his consent. None of the available documents authorizing the privatization of the jail contain Sheriff Del Toro's signature. Thus, it appears that Sheriff Del Toro "threw in the towel." He simply dropped his opposition. After his term had expired he was hired by DDC to serve in executive level positions—Warden of the Crystal City Detention Center and Vice President of Operations, Planning and Programs (Del Toro, 1996).

Consolidated Financial Resources Incorporated (CFRI) had been the lessor for the jail since 1987. They were well aware of the county's financial difficulties in making the lease payments. Although, it is unclear who first approached whom about privatization of the jail, there is no doubt that CFRI executives recognized jail privatization as a lucrative business opportunity. DDC had been formed in 1988 but did not enter the confinement business until 1992. By then, Tom Shirey headed both DDC and CFRI (Consolidated Financial Resources Incorporated, 1985, 1991; Dove Development Corporation, 1998, 1992). Under Shirey's leadership these companies courted Frio County to privatize the jail. These efforts apparently paid off. No record of other bidders or the selection process has been found. Furthermore, none of the local officials involved could "recall" exactly how DDC had been selected despite a requirement for a competitive bid process. From all appearances, DDC was selected as a sole source contractor. The selection seems based almost solely on Shirey's prior relationship with county officials. The owners of DDC, through their involvement in CFRI, held the lease on the new jail and could gain title to the facility if the county defaulted on its lease-purchase payments. Quite simply, Tom Shirey, had a larger ownership stake in the facility than the county through the companies he controlled.

In Frio County, we see perhaps the worst possible combination of factors leading to the privatization decision:

- A policy motivated by ethnic politics and political animosity;

- A need to distance the Commissioners Court from the policy decisions that lead to the financial problems that plagued the new jail;

- Possible co-optation of the Sheriff's opposition to jail privatization;

- A naïve county government responding to political expediency;

- Little or no research or study by county officials to determine the county's need, the viability of privatization as a policy option, or the operational issues involved;

- The selection of a contractor without a competitive process;

- The selection of an inexperienced provider based on good ol' boy relationships with county officials;

- An under-capitalized management company;

- The hasty development of a contract that strongly favored company interests;

- No clear performance standards or contract monitoring requirements;

- Total privatization of the public sector mission; and
- The creation of a private monopoly over detention services.

The New Jail: Under Private Management

The original contract with DDC was for a two-year period from September 1, 1992 to September 1, 1994.[6] A signed and dated copy of the contract could not be located.[7] The contract allowed Frio County to use up to 10 beds/day for local offenders free of charge. Thereafter, the county would pay DDC $23/day for each bed that exceeded the 10 free beds/day. DDC agreed to pay the county a "good will" incentive up to $4/per compensated bed day based on the average daily rate paid for all inmates, including local offenders (Operations and Management Agreement, 1992:3, Schedule 1). From the DDC perspective, this incentive would encourage local officials to reduce the number of beds used by the county for local offenders and might ensure continued political support. Under the contract, revenues would come to Frio County and be placed in a fund account from which DDC would be reimbursed based on monthly invoices.

A little more than one month after privatization, CFRI/DDC executives asked the county to support construction of a new minimum-security detention facility in the county. After discussion, the Commissioners authorized new financial services from CFRI. They also directed that a letter be sent to the Texas Commission on Jail Standards requesting approval for CFRI to finance a 1,000 bed detention/prison facility to house Texas Department of Corrections (TDC) "paper-ready" inmates (i.e., state inmates held in local jails because of insufficient prison bed space). Despite these efforts, nothing ever came of it and the idea of a new 1,000-bed private facility quietly disappeared. However, another motion on behalf of CFRI/DDC also passed that day. This one extended the contract for prisoner care from two years to five years (Frio County Commissioners Court, 1992c). Although the County Attorney's notes dispute the official record on some of the details, it is clear that DDC had arranged a contract extension from two years to five years in less than one month after signing the first contract (Smith, undated:1). No one has provided a clear rationale for the contract extension but it appears that DDC wanted the extension to finance remodeling of the Sanders Unit and increase the number of beds for lease (Woods, 1998).[8]

Between October and the end of December 1992, DDC brought the inmate population up to full capacity. When renovations of the Sanders Unit were completed in January 1993 the capacity rose by 30 beds to 196 beds. Over the next 18 months, most of the contract inmates were state inmates from Harris County billed at a rate of $35.25/inmate day (Texas Department of Criminal Justice, 1992:3). The Harris County jail, like many other local Texas jails, had become overcrowded with backlogged state inmates who could not be admitted to the state prison system under the population restrictions imposed by the Federal Court (*Ruiz v. Estelle*, 1982; *Ruiz v. McCotter*, 1986).[9]

By late 1993 and early 1994 the Texas officials had become desperate to alleviate the backlog of "paper ready" inmates in local jails. Recent projections indicated that the state would have 35,000 state inmates in local jails by June of 1994. Approximately, 15,000 new state jail beds would come on-line by the end of August. However, that would still leave another 20,000 state inmates in local jails. The state was also in the process of building 76,000 new state prison beds but they would not be available for at least another year. In the face of dire shortages in prison capacity Governor Ann Richards, Lt. Governor Bob Bullock and House Speaker Laney pushed through legislation to provide emergency relief. As envisioned, the legislation would provide grants to selected counties for temporary inmate housing. Up to 7,500 inmates, from the most crowded county jails, would be housed in temporary county facilities at state expense for a 90-day period between June 1 and August 31, 1994. It would be up to the counties to decide how best to use state grant funds to meet the objectives of the program. They could use the funds to build permanent facilities, buy tents, rent portable units, or use other means acceptable to the Texas Department of Criminal Justice (TDCJ) to house and supervise inmates. The state would pay up to $30/inmate day for care and supervision. TDCJ sent grant contracts to 26 interested counties on April 13, 1994 (Overcrowded county jails . . ., 1994). Frio County was one of those counties.

On March 14, 1994, almost exactly a month earlier, CFRI/DDC officials began to position themselves for an expansion of the Frio County jail. At Commissioners Court, they proposed a 130-bed expansion to the Main Jail and a motion to that effect passed. A few weeks later the Commissioners Court approved another motion to increase the size of the expansion from 130 beds to between 150 and 200 beds (Frio County Commissioners Court, 1994a, 1994b). The next day, the San Antonio Express News carried a story with the headline "Frio County approves temporary prison beds" (Flores, 1994:4A). The article states:

> Prompted by a state proposal to create 7,500 temporary prison beds for inmates held in overcrowded facilities, the Frio County Commissioners Court unanimously approved a plan Monday to build space for up to 160 beds adjacent to the Frio County Detention Center.
>
> [Judge] Williams said the county took the step after being asked by state officials if the county was interested in the project.

> The Commissioners Court approval of the project came less
> than two weeks after state leaders proposed building 7,500
> temporary prison beds in counties . . . .
>
> In Frio County's case, the temporary jail space ultimately would
> be converted into a permanent facility, which in turn could be
> used to house county, state, or federal prisoners, according to
> Williams. . . . [added]

At an *"emergency meeting"* of the Commissioners Court on April 19,
1994 a resolution to enter into a sole source contract with Dove Development Corporation to construct "a temporary detention facility" for
felony prisoners from the TDC was approved. However, two incidents
on the same day made it clear that Commissioners had a permanent
(rather than temporary) facility in mind. First, they approved the eminent domain acquisition of land adjacent to the Main Jail (Frio County
Commissioners Court, 1994c). Second, a new lease-purchase agreement for $1 million was signed between CFRI and Frio County. Then
Judge Williams and the Commissioners Court pledged ad valorem tax revenues as collateral for a $1 million bank loan made to CFRI. The funds
would purchase equipment and furniture for the facility expansion
(Consolidated Financial Resources Incorporated, 1994:1, Exhibit A;
Smith, 1994a).[10]

Tom Shirey and others at Dove Development Corporation were certain that the county would get a state grant. They started work on the
project on April 14, 1994—five days before the Commissioners Court
authorized it and 11 days before the state made the funds available
(Dove Development Corporation, 1994; Texas Department of Criminal
Justice, 1994). Both Frio County officials and executives with DDC,
undoubtedly, hoped that the state-funded expansion would make the
facility self-supporting. The decision to build permanent rather than temporary facilities was described in Frio County documents:

> Dove Development, in concert with the court, decided it made
> more sense to build and furnish something of a more perma-
> nent nature rather then build a temporary facility that would
> have to be renovated and updated in order to be licensed by
> the State for permanent use. Research by Dove and the court
> showed that a permanent structure could be built for the 1.33
> million dollars provided for in the State's temporary service
> contract but that it would take additional Frio County dollars
> to furnish it. The benefit to this scenario would be that Frio
> County would have a permanent facility for their use at the end
> of the contract. . . .

> It was our decision to build a permanent structure based on the benefit of having a permanent facility at a cost of around one half of the total added value to Frio County and use Frio County's money to furnish it. (Frio County, undated:1, 2)

This was clearly a good deal for Dove Development Corporation. The combined value of the state grant and lease-purchase funds for equipment and furnishings totaled $2,333,332. These funds were to provide capacity to house up to 336 state inmates for a 90-day period between June 1 and August 31, 1994 (Texas Department of Criminal Justice, 1994; Smith, 1994a). The primary requirement for the $1.33 million state grant was that the county had to be ready to house inmates within 45 days after authorization. Frio County passed the responsibility for compliance to DDC by subcontract. The county simply acted as a pass-through agent for state funds transferred to DDC. In exchange for the financial support and pass through services, DDC agreed to pay Frio County one dollar per day per prisoner for inmates housed in the county (Frio County, undated:1; Frio County, 1994b:1).

The eminent domain resolution passed on April 19, 1994 was intended to ensure that there was sufficient land adjacent to the existing jail for construction of the full 336-bed expansion. The language of the resolution is unequivocal: "WHEREAS, maintaining on jail and detention center in a single unit in a single location is of utmost importance and there is no practical alternative; . . ." (Frio County, 1994a:2). Yet, over the next few days DDC argued that there was insufficient land to build the full 336-bed expansion next to the jail (Frio County, undated:1). There is no record of these discussions but DDC was persuasive enough to prevent the eminent domain resolution from being exercised.[11] DDC also successfully limited the size of the expansion to 96 beds at the Main Jail in Pearsall. Later it was learned that the remaining 240 beds would be built in Zavala County adjacent to another detention facility managed by Dove Development Corporation. The facility would later become known as "Crystal City II." The argument that there was insufficient land adjacent to the Frio County Jail for the full expansion has not been borne out. The subsequent contractor—Correctional Services Corporation—has expanded the facility to approximately the same size that the full state funded expansion would have required. Clearly, the constraint of available land adjacent to the jail was not the issue that forced the Commissioners to approve building 240 prison beds in Zavala County.

A year earlier, DDC had negotiated an inter-local agreement between Frio County and Crystal City to operate a separate jail facility in Zavala County (Dove Development Corporation, 1993). Crystal City, the county seat in Zavala County, is approximately 60 miles from Pearsall. The only document authorizing DDC to construct the Crystal City II facility from grant funds is a Frio County Resolution is dated June 13, 1994—

roughly two weeks *after* the mandatory completion date for the project (Frio County, 1994b). Interestingly, the resolution states that "the Crystal City Temporary Facility shall be *owned* by DDC" (Frio County, 1994b:2, emphasis added). Based on a draft contract ("Agreement Concerning Temporary Detention Facilities" dated June 9, 1994) the resolution reflected an earlier contractual understanding that the Crystal City II facility would be owned by DDC. In return, the county would be paid $1.50 per inmate/day. This additional revenue stream would also serve as another incentive for local officials to help keep the new DDC facility as full as possible (Frio County, undated:6). These transactions benefited DDC in two ways. They gained ownership of a fully operational confinement facility at little or no direct cost to the company and dramatically increased the profitability of the Frio County facility they managed. Furthermore, the collateral for the $1 million loan to CFRI/DDC was a pledge of ad valorem taxes from Frio County and the county agreed to repay the loan through additional lease purchase payments to CFRI (Consolidated Financial Resources Incorporated, 1994:1).

Although the stated purpose of the loan was to purchase equipment the contract listed a real property item—a sewage treatment plant for the Crystal City II facility—as plumbing equipment (Consolidated Financial Resources Incorporated, 1994, Exhibit A). Of the total loan amount, $122,805 was spent on the wastewater treatment plant (Mimlitch, 1994). Another $863,550 was spent on items identified only as fencing, electrical, heating, ventilation, air conditioning, laundry, and plumbing equipment. There are also no purchase requisitions to document the items ordered, with unit costs and total costs. There are no records of equipment warrantees or whether the equipment was new or used. There is no inventory of the items or quantities received and no record where the items were placed. It would be impossible to identify what was ordered, what was received, or to take an inventory of these items. The actual existence of the items purchased with loan funds cannot be verified because the paper trail ends with documents, signed by Judge Williams, authorizing payment of undocumented billings submitted by Tom Shirey.

On December 2, 1994 Commissioner Espinosa sent a letter to Mr. Shirey, President of Dove Development Corporation requesting an itemized listing of expenditures funded by the State Grant and the $1,000,000 loan (Espinosa, 1994). Nearly two months later Mr. Shirey responded with a letter to County Judge Garcia, the successor to Judge Williams (Shirey, 1995). The attachments to that letter show that Judge Williams signed the payment authorization of each billing but did not provide the itemized list of the purchases requested by Commissioner Espinosa. Over the next four years, Frio County officials made numerous requests to CFRI/DDC officials for a detailed accounting of these funds but such an accounting has never been provided despite repeated promise to do so (Frio County Commissioner's Court, 1995a; Garcia, 1999a; Smith, 1995, 1999).

There are other indications of possible misuse of public funds. Of the $986,355 in expenditures documented by Mr. Shirey, $884,017.50 was paid to either *Governmental Construction Company* (May 5, 1994—invoice #050594—$300,000) or *Government Construction Company, Inc.* (May 26, 1994—invoice #052694—$400,000; June 21, 1994—invoice #062194—$163,550). Another $20,467.50 was billed to Frio County by *Governmental Construction Company* (Mimlitch, 1994). The address on all invoices, regardless of company name on the invoice, is P.O. Box 228, Greenville, TX 75403.

Government Construction Company, Inc. was originally named Public/Private Construction, Inc. (Public/Private Construction, Inc., 1994). Its articles of incorporation were filed with the State of Texas, Office of the Secretary of State on April 14, 1994 (Public/Private Construction, Inc., 1994:1). The filing was five days before Frio County signed the lease purchase agreement with CFRI to repay the $1 million loan supporting the $1.3 million grant for temporary housing of "paper ready" prison inmates. CFRI's first billing for $699,999.60 for project start-up was dated the same day. When the facility expansion project was officially authorized, Government Construction Company, Inc. had been in business less than two weeks. The owner and single member of the board of directors was David Thomas Shirey, Jr. (Article of Incorporation of Public/Private Construction, Inc., 1994:3). He also used the name Tom Shirey (Articles of Amendment to the Articles of Incorporation, 1994). David Thomas Shirey/Tom Shirey had served as either the President or Treasurer of Consolidated Financial Resources, Dove Development Corporation and Government Construction Company.

Two years later, in 1996, an Assumed Name Certificate was filed with the Secretary of State, Corporations Section to allow Government Construction Company to conduct business under the name "*Dove Correction Services Company*" (Government Construction Company, Inc., 1996). D.G. Greiner signed the Certificate as President of Government Construction Company, Inc. He has long been an associate of Tom Shirey and served in various executive capacities, with both CFRI and DDC (Frio County Commissioners Court, 1995b, 1995c).

The other firm—*Governmental Construction Company*—was paid $320,467.50 but has never been registered as a corporation in Texas (Bomer, 1999). The mix-up was probably due to an uncorrected typographical error when Shirey or one of his associates generated the letterhead for the first two billings on their computers for Government Construction Company, Inc. Apparently, the company was so new they had difficulty getting the name right on the billings.

For DDC these deals were a windfall worth more than $2.3 million to the company in new confinement capacity that they either controlled or owned at public expense. These deals also provided DDC with the potential for substantial profits over the long term from competitively priced lease rates, due to their low overhead costs. From the perspective of CFRI/DDC executives at the time, these deals must have seemed too good to be real—but they were real. Everything was stacked in their favor. It was quite literally a "steal."

The Williams Unit

Early in June 1994 the 96-bed expansion to the Frio County Jail was dedicated as the "The Williams Unit" and opened. It was named after County Judge, Sid Williams. Although, the Williams Unit met the minimum standards for occupancy and was certified by the Texas Commission on Jail Standards, it was actually built to a lower standard than either the 166-bed Main Jail or the 30-bed Sander's Unit. The building contained two large open dormitory areas cordoned off from an internal access corridor as well as the entry and exit doors by chain-link fences. Subdivisions within each dormitory area were also constructed of chain-link fence from floor to ceiling. Each of these "housing areas" were supposed to be supervised by an officer stationed in a nonsecure remote observation office. The remote observation post did not allow officers an unobstructed line of sight into the bathroom and shower areas. The design required two officers at all times for minimally adequate supervision. The author visited the new building many times but only on the first visit was a second officer observed on duty in the building.

The Williams Unit had been built about 50 feet from the existing main jail. Between the two buildings was an open space. This area was fenced in to provide an outside recreation area and a traffic control corridor between the two buildings. The fencing for the entire area was constructed of pool-quality chain-link fencing. Because only a single fence was installed, the recreation area could be approached from the street. There was no "ceiling" fencing in the "yard area" to prevent contraband from being thrown into the area from the outside. The fence did not have razor wire along the top to discourage inmates from climbing over the top, and had not been embedded in concrete footings to make it difficult to crawl under the fence. A basketball hoop was placed next to the new building. The metal post supporting the basketball hoop was placed about two feet from the building and allowed direct access to the roof if anyone cared to climb the pole. If an inmate had climbed to the roof it would be an easy jump to freedom. It is clear that DDC failed to provide the level of professional security needed to house long-term inmates at this facility. The security problems at Dove Development Corporation facilities became common knowledge when there were two successful escapes from their facilities within three months. Three Utah inmates ran out the front door of the Crystal City facility on October 14, 1995.[12] Three more Utah inmates escaped from the Frio County facility on January 18, 1996—this time, by scaling the fence in the recreation area between the Main Jail and the Williams Unit.[13] After the second escape, Dove Development Company built a second perimeter fence around the Williams Unit and the recreation areas between the Main Jail and the Williams Unit. Once again, razor wire and cement footings were not used.

Despite security problems and poor construction, the Williams Unit improved the bottom line economics of the jail. For the first time, the number of beds available for lease were sufficient to support both operational and lease purchase costs at the lease rate charged. By the end of 1994, income from leased beds covered all facility costs (see Figure 8.2). If the jail had not been expanded it would never have generated income to be a self-supporting facility. However, this rosy financial picture would not last long.

Loss of Texas "Paper-Ready" Inmates and Financial Disaster

Almost immediately after the Williams Unit opened in June 1994, the number of beds leased to the State of Texas began to decline. The County Attorney, James W. Smith, informed the Commissioners on January 23, 1995 that many of the new state prisons were nearing completion and that all State inmates would be gradually removed over the next several months (Frio County Commissioners Court, 1995b). By the end of January, the number of beds leased had declined to about 200 beds/day. By late August 1995, less than 20 beds/day were leased to the State. As Table 8.1 and Figure 8.2 indicate, the decline in leased beds pushed the jail into a financial tailspin—income declined and debts mounted for both the company and the county. It became progressively more difficult for DDC to meet its financial obligations to the county and local suppliers. The company also began having difficulty finding new clients to lease the empty beds. Their difficulties in leasing beds were due to two fundamental problems. DDC had begun to earn a negative reputation in correctional circles, which undercut their efforts. Secondly, Justice of the Peace Carlos A. Garcia defeated Judge Williams in the March 1994 primary election. This event signaled the loss of political support for the company in Frio County.

The Warden of the Frio County Jail from 1994 through December 1996 was Darrell Woods. Warden Woods was a former official with the Texas prison system. He joined Dove Development Corporation in August 1993. At that time, Bobby Ross and Larry Young managed the facility for DDC. According to Woods (1996), both Ross and Young resigned when it became evident that neither Shirey nor any of the other CFRI/DDC executives understood confinement and would not establish the programs and services needed to manage long-term prison inmates. Shirey immediately appointed Woods to the position. Early in his tenure as Warden, Woods began to push for the same kinds of programs and services that Ross and Young had tried to establish. He encountered the same resistance and began to understand that his real role within the corporation was not as Warden but as a "front man" (or shill) for the marketing effort (Woods, 1998). Woods could speak the language of corrections with state correctional executives. This was valuable to the company and helped to establish credibility with prospective client agencies. However, it became apparent to him that his superiors expected him to sell the beds by whatever means possible—"Tell them what they want to hear to about programs and services to fill the beds. Dove people knew that states might not enforce these issues if everything else is OK" (Woods, 1998).

On November 27, 1995, Warden Woods sent a letter to Tom Shirey detailing what he saw as a set of serious institutional management problems that needed to be addressed if they were to consistently fill the beds at the Frio County jail. His opening paragraphs frame the issues clearly:

> I understand that we . . . are currently experiencing a difficult financial transition period. However, this does not excuse us from the obligation of managing and maintaining, in an appropriate manner, the detention facilities we currently operate. Case law in the area of corrections does not recognize not having funds . . . as a viable defense against legal actions taken by inmates. . . . Most decisions made in Greenville . . . are . . . made by persons with little or no practical experience in the day to day operations of a correctional facility.
>
> . . . It seems our current philosophy is to get more inmates, generate more revenue, and then figure out what to do in the area of facility . . . and inmate management after the inmates are here. . . . Those inmates . . . are expecting certain basic conditions of confinement to be met. These conditions being access to courts, medical services, dental services, psychological services, religious services, work assignments, and pro-

grammatic activities to include recreation, GED, substance
abuse [treatment] and vocational training. When these basic
conditions are not met upon arrival, it is extremely difficult,
from an inmate management standpoint, to ensure that the
facility operates within acceptable correctional standards.
(Woods, 1995:1 [added])

Management of the Frio County jail became extremely complex during the fall of 1995 through 1996. The facility was required to follow jail
standards because it was classified as a jail but it also functioned as a prison
for state prison inmates. The facility held local offenders awaiting trial as
well as sentenced inmates from several other jurisdictions at the same
time. At times the facility housed out-of-state prison inmates, out-of-county jail inmates and local offenders simultaneously. Each jurisdiction
imposed different standards based on the minimum requirements in their
jurisdiction.[14] Woods (1995:3) makes this comment in his letter: ". . . housing several different types of inmates in one facility is a monumental task.
. . . In effect, you [are] running 3 or 4 institutions within one."

One month before Woods' letter to Tom Shirey, three inmates
escaped from the Crystal City II facility. Then, three months later, three
more inmates escaped from the Frio County Jail. These escapes made
national news and the negative publicity probably signaled the end of the
company as a private correctional contractor. However, from Woods'
(1996, 1998) point of view, these incidents were symptomatic of chronic management problems that CFRI/DDC executives would not address:
insufficient staff training, insufficient staff per shift to maintain security
and operate inmate programs, and inadequate security fencing.

Part of the reason Dove Development Corporation had difficulty in
filling its beds in 1995 and 1996 was that correctional agencies were
beginning to understand what Woods already knew—Dove Development
Corporation was not interested in actually running a professional facility. Instead, they used the language of quality to build credibility and
entice potential client agencies but once the inmates were at the facility the company was mainly interested in earnings and minimizing
expenses. One year later, Shirey asked for Warden Woods' resignation.

DDC Begins to Lose Political Support

The second problem faced by Dove Development Corporation was
political. As mentioned earlier, Justice of the Peace Carlos A. Garcia was
elected as County Judge defeating DDC's political patron—Sid Williams.
When it began to appear the Garcia might win in the primary, DDC made
a direct offer of $2,000 to Carlos A. Garcia as a campaign contribution.
But Garcia refused the offer because he did not want to be indebted to
DDC. It was precisely the kind of special interest politics that he

opposed (Garcia, 1999c). With the primary win, Garcia became the County Judge Elect—he would be unopposed in the November general election. His election signaled the end of Anglo-dominated ethnic politics and political support for DDC in Frio County.

Judge Garcia was the first Hispanic candidate for County Judge to be elected at large. Additionally, Gloria Cubriel, former Jail Administrator under Sheriff Del Toro, defeated the long-term County Clerk—Mona Hoyle. For the first time, the majority Mexican-American community gained control of the political structure of the county. But this did not happen by accident.

There had long been suspicions among residents of Frio County of voter fraud in the County Clerk's office (*Honorio Gonzales, et al. vs. Humberto Berrones et al.*, 1986; Roberts, 1996; Rodriguez, 1993; Trevino, 1992). In the 1992 primary Commissioner Adolfo Alvarez lost to Pedro (Pete) Espinosa by 23 votes. He filed suit against the County Clerk Mona Hoyle, Pete Espinosa, and others alleging mishandling of ballots, insecure ballot boxes, and voter fraud (*Adolfo Alvarez, Sr. v. Mona Hoyle, et al.*, 1992). Although this case was dismissed in 1993, it does indicate the extent to which there was broad suspicion of ballot rigging in the County Clerk's office by manipulating the count of absentee ballots. As one Commissioner explained in confidence: "If you wanted to get elected you had to deal with Mona Hoyle." Rightly or wrongly, she was widely perceived to be one of the major power brokers behind Judge Williams.

When Judge Garcia ran for County Judge, he was aware of this perception and decided to guard the ballots himself. He had an office in the County Courthouse and could "work" in the Courthouse after hours and keep an eye on late-night activities within the County Clerk's Office. For the 30-day period leading up to the primary during which absentee ballots were being collected, Garcia stayed overnight in the Courthouse (Cubriel, 1999; Garcia, 1999d). Other people watched outside the Courthouse to let Garcia know when someone entered the building at night. He recalls several occasions when Mona Hoyle arrived at the Courthouse after midnight. As he describes it, she would leave as soon as he would say "Hello." He claims that at times she had her key in the door when he made his presence known and she re-locked the door and left without ever entering her office (Garcia, 1999d). Many residents now believe that the 1994 election was probably the first honest election Frio County had in quite a number of years.

On January 1, 1995, Judge Garcia and Gloria Cubriel took office as the County Judge and County Clerk. Between the primary election and the inauguration it appears that many county records were discarded or destroyed by the Williams Administration. Maintenance workers at the County Courthouse found hundreds of tapes of Commissioners Court meetings in a dumpster (Cubriel, 1999b; Garcia, 1999b). They notified Judge Garcia, who retrieved the tapes. He notified Mona Hoyle, the County Clerk, and has since retained them on file. When Judge Garcia took office, he found that the County Judge's Office has literally been stripped of records. Everything except school records had been removed. The file cabinets were empty. Computer hard drives in both the County Judge's office and the County Clerk's office had been removed and other computers were missing. Information from courthouse staff indicated that these records and equipment had been discarded or removed at Judge Williams direction (Cubriel, 1999; Frio County Commissioners Court, 1995f; Garcia, 1999b). The missing paper and computer files have not been found.

After the loss in the 1994 primary, Judge Williams spent the summer developing the budget for the next fiscal year starting in October. During the budgeting process Commissioners, under Williams leadership, cut the Sheriff's operational budget for local prisoner care from $514,000 in FY 1993-94 to $335,000 for FY 1994-95. At the time, DDC had just opened the new 96-bed Williams Unit and the jail had become totally self-sustaining for the first time. No rationale for the budget cut has ever been presented.[15] Sheriff Burris had originally supported the privatization of the jail. The privatization decision by Judge Williams had taken place before he took office and Williams had been his political patron. However, Burris gradually became dissatisfied with the company's performance. DDC routinely violated provisions (sections 7.02 and 7.03) of the contract by failing to consult with the Sheriff's Office in selecting inmates for transfer to the facility (Operations and Management Agreement, 1992:7). They also discontinued reports that informed the Sheriff of each inmate's confining offense, length of sentence, and custody (risk) level. The company ignored the sheriff's repeated request for such information (Burris, 1996).

Sheriff Burris began to ask a lot more questions about DDC's role in the county, their security practices and their violation of the contract (Burris, 1996). In the process, he alienated Judge Williams and lost his political support. Judge Williams never informed the Sheriff that the prisoner care budget had been cut by $179,000. This would later create a financial crisis for the Sheriff's Office and the Garcia Administration (Frio County Commissioners Court, 1995h). As a result of the budget crisis the county nearly defaulted on its lease purchase contracts. If the county had defaulted on the contract, title to the facility would have been transferred to CFRI and Tom Shirey. The company would have gained ownership of the facility at a fraction of the cost originally financed. Had this happened the lease rates for beds would have been exceptionally competitive and the low overhead costs would have made the facility highly profitable.

The Sheriff did not notice the budget cut until March or April of the next year when it became obvious that the account was nearly out of funds. Shortly after taking office, the Garcia Administration faced a financial crisis. Given the missing files and equipment in the County Judge's and the Clerk's offices, it is hard to interpret the budget cut as anything other than a deliberate strategy by the Williams Administration to embarrass a troublesome Sheriff and the new administration. Williams may have wanted to create a public image of incompetence in the Sheriff's Office and the Garcia Administration. From Williams' point of view, an image of incompetence might help defeat Burris in 1996 and Judge Garcia in 1998. The budget crisis engineered by Williams may have had another purpose, forcing the county into default so that ownership of the jail would be transferred to CFRI. Judge Williams, the political patron to CFRI, knew that a financial crisis might lead to the county's default on its lease-purchase contracts and that would transfer ownership of the jail to CFRI and serve Tom Shirey's interests. Given the history of "good ol' boy" backroom deals and ethnic politics in Frio County, this is not unreasonable speculation.

A New Political Culture: The Garcia Administration

One of the changes the Garcia Administration made when it took office was to ensure a legitimate and accurate public record of all Commissioners Court meetings. The new administration began to record and transcribe Commissioners Court meetings in their entirety (Frio County Commissioners Court, 1995a). Once approved by the Commissioners Court, the minutes were posted to the county records. This offended the three Commissioners held over from the Williams Administration. They complained that the details of their discussions were not needed and should be briefly summarized as had been done by Judge Williams and Mona Hoyle (Frio County Commissioners Court, 1995d, 1995e). Judge Garcia and Gloria Cubriel recognized that the brief summary style hid more than it revealed about Frio County government and local politics. They were undeterred and continued to provide a full written record of these meetings.

Judge Garcia also refused to use the politically coercive strategies commonly used by Judge Williams. Garcia wanted a more open and democratic form of government in Frio County (Garcia, 1999c). For the next 24 months the Commissioners Court consistently split, two to three, on policies that conflicted with those previously set by the Williams Administration. The three incumbent Commissioners perceived the non-coercive political style used by Judge Garcia as a weakness and systematically blocked every effort to restructure the contract with DDC or bring the their political influence under control. There was only one other commissioner on the court who supported Garcia and motions that threatened DDC corporate interests were routinely voted down. Commissioners Lindsey, Berrones, and Siller were able to block many of Garcia's motions from coming to the floor for discussion.

County Auditor, Mary Hornbostel had first called the financial problems with the prisoner care account to the attention of the Commissioners Court in December when Judge Williams was still in office. However, her concerns were ignored. On February 13, 1995, she again called the problem to the attention of the Commissioners Court. She reported that the Sheriff's Office had been ". . . under budgeted by over $300,000 for prisoner care, we're going to be running out of money, probably in March, for . . . care of . . . county prisoners . . ." (Frio County Commissioners Court, 1995i). This alerted Judge Garcia and the Sheriff to the problem. At the end of March, Sheriff Burris directly addressed the problem with the Commissioners (Frio County Commissioners Court, 1995j). He explained:

> . . . We were budgeted $335,000 for prisoner care and to this point it looks like we've spent $225,000 . . . I have projected the payment for this month . . . to Dove Corrections . . . [to be] $48,000. . . . It's going to leave me with a projected balance of $62,000 . . . [and only] about half way through our fiscal year. I've just been made aware that we have a $67,000 medical bill with Dove.

> . . . I have written to Commissioners and asked for an amendment to the contract with Dove. What I'm asking for is 60 free beds. I would like for the 60 free beds to run through the term . . . of the existing contract. . . . it is a lot, but in the past the County has been giving and giving to Dove.

> . . . I need help, because . . . at midnight I'm going to be out of money. And I don't want a tax increase and I know you don't want a tax increase, but I need help today. . . . I don't want it coming back at the end of the year and somebody pointing the finger at me, like they did another gentleman (i.e., former Sheriff Del Toro) that is present with us today; and telling me that the tax [hike] is my fault like it was his fault, because its been brought to the court's attention [just as] he brought [problems] to the court's attention . . . when he was in charge. [added]

Later during that same meeting a motion was made to approve an amendment to the DDC contract for 60 free beds for local inmates from April 1, 1995 to August 30, 1997. Unexpectedly, the motion passed. Commissioner Siller had voted against Dove Development Corporation's interests. If Dove agreed to this amendment it would reduce the number of income earning beds below the break-even point. DDC had earlier argued that it could not make enough money with the available lease beds and persuaded the Commissioners to reduce the number of free beds from 30 to 10 beds per day. It was unlikely that DDC would accept an amendment to decrease their income by increasing the number of free beds from 10 to 60 per day.

The last two motions of the meeting also passed. The first authorized the formation of an Ad Hoc Committee to thoroughly study the financial problems and review all the contracts and separate agreements between DDC (doing business as Frio Detention Management) and the county. Judge Garcia appointed four members to the committee. Bleecker Morse, a local beverage distributor, was selected as Committee Chairman. Over the next couple of months, this committee would delve into nearly every aspect of the county's relationship with DDC. The second motion proposed a moratorium on the accumulation of debts between the company and the county. It was requested by Tom Shirey. The moratorium was approved, but lease payments were not made and the county was pushed closer to financial default.

Shirey and other CFRI/DDC executives did not recognize that the political terrain in Frio County had changed when Judge Garcia was elected. They acted as if Judge Williams were still in office and worked through the three Commissioners solidly in their camp to get the things they wanted done (Garcia, 1999c; Hornbostel, 1996; Morse, 1996). When asked about this corporate behavior, Warden Woods (1998) remarked, "Dove felt that they had enough Commissioners on their side to control decisions in Commissioners Court, Judge Williams still controlled the majority on the Court and had Sorenson as County Engineer."[16] Warden Woods was not the only one to make this observation. It was clear to many local political observers that Sid Williams still controlled the Commissioners Court through the loyalty of Commissioners Lindsey, Berrones, and Siller and County Engineer Sorenson.

Judge Williams often did things informally, without approval of the other Commissioners who would "go along" with his decision because of the coercive power he held (Berrones, 1998; Roberts, 1996; Woods, 1998). One Sunday late in April 1995, two high-ranking DDC employees tried to use the "good ol' boy" approach that worked with Judge Williams on Judge Garcia. Vice President of Operations (and former Sheriff) Gabriel Del Toro and Warden Darrell Woods went to Judge Garcia's home with a "contract" to fill the jail with Utah state prison inmates. They wanted Judge Garcia to authorize the contract without review, discussion and approval by either the County Attorney or the Commissioners Court (Del Toro, 1996; Garcia, 1999c; Woods, 1998). This was precisely the kind of back room dealing that Judge Garcia wanted to replace with a new, more transparent, political tradition. Furthermore, he was personally offended by their assertion that it would be irresponsible if he did not immediately sign the agreement. Judge Garcia refused to make such a commitment without a legal review of the contract and appropriate hearings. The following day, Commissioners Lindsey and Berrones tried to hold an *"emergency meeting"* with the voting majority to approve the Utah contract without Judge Garcia's knowledge (Frio County Commissioners Court, 1995k). When Garcia learned of the meeting, he intervened by informing the Commissioners that there was no basis for an emergency meeting. The attempt by Lindsey and Berrones to circumvent a public hearing failed. Shirey's role in this event was revealed at the next Commissioners Court meeting when he defended the "emergency meeting." He stated that:

> . . . the contract was the same one . . . brought before the Court, two months ago, with a few changes. . . . The crisis . . . [was that] the Jail [cannot] pay for [itself], with the current . . . shortage of prisoners. It can't stand that for very long. Utah had been here and looked at the Jail, they were happy with it and they had given [us] a deadline . . . last week sometime. We kept begging off another day, another day . . . that's the reason we felt it is was an emergency . . . [for] Frio County because it put this contract with Utah in jeopardy, which is the base for the revenue to make the payments. (Frio County Commissioners Court, 1995k [added])

Judge Garcia responded:

> Mr. Shirey you came before the Court, you asked for permission to look for "out-of-state prisoners" and you were given permission, but you were to come back to Commissioners Court and advise the Commissioners of progress and what the situation was. Now what happened last week, you didn't come before Commissioners Court . . . you sent two of your employees . . . to me to sign a contract and [they tell me] that an airplane [is] ready to haul those prisoners from Utah down here. All I told them was, "we have to go to Commissioners Court for this, and I'll see if I can get something started." When I phone[d] Mr. Smith in Austin . . . I told him that I didn't see an emergency existing [and] that I would like to wait for him to be present when . . . that contract would be signed. He replied "Okay, we'll just . . . do it Monday," which was today. (Frio County Commissioners Court, 1995k, [added])

This incident made it glaringly apparent that DDC did not recognize the emergence of a new political reality in Frio County. Their assumption that Judge Garcia would, when pushed, respond like Judge Williams appeared arrogant. In so doing, they further alienated Judge Garcia.

At the same meeting the Ad Hoc Committee presented their preliminary findings to the Commissioners. Committee spokesman Roger Trevino opened his presentation with the following statement:

> It has been brought to light that Frio County although . . . in partnership with Dove, is *not a true partner* because we can't even get their financial statement. [It] has been brought to light by our Sheriff that Frio County is losing . . . anywhere from $30,000 to $50,000 . . . a month because of the contract with Dove Corporation. (Frio County Commissioners Court, 1995l, [emphasis added])

Trevino went on to explain how negotiations with DDC and the Sheriff broke down over the number of free beds and the daily rate to be paid for county inmates. Consequently, the Committee was not ready to make detailed recommendations for contract amendments. However, they did have some important observations about the contracts and the meetings where these contracts were approved. Trevino explained:

> . . . all of the contract(s) with Dove Corporation may be illegal. They may all have violated the Open Meetings Act. . . . all of the meetings with Dove Corporation to approve/disapprove and to amend contracts have been in . . . 'EMERGENCY MEETINGS' . . . if this was so and it was not a stated emergency as prescribed by law then these meetings were illegal as per opinion of the Attorney General. . . . the AD HOC COMMITTEE's recommendation at this time is to table any new contracts or amendments to contracts with Dove Corporation and continue the moratorium until this Commissioners Court can . . . ask the District Court or the Attorney General to (1) appoint an independent counsel or have our District Attorney look into these allegations and (2) to . . . have the Court hire independent counsel or . . . the Attorney General . . . look into the possibility of severing the contract with Dove Corporation, if a valid contract exists. (Frio County Commissioners Court, 1995l)

After a very lengthy and contentious discussion about DDC's contract, role, and behavior within the county, Commissioner Berrones introduced a motion to approve the Utah contract. The motion failed. Commissioner Siller once again served as the swing vote in voting against the motion (Frio County Commissioners Court, 1995g). It was a dramatic turn of events. Siller rarely voted against Dove Development Corporation. Over the next 18 months, DDC won most of the political battles because of their entrenched political support on the Commissioners Court. However, the rejection of the Utah contract and DDC's inability to maintain a sufficient number of inmates to generate the income needed signaled that DDC's days in Frio County were numbered.

The 1996 Primary: The Majority on the Court Shifts Away from DDC

The balance of power on the Commissioners Court shifted against Dove Development Corporation with the 1996 primary election. Commissioners Siller and Espinosa were defeated. Commissioner Adolfo Alvarez, Sr. replaced Espinosa and Commissioner Chuy Salinas replaced Siller. Both, supported Judge Garcia and shifted the balance on the court—three to two—against the company. Quite simply, DDC had lost its base of political support and protection. Tom Shirey now recognized that DDC would not be able to hang on in Frio County and began to look for another firm to take over their confinement operations.

Sheriff Burris had thought that Frio County might resume public operation of the jail. However, resuming public operation of the jail was more easily discussed than achieved. During the contentious May 8, 1995 Commissioners Court meeting, Sheriff Burris was asked by Commissioner Lindsey about his intentions to take the jail away from DDC. The Sheriff responded by saying "If they [DDC] are not 'legal,' by all means. . . ." Commissioner Lindsey's response pointed out the economic problems with resuming public control of the jail, ". . . all those people will have to be let go . . . how are they going to stay there if we don't have a budget for them. Where will you [i.e., Sheriff Burris] get the money? . . . The money is not there, . . . we don't have [the] budget to run that Jail" (Frio County Commissioners Court, 1995m).

On this point, Commissioner Lindsey was right. Frio County did not have the resources to resume public operation of the jail. The payroll, the training, local prisoner care costs, and daily management were beyond their capacity. Having made the privatization decision in 1992, Frio County officials concluded that they could not resume public management of the jail. There was no going back. The public infrastructure to support such an operation had been lost. The county had only one real option: find another private corrections contractor to take over the contracts. The jail would remain privatized; however, they needed an operator that would work with the county, comply with its contracts, and ensure that local confinement needs are met. With this realization, the search for a new contractor began in earnest.

The Solution—A New Contractor

Within a year, Correctional Services Corporation (CSC) replaced Dove Development Corporation. Since then CSC has developed a much more constructive relationship with the county and corrected the operational problems that DDC had ignored by:

- installing high security double fence systems (topped with razor wire and embedded in a concrete footing),

- creating a large outdoor recreational area,

- renovating an interior recreational court yard into a multi-purpose program area,

- increasing the number of security and program staff on each shift,

- offering the standard array of programs and services offered in prisons and

- separating local jail inmates from prison inmates.

As of the spring of 1999, CSC appears to be performing very well and Frio County officials are happy with the way they have alleviated the public debt accumulated through lease-purchase contracts with CFRI. Recently, the county and CSC negotiated a 12-year lease. Based on the long-term lease, CSC has added another expansion (99 beds) to bring the total capacity at the Frio County Jail to 391 beds (Texas Commission on Jail Standards, 1999).

Frio County has come through a very difficult time. The original contractor hired by the county turned out to be an unscrupulous firm and was apparently facilitated by official corruption. CFRI/DDC took advantage of every opportunity they could find to exploit the county for corporate gain. The county nearly went bankrupt in 1996 and 1997 when it narrowly avoided default on its lease-purchase contracts with CFRI. Had that occurred, CFRI/DDC would probably own the facility and still be in the confinement business.

Frio County is now recovering financially. The latest expansion of the Frio County Jail by Correctional Services Corporation was completed at CSC expense. At least to this point, CSC has proven to be an honorable partner and has lived up to its obligations and commitments under its contract with the county.[17] Frio County now has a detailed contract that provides a more balanced distribution of power between the county and the company. The county has hired several consulting firms to help them ensure that public interests are reasonably protected in their dealings with CSC. In short, they are now dealing from a position of knowledge, strength, and honesty. They have more than a symbolic means to hold CSC accountable. County government is still dependent on a private contractor for local jail services and they still hold a local monopoly position, but their relationships with the community are more closely monitored. The private sector abuses of the past could reoccur but it appears much less likely under current conditions. A lot has changed since DDC first arrived in Frio County—there is a more honest county administration, greater transparency in the formation of public policy, a detailed public record, and a more knowledgeable community.

Lessons from this Cautionary Tale

Several lessons for criminal justice privatization can be drawn from this case. First, private providers can become politically entrenched and make it difficult (if not impossible) to modify contracts, impose controls, or terminate the contract despite serious performance problems. This is especially problematic when the contractor has established a monopoly over production of a public service. This is what happened in Frio County. The contracts, agreements, and amendments were strongly to the disadvantage of the county. The contracts did not include contract monitoring as a safeguard or require public disclosure of the nature and scope corporate relationships with local officials. All of these problems were exacerbated by apparent public corruption. DDC controlled the formation of public policy related to the jail through their influence with Judge Williams and other Commissioners for four years. In April, May, and June 1994, Judge Williams signed payment authorization for nearly $900,000 in public expenditures to a start-up construction company owned by Tom Shirey who also owned or controlled Consolidated Financial Resources, Inc. and Dove Development Corporation. Shirey has never fully accounted for these expenditures. Although, circumstantial evidence suggest, that these funds were misused, it is now impossible to determine whether they were actually misused. At the conclusion of these transactions, Shirey gained ownership of an operational 240-bed confinement facility at public expense. Direct contractor involvement in the political affairs of a jurisdiction should be grounds for contract termination or being declared ineligible for contract renewal. Such political involvement must be made transparent.

Another lesson from this case is the need for clearly specified standards of performance. The contract in Frio County only specified five performance issues:

- the daily billing rate for local inmates,
- the daily fee (= $1.00 per day per inmate) paid to the county,
- a prohibition against housing violent offenders,
- a requirement that the Sheriff approve all inmates transferred to the county jail, and
- continued certification by the Texas Commission on Jail Standards.

The contract subordinated public interests to corporate interests. Furthermore, DDC routinely violated its contract to increase the occupancy rate of the facility. The company promised out-of-state agencies that inmates would have access to an array of programs and services that were never actually provided. Such corporate behavior points out the critical need for clearly defined performance standards and contract monitoring provisions in privatization contracts. Government is a public entity with an affirmative responsibility to ensure public funds are not misused, wasted, or inappropriately paid out. The government does not have a duty to ensure corporate earnings, profit margins, or sweetheart deals allowing corporate profits at public expense. Contractors who do not like the standards set or oversight requirements do not have to submit a bid. Contractors also do not have to sign contracts with provisions they consider unfair or unprofitable.

A third lesson is that contract termination must be a meaningful option at all times. This means that jurisdictions must structure their contracts to ensure that public operation could be resumed if needed. Conditions for "just cause" contract termination should include deliberate or chronic contract violation, chronic sub-standard performance, hiring of unqualified personnel, conflicts of interest, manipulation of inmate sentences to increase length of stay, falsification of reports, refusal to provide evaluative data about performance and costs, and direct involvement in local politics. In Frio County, several of these conditions existed simultaneously but corrective actions were blocked politically by politicians supportive of, or controlled by, the contractor. Political power appears to have been misused to protect the company at the expense of public interest. Over time the county lost the operational and financial capacity to resume public operations. As a result, the threat of contract termination was never a viable option and company officials knew this. County officials found that they were unable to return to public operations. In the end, they willingly turned to another private contractor. This outcome represents a loss of local sovereignty over an important public service.

Finally, county officials mismanaged county resources and failed to use rudimentary precautions in obligating public funds. Even the most basic checks and balances over public expenditures were lost under Judge Williams. The Commissioners Court served largely at his pleasure, they did what he wanted or they paid for it politically. He appears to have used "*emergency meetings*" to circumvent the spirit of the Open Meetings Act and get things passed without publicity. He authorized actions in the name of the Commissioners Court without actual approval and signed payment authorizations without sufficient documentation to provide a paper trail. With respect to DDC, nearly all of his actions benefitted DDC economically at the expense of the county. The repeated financial deals with CFRI left the county heavily in debt while three firms managed by Tom Shirey were enriched.

This case study exemplifies the potential for private contractors to abuse the public trust when they are allowed to assume monopoly or near monopoly positions in a jurisdiction unprepared to control such private power. It also demonstrates how local politics and corruption can protect private interests at the expense of public interest. This case highlights the need for policymakers to carefully assess local needs, weigh the potential benefits and risks, and make informed policy decisions when criminal justice privatization is considered.

Endnotes

[1] Although Bobby Ross was appointed President of Dove Development Corporation in late 1992 or early 1993, he worked under the general supervision of David Thomas Shirey, Jr. (also known as Tom Shirey) President of Consolidated Financial Resources, Inc. When it became clear to Ross that he would not be allowed to develop the range of programs and services needed to manage long-term inmates he resigned from Dove Development Company and formed his own private jail management company (i.e., The Bobby Ross Group). As of the 1997 census of private prisons and jails, The Bobby Ross Group managed five jails in Texas (Thomas & Bolinger, 1997).

[2] Data collection for this case study was conducted between 1993 and 1999 by the author and several research assistants. Although monthly longitudinal data were collected on the operations and management of the Frio County Jail and the county justice system, this chapter concentrates on the data revealed by extensive archival research and personal interviews of knowledgeable citizens, public officials, and corporate executives. A book on this case is under development.

[3] Annual operating cost could have been estimate by comparison with jails of comparable size in south Texas and the southern United States. The lease-purchase payments for a 15-year payment plan for the construction and furnishings could also have been calculated at various interest rates. Had Frio County officials obtained these estimates they could have estimated the number of beds needed to be competitively priced or the price they would need to charge for the available beds in order to be self-supporting. They apparently did neither. It is now clear that they would have had to charge $54.46/inmate day with 100 percent occupancy of 126 beds (retaining 40 beds for Frio County use) to "break even." Lease costs were $704,440/year and operational costs at full capacity were roughly $1.8 million/year. A higher rate would be needed to generate excess funds. Yet, the competitive daily rates for confinement services are typically between $30 and $40/day. At $30/inmate day the county would need 228 beds with 100 percent occupancy to cover operational costs and lease payments. At $40/inmate day 171 beds would be needed. In short, basic policy analysis was not conducted.

[4] Frio County has historically been dominated by the Democratic Party. For all practical purposes there is no Republican opposition in the county. Consequently, the primary elections determine the outcome of general elections later in each election year.

[5] Judge Williams, Commissioner Lindsey, and Commissioner Berrones voted to strip Sheriff Del Toro of the "Sheriff's House." While Commissioner Moreno abstained and Commissioner Alvarez was absent.

[6] Although the record copy is undated as to the start date, Dove Development Corporation did assume management responsibility for the jail on September 1, 1992 and notes by County Attorney James W. Smith verify the start date of the two-year contract as September 1, 1992 (Smith, undated:1).

7   The record copy of the contract on file at the County Clerk's Office is signed but undated. Furthermore, it is unsigned by either the outgoing Sheriff (Del Toro) or the Sheriff Elect (Burris).

8   Once DDC had verbal agreements on the contract extensions they renovated the Sanders Unit to increase the capacity of the jail to 196 beds. These contract extensions were not documented in writing until December 22, 1995—three years later (Operations and Management Agreement, 1995). The contract extensions applied to both the Sanders Unit and the Main Jail.

9   *Ruiz v. Estelle*, 679, F. 2d 1115, 1126 (June 23, 1982) and *Ruiz v. McCotter*, Memorandum Opininon and Order, December 21, 1986 forced many reforms upon the Texas Department of Corrections. One of these was strict limitation of prison populations. At the time these cases were decided Texas prisons were routinely filled beyond their rated capacity by 35 percent to 50 percent (Martin & Ekland-Olson, 1987:140, 240). These population restrictions forced a massive increase in prison capacity during the mid-1990s. The backlog of state prison inmates filled the privately operated Frio County jail for 16 months between June 1994 and September 1995.

10   This lease-purchase agreement would later become a source of great conflict between CFRI/DDC and county officials.

11   James W. Smith, the current Frio County Attorney, was also the County Attorney in 1994. His recollections as to why the county changed from an unequivocal commitment to a single site to splitting the 336 beds between Frio County (96 beds) and Crystal City (240 beds) are unclear. He states that he never has understood how or why the Commissioners made this decision. Furthermore, he noted that the Commissioners Court resolution of eminent domain was non-binding and did not require mandatory action or formal removal of the resolution if it is not pursued (Smith, 1999b). County Attorney Smith cited Brooks (1989:148) as the basis for this view.

12   The escape from the Crystal City facility involved three inmates "trustees" working outside the facility security perimeter painting the jail lobby. The inmates were left unsupervised after lunch and took the opportunity to escape. The inmates were Utah prisoners. One was serving a life sentence for spousal homicide, another was serving life for sodomizing a child and the third inmate was doing time for theft and escape. All were recaptured within three weeks (Maffly, 1996:B1, B4).

13   The escape from the Frio County facility involved three inmates serving life sentences. Two for murder and one convicted for robbery as a career criminal under Utah law. All were recaptured within a week. One inmate was recaptured an hour after the escape but escaped again from the vehicle sally port area while the arresting officer was securing his weapon in a lock box. He later stole a dump truck and was recaptured in Austin, TX on January 22, 1996 (Maffly, 1996:B4).

14   Public agencies cannot use contractors to do what they are prohibited from doing or to provide services below the minimum level authorized in their state or locality. Consequently, confinement contracts with out-of-county or out-of-state jurisdictions may impose different rules, regulations, privileges, rights, and responsibilities than are imposed by other jurisdictions. In a facility housing offenders from multiple jurisdictions, managers are faced with situations in which inmates from different jurisdictions must be treated differently by contract. This can create

hostility and confrontations among inmates and present one of the most difficult facility management challenges possible to the contract manager who operates the facility. This is precisely the situation faced by Warden Woods in 1995-1996.

[15] Commissioner Lindsey would later explain that the budget cut was accidental and they planned to correct it later. However, the Commissioners never did correct it and it is hard to miss a 40 percent reduction in the prisoner care budget since it one of the largest budget items within the Sheriff's Office.

[16] The Warden Woods reference to Mark Sorenson, County Engineer reflects the common understanding among many people in Frio County that Sorenson served an enforcer role in Williams Administration (Del Toro, 1996 and many others). In Frio County, like many poor Texas counties, the County Road and Bridge Department has the most discretionary money available for political uses by County Judges. State highway funds provided a pool of capital that could be spent or not spent based on the political assessment of the County Judge. In Frio County, Judge Williams used the Road and Bridge budget politically to reward those who supported him with road repairs and other tangible community projects in that their precinct. Of course this provided visible evidence to voters that their Commissioner was politically effective. Judge Williams could also punish those who didn't support him by denying their district needed repairs (Alvarez, 1998; Berrones, 1998).

[17] On August 28, 1999 two inmates escaped from the CSC managed facility in Pearsall, TX. As of the completion of this chapter neither inmate had been recaptured. At this point it is unclear how the escape occurred.

9

The Corrections Corporation of America aka The Prison Realty Trust, Inc.

Alan Mobley and Gilbert Geis
University of California, Irvine

The Corrections Corporation of America (CCA) is the largest private prison entrepreneur in the United States and, undoubtedly, in the world as well. Based in Nashville, Tennessee, CCA has existed since 1983, time enough to discern a sense of its mission and its ethos and to examine its experiences. This chapter primarily considers some of the more distressing episodes in the corporate life of CCA. Part of the reason for such a focus on failure is that success stories, though they may get some passing attention, rarely capture headlines. Much more importantly, CCA is a far-flung enterprise and difficulties that have arisen in its prison operations need to be gathered together for analysis in regard to judgments concerned with the privatization of prisons.

The record of CCA must be scrutinized with an awareness of the performance of state-run penal facilities. If government-operated correctional facilities had an even halfway decent record they would not have been as vulnerable to encroachment by groups such as CCA. State-run prisons are marked by overcrowding, inmate suicides, escapes, brutality, and explosive riots. These circumstances have given them a deservedly unsavory reputation and made them easier targets for takeover. Other considerations as well, particularly speculative cost-benefit analyses and the astounding escalation of recourse to imprisonment in the United States, have played into the emergence and growth of privatized corrections. There are, for instance, now about 1.8 million persons confined in penal facilities in the United States, a figure double the total of a decade ago.

We cannot as yet provide more than faint indicia of the "success" and the "failure" of privatization on the basis of our brief case history of a particular corporate entity. For one thing, elements of such judgments hinge upon very intricate and, almost invariably, rather inconclusive comparisons, in large part because of the difficulty of locating satisfactorily equivalent representations of the two approaches to corrections. The episodes we detail below offer lessons only about possible shortcomings in the privatization approach. Whether these shortcomings are remediable and will be remedied remain open questions.

Financial issues are often at the center of the privatization debate. Complicated calculations of savings or losses to taxpayers underlie much of the discussion. Claims have been made backing both sides of the fiscal debate concerning the costs of privatization (Logan, 1992; General Accounting Office, 1996; McDonald, Fournier, Russell-Einhorn & Crawford, 1998). Although these matters can be of great concern to both citizens and shareholders, they are not considerations to which most of the following pages will be devoted. While the evidence on taxpayer savings from privatization remains mixed, the prevailing opinion continues to be that most private prisons save the state some money, at least in terms of direct outlays. Yet Douglas McDonald (1990:91), after considerable study, concluded that "the claims of the private sector's superior cost-effectiveness . . . are less robust than they might first appear." Beyond that, it can be said that the financial rewards for CCA itself have been extraordinary, indeed spectacular.

Finally, this introduction would be inadequate without our personal testimony that on ideological grounds we are opposed to private prisons and, more generally, that we are dismayed by this country's increasing reliance on imprisonment to solve what we see as pressing social problems. We would add that although we are by no means enamored with the way that state-run correctional facilities are operated, we would prefer, perhaps naively, to seek as a first recourse to reform that system rather than to turn it over to private profit-generating enterprises. Our bias may very well bear upon those things that we report and the manner in which they are reported. We shall try assiduously to keep our personal beliefs under control, but it seems essential to place them on record.

The Evolution of CCA and The Prison Realty Trust

The renaissance of private prison management has its roots in the variety of circumstances addressed in other contributions to this volume. The particular story of Corrections Corporation of America exemplifies many elements of the economic and ideological debate that has coalesced around prison privatization during the past 15 years.

Thomas W. Beasley and Doctor R. Crants, two Nashville businessmen, lawyers, and members of the 1966 West Point graduating class, founded CCA in 1983. Beasley and Crants were attracted to the field of corrections by the fact that American prisons were beleaguered by court orders mandating lower facility populations while at the same time public and political opinion was pressing toward the incarceration of a larger percentage of the American population. The ballooning ranks of prisoners was the result primarily of the increasing incarceration of nonviolent offenders, most particularly drug users who in previous times would have been enrolled in treatment programs or other alternative approaches to imprisonment. CCA entered the fray, promoting privatization as a solution: "You just sell it like you were selling cars, or real estate, or hamburgers," Beasley has said (Schlosser, 1998:70). The firm sometimes has used arguable campaign tactics to gain marketshare, stating that its main competitor, the government, "can't do anything very well" (Bates, 1999:593).

Persuaded that the era of "big government" was over, CCA's founders sensed that the approximately $35 billion spent each year in the United States on corrections represented an attractive opportunity for private business. By the end of 1989 CCA had a contracted caseload of 3,448 beds. Expansion in the 1990s was remarkably vigorous: CCA now has 71,851 beds in 81 facilities, making it the sixth largest prison system in the country. It owns and operates 44 prisons and jails and manages 35 others (PR Newswire, 1999a), employing more than 14,000 persons (Wilson, 1998).

CCA's success in acquiring contracts did not go unnoticed on Wall Street. From 1992 through 1997, CCA shares showed a compound annual growth rate of 70 percent, making the company one of the five top performers on the New York Stock Exchange (Johnston, 1998). The value of its shares rose from $50 million when it first went public in 1986 to more than $3.5 billion at its peak, which was toward the end of 1997. Crants owned 1.6 million CCA shares, while Beasley controlled well over two million (Vickers, 1999). CCA's largest stockholder—with 16 percent of the common stock—is Sodexho Alliance, a facilities management and food services conglomerate headquartered in France. Sodexho is also CCA's partner in UK Detention Services, a private prison company based in Europe. The French company also holds a majority stake in Sodexho Marriott of North America, whose board of directors includes Crants.

CCA's stock recently has moved downward. Perhaps in anticipation of this turn, just weeks before the decline in stock price Crants and Beasley sold 200,000 and 122,000 shares, respectively, saving themselves millions in losses (Corrections Corporation of America, 1998d;

Schlosser, 1998). Further declines have followed since CCA shareholders approved a complicated plan that allowed the company to be merged into CCA Prison Realty Trust (PRT), a real estate investment trust, or REIT, that had been spun off by CCA into a separate company in mid-1997. REITs are corporate entities that pay no federal taxes—estimated for CCA to be about $50 million in 1998—but they are required to distribute to shareholders at least 95 percent of what would have been their taxable income (Johnston, 1998). PRT's founding president was Robert Crants III. The 28-year-old Crants is Princeton-educated, a former Goldman Sachs REIT specialist, and son of CCA Chairman Doctor Crants.

The merger was accomplished over the objections of several of the nation's largest pension funds whose managers claimed that the deal was not in the best interest of shareholders but rather that it favored company executives (Hartmann, 1998). The Prison Realty Corporation, the newly formed REIT, is publicly traded under the symbol PZN, with PrisonR its newspaper listing. One wonders if the recent acquisition by CCA of one of its competitors, U.S. Corrections Corporation, will result in the company's market listing evolving further into PRISONS-R-US.

The stock price for Prison Realty at the time of the new arrangement was in the low 30s. The company received some "buy" endorsements after analysts were told that PZN would pay CCA $400 for each bed in facilities that PZN acquired and farmed out to CCA to run. Later it was announced that the original $400 figure had been renegotiated to $4,000. PZN's stock price then cascaded downward into the low teens (Associated Press, 1999).

Company officials have also admitted that the costs to operate and develop prisons are much higher than those represented to shareholders in connection with the merger. Some people expressed puzzlement: "How the company could not have known about an $80 million shortfall is beyond me" (PR Newswire, 1999b:1). A person associated with Legg Mason Securities, said: "The way they disclosed the problem is very disappointing. It raises serious questions about the credibility of the management team. People are debating whether these guys are incompetent or thieves" (PR Newswire, 1999b:1).

Nevertheless, CCA plans to move forward and take advantage of its REIT affiliation by buying additional government-managed prisons, a strategy believed to provide a more stable, if slower growing business than the current focus on negotiating contracts to manage such facilities (Skerrert, 1998). Management chores will fall to now-private CCA, whose officers and directors are nearly indistinguishable from the REIT's. A CCA board member has declared that there is nothing for clients to fear from the corporate restructuring: "It's the same company. It's just a different way of doing business" (Thompson, 1998:B4).[1]

Lobbying for Lucrative Leverage

Soon after its formation, CCA had "achieved a certain notoriety because of its political and financial ancestry" (Ryan & Ward, 1989:13). Beasley was the former chairman of the Tennessee State Republican Party, and his new company was backed by capital supplied by the Massey Burch Investment Group, which funded the Kentucky Fried Chicken operation. Massey Burch, more relevantly, had founded the Hospital Corporation of America (HCA), which, like most HMOs, is now under almost constant consumer siege.

The blueprint for the operation of CCA generally followed much the same lines as the HMOs. Service is not to be driven by need but by cost. As one critic puts it: "Private prisons companies are more concerned with doing well than with doing good" (Robbins, 1986:25). In a 1997 prospectus, CCA was quite forthright about its overarching aims: "The Company's primary business objectives are to maximize current returns to shareholders through increases in cash flow available for distribution and to increase long-term total returns to shareholders through appreciation of the value of the Common Shares" (Prison Realty Trust, 1997:24). Costs are to be kept under control by bulk purchasing and, most importantly, by control of wages and benefits. About 60 to 80 percent of the operating costs in correctional facilities are represented by wages, and CCA routinely pays about 15 percent less than state-run facilities, though its administrators usually earn a great deal more than their state counterparts (Schlosser, 1998).

Tennessee Tactics

In 1984, a Tennessee court threatened to order the immediate release of 300 inmates from the state prison system if some arrangement to reduce violence was not put into place. The predicament worsened a year later when a policy calling for new prison uniforms with stripes along the pants legs led to disturbances throughout the system, causing $11 million in damages (Associated Press, 1985).

Seeing an opportunity where others saw disaster, CCA offered to buy the entire Tennessee prison system for $50 million down and $50 million over the next 20 years, along with another $150 million it would spend on improvements and new construction. For its operation of the prisons, CCA was to be paid from the state treasury a sum not to exceed the $175 million annual operating budget of the corrections department (Cody & Bennett, 1987). While the proposal was being considered, it was discovered that the wife of Lamar Alexander, Tennessee's governor, and Ned McWherter, the speaker of the state Assembly and later Alexander's successor as governor, had invested money in CCA and together owned

1.5 percent of the company's stock (United Press International, 1985). The list of original stockholders also included current and former Alexander cabinet officials. Conflict of interest charges led Ms. Alexander to exchange her shares for an equivalent amount of another Massey Burch-financed company. She eventually sold these for a six-figure profit (Marcus, 1995:A19). Ultimately, CCA's purchase offer was rejected by the state legislature (see further discussion in Hallett & Lee, this volume).

Today, CCA's lobbying tactics in Tennessee continue apace. The wife of the speaker of the legislature is the company's chief lobbyist in the state (Aucher, 1997), while a son of the county employee responsible for monitoring a CCA work farm near Chattanooga was put on the CCA payroll. In addition, five state officials, including the governor, the House speaker, and the sponsor of the privatization bill, are partners with Beasley in several barbecue restaurants (Bates, 1999).

Elsewhere, CCA is equally aggressive. Crants and other CCA employees have made substantial campaign contributions to Governor Tommy Thompson of Wisconsin, whose state leads the nation in prisoners outsourced to other states (Jones, 1998b:1), and to Governor Frank Keating of Oklahoma, a state where the majority of medium-security beds are in private hands (Swope, 1998). CCA broadened the scope of its political reach in 1997 when it added Joseph Johnson to its board of directors. Johnson had been a long-time Washington DC Council member and former mayoral candidate John Ray's top political strategist. Before that, he was National Campaign Manager for the presidential campaign of Governor Douglas Wilder of Virginia; and in the 1980s he served as Secretary of Health for the state of New Mexico, and Executive Director of Jesse Jackson's Rainbow Coalition. Along with his appointment to the board, Johnson was given options on 140,000 shares of company stock, at least 80,000 of which was priced at $18.25. The closing price of CCA stock the day the options were granted was $32.50, providing Johnson with an immediate windfall of more than $1 million (Corrections Corporation of America, 1998d:30). The rationale for the stock award reads as follows:

> The company granted Mr. Johnson the Option in consideration for his extensive efforts in building and facilitating the Company's business relationship with certain governmental departments, agencies, and entities. (Corrections Corporation of America, 1998d:30)

The Youngstown Debacle

Events that took place in 1997 and 1998 at CCA's Northeast Ohio Correctional Center (NOCC) in Youngstown expose a dark side of private prison management. Problems that led to violence at the facility have been detailed in a post-mortem review conducted by a committee headed by a federal government official. Among a variety of matters, the committee pinpointed the curious manner in which CCA entered into a full-service detention contract with the District of Columbia, virtually bypassing the competitive process said to be an especially advantageous aspect of prison privatization:

> The immediate need for prison bed-space by [District of Columbia Department of Corrections] officials, coupled with the desire by CCA to fill its new vacant prison facility in Ohio, led to a request for bids that . . . virtually eliminated competition (Clark, 1998, chap. 2:1).

What followed in Youngstown may be no more than a private-prison analog of the considerably more awful events that in earlier years marked the life stories of state-run prisons such as that in Attica, New York (Wicker, 1975) and Jackson, Michigan (Martin, 1954) and, more recently, at the Corcoran facility in California (Gladstone & Arax, 1999). Alternatively, Youngstown may be the result of something else, the drive by private managers to maximize profits. The escapes, murders, and assaults that plagued the Youngstown prison were blamed on inadequate numbers of staff and inexperience on the part of those staff present. It is reasonable to attribute the penny-pinching on personnel to attempts by managers to lower costs by downsizing their operation. But the brutality that followed, where guards were instructed by management to engage in violent, degrading treatment of inmates (Clark, 1998) is typical of any prison, public or private, that is out of control.

Court and financial pressures bearing upon the District of Columbia led to the decision to dismantle parts of its Lorton, Virginia correctional complex and transfer 1,700 medium-security inmates to the CCA-operated prison in Youngstown, a site said by CCA officials to be "within a reasonable distance for families to visit District inmates" (Ray, 1998:A20). We should perhaps note that 300 miles may be a reasonable distance for families with corporate-provided chauffeurs and paid-for airline trips. But for the poor families of the predominantly African-American prisoners the cost of the trip often was prohibitive. The prisoners' considerable distance from home likely was an important contributor to the trouble that exploded at NOCC.

The prison had been built for $57 million by CCA on an abandoned industrial site sold to the company by the city of Youngstown for $1. The city gave CCA a 100 percent tax abatement for three years as an additional incentive to place the prison in their economically troubled area (Clark, 1998, chap.1:2). As a sign of the prosperity to come the spanking new prison featured a sign in front displaying CCA's daily stock price.

Within 14 months of the Youngstown facility's opening there were two fatal stabbings and 47 assaults, 20 of them involving knives. Assault victims were about evenly divided among inmates and guards. The violence went unreported to local authorities but became known after some of the injured prisoners were taken to a hospital. The lack of communication between the prison and local officials occurred despite a contract provision that called for the police to investigate all serious felonies within the facility (Tatge, 1998b). One prisoner was stabbed to death by inmates who were supposed to be shackled but who had obtained keys to remove their restraints. The other murdered man, Bryson Chisely, was a medium-security prisoner housed in a segregated protective custody unit. Chisely's wife had complained to CCA officials both in Youngstown and Nashville that he was in danger. She had also written to members of the D.C. Council, telling them three weeks before her husband was slain that "he fears for his life" (Jaffe & Brooks, 1998:A8).

Shortly after CCA spokespeople declared they had things under control at Youngstown, six men escaped (all were eventually recaptured); five were convicted murderers. They had cut through two 12-foot fences and evaded surveillance cameras and a defective motion detector. An employee was believed to have helped the inmates flee (Tatge, 1998b).

The investigative report prepared for the federal Department of Justice by a team headed by D.C. Corrections Trustee John Clark faulted both the District government and CCA. The $182 million, five-year contract between D.C. and CCA was negotiated, the report indicates, at a "somewhat inflated price" and marked by "weak requirements on the contractor and minimal provisions for enforcement." District of Columbia prisoners had been transferred to Youngstown at a pace that created chaos. A total of 904 inmates had been moved in 17 days, before any policies were established and before the security system had been set up. The CCA staff was inexperienced and poorly trained, and there were few educational and work opportunities for inmates. In the words of the Clark Report: "The District's rush combined with CCA's awareness of lack of competition proved to be advantageous to the company and cost D.C. more than $27 million over the life of the contract" (Clark, 1998, chap.2:3). CCA's successful lead lobbyists on the project were John Ray, late of the D.C. Council, and Joseph Johnson.

For its part, CCA responded, as it routinely does to problems, with a practiced calmness and reassurance that glitches were to be expected, and that they would remedy them in the future. "The idea was to move folks to a much safer environment [than Lorton]," said a CCA board member. "That was all we had to achieve. We had some problems, early on problems that we have addressed and will continue to address. But we'll never be a problem-free facility" (Thompson, 1998). The former mayor of Youngstown who had helped bring CCA to the city to create job opportunities was not placated. He termed CCA the "most deceitful, dishonest corporation I have ever dealt with" (Jaffe & Brooks, 1998:A8).

CCA's public declaration failed to address the allegation that the company conspired with D.C. officials to ship numerous violent, maximum-security prisoners to Youngstown, a move at odds with the contract that permitted the transfer of only medium-security prisoners. Neither D.C. nor CCA officials at Lorton had furnished the records necessary to show that many of the men were dangerous and that some were to be separated from one another. D.C. and CCA had created a classification system for Lorton inmates that lowered some prisoners' custody level from "high" or "maximum" to "medium" and "high-medium" (Clark, 1998), a security designation heretofore unknown, but one which the colluding officials thought would legitimate transfer to NOCC. Youngstown's mayor commented: "Under this company's classification system, Jack the Ripper would be classified as medium-security" (Tatge, 1998b). The attorney representing the inmates put it another way: "Instead of removing a lot of maximum-security inmates, they have just called them something else" (Tatge, 1998a:5B). An independent consultant appointed by the courts found that 319 of the 1,700 inmates were incorrectly classified. For their part, CCA had willingly accepted all comers to NOCC, well aware that the more beds it filled the greater would be its profit.

Unsound correctional practices as detailed in the Clark Report were surely at the root of the NOCC fiasco, but how such a situation was allowed to develop remains a point of contention between CCA leaders and Youngstown city officials. NOCC is a state-of-the-art facility planned as a showpiece for the CCA way of corrections. An accreditation team of the American Correctional Association had given the facility a near perfect rating, even with the mayhem of the first 15 months. Company officials hoped that the 1,700 D.C. inmates sent to NOCC would be but a first installment, since the entire Lorton complex of prisons had to be closed by December 31, 2001. A creditable showing at NOCC would have put CCA in the driver's seat to essentially assume control of D.C. corrections and to prove that it could do what it proposed all along— operate a jurisdiction's complete correctional system.

Jolts in Other Jurisdictions

Youngstown was not the only CCA trouble spot, though it was the most egregious. The need for CCA to keep up its image in order to retain and obtain business can on occasion lead to controversial and seemingly self-serving (rather than socially desirable) tactics.

Tennessee

CCA has been sued for inmate abuse, including the misuse of electric stun guns at its Whiteville, Tennessee facility. Allegations of excessive force against Wisconsin prisoners housed at Whiteville were repeatedly and vehemently denied by CCA until a Wisconsin state delegation investigating the matter uncovered convincing evidence. In response, CCA admitted wrongdoing and dismissed eight employees, including the prison's director of security. Wisconsin officials have asked the FBI to investigate a cover-up (Jones, 1998a:1).

CCA's reticence to own up to problems or to allow oversight at Whiteville would come as no surprise to Ohio authorities. When two legislators in that state tried to go into the NOCC to make a spot inspection, prison employees refused them entry because a pair of Ohio corrections officers were accompanying them. The incident led one lawmaker to observe sarcastically: "Turns out it's a lot easier for prisoners to get out than for the lawmakers to get in" (Turnbull, 1998:2A).

In another incident, in mid-1998 CCA abruptly transferred inmate Alex Friedmann from its lockup in Clifton, Tennessee. Friedmann said that he had been accused of "efforts to degrade CCA with negative articles" published in "outside sources" (Bates, 1998a:5). The CCA warden thought he had his finger on the problem: "Alex is intelligent," the warden said, "but once he gets in his mind that something's wrong, he's going to hit it with a vengeance, forever and ever, amen." Friedmann's sin was that he had been quoted in a cover story published in *The Nation* (Bates, 1999) that criticized CCA's operation of the facility. He lost an appeal seeking administrative remedy on the grounds that he had made "a deliberate effort to disseminate material which is negatively oriented to the prison operating company," apparently something not to be tolerated by CCA, despite First Amendment guarantees (Bates, 1998a).

The Friedmann incident is especially interesting as it mirrors a much-publicized event marring the otherwise exemplary career of the current CEO of CCA, J. Michael Quinlan. Quinlan was director of the Federal Bureau of Prisons from 1987 to 1992 under presidents Reagan and Bush. Shortly before the 1988 presidential election, an inmate at the federal prison in El Reno, Oklahoma contacted media sources alleging that he once sold marijuana to Bush's vice-presidential running mate, Dan Quayle. Nina Totenberg, a correspondent for National Public Radio, got in touch with members of Quayle's staff regarding the inmate's charge. They maintained that there was no truth in the report. A senior Quayle advisor then called Quinlan to discuss the matter. Soon after, the inmate, Brett Kimberlain, was placed in administrative segregation and held incommunicado until after the election. Quinlan insisted that political motives played no part in his decision to order Kimberlain segregated. He said that he was told Kimberlain feared for his safety and that the transfer to protective custody had been at his own request. Both Kimberlain and Totenberg refute Quinlan's account. An investigation of the matter by the inspector general of the Justice Department concluded that the extraordinary intervention of the bureau's chief in disciplining an inmate was inappropriate (Isikoff, 1991:A3). Quinlan resigned his post as director before the inspector general's report was made public, citing health reasons (Ostrow, 1992:A39).

North Carolina

The high business tide upon which CCA has been riding can be illustrated by its experiences in North Carolina. The company contracted to build a facility in rural Pimlico County, near the Atlantic Ocean coast, and another in the mountains on the Mitchell-Avery county line. The rationale for going private offered by a Republican state representative is the usual one: "The private sector can provide services and facilities at much less cost to the taxpayer and provide the same level of service" (Gray, 1998:1). The legislator also noted that the innovations wrought by CCA can impel improved state procedures; thus, the state, following CCA's lead, had begun to use preset concrete and steel cells, making construction cheaper than when done with more traditional methods.

The peculiar aspect of the North Carolina CCA involvement is that the state does not have run-down hellholes for prisons nor is there a public employee union whose wage levels can be undercut. The Department of Corrections runs a most unusual operation, one that not only pays for itself, but contributes about $1 million a year to the general fund and $500,000 to the program to compensate crime victims. But as often has been the case, CCA negotiated a notably sweet deal, stipulating that the state will assign to its facilities only able-bodied inmates who are willing to work. "They're not obliged to take mad or mean convicts or sick ones," complained one state prison superintendent. "If I can go through and pick the best prisoners, I can run a cheap prison too" (Gray, 1998:1).

Others have seconded concerns with "cherry picking," and accuse CCA of taking in only the healthiest and most docile inmates. "When a prisoner falls ill or proves troublesome, CCA simply ships him back into a state-run prison, where the bill is picked up by taxpayers instead of company shareholders" (Bates, 1999:598). Not only can this selection process make the operation of CCA prisons less costly, but facilities can be rendered less hazardous places in which to work and to "do time." This practice would surely produce a noticeable disparity between the quality of CCA and public institutions, with public facilities finding themselves in an ever more precarious predicament because of the congregation inside their walls of the most needy and aggressive inmates.

CCA apparently plans on plucking not just the "best" prisoners from public penal systems, but the best prisons as well. As mentioned earlier, the new Prison Realty REIT has as its goal the acquisition of penal facilities, primarily those now publicly owned. By purchasing the best prisons and stocking them with the least costly prisoners, CCA stands poised to outperform public facilities in terms of cost and safety. As older, more hazardous government-operated prisons become ever more expensive to run, CCA will be able to portray itself as an efficiency-oriented, cost-cutting corporate savior, instead of, as some view it, as a politically savvy and highly skilled poacher of prisons, extracting the pick of state correctional systems.

CCA facilities might then be used as rewards for cooperative prisoners, even as the company verges on becoming the gilded revolving door through which state-trained prison workers pass. Kathleen Hawk, the present director of the Federal Bureau of Prisons, recently voiced to Congress her concerns over the potential departure of a large percentage of the bureau's executive staff (Hawk, 1995). The latest case of a senior civil officer leaving for the private-prison sector is the early retirement of Percy Pitzer, a 48-year-old warden. Pitzer became the new head of CCA's troubled Whiteville, Tennessee facility (Jones, 1998a:1). Michael Quinlan, Hawk's predecessor, traded his $123,100 annual salary for a CCA compensation package that included $3 million in stock (Hallihan, 1997:A26).

Healthcare: Florida, Tennessee, and Ohio

The attempt by CCA to avoid paying medical costs is indicated by a 1994 arrangement under which prisoners in the Hernando County Jail in Florida had to bear the expense for their own healthcare. The money was taken from a prisoner's account; if the inmate had no funds he left prison with a debt that the county could seek to collect by seizing property or other assets. This procedure was said by the resident prison doctor to encourage inmates "to find the most appropriate way to treat their problems. They learn to treat minor medical conditions [themselves] and to seek professional care when necessary" (Stern, 1998:41-42).

A Tennessee contract with CCA bars prisoners with AIDS from being sent to a CCA facility and places a $4,000 per inmate cap on medical services; if the cost is greater the excess has to be paid by the state (Aucher, 1997). In regard to the CCA facility at Clifton, Tennessee, the mother of a deceased 28-year-old inmate claims CCA reduced its average daily medical care costs from $3.07 per inmate per day in 1994 to $1.68 per inmate per day in 1997. The facility's medical expenses stayed the same during that period—around $1 million—even though the inmate population grew from 1,000 to 1,500 (Associated Press, 1998c).

In addition, 250 of the first 900 prisoners to enter NOCC at Youngstown in its first 17 days required chronic health care treatment for ailments such as asthma, HIV, diabetes, high blood pressure, and heart disease. Not a single prisoner was turned away by CCA even though the medical department was overwhelmed by the pace of new arrivals and incapable of meeting their healthcare needs (Clark, 1998:21).

South Carolina

State officials refused to renew a contract with CCA to run a juvenile detention facility when child welfare advocates claimed that the company's employees were mistreating some boys and had confined as many as 18 in a one-person cell where they had only cups for toilets. One boy was said to have been hog-tied on at least 30 occasions. CCA has filed a suit in court seeking to recover $12 million it spent to renovate the facility and build wilderness camps. Said a CCA spokesperson, "We did the best that could be done under the circumstances. We're proud that we prevented South Carolina from paying substantial fines" (Corrections Professional, 1997:2).

Texas Tribulations

CCA's Houston Processing Center for suspected illegal immigrants, with a design capacity for 411 beds, also brings into question the quality of the facilities that the corporation creates and runs. The Houston Center was built in April 1984 and represents CCA's first design, construction, and management contract. The following sketch, though perhaps telling, has to be read with some caution, since it is the product of a site visit by members of the British Prison Officers' Association, hardly a neutral source:

> The inmates were...in large dormitories each containing between 540 and 600 beds with no privacy whatsoever, no lockers, no screening around toilets or showers which were open to view by both male and female staff. . . .The few officers we saw were scruffy and thug-like in appearance. . . . [W]e have never witnessed such shocking conditions, which considering the state of some of our prisons, is a terrible condemnation. . . .We have never seen so many prisoners obviously confused and despairing. (Ryan & Ward, 1989:49-50)

The British report might be seen as a warning sign regarding what was to occur later, when two sex offenders escaped from the facility. One of the two escapees was serving time for sexual abuse, the other for beating and rape of an 88-year-old woman. They climbed a fence topped with razor-wire and, once outside, assaulted a guard and stole his car.

CCA had sought to increase the Houston's facility's population (and profitability) when it found itself receiving fewer immigrant detainees. On its own initiative, CCA brought in 244 sex offenders from Oregon— "some of the worst Oregon had," according to one Texas legislator (Turner, 1996:33). State and local officials were unaware of the transfers, since the facility previously housed only federal offenders. "Who the hell would have thought that someone would do something like this?" a Texas state legislator said, referring to the Oregon transportees (Bardwell, 1996:1).

Meanwhile, in 1996, at the 1,000 bed CCA-run facility in Eden, Texas, a disturbance led to the injury of 17 persons. The inmates said that they were protesting against poor food, inadequate recreation, and what they regarded as other subpar institutional conditions (Turner, 1996). Pressure to provide decent arrangements and still come in under budget has apparently been too much for CCA at some of its Texas facilities. The company recently announced that it is in the process of closing three of them (Hallihan, 1998).

Issues of Evaluation

Social science and economic evaluations of the consequences of prison privatization presents a formidable challenge. As Adrian James and his colleagues aptly observe: "[T]here are no simple and yet truthful answers which encompass the myriad of complex practical, moral and theoretical questions raised by an initiative such as contracting-out . . . not least because the data are open to various interpretations" (James, Bottomley, Liebling & Clare, 1997:169). John Donahue adds a point particularly relevant to our scrutiny of the activities of CCA:

> Ideologically fervent commentators of every political stripe too often neglect . . . [the fact] that no set of studies can prove any universal assertion about either public or private institutions. . . . The best that any empirical survey can hope for is to find some suggestive tendency in the way the evidence falls. (Donahue, 1989:57)

In an early attempt to quantify the relative advantages of private and public prisons, Charles Logan measured 333 indicators of quality of confinement. He derived his numerical evidence from institutional records and surveys of inmates and staff at two New Mexico facilities, one run by CCA, and the federal institution at Alderson, West Virginia. All three prisons held female inmates and were deemed to be "of high quality." The private CCA-operated facility was said to have "outperformed its governmental counterparts on nearly every dimension" (Logan, 1992:577).

Logan's findings have been called into question by critics (Ryan, 1997). Furthermore, the New Mexico Department of Corrections later accused CCA of overcharging the state nearly $2 million for its running of the facility. It did so, the New Mexico officials said, by including in its $95 fee for each inmate each day $22 that represented debt service. It was also charged that the women inmates in CCA's New Mexico facility lost good time credits at a rate nearly eight times higher than men in the state-run facility (Bates, 1999). As Jerome Miller says, "The problem is all the incentive in privately run prisons is to keep them full and to get as many people in there for as long as possible" (Hammack, 1995:G1).

Although Logan himself lists shortcomings of his study that might render the findings suspect, he is unwilling to touch the issue of recidivism, that is, the success experienced by inmates in the different facilities upon their release. He offers this defense of his decision to bypass outcome measures:

> The criteria proposed here for comparative evaluation of prisons are normative, rather than consequentialist or utilitarian. They are based on a belief that individual prisons ought to be judged primarily according to the propriety and quality of what goes on inside their walls—factors over which prison officials may have considerable control. (Logan, 1992:579)

He adds: "It is neither fair nor methodologically feasible to compare Prison A with Prison B in terms of external outcome—that is, in terms of each one's relative contribution to crime control" (Logan, 1992:579). It is this methodological complexity that leads us to regard skeptically the purported first-ever recidivism study comparing private and state-facilities. This study found both a lower re-offending rate and less serious offenses after one year for inmates released from private compared to public facilities (Lanza-Kaduce, Parker & Thomas, 1999). Aside from the overly short time span of the study, it takes for granted the problematic equivalence of the facilities. In addition, the Florida Ethics Commission ruled that one of the authors, Charles Thomas, had a conflict of interest in his work on private prisons. He has or will receive more than $3 million in cash, stock options, and fees for serving on the Prison Realty Trust Board of Trustees (for further details see Geis, Mobley & Shichor, 1999).

The matter of recidivism measurement is not, however, unfeasible methodologically. It can be carried out rather elegantly by recourse to random assignment, the most powerful experimental tool science possesses. A pool of eligibles can be created on a random basis: Prisoner A can be placed in a private prison and Prisoner B in the state-run facility to which it is being compared. There inevitably will be glitches in the purity of the design (knowledge that their assignment was randomly determined, for instance, may disproportionately affect the members of one or the other group). Also, of course, such work takes time for the outcome to become known. We suspect that recidivism may not differ greatly between private and state run institutions, but we are not certain. There are hypotheses that cut both ways. Some say, for instance, that juvenile recidivism is encouraged when locked-up delinquents discover that they can manage quite well in an affable institution; the obverse is that less indulgent facilities create a stronger sense of not desiring to repeat the experience.

Staffing Private Prisons

CCA officials and spokespersons often insist that staffing difficulties, common enough in any pioneering endeavor, lay at the root of difficulties that the company has experienced at various sites. They maintain that such things as staff inexperience are no more than a temporary difficulty that in time will be resolved.

It is arguable, however, whether CCA staff difficulties represent only a short-term problem. Staffing issues are crucial to CCA and all private prison companies since personnel costs are at the core of the industry's profitability. Private prisons aim to operate more cheaply than public prisons by lowering costs, especially labor costs which, as noted earlier, account for approximately 60 to 80 percent of total expenses (Schlosser, 1998). This can be done in three ways: (a) by employing fewer workers than state prisons; (b) by paying the same or a similar number of workers less; or (c) by doing both simultaneously. Any of these approaches can exacerbate long-standing problems of prison management.

Employing fewer workers per shift is standard procedure for CCA operations. Technology allows a very small number of guards to oversee large prison populations, but only if prisoner movement is tightly constrained. In CCA's Youngstown facility, for example, a typical day found inmates contained in their two-man cells, within the dayrooms of 36-man pods, or within recreation areas along with the 216 men from their adjacent housing units (Clark, 1998). Using such tactics, even a prison of 2,000 or more inmates theoretically can be managed with no more difficulty than a jail with a 200-person population. Such a high level of containment over a prolonged term, however, breeds apathy, despair, and violence (Johnson & Toch, 1982).

The alternative, employing a higher number of less well-paid staff, permits a more fluid prison operation, as larger numbers of prisoners can be set in motion simultaneously while appropriate levels of staff supervision are maintained. This approach both permits and demands activities to fill idle hands and minds, and it makes the orderly running of the institution more dependent on staff personnel, particularly on line staff, and less reliant on architecture and technology.

More of a human touch increases the options available for programming, work assignments, and other activities, but it also looms as a potential liability. Employees often are responsible for the illegalities that transpire behind prison walls. Staff members import drugs, weapons, escape tools, and other contraband into prison facilities, and staff allow prisoners to engage in officially proscribed activities, such as the sanctioned killings recently reported at a California state facility (Gladstone & Arax, 1999:A3). Persons from all social classes and of all caliber working in prisons have proven vulnerable to being corrupted by the near absolute power of their positions (Haney & Zimbardo, 1998). Poorly trained and poorly paid employees of CCA prisons must surely be prone to such potentially deadly mischief.

Systems such as the Federal Bureau of Prisons have tried to lessen the allure of employee opportunism by paying staff relatively well, offering benefits representative of the middle-class, and by promoting an inclusive "bureau family" atmosphere. Staff members who see the bureau as a career and not transient employment probably stand a much better chance of resisting temptations. Nonetheless, even prisons and prison systems offering the highest wages have great difficulty retaining employees. No doubt it is the nature of the work (not just the stigma of it) that drives people away. What then can the likes of CCA expect from line staff? Paltry wages, few benefits, and no retirement plan do not command much loyalty in today's economy, particularly when the work is so difficult and potentially dangerous.

CCA no doubt expects very high rates of staff turnover, meaning that CCA prisons may be perpetually manned by inexperienced crews. Since acute prison problems such as assaults, riots, brutality, and homicides are often the result of poor decisions made by inexperienced staff unfamiliar with procedures, institution staff may emerge as CCA's greatest liability. It is a curious situation where prison managers are compelled by their corporate responsibilities to see prisoners as capital assets and employees as costly threats to corporate profitability.

Conclusion

An examination of prisons operated by CCA involves, at its heart, consideration of the real and possible virtues and deficits of the two major economic and ideological positions of our times, capitalism and state socialism. Scrutiny of the achievements and setbacks of CCA obviously cannot resolve that larger and formidable debate, which at its core is both a moral and an empirical issue. But it can provide information bearing upon it, and can offer facts and judgments that might be relevant to legislative enactments, court decisions, and public attitudes concerning private prison operation.

On one side of the ideological battlefield stands the extraordinarily powerful critical analysis of the dynamics of capitalism propounded by Karl Marx and Friedrich Engels. Put into the context of responsibility for prison management, it insists that the press of private enterprise inevitably and inexorably will be toward exploiting those it employs and supervises. In prisons, profit-driven corporate employers will tend to look to their own benefit when negotiating staff size, experience, salaries, and benefits, and the maintenance expense of prisoners. Every cent saved is a cent that reflects favorably on the managers and contributes to an escalation of corporate profits and the enhanced wealth of stockholders.

Shareholders likely will know little and care less about how the private prisons are operated. Profits are regarded as their rightful reward for having risked their money in the hope that the organization they bought into will pay off. Such profits, going into the pockets of private citizens, are not seen as subtracting from either prison or public funds but rather are regarded as a consequence of savings achieved by operational skill and intelligence. Private prison corporations have been able to ignore the need for voter approval for bond issues to build new prisons. If the public were directly confronted with the fact that punitive penal policies were being paid for by increasingly heavy burdens on their personal incomes, they might well re-examine their support of such policies. As it is, CCA and other companies allow legislatures to have prisons built, still at public expense, but without public consideration and formal approval.

There are, of course, limits beyond which profit-making cannot reach. Wages and benefits, for instance, must be enough to attract reasonably competent workers. Prisoners may not have the status of medical patients at health maintenance organizations who can stir up a mountain of agitation if they believe they are being ill treated. But, though unable to vote and carrying a social stigma, prisoners nonetheless must be kept sufficiently satisfied so that they do not riot or otherwise call attention to what they may see as inadequacies of the private regime (Sykes, 1957).

If a profit is made from the operation of government-operated prisons (and that is unlikely), that sum would be returned to the state to be used to upgrade prisons, or, more likely, to be incorporated into the government's general operating budget. There is no notable incentive in public prisons to be particularly careful, much less adventuresome, in regard to the reduction of expenses and the burden of work. Prison staff typically unionize and press for the best working arrangements that negotiations can secure. Prisoners, under this arrangement, remain relatively powerless unless they adopt attention-gathering (and dangerous) tactics to seek to call attention to and gain sympathy for what they regard as unacceptable conditions.

Free-market economic theories suggest that CCA will continue to improve its operations and remedy failures out of its own corporate self-interest. But CCA appears to have a marked predilection to repeat the mistakes of its past. Although it operates one of the largest prison systems in the country, it discourages the circulation among its institutions of written reports detailing problem areas. Lapses in security, escapes, management blunders, and even circumstances leading to injury and death are later repeated in other institutions because of this lack of communication.

An incident involving Washington DC inmates transferred from Ohio to another CCA facility provides a chilling example. In August 1998, five months after the Chisely killing, two inmates who were supposed to be separated from one another were housed on the same tier and removed from their cells at the same time. Both produced weapons and one, Corey Smith, was killed. The survivor had removed his handcuffs, presumably through the use of a tool, and attacked the other. How could a homicide so remarkably similar to one at Youngstown occur? The answer lies in the fact that CCA took no steps to warn receiving prisons about the strategies peculiar to the most violent D.C. prisoners. Not only does the company prohibit the dissemination of reports following mishaps, corporate policy forbids the very writing of such reports out of a concern that written documents could be used in litigation (Clark, 1998, chap. 7:3).

This bottom-line-oriented policy almost surely permitted what the Clark Report (1998, chap. 2:16) called "a carbon copy . . . of the Chisely case." Other maximum-security inmates shipped from Youngstown attacked and beat five guards at the CCA Estancia, New Mexico prison. That institution, like Youngstown, was said to be intended only for minimum- and medium-security inmates (Beyerlein, 1998). But perhaps the most distressing incident occurred at the Clifton, Tennessee CCA site, where four inmates convicted of crimes such as rape and murder escaped into the surrounding community. They fled through holes cut in both perimeter fences while on the recreation yard in a re-enactment of the mass escape at Youngstown. Once again a staff member, this time a supervisor, is suspected of facilitating the escape (Warren, 1998).

The following quote epitomizes the way in which CCA presents itself in a press release: "A safe and secure correctional environment for staff, inmates and the community is paramount at ALL CCA facilities, all of which have numerous features designed to provide that secure environment" (Tatge, 1998c:4B).

The evidence that we have accumulated in this chapter indicates that in many respects the company has seriously failed to realize the goals that it claims to have set for itself. The Clark Report tells how it views CCA's work to date: "[CCA] has not demonstrated the capability to identify and correct its own problems. Numerous major changes have been spurred primarily in reaction to intervening negative events or external forces" (Clark, 1999, chap. 7:4).

Prisons may be a ""necessary evil" to hold captive persons who truly represent a serious threat to other human beings, people who deserve better. In the United States, we seem to have concluded, senselessly, that the only cure for the maladies that are characteristic of prisons are more prisons. We have failed to attend to the horrors of imprisonment and to the fact that there are more effective and more decent alternatives. Private companies see prisons as a source of financial profit, with their income dependent on a flourishing trade in more prisons and more prisoners. If the early history of CCA is a fair indication, the movement to privatize prisons will only worsen rather than relieve a problem desperately in need of correction, and not a euphemistic parody of the term.

Endnote

[1]   See Chapter 3 in this text for later developments.

10 Public Money, Private Interests: The Grassroots Battle Against CCA in Tennessee

Michael A. Hallett
University of North Florida, Jacksonville

J. Frank Lee
Middle Tennessee State University

> *The politics of corrections has never been played out in the sort of pluralistic universe that defines much of the rest of U.S. public policymaking.*
> —John DiIulio, 1993:279

In 1997, Tennessee became the epicenter of one of the major public policy shifts of our time in criminal justice, prison privatization. That year, the Tennessee legislature gave serious consideration to the largest-ever privatization proposal on record, a contract for privatizing the *entire* Tennessee state prison system—with an inmate population approaching 20,000. On April 29, 1997, executives from Corrections Corporation of America (CCA) escorted key members of the legislature's Select Oversight Committee on Corrections to a private meeting at the Crown Plaza Hotel, across from the state capital in downtown Nashville. News reporters who accidentally learned of the meeting were politely asked to leave (Wade, 1997a:A-1). On April 30, 1997, executives from Wackenhut Corporation arrived in Nashville to take six members of the House *Ways and Means Committee* out to dinner.

So began the latest effort to "privatize" the Tennessee prison system. It had been tried before, when in 1985, after a Federal Court order forced the state to spend an additional $380 million on prison renovation

227

and construction, Tom Beasley—former chairman of the Tennessee Republican Party—proposed to then Republican Governor Lamar Alexander, that his company (CCA) could "lock them up better, quicker, and for less" than the state (Kyle, 1998:88).

The major opponent to the latest effort to privatize Tennessee's prisons became the Tennessee State Employee's Association (TSEA), for whom the lead author was a hired consultant during the initial stages of the debate and delivered a report to the legislature against privatization on their behalf (Hallett, 1997). TSEA is a state public employees' union, roughly 4,500 members of whom work as correctional officers in the state's prisons. Tennessee's experience with the effort to "privatize" its prisons affords a unique vantage point on both the national public policy debate about prison privatization, as well as an important perspective on a global trend toward the transfer of public wealth into private hands—all in the name of efficient administration of government.

This paper argues three main points about the recent Tennessee experience with prison privatization. First, the Tennessee print and broadcast media's characterization of the TSEA as having successfully fended off "big money and power" in the battle for control over Tennessee's prison system is inaccurate (Locker, 1998; Humphrey, 1997). As this paper will show, the effort to privatize the Tennessee prison system suffered three separate defeats that unfortunately cannot be attributed to the vociferous grassroots efforts of the TSEA.

Second, as a result of the machinations surrounding the Tennessee initiative, the citizens of Tennessee have yet to be provided a real and substantive debate regarding the fundamentals of prison privatization (i.e., Constitutional issues, incentive structures of for-profit service providers, per diem cost assessments, contract monitoring and liability issues, legislative versus executive control over the contracting process, etc.). Specifically, despite calls for openness and accountability in the bidding process, CCA and Wackenhut submitted their bids to a consultant, hired by the Tennessee legislature's Select Oversight Committee on Corrections (SOCC), and claimed "proprietary interest"—arguing that each company's proposal amounted to *secrets of trade* and that each company was therefore entitled to keep the specifics of their proposals private. In short, activists demanding the right to cross-examine proposals ceding public control of Tennessee's prison system were denied the opportunity to do so.

Third, CCA's own attribution of the TSEA as the "victor" in this most recent battle, strategically overstates the power the TSEA was able to exert in the policy arena. Specifically, CCA's attribution of a TSEA "victory" distracts from the very real role that mismanagement of CCA prisons in Tennessee and elsewhere played in driving the final stake through the heart of the initiative (Humphrey, 1998:A-1; Wade, 1998b:B-1).

This research was conducted by way of interviews with legislators and activists, as well as through archival research. While the recent effort to privatize Tennessee's prisons was unsuccessful, the alliances and connections laid bare by the attempt offer insightful vantage points for the effort to defeat future prison privatization initiatives elsewhere. It is our hope that this chapter will alert academics and policymakers to some of the lessons learned in Tennessee.

Insider Politics: Context of Tennessee Prison Privatization

The genesis of prison privatization in Tennessee must be understood in no uncertain terms as having been "mobilized" from within. A theoretical framework for understanding public policy approaches to social problems that deals specifically with policy initiatives sponsored by political insiders is "agenda setting," as developed by Cobb and Elder (1972). Agenda setting is defined as "the process by which demands of various groups in the population are translated into items vying for the serious attention of public officials" (Cobb, Keith-Ross & Ross, 1976:126). An "agenda" is a "general set of political controversies that will be viewed at any point in time as falling within a range of legitimate concerns meriting the attention of the polity" (Cobb & Elder, 1972:14). Agenda setting is regarded by many as the most important element of the policy process: "The determination of what does and what does not become a matter of governmental action, ultimately becomes the supreme instrument of power" (Palumbo, 1994:40).

The key sponsors of each initiative to privatize Tennessee's prisons, both in 1985 and in 1997, were long-time political insiders, either current or former business partners, or otherwise connected through marriage or progeny. Tom Beasley and co-founder of Corrections Corporation of America, Doctor R. Crants, were roommates at West Point. Beasley is a former chairman of the Tennessee Republican Party. He occupied that position during the tenure of Republican Governor Lamar Alexander. Lamar Alexander was Governor in 1985, when CCA first proposed privatizing the entire Tennessee prison system. Early investors in CCA included Lamar Alexander's wife, Honey Alexander, and Lamar Alexander's successor as Governor, Democrat Ned McWherter. At the time of CCA's founding, Ned McWherter was the long-standing Speaker of the Tennessee House of Representatives.

In the most recent effort to privatize Tennessee's prisons, CCA worked directly with Representative Matt Kisber, who sponsored the bill, and who is part owner of a Nashville restaurant with current Speaker of the House Jimmy Naifeh (Locker, 1997c:A-1). Naifeh's wife, Betty Anderson, as well as current Republican Governor Don Sundquist's wife,

Martha Sundquist, and the Sundquist's three adult children, are business partners with Naifeh and Kisber in a Nashville restaurant (Locker, 1997b:B-3). Governor Sundquist is on record as supporting prison privatization. Perhaps the most unseemly political connection in the affair, however, and certainly the connection that drew the most attention, is the fact that the wife of the Speaker of the House and long time supporter of prison privatization, and business partner of Beasley and Kisber, is none other than Betty Anderson—CCA's chief lobbyist in the Tennessee legislature. All of this perhaps makes unsurprising the fact that Crants and Beasley were leading contributors to Governor Don Sundquist's re-election campaign in 1998—as well as contributors to Naifeh's, Kyle's, and Kisber's re-election campaigns (Locker, 1997b:B-3).

Back in 1985, then Governor Lamar Alexander was forced to call the Legislature back into a special session to deal with a Federal Court order placing a cap on the state's prison system. Like many states in the late 1970s, Tennessee began its own crusade to lower crime rates through the implementation of mandatory minimum sentencing. Predictably this created the tremendous overcrowding which led to the Federal court order placing caps on the prisoner population. By 1985 the situation reached a crisis point, with rioting and several deaths, and the declaration of the state's oldest prison at Nashville unconstitutional. Tennessee found itself very quickly in need of at least 7,000 additional prison beds, and called for spending an additional $380 million to build six new prisons (Select Oversight Committee on Corrections, 1995).

It was during this period, during the special session, that Beasley introduced CCA's first proposal to manage the state's prison system. Said Beasley in 1985:

> Our proposal is simple—we will pay the state for the right to manage the system under the state's supervision; we will spend private capital to improve the system and draw our profit out of more efficient use of the state's regular operating budget. That is a $250 million—one quarter of a billion dollar turnaround in the state budget—without a tax increase! We believe this is absolutely a win/win situation and an unprecedented opportunity to make Tennessee a leader in this most difficult area (Corrections Corporation of America, 1985:2).

Sensing a potential battle for control over the correctional system with the Governor, the state legislature saw fit to create the Select Oversight Committee on Corrections (SOCC), "a 10-member joint Senate and House committee charged with reviewing corrections plans, both capital and operational, to help ensure that the state delivers a correctional system that is effective and efficient" (Kyle, 1998:89). Fearing that too abrupt a move to privatize was shortsighted and legally risky, the legislature passed the Private Prison Contracting Act of 1986, which "limited the opportunity to privatize to a single, 180-bed state prison already under construction by the state" (Kyle, 1998:89).

Beasley's 1985 plan offered the state $100 million in cash for the right to manage the entire system with a 99 year lease, with the proviso that $250 million in capital expenditures be provided by CCA in exchange for a sum equal to the entire adult correctional budget for fiscal year 1986-87—approximately $170 million (Kyle, 1998; Chesteen, 1998). Concerns about the Constitutionality of prison privatization, as well as public opposition from AFCME and a Democrat-dominated legislature, helped forestall the push toward privatization. The Private Prisons Contracting Act of 1986, however, left the door open for the privatization of future prisons (Kyle, 1998; Select Oversight Committee on Corrections, 1995).

Finally, in 1991, then Governor Ned McWherter authorized a contract for CCA to run the South Central Correctional Center in Clifton, Tennessee. The initial contract was for a three-year period (1991–1994) mandating that "the performance of the contractor shall be compared to the performance of the State in operating similar facilities" (Select Oversight Committee on Corrections, 1995:2). "The objective was to compare public and private operation at basically the same type of physical plants." (Select Oversight Committee on Corrections, 1995:2). The legislation required a comparison of the performance and cost of the private operation to that of the State operation. Specifically, South Central would be compared to two other Tennessee facilities, Northwest Correctional Center and Northeast Correctional Center. "Importantly, for this comparative evaluation process, the three facilities being compared are nearly identical in physical space, design of housing units, infrastructure, support buildings, and administrative core" (Select Oversight Committee on Corrections, 1995:2).

At the conclusion of the three-year contract, a report by the Select Oversight Committee on Corrections (SOCC)—a report the U.S. General Accounting Office described as among the best comparative evaluations they've seen—became the subject of much controversy in the privatization debate (General Accounting Office, 1996). While Tennesseans were never provided a thorough presentation of the estimated costs of the proposed operation of the *entire* prison system, several studies of individual Tennessee facilities existed by the time of the most recent debate.

Tennessee Cost Assessments

As privatization advocate Charles Logan notes, "among claims made for the superiority of proprietary [private] prisons, the most frequent and most salient . . . is that they will be less expensive, or at least more efficient" (Logan, 1990:76). Not surprisingly, stakeholders on both sides of the privatization debate cling to reports which each finds favorable. Part of the problem is that calculating costs for prison systems across jurisdictions is a *very complex matter*—requiring a conflation of comparison costs between multiple facilities often differing in jurisdiction and type of inmate. This results in an "apples and oranges" kind of comparison that critics argue is neither reliable nor valid (Camp & Gaes, this volume; Shichor, 1995; General Accounting Office, 1996). The two primary claims about the cost-utility of privatization of prisons, however, are clear (see Shichor, 1995):

1. Private contractors claim they can operate prisons more cheaply and efficiently than state-based providers, resulting cost-savings for taxpayers; and that,

2. The quality of services provided by private vendors will be greater than or equal to those offered by state-based providers.

While there are situations and conditions (e.g., in *construction* of prisons) for which the evidence suggests that private prisons are more cost-effective than state prisons, the data are not uniform across the sites and generalizations about the private operation of prisons cannot be made across jurisdiction or region of the country (Shichor, 1995:136; see also Thomas, 1996c). For example, prison facilities differ in terms of institutional history and geographic location as well as in terms of overcrowding, history of violence, classification level of inmates, history of court intervention, and relative emphasis placed on achieving American Correctional Association (ACA) accreditation. *Thus, when privatized facilities are found to be more cost effective, the salient question is— why and under what conditions?* Because the essential argument in favor of prison privatization is that private vendors can provide "more for less," clearly some explanation is in order regarding exactly how private vendors accomplish this goal (see Camp and Gaes in this volume).

The first thing that must be stated about costs, as even key proponents of prison privatization like Charles Thomas concede, is that *costs are a highly regional phenomenon.* That is, when comparing costs it is vital that the comparisons be made between as-near-similar institutions as possible (Thomas, 1996c:12, fn20; GAO, 1996:5). It would be patently unfair, for example, to compare the costs of operating a prison in the rural South to the costs of operating a prison in Houston, Texas, or California—as this would greatly distort the averages.

Silverdale

The first-ever evaluation of the cost effectiveness of privatization of prisons, as it turns out, took place in Tennessee. In fact, the first contemporary county-level prison privatization contract in the United States was awarded in 1984 in Hamilton County, Tennessee, for the Silverdale Detention Center. A 1989 study of the facility claimed a 4 percent to 8 percent annual savings on the private facility (Logan & McGriff, 1989) with a subsequent re-examination of the same study (McDonald, 1990) stating that the actual savings was between 5 to 15 percent.

The Logan and McGriff study is by far the one most cited in favor of the argument that privatized facilities are in-fact cost effective—and Silverdale is by far the single-most evaluated private prison facility in the United States (see Logan, 1990; McDonald, 1990; Thomas, 1996c). Because of the frequency of its evaluation, Shichor (1995:214) refers to Silverdale as a "showcase" facility for the private corrections industry— "meaning that conditions may be different there than in other institutions because the company wants to prove the advantages of privatization." Silverdale had numerous operational and cost problems initially, however, with the Select Oversight Committee on Corrections noting: "There was an initial apparent lack of clarity regarding authority and responsibility, as it related to 'care, custody, and control' by the private operator" (Select Oversight Committee on Corrections, 1995:18).

As the August, 1996, General Accounting Office report *Private & Public Prisons* points out, one of the key difficulties in accurately evaluating costs between facilities is that facilities tend to greatly differ (Thomas, 1996c:12, fn20; Thomas, 1995; General Accounting Office, 1996:8). Each of the above-mentioned studies of Silverdale has been much criticized, both by the General Accounting Office and by independent scholars. In the first instance, concern developed that hidden costs were not factored into the analysis of the private facilities while they were used in analysis of the public facilities (Shichor, 1995:211). In a second study (General Accounting Office, 1996:30), a researcher sought to assess the quality of service from the inmates' perspective. While the study showed remarkably high inmate satisfaction with services at Silverdale, several major flaws in the study have been exposed.[1]

The Select Oversight Committee on Corrections Study

The U.S. General Accounting Office (GAO) report on prison privatization closely examined five studies in California, Texas, Washington, Tennessee, and New Mexico of the cost effectiveness of prison privatization (General Accounting Office, 1996). A central focus of that report was the Tennessee Select Oversight Committee on Corrections' evaluation of Tennessee's South Central Correctional Center (SCCC), run by CCA, and the Northeast and Northwest Correctional Centers, also located in Tennessee and run by the state, as authorized by the Private Prison Contracting Act of 1986. The SOCC's evaluation became central to the debate on prison privatization primarily because it purported to find virtually no difference in the cost or delivery of services between the public and the private facilities. In other words, the Select Oversight Committee on Correction's own evaluation offered little support for the argument of Tom Beasley: that his private company could "lock them up better, quicker, and for less."

It is worth noting here that the Select Oversight Committee on Corrections' report *also found* a higher rate of injuries to staff and prisoners at South Central, the CCA facility. States the report:

> The number of injuries to staff and prisoners is a measure of the security and safety of the facility. During the fifteen-month evaluation period, South Central Correctional Center reported significantly more injuries to prisoners and staff than either North East Correctional Center or North West Correctional Center, with 214 injuries reported at SCCC, 21 and 51 at North East Correctional Center and North West Correctional Center, respectively. The use of force is also reviewed when looking at the security and safety of a prison. The facilities have significantly different reported incidents of the use of force. South Central Correctional Center had 30 reported incidents, North East Correctional Center 4, and North West Correctional Center 6 (Select Oversight Committee on Corrections, 1995:viii).

The Select Oversight Committee on Corrections study, titled *Comparative Evaluation of Privately Managed CCA Prison and State-managed Prototypical Prisons*," was conducted in two phases, one assessing operational costs and the other assessing quality of service. The study compared three multi-custody (minimum to maximum inmate classification) prisons for male inmates. Findings from the study include the following:

> Using data that covered July 1993 through June 1994, the study concluded that the costs of operating the private and both state facilities were virtually identical. Specifically, the comparison showed that the average daily operational costs per inmate for the private prison were $35.39, versus $34.90 and $35.45, respectively, for the two public prisons (as cited by General Accounting Office, 1996:25).

> As can be seen from comparing the daily operating cost after adjustment for the variation in average daily census, the daily

operating cost of the two state facilities is $32.65 compared with the CCA cost of $33.25. This translates into an average annual cost of $11,917 per inmate day versus an annual cost per inmate to CCA of $12,136 or a difference of approximately 1.84%. The cost after adjustment for the allocation Department of Correction Central Office Cost to the three facilities shows an average cost for the state facilities of $35.23 per day versus $35.39 for the CCA facility, or a difference of less than one half of 1% (Select Oversight Committee on Corrections, 1995:2).

While there is still much haranguing about the quality of the study, several evaluations of the SOCC study have praised it, particularly that by the GAO.[2] The General Accounting Office, in its review of the SOCC's study, not only evaluated the SOCC's study itself; it also examined several other reviews of the SOCC study. A Washington study comparatively assessed the quality of services at the selected private and public prisons in Tennessee and Louisiana and two multi-custody male facilities in Washington. "The study concluded that the private and public prisons in the respective states (Tennessee and Louisiana) generally were similar in quality of service" (General Accounting Office, 1996:27). The Washington study found that: "The unadjusted operational costs of the three Tennessee facilities were similar. However, after adjustments to equalize the numbers of inmates, the private facility's average daily operational costs per inmate ($33.61) were slightly lower than the comparable costs for the two public facilities ($35.82 and $35.28, respectively)" (General Accounting Office, 1996:26).

In short, both the GAO and the Washington studies amounted to detailed re-assessments of Tennessee's own Select Oversight Committee on Corrections' evaluation of three facilities. All three of the studies address the cost-effectiveness and operational quality of the privately run prison versus the two owned and operated by the state. The GAO stated about the SOCC study:

"The overall performance scores were 98.49 for the private facility and 97.17 and 98.34, respectively, for the two public facilities" (General Accounting Office, 1996:25).[3]

Tennessee's 1997-98 Privatization Initiative: Three Public Deaths

Death Number 1

Unfortunately, details like those offered above were not the central issues driving the privatization debate in Tennessee. While the Tennessee media were quick to declare TSEA the victor, several crucial elements of the debate were never given adequate hearing. Certainly the story of "secret meetings" that broke on April 29, 1997, marked the beginning of the debate—and gave those politicians involved much to answer for from a suspicious press. A little noted point about those meetings, however, is the fact that Linda McCarty, Executive Director of the TSEA, and her legislative aide, Jo-Ann Davis, were also present on at least one occasion.[4] Several of the State's newspapers published editorials critical of the secret "closed-door" nature of those early meetings (Wade, 1997a, 1997b).

It was not the exclusion of the TSEA, however, that proved to be the critical element in the first failure of the initiative—it was the exclusion of key members of the Democratic Caucus in the Senate. At least three Senators, including Senator Steve Cohen, abruptly left when it became clear that the meeting was not open. When asked by a reporter (who had been excluded from the meeting) about the reason he was leaving, Cohen stated: "Enough has been done already that's not in the public eye. I don't think in the last three years we (Senate Democrats) have had a meeting on this issue. The bill has been done so much in secrecy at this point, everything ought to be open" (Sher, 1997:A-1).

By the time the bill's sponsors sought to rally the support of other legislators in early May, 1997, only weeks remained until the end of the session at the end of the month. After the SOCC completed its review, the bill would have had to pass through both the house and senate government and finance committees, and finally through the full legislature. While the SOCC held two subsequent public hearings on the issue during this stage of the initiative, these hearings generated more heat than light—with a preacher from Memphis being escorted from the forum, loudly berating the relationship between the House Speaker and CCA's chief lobbyist. The lion's share of the hearings, however, were devoted to statements made by correctional officers organized by the TSEA. During these first hearings, TSEA firmly made the point that the SOCC's own study of South Central Correctional Center provided little evidence of either cost savings or enhanced performance. If savings could not be compellingly demonstrated for one facility—a primarily minimum security facility, at that—TSEA argued, how could the state rush to judgment on an effort to privatize the entire system?

Undeterred, Lt. Governor John Wilder introduced the bill in the Senate, attempting to unify Senate Democrats and appease criticism by the rank and file in the legislature. Said Wilder: "Some members of the Senate feel like they were left out. But nobody has been left out. The bill is now filed. This is the first official action. . . . Now it's going to Corrections Oversight and that's where it's going to be reviewed. I want the Senate to know the speaker is not pushing, the Speaker is presenting" (Locker, 1997a:B-1; Wade, 1997c:B-1). After several meetings by the legislative sponsors attempting to revise various elements of the bill in time for a vote before the end of the session, too much time had passed and Senator Jim Kyle announced that the bill could not be considered until July (Ferrar, 1997:A-4). Said Kyle: "The committee is going to come back in July and begin delving into this issue in an orderly fashion" (Locker, 1997d:B-1).

The first public death of the (1997) effort to privatize Tennessee's prison system had occurred. Mismanagement on the part of the bill's legislative sponsors, who relied on insider connections and a pro-privatization Governor to carry the bill forward—rather than on effectively lobbying the bill to the rank and file members of the House and Senate—proved to be the pivotal undoing of the initiative at this stage. As one Senator put it to us off the record, "That bill was dead on arrival— the most ineffectively lobbied bill I have ever seen. There was the sense that this came down from the top. . . . Now, we have big egos in the legislature and we don't like to be left out . . ."

The Second Death

In July, the SOCC did indeed come back to the issue more systematically, holding additional hearings, during which private correctional service vendors presented their arguments in favor of privatization. The primary argument made by these vendors was that privatization would introduce "fair competition" into the operation of corrections and that such competition would enhance the performance of state-operated facilities as well as save the state money. It would be unwise, argued the six other vendors aside from CCA, to offer a contract for the entire state to a single company. Multiple vendors and a gradual phasing-in of privatization would offer the State more protection and a better bargaining position (see Gilbert's Chapter 3 "How Much Is Too Much Privatization of Criminal Justice?," this volume).

Estimates on the amount of money to be saved varied wildly, with initial claims by CCA of saving $100 million, to revised claims of savings of up to $25 million. No specific numbers were ever presented, however, in part because the State had yet to issue an RFP specifying precisely what services and facilities it wanted to contract for. The hired consultant to the SOCC ultimately suggested scaling back the initial proposal to privatize the entire system, to privatizing 60 to 70 percent of the system.

Other changes to the initial bill included a phasing-in of privatization, with ultimately 30-40 percent of the State's prisons to be kept under State control. In other words, there would be no immediate carte-blanch transfer of the entire prison system to a single private company. Moreover, there was wide agreement that private companies would be required to offer jobs to all current state prison system employees— though they could require work transfers to other facilities, a lessening of employee benefits, and the possibility that eventually some jobs would be eliminated.

By far the most important development during this stage of the initiative, however, was Governor Don Sundquist's proposal to restructure state oversight of corrections, with the creation of a new executive branch state agency, the *Tennessee Department of Criminal Justice*. Under Sundquist's proposal, the Governor would retain sole authority to authorize which prisons would be privatized or closed, as well as the terms under which privatized facilities would be managed, opened, and contracted for. Sundquist would also keep total control over the monitoring of contracts to private prison vendors, with monitoring officials from the new *Department of Criminal Justice* being part of the executive branch.[5]

In late October, 1997, Democratic Senator Jim Kyle, Chair of the Select Oversight Committee on Corrections, remarked about the possibility of the Governor gaining complete control of the proposed privatization apparatus for the state: "As chairman of this committee, I'm uncomfortable with that idea" (Wade, 1997d:B-1). At that point the Committee adjourned, scheduled to return to take a final vote on the legislation November 4-5, 1997. Meanwhile, the SOCC's consultant issued a report to the committee drawing into question vendors' claims that they could save the state up to 50 percent of its correctional operating budget. He also noted that the state's own Department of Corrections, if also allowed the flexibility of closing older facilities and building new ones, could cut its own costs by 30 percent.

On November 5, Senator Kyle announced: "The consensus on the committee is that there should be joint legislative and executive branch decisionmaking on this venture. . . . Now we're waiting for the sponsors and the administration to come to an agreement" (Wade, 1997c:B-1). Here a key difference of opinion emerged between the bill's legislative sponsors and the SOCC, with co-sponsor of the bill Representative Matt Kisber stating: "I feel that the executive branch, and the governor as the CEO of the executive branch, has to have the responsibility to run the departments vested in the administrative branch" (Wade, 1997d:B-1). The legislature broke for holiday recess, with no action being taken on the bill. Later that day, Governor Sundquist issued a statement: "I'm not in favor of any dilution of my authority over prisons" (Wade, 1997d:B-1).

After the holidays and with the legislature back in session, Governor Sundquist indicated his intention to throw his full support behind yet a newer version of the bill drafted by his staff. This newest bill would be co-sponsored by Representatives Kisber and Walley, Lt. Governor John Wilder, and Senate Republican leader Ben Atchley. In Sundquist's new proposal, up to 70 percent of Tennessee's prisons could be privatized and would be monitored under the supervision of a to-be-created *Tennessee Department of Criminal Justice*—which would remain under the jurisdiction of the executive branch. In preparation for the debate, Sundquist appointed a five-member "advisory council" on prison privatization, including himself, Lt. Governor John Wilder, House Speaker Jimmy Naifeh, Finance Commissioner John Ferguson, and Comptroller William Snodgrass (West, 1998a:A-1).

With legislative leaders from the SOCC having invited a compromise from the Governor and legislative sponsors before the holiday recess— legislative support for the effort was waning (Associated Press, 1998a; Wade, 1997e). In an effort to bolster the bill, Lt. Governor John Wilder called another meeting—*to which all 132 Tennessee legislators were invited*—outlining the specifics of Sundquist's proposal. By early March, SOCC members were hinting at their disapproval, with SOCC member Senator Bob Rochelle stating: "The (Governor's) bill does not state any purpose, objective or goal the state is trying to accomplish by reorganizing the Department of Correction or expanding the state's authority to contract for prison management services" (Associated Press, 1998a:A-12).

On March 31, 1998, co-sponsor Ben Atchley conceded Sundquist's bill did not have the votes for passage in the Senate's *State and Local Government Committee*. "We still have some work to do here," he stated (West, 1998b:A-7). Atchley indicated, furthermore, that many legislators remained opposed to giving prison control to a new Commissioner of Criminal Justice who worked for the Governor under the auspices of a new *Tennessee Department of Criminal Justice* (West, 1998b:A-7).

Unable to garner the necessary committee votes, Sundquist's refusal to compromise effectively put the privatization initiative back to square one. Stated Atchley: "We lost the momentum. I think a fresh start may be what's needed" (Associated Press, 1998b). Atchley's co-sponsor Lt. Governor John Wilder stated: "It's not ready to be passed. It's not over yet, but it's over for this session" (Locker, 1998:A-1). A statement released on April 14 by the Governor read: "The Governor still supports the concept of prison privatization and he plans to work legislatively and administratively to see that it happens" (Locker, 1998:A-1).

The Third Death

With Lt. Governor John Wilder's promise to revive the privatization effort in the next legislative session quite clear, Tennesseans expected more wrangling over the issue in the Fall of 1998. Despite facing a re-election bid that November, Governor Sundquist was the strong favorite for re-election, facing a little known Democrat with one-tenth of the funding of the Governor for his campaign. What Sundquist could not have predicted during this third phase of the initiative, however, was that CCA would provide the worst possible backdrop for political supporters of privatization: A seemingly unending series of news stories about escapes, murders, and riots in CCA facilities in Tennessee and around the country.

The first and most dramatic incident impacting local perception of CCA's competence was the dramatic set of events, which took place at the Northeast Ohio Correctional Center in Youngstown, Ohio. Several high-profile escapes and stabbings at that facility received intense media coverage in the Tennessee press. The local media immediately sought the reaction of legislative leaders to the events at CCA's Youngstown facility. Most damaging in the reports from Youngstown were allegations (subsequently proven) that the incidents involved inmates illegally transferred from Washington, DC. Reports of high employee turnover and extreme violence at Youngstown saturated the news in Tennessee and raised additional questions about whether out-of-state inmates should be housed in Tennessee. There were roughly 1,600 out-of-state inmates in CCA facilities around the state at the time of the Youngstown incidents.

A number of reporters and one state senator, Pete Springer, traveled to Ohio to investigate the incidents. Senator Springer later returned to Ohio to offer testimony to the Ohio Legislature on prison privatization problems in Tennessee (Hartmann, 1998:E-1). A key concern for Senator Springer was that the Youngstown incident seemed to revolve around a failure to select inmates for transfer according to their custody classification; that is, a failure to transfer the types of inmates specified in the contract. Springer made this a key plank in his re-election campaign, underway at the time. Representative Phil Pinion, a member of the SOCC stated in the aftermath of these events: "The reaction I've gotten from members of the Tennessee legislature and the general public is it looks like we don't need to be going into something like privatization especially after what happened in Ohio," (Wade, 1998a:B-1),

In addition to the events in Ohio, however, several embarrassing and ill-timed incidents plagued CCA facilities in Tennessee. First, on September 4, 1998, a rapist managed to escape from Hardeman County Correctional Facility. Two weeks later, reports of a racially motivated stabbing incident at the same facility made headlines here. While the initial story released by CCA after the incident was that one inmate was hurt, a follow-up story indicated that the event was racially motivated and involved "about 70 inmates" (Aldrich, 1998:A-11).

Facing an election in roughly two months, key sponsors of the bill started to waver. Matt Kisber—sponsor of the original privatization legislation in 1997—stated in response to the reports from Youngstown:

> I think there is no question that the problems in Ohio make legislators more uncomfortable since they do not have information as to what is the cause of the problems and what could be done to prevent them. My advice to any private contractor doing business with a government entity is that disclosure is the best disinfectant. If there are problems, being under the

light of sunshine tends to help find solutions to them . . . If its
going to save money but risk public safety, that's not good
enough (Aldrich, 1998:A-11).

Kisber's public withdrawal was a serious blow: "Any time a primary
proponent of an issue this controversial drops out, it does raise some
concerns," said Representative Page Walley, a co-sponsor of the revised
bill (Wade, 1998a:B-1). While first sticking firmly behind privatization—
despite news of the events at Youngstown and in Tennessee, by the end
of the month Governor Sundquist himself announced he would not
pursue legislation authorizing prison privatization in the next legislative
year, 1999. "There has been a lot of coverage and focus on recent incidents, on incident reporting and notification. There are some fair questions that have been raised that we think should be answered . . . and we
didn't do a good job of quantifying cost savings" (Wade, 1998b:B-1).

Discussion: The Assault on Community Values

The mismanagement on the part of the privatization initiative's legislative sponsors—and on the part of CCA itself—had more to do with
the recent demise of the proposal to privatize Tennessee's prison system
than did any grass-roots level opposition to privatization organized by the
state employee's union or that of other activists. The Tennessee State
Employees Association was vocal with legislators and visible with
protests, but this public activism had little to do with the actual failure
of the privatization effort. Betty Anderson, chief lobbyist for CCA, stated after the bill's withdrawal: "I have to congratulate the state employees
group. They did a good job amassing their numbers" (Locker, 1998:A-1).
Her statement belies CCA's own role in driving the final stake through
the heart of the initiative. While the effort to privatize Tennessee's prisons did not provide for a thorough debate on the substantive issues of
prison privatization—it did raise serious concerns about the efficacy of
grassroots politics in correctional public policymaking.

Privatization Rhetoric: Fair Competition
and The Free Market

One of our main concerns about the rhetoric used in support of
prison privatization in Tennessee—that remained unchecked in the
public debate—is the notion that service vendors in the private prison
industry are somehow exemplary of the "free market." A key argument
put forward in favor of privatization in Tennessee was that allowing private vendors to manage state prisons would provide for "fair competi-

tion," with private vendors saving money and thereby forcing the state-run prisons to operate with more efficiency for fear of losing their own contracts. In other words, by expanding the number of "service providers" beyond the traditional state-run prison system, privatization proponents argued something like the "invisible hand" of free market competition would keep costs down.

Of course, a detail not pointed out by privatization proponents in Tennessee is the fact that the traditional free market formula for fair competition is one in which those taking the most risk stand to gain the most profit (not to mention that risk exists in a free market because of a proliferation of comparable market competitors) (see National Institute of Justice, 1987). In the private prisons industry at the time, however, CCA clearly had a near *monopoly* on the industry, dominating 52 percent of the market. In the case of the private prison industry, we find that economic benefits of privatization are retained by private contractors while the risks of privatization are socialized and transferred to taxpayers who take on the lion's share of risk (e.g., legal liability/cost of increasing incarceration/need for more prisons). In all the discussion of efficiency, it is worth remembering that the most efficient prison operation would not include a "profit margin"—just a "cost margin."

The rhetoric of privatization provides a set of strategies that play upon the public's loathing (and misunderstanding) of crime and criminals—in order to bilk the public out of ever-diminishing collective resources and transfer public wealth into private hands. Public hatred of criminals provides the best possible basis for converting public money into private hands, without getting the public to question the transfer.

What concerns us most, however, about the privatization paradigm is the utter *passivity* engendered by its adherents. There is no individual citizen-based action plan whatsoever with regard to *reducing* crime. Beyond proposals inevitably prescribed by the relatively few people capable of making short-term profit on crime, in our view government facilitation of prison privatization amounts to government malfeasance of duty (e.g., by government's failure to devise means by which crime is reduced, rather than accommodated and profited on through privatization).

At its current stage of development, the debate about prison privatization is preoccupied with short-term "micro-management" issues such as per diem costs, contract monitoring, cost savings through employee benefit reductions, etc.—and not at all attentive to the longer-term "macro-policy" issues raised by its emergence. Essentially we are missing the forest for the trees—in that we have given over any deliberation on ways to reduce crime in favor of making profit on ever larger numbers of offenders.

Fixing some social problems might not be profitable; additionally, infrastructure spending has commonly been understood as a long term investment strategy (Palumbo, 1994). In the privatization paradigm, however, citizen/consumers are expected to sit back and wait for what the market offers up—with only passive concern for the collective amelioration of social ills beyond what the market supports. In sum, strategies for *profit taking* on human beings come before strategies of *investment* in human beings.

EPILOGUE—Contracting with Cities and Counties: Privatization Through the Back Door

The old adage from the 1960's "THINK GLOBALLY, ACT LOCALLY" applies well to CCA. While foregoing (for now) the effort to gain control of the state's entire prison system, CCA has still managed to acquire more than 7,000 beds in Tennessee by contracting with counties and cities for jail space. Tennessee currently has roughly 20,000 inmates in the state system—and CCA has more than 7,000 prisoners at the "local level"—many of whom are state prisoners from other states. By contracting with the counties, CCA circumvents the need for either legislative authority or executive order required for democratic approval of prison privatization as a correctional policy (see National Institute of Justice, 1987, for a critique of this practice). In the facilities CCA currently operates in Tennessee, they house inmates from other states. Local politics being less public and cumbersome than state politics, targeting job-hungry and/or impoverished rural jurisdictions has proven to be an effective strategy for the private prison industry all over the country.

Correctional privatization seems to be shifting towards a new grassroots politics in which the emphasis on market expansion may be increasingly concentrated on attaining excess capacity in local confinement facilities. Those opposed to correctional privatization will soon need to fragment their efforts and mobilize at the county and city level—jurisdiction by jurisdiction.

Endnotes

[1]   First, in surveying of the inmates, the researcher had a prison chaplain distribute questionnaires to those he thought capable of answering them. In other words, routine random assignment was not followed in the research, hopelessly biasing the data produced. Moreover, because the research subjects in this case were literally members of a "captive audience," concerns have been raised about the possibility that inmates provided information to the authorities that they felt "they might want to hear" (see Shichor, 1995:212-214).

[2]   About the several studies of prison privatization the GAO examined:

> These studies offer little generalizable guidance for other jurisdictions about what to expect regarding comparative operational costs and quality of service if they were to move toward privatizing correctional facilities. First, several of the studies focused on specialized inmate populations, such as those in pre-release situations that limited their generalizability to a wider inmate population. Second, methodological weaknesses in some of the comparisons—such as using hypothetical facilities or non-random survey samples—make some findings questionable, even for the study setting. Third, a variety of differences in other states and regions could result in experiences far different from those of the states that were studied. For example, cost of living and a state's correctional philosophy could affect the comparative costs and quality of private and public facilities from state to state. Finally, the age or maturity of the private system could affect the relationship between private and public facilities in terms of costs and quality (1996:4).

[3]   Why GAO chose to play down the SOCC's findings of higher incidents of violence with staff and inmates is unclear. It remains equally unclear why Tennessee's Select Oversight Committee on Corrections failed to more critically examine the higher rate of injuries due to violence in the private facility: "During the fifteen-month period, SCCC reported significantly more injuries to prisoners and staff than either NECC or NWCC, with 214 injuries reported at SCCC, 21 and 51 at NECC and NWCC respectively" (Select Oversight Committee on Corrections, 1995:66).

[4]   Personal conversation, May 1997.

[5]   This, of course, violates a fundamental guideline for privatization offered by the U.S. Department of Justice—that independent monitors be part of the legislatively authorized use of privatization.

11 The Right to Profit: Promoting Economic Gain in the Name of Public Interest

Steven Jay Cuvelier and Dennis W. Potts
Sam Houston State University

Private contractors provide most products consumed by the government, from jet fighters to paper clips. And while there are instances in which the relationship between the public and private sectors may be called into question on moral or ethical grounds (Christie, 1995), few would suggest that the government should get into the business of manufacturing products for itself. So, if it is appropriate for the government to contract for consumables in virtually all areas of its operation, why should there be any problem with contracting for criminal justice services as well?

In many cases, the answer to this question is clearly "nothing." Many private sector services add value to the functions of criminal justice operations. Drug testing, electronic monitoring, ignition interlock devices, and psychological services are a few areas in which the private sector supports the administration of justice. In their ancillary roles, private providers offer expertise and specialty services more cost-effectively than individual government agencies could provide for themselves. This would be most likely observed where an economy of scale enables private providers to amortize their costs across a wider client base than may be available to a given governmental agency (for example an electronic monitoring provider serving many probation departments). The private sector must, at very least, sell the *perception,* if not the reality, of cost-effectiveness, when marketing services to government.

A key marketing strategy is not to sell a product directly, but to sell the *need* for the product one provides. While selling a need to private consumers is commonly accepted, selling a need when the public interest is involved is tantamount to setting public policy. For example, a provider of electronic monitoring services or ignition interlock devices may seek to persuade decisionmakers to change laws or practices in ways that broaden the use of, or lengthen the time that individuals are kept under, technological control, selling this on a public safety rationale. The motive is profit but the stated rational is public safety. What elected official would take a stand against public safety? Under these conditions, differentiating between a marketing strategy and a policy manipulation may well depend upon which side of the profit-making fence one is standing.

Public interest is a key factor in considering the appropriateness of private involvement in a governmental function. Gilbert (1996a:17) defines public interest as "the institutions, practices, and values that promote the well being of every member of society: the common interests and values we share; the public goods and services we provide; and the sacrifices we make for others." As the profit motive enters into a government function, economic interests may supplant public interests and the sovereignty of government may be lost through the policy manipulations of profit-seekers (see Gilbert 1996a, 1996b for a discussion of these issues).

This chapter illustrates the interplay of economic and public interests in pretrial release by examining the actions of the bail bond industry in confronting the trend toward government-sponsored pretrial release programs. An examination of the commercial bail industry's response to this trend provides a unique opportunity to study private sector response to policy changes that have brought increased governmental involvement in areas of established private sector function. This examination may offer insight into the private sector response in many areas of criminal justice play, should the public interest turn to favor less profitable alternatives.

This chapter is organized into four parts. The first part briefly reviews the history and development of bail and pretrial services agencies (PTSAs). The second part examines the nature of the conflict between the private and public sectors, with special emphasis on Harris County (Houston), Texas, and the actions taken by members of the bail insurance industry. The third part builds a conceptual framework to better understand the underpinnings of this public/private sector conflict. And the fourth part concludes by connecting the actions taken by the commercial bail industry to the potential for future public/private sector conflicts in other areas of criminal justice.

The Private and Public Side of Pretrial Release

Unlike most areas of criminal justice, arranging pretrial release has historically been a private sector function, that has experienced a shift in public interest and increased involvement by government. This section examines the development, role, and relationship between commercial bail and pretrial services agencies.

The Development of Commercial Bail

The American system of bail springs from British common law, rooted in Anglo-Saxon traditions. Bail appeared in a recognizable form in the Assize of Clarendon in 1166, was refined in the Magna Carta in 1215 (Goldkamp, Gottfredson, Jones & Weiland, 1995), and by 1689 the English Bill of Rights included a prohibition of excessive bail (Goldfarb, 1965:27). The English system of bail was based upon personal surety, where persons, typically family members, would pledge property to the court as assurance that the accused would appear for trial. The bond that the accused was held by was, in the end, a social bond. The strength of the relationship between the accused and the sureties measured the strength of constraint placed upon the accused.

The American justice system imported the bail concept, with the prohibition of excessive bail written into the Eighth Amendment of the American Constitution (Goldfarb, 1965:22-27). The Judicial Act of 1789 further authorized bail for all but capital offenses (Goldfarb, 1965:29). But the translation of bail from an island nation to a largely unexplored continent changed the administration of bail significantly. With relatively low levels of mobility and long-standing family roots, the English system worked off of the interpersonal constraints of family to assure the defendant's appearance in court. In the United States, the presence of family ties and property were not as common. The accused often did not have the property or the family connections to stand as sureties for the court. But certain citizens, with the means to do so, would stand in as sureties for the accused, for a fee. Like a banker making a loan, the surety would collect sufficient fee payments and collateral to cover the risk of forfeiture and make a profit (Goldfarb, 1965:100).

While the American system of bail still evinces its English roots, the retreat from interpersonal to financial assurances markedly changed its function. With the gap between the financial demands of bail and the large number of defendants who could not raise the amount of money to secure a bond created a profitable opportunity for entrepreneurs. Goldfarb (1965:95) suggests that the growth and development of the bail industry was aided when judges set bail at $1,000, intending that the defendants would be required to put up $100. This indicates a degree of accommodation between the public and private sectors. The private sector filled a void created between the offering of bail and defendant's ability to post bail. The public sector, in turn, seems to have anticipated, and thereby encouraged, the use of commercial bail.

In time, bail bonds posted by insurance companies, backed by large cash reserves, began to supplant the private bail agents' pledge of personal property. Bail insurance company agents function in much the same way as traditional bail agents, but they act only as representatives for the surety company. All bail agents function as marketing representatives, a role that includes identifying and contacting customers, and executing contracts for bail. As with any business, a key objective of these surety companies is to maximize gross revenues while minimizing administrative overhead and exposure to financial loss.

The bail agent is the only non-public actor who directly affects the administration of bail and exerts perhaps a stronger influence on the defendants' bid for freedom than any other non-judicial actor (Wice, 1984:50). The only time forfeiture occurs is when a defendant fails to appear in court. If a defendant is arrested for another crime while out on bail, the agent can surrender the bond, thereby escaping liability. Alternatively, if the court sets bail for the new charge, the defendant is likely to turn to his or her original agent for the new bond. The bail agent's profit is not compromised by new offenses committed by a client, only the client's failure to appear in court. Is it any wonder that bond agents hire bounty hunters to recapture bail jumpers, but do not include supervision for their clients?

The American system of bail has had many outspoken critics and would-be reformers over the years (e.g., de Toqueville, 1969; Beeley, 1927; Goldfarb, 1965; President's Commission on Law Enforcement and Administration of Justice, 1967; Wice, 1984). Nevertheless, today some 8,000 licensed bail agents take in more than $4 billion annually (Chamberlin, 1998:14), netting a profit of about $400 million (Parenti, 1997:23).

The Bail Industry's View of Its Role

George L. Will, then Executive Director of the American Society of Professional Bail Bondsmen, testified before the Senate Constitutional Rights Subcommittee on behalf of the commercial bail industry in 1964. In his testimony, Will made the following assertions (Goldfarb, 1965:119-123):

1. [Bondsmen] have ensured that the American citizen receives equal justice under the law by enforcing his attendance to the courts.

2. The bail bond system is the very foundation of justice, in that it ensures that the machinery of justice does not break down.

3. The role of the bondsman is to release good risks. The business is so highly competitive that any good risk can secure a bond.

4. The bondsman performs a valuable service that is available to all.

5. If a "mistake" is made [a defendant fails to appear] the bondsman "pays" for his mistake by forfeiting the bond to the court.

6. Bondsmen save the taxpayers millions of dollars a year.

7. The poor indigent is the poorest risk, and it is for this reason that he remains in jail pending trial . . . [because] . . . there is no such thing as a "good risk indigent."

8. It is not the fault of the bondsman that indigent defendants languish in jail, but the courts for violating the defendant's constitutional rights to a speedy trial.

9. Who should control the keys to the jail? The independent businessman or the social parasite [public servant] who infiltrates government and lives off the fruits of another's labor and business.

10. If government can seize control of a business that has served the public for more than 100 years, they can and will socialize every business and profession. In essence, government encroachment on the bond business is an attack on free enterprise.

Based upon the line of argument used more recently by representatives of the bail insurance industry, we will find in a coming section that the industry's position has not changed substantially in the last 30 years.

The Commercial Bail Industry's Position on Pretrial Services Agencies (The Manifesto)

A recent publication titled *Methods of Exposing the Fraud of Pre-Release* outlines a method of attack by which bail agents can undermine government-sponsored release alternatives. Published by *Bail USA*, a Pennsylvania bail company, this manifesto recommends the following steps:

1. Meet with [local] bondsmen . . . Secure their commitment to support the effort [and] select . . . a liaison person.

2. Gather data and/or statistics from the county (example: single sensational examples of misuse of OR release, PTSA budgetary information) . . .

3. [Confer] with most . . . receptive (generally, the most conservative) . . . elected officials [who] control the purse strings.

4. Meet with the elected official and "educate" him on such things as:

    a. who we are and why we are there,

    b. the economic and public safety "costs" of public bail,

    c. how other counties . . . are . . . challenging [free bail] as not being proper use of tax dollars, and

    d. how using our industry is a far better choice. Gently encourage him to put [these issues]: on the . . . hearing. Arrange to address the board at that meeting. Keep at this with any necessary official until this step is accomplished.

5. Appear at the county board of commissioners/supervisors and make a presentation, urging a "review" of the actual effectiveness, value, and track record of [the pretrial services agency].

6. Follow this up with [a] memorandum, zero in on economics and recidivism.

7. Support this "encouragement to examine" by personal contacts to conservative county officials and state legislators.

8. Continue to send county officials selected data at timely intervals-keep the issue alive with them. Offer "support" if needed or desired.

9. Keep local bondsmen and liaison fully apprised, and "coach" liaison on exactly what bondsmen can do to help because during all of this, good public relations actions, are central.

10. Maintain heavy monitoring and follow until [the] goal (cutting PTS budget) is achieved.

11. Meet with professional groups and associations, get the message out there. Raise public awareness of this abuse of tax dollars.

This manifesto outlines a plan of attack in which the local bail agents organize into a political action committee and launch an 'information' blitz, targeting the decision-makers who will be most receptive to their cause. The plan clearly uses a message of concern for the public interest to mask their economic motivation of suppressing competition. Bail agents find allies in conservative politicians who would readily favor public-choice economics (Gilbert, 1996a:16). From this perspective, the private sector is assumed to be more effective and efficient than government bureaucracies. By starting with the assumption that private industry best serves public interest, bail agents may engage in a smear campaign against pretrial agencies without putting their own performance to the test. We will refer to these directives as we examine the commercial bail industry's attack on the Harris County Pretrial Services Agency as we discuss the conflict between private and public pretrial release.

The Development of Pretrial Services Agencies

A milestone in bail reform came in the form of the Vera Foundation's Manhattan Bail Project (Ares, Rankin & Sturz, 1963), initiated in 1961. Through interviews with defendants prior to arraignment, project workers sought to identify defendants who would be good risks for personal recognizance release. The reported success of the project served as the model for the formation of pretrial services agencies and the popularization of "community ties" as an alternative to wealth as a measure of trustworthiness.

Pretrial services agencies were born out of the recognition that the commercial bail business was not serving the wide range of defendants, but catering to those with the financial means to afford the bail agent's service. In principle, one cannot lay blame on the private sector for turning away unprofitable business; social justice is a responsibility of government. Making release through pretrial services agencies possible to trustworthy but indigent defendants is not a major point of contention, even from the bail agents. But, extending the concept farther, how do you justifiably deny a release through a pretrial services agency to someone on the basis that the defendant has money to pay a commercial bail agent? Can the government legitimately deny low-cost release alternatives to defendants on the basis of financial means?

The concern for indigent offenders in the 1960s was replaced in the 1970s with a concern for the victim. The ideology that all defendants are entitled to consideration for pretrial services release was replaced with the belief that public safety is also a consideration in release decisions. In *Williams v. Illinois* (1970), the Court held that use of fines in lieu of jail denies equal protection of the law to the indigent. The inability to raise a certain amount of money does not justify imprisonment. In *Tate v. Short* (1971), the Court held that to imprison an indigent offender for nonpayment of a fine imposed in lieu of jail was also unconstitutional. Because imprisonment was imposed solely because of indigency.

The District of Columbia Court Reform and Criminal Procedure Act of 1970 (Pub. L. No. 91-358, 84 Stat. 473) legislatively created a new purpose for bail. Bail should be denied to defendants who would pose a danger to other persons or the community. The Federal Bail Reform Act of 1984 (18 USC §3142(e)) permits pretrial detention of defendants on the finding that "no condition or combination of conditions will reasonably assure . . . the safety of any other person and the community." This act allows preventative detention in federal criminal trials. *United States v. Salerno* (1987) affirmed that the constitutionally acceptable goals of bail include public safety. The majority opinion held that preventive detention is not punishment and therefore not prohibited by the Fifth Amendment, nor does it violate the Eighth Amendment's prohibition against unreasonable bail. While Gain (1989) suggests that there is more at issue than the decision addresses, the case has nevertheless affirmed the centrality of public safety in the pretrial release decision. This affirmation places great weight upon the system's ability to gather and process information, and the ability of behavioral science to devise valid assessments of risk.

The Pretrial Services Agency Role

Pretrial services are provided as an administrative support to judges. Pretrial services officers (PTOs) do not make release decisions. They are often the first to learn of personal information regarding the defendant. On the basis of this information, certain recommendations may be offered to the judge. The primary function of the PTSA is to provide whatever support the judges require in making appropriate pretrial decisions about the release of particular defendants. In addition, PTSAs provide administrative support to judicial oversight of released defendants, providing supervision, drug testing, and many other services the judge may order as a condition of pretrial release.

The Pretrial Services Agency View of the Commercial Bond Industry

As governmental agencies, PTSAs do not actually make public statements, however, through the National Association of Pretrial Services Agencies (NAPSA) and the Pretrial Services Resource Center (PSRC), the points of view that represent a significant number of the people working in PTSAs may be heard. Much of the philosophy underlying government sponsored pretrial release is echoed in the writing found in the newsletters and literature disseminated by these two national organizations.

> . . . never leave the high ground. Bonding for profit is wrong. Every national organization that has examined criminal justice has called for its abolition. It shares characteristics of slavery, racism, and sexism, and as such, should be eliminated. (Henry, 1993:2)

In other publications, the pretrial services community disseminates information intended to counter detractors' claims regarding the use of pretrial agency releases Kennedy (1994:13-16) offers six strategies for addressing assertions by proponents of the bail industry:

- Frame the argument about pretrial release options to reflect real issues. Instead of answering claims of high costs and failure rates, assert that PTSAs supply information and assistance and screening to the judge for defendant management purposes.

- Collect and keep accurate local pretrial data.

- Keep up with the literature on bail bonding and pretrial release.

- Enlist the support of others who are opposed to commercial surety bail.

- Educate others about the benefits of pretrial services agencies.

- Cite other types of financial release. When there is a call for financial obligation, there are other forms of financial release, such as deposit bail.

The PSRC's strategy has a number of similarities with the commercial bond industry strategy, however the actions are more clearly defensive. There is no suggestion of assailing the commercial bond industry, but rather, fending off attacks. This is understandable in that a government agency that attacks a private sector rival would raise serious issues regarding the role of government in the private sector. Yet, when the private sector assaults the public, the reverse question is rarely raised.

The Conflict Between the Private and Public Pretrial Release: The Harris County Experience

Typically, conflict occurs when two or more entities vie for a common goal that only one may achieve. In terms of the bail bond business, commercial bail and PTSA activities are only indirectly related. Commercial bail's 'competitor' is actually the judge. It is a judicial decision to offer pretrial release, PTSAs gather information to facilitate decision-making and provide the operational means to act on the judge's decision. PTSAs also address the public safety concerns by providing supervision services and allows non-market values to operate in making eligibility for pretrial release available to everyone, not just those with financial resources. But the bail agents cannot take the judges on directly. So, they attempt to limit the judge's choices by trying to discredit the PTSA, or cast doubt as to the effectiveness or ethics of the PTSA and its employees. Bail agents seek to maximize profits by undermining confidence in a governmental agency whose primary responsibility is to provide decision-making information to judges and carry out judicial wishes as to the disposition and supervision of pretrial populations.

In sum, bail agents and PTSAs operate in very different niches in the criminal justice system. Whereas the bail agents are independent business persons, doing the business the market will bear, the PTSAs operate as executors of judicial decisionmaking by providing defendant information, facilitating court-imposed measures, such as drug testing and supervision. It is actually the judge that is responsible for executing the personal bonds that are in direct competition with the commercial bond agents. Realistically, the bond agents cannot afford to alienate the judges so their attack must be indirect, attempting to undermine the infrastructure that makes the personal bond a viable option for the courts.

The Precipitating Event

It is not uncommon for criminal justice policy to result from one or more precipitating events. These events are usually tragic, highly visible, occur at just the right time, and are accompanied by a motivated leadership cadre ready to galvanize support for a particular position. But the importance of each event to the development of criminal justice policy lies not in the event itself; it lies in the applicability of the event to a particular political or policy agenda.

We begin our examination of the conflict in Harris County by recounting two tragic crimes committed by defendants who were out on bail awaiting trial. In each case the victim was a woman who was surprised in a public place and shot to death, but the individual tragedies were themselves not at issue. One criminal event assumed greater significance as the focal point for a bail industry attack on the pretrial services agency.

May 15, 1994

Dr. Beth Peavy stopped at a Houston convenience store for gasoline and candy. She was approached by Tony Dixon, a mentally impaired 17-year-old who was about to carry out a barely conceived carjacking. Dixon shot Peavy at least five times with no apparent warning, dragged her body from her car, and drove away from the scene.

Dixon, who had no history of violence, was on a personal bond administered by the pretrial services agency, awaiting trial on a burglary charge. At the time of the murder, Dixon was home on a pass from the distant shelter where he was living while awaiting trial (Bardwell, Makeig, Liebrum, Milling & Johnson, 1994).

June 12, 1995

Soon after the end of their relationship, Clinton Dillard lured Mable Ann Edison to a motel room where he pointed a shotgun at her and held a knife to her throat. Edison talked her way out of the situation and filed charges. But Dillard secured a $10,000 surety bond release on June 1ˢᵗ.

On the afternoon of June 12, 1995, Edison left her office at a downtown Houston bank. While walking to her car, Edison was approached by her ex-boyfriend, Dillard. After a brief argument, Dillard produced a shotgun he had been hiding in a pillow, chased Edison down, shot her repeatedly, and fled.

Two days after the murder, while Dillard was still at large, the bondsman filed an affidavit of surrender, thereby sparing himself the cost of forfeiture on the original charges (Vara, 1995; Asin, 1996).

Both of these tragic stories are true and the events occurred in Houston barely one year apart, but the impact of each on the criminal justice system was strikingly different. Peavy's murder precipitated a concerted effort to abolish pretrial agency release and ended with the death penalty for Dixon. Edison's murder seemed to pass quietly from public attention with a life sentence for Dillard.

What explanations are there for the differences in public reaction to these two tragedies? While certainly the public fear of crime is most deeply felt in Peavy's tragic end, we also see a private sector influence that cannot be ignored. The case of Dr. Beth Peavy became a tool by which the bail industry sought to gain market share at the expense of the Pretrial Services Agency. Much publicity was brought to Dr. Peavy's murder by bail industry representatives for the purpose of discrediting the PTSA, in the bid for a market share, Tony Dixon was tried in the court of public opinion extensively before being brought to trial. One can only speculate on the influence the publicity could have had on the outcome of his case.

A Chronology of Events

We can see the bail industry's battle plan develops in a series of events that unfolded around the time of Dr. Peavy's murder. Arranged here as a chronology with running comments, it is interesting to see the pattern and frequency of the assault. Keep in mind the bail industry's "manifesto" discussed in the previous section and see how it is followed through these coordinated steps.

May 13, 1994
Jerry Watson, in his role as General Counsel of the National Association
of Bail Insurance Companies (NABIC), writes to Administrative Judge
Miron Love:

"For a while now, there has been a 'volume reduction' in our number of
bonds written. When we inquired of our agents, the consistent answer
was, 'they're getting out on pretrial release. . . . The answer made no
sense to us, since a classic pretrial release program should not adverse-
ly impact upon our business. Pretrial release was designed to secure the
release of the defendant who meets three qualifications: (1) a pure
financial indigent who[,] (2) is a non-serious offender[,] and (3) is not
a multiple-offender."

The letter goes on to charge that the Pretrial Services Agency "*does not
even inquire as to the defendant's ability to pay for his own release*
[emphasis in original]. So, rather than the person who got himself
into jail paying to get himself out of jail, the Harris County Taxpayer is
paying for that." Additionally, he suggests that the Pretrial Services
Agency "*now releases by % [sic] of defendants assigned to each
Court*" [emphasis in original] and that the Agency "is regularly releasing
persons (a) with prior convictions, or (b) on parole, or (c) charged with
violent crimes, or (d) charged on serious drug offenses, or (e) who do
not even live in Harris County, or (f) some combination of the above."
Finally, he charges that "*a majority of the sexual assault cases are
released through PTR*" [emphasis in original] (J. Watson, letter, May 13,
1994).

Item #2 of the manifesto (gather data and/or statistics) is fulfilled.
This is a wholly uninformed position insomuch as it presumes the old
Vera model in defining the class of clientele for which pretrial programs are designed, but fails to consider the impact of Supreme Court
decisions, establishing the principle of equal protection, regardless of
financial state. Additionally, U.S. District Judge James DeAnda, in *Alberti v. Sheriff of Harris County* (1975), ruled that the Pretrial Services
Agency had to consider all defendants, not just the indigent, when
screening for pretrial bond eligibility. A number of allegations seem to
have been simply made up or at least vague enough to defy verification.
Finally Watson seems to have overlooked the point that it is the presid-
ing judge, not the Pretrial Services Agency that releases defendants.

May 15, 1994
Dr. Peavy is murdered by Dixon, a pretrial releasee.

May 17, 1994
Gerald Monks, a local bondsman, and longtime PTSA critic, writes an open letter to the judges and commissioners of Harris County.

"MY FRIEND AND THE SCHOOL MATE OF MY SONS ATTORNEY MIKE AND PAT MONKS was brutally murdered by a criminal out on a Harris County Pre-trial Release Agency bond, an Agency controlled by a small group of Judges and financed by the Taxpayers of Harris County. A Harris County financed criminal killed her. Someone must take the responsibility! . . . I have begged and pleaded with Judges and Commissioners for years to eliminate the Pre-trial Release Agency because it promotes crime, does not reduce jail populations, [and] it eliminates private attorneys. It does not guarantee appearance in court. Yet they pander to bureaucrats, and court appointed attorneys, grabbing more tax dollars. . . . I guarantee you this crime would not have happened if the defendant had been controlled by a bail agent. . . . All should be defeated who voted more money for this Agency. They were wrong and should pay the price. . . . I will remember Beth and do whatever I can to defeat those who financed this brutal murder" (G. Monks, letter, May 17, 1994).

Some amount of correspondence from members of the bail industry to the judiciary was exchanged in an attempt to distance themselves from Monks. Clearly, they wanted to isolate the PTSA, but not alienate the judges. However, how could any elected judge not consider the threat of adverse publicity if one is too outspoken in support of the PTSA?

May 18, 1994
Harris County Commissioner Jim Fonteno requests information from PTSA Director Charles Noble concerning details on all personal bonds "issued" by the PTSA from January 1, 1992 through January 1, 1994 (J. Fonteno, personal communication, May 18, 1994).

May 26, 1994
Noble replies to Fonteno. Noble notes that the total liability for "personal bonds judicially granted through" the Agency for the indicated period was $937,016. For comparison, Noble also tells Fonteno that the negotiated liability for surety bonds for the same period was $7,592,671. The figures supplied by Noble indicate that the Agency accounts for 16% of the bonds written and 11% of the outstanding liability, while surety accounts for 68% of the bonds and 89% of the liability (C. Noble, personal communication, May 26, 1994).

May 1994

Shortly after Noble's May 26, 1994 communication is received, Fonteno reiterates his original request, adding "YOU DID NOT ADDRESS WHAT MY LETTER REQUESTED. I AM NOT INTERESTED IN SURETY BAIL BONDS AT THIS TIME" [upper case in original] (J. Fonteno, personal communication, specific date unknown).

June 2, 1994

Fonteno acknowledges receipt of the revised report and requests additional information, advising Noble, "[i]t's my understanding you will have this information by Monday, June 6" (J. Fonteno, personal communication, June 2, 1994).

June 6, 1994

A 450-page report is delivered to Fonteno's office, providing the requested information on 14,352 personal bonds (J. Barr, letter, June 14, 1994).

June 7, 1994

A full-page advertisement in the *Houston Chronicle* reads: "Today, an Accused Criminal Walking the Streets Will Commit a Crime. And YOU Paid for Their Freedom." The ad, placed by the American Legislative Exchange Council (ALEC) "highlights four specific instances in which crimes were committed by defendants on personal bond before citing [release] figures for specific charges" (J. Barr, letter, June 14, 1994).

Jerry Watson would later acknowledge that the information provided to Fonteno by the PTSA over the preceding two weeks was delivered to the ALEC and was used in this advertisement (Watson, 1995).

In subsequent testimony, Fonteno denies supplying data to ALEC representatives, but other testimony suggests that their information came from his office (See Watson's testimony). Whether knowing or not, item #3 of the manifesto (meeting with Supervisors/Commissioners) proved to be effective.

At this time, a telephone interview with Elizabeth McLanen, ALEC Director of Media Relations was quoted as claiming many Texas state legislators among the organization's members, and that Gerald Monks (the writer of the open letter to the judiciary and a long-time critic of the PTSA) was a "private sector member" of ALEC's Criminal Justice Task Force. Another ALEC official, Bill Myers, indicated the organization's intention to launch similar (anti PTSA) campaigns in other major Texas cities (J. Barr, personal communication, June 14, 1994).

June 8, 1994
At a Harris County Bail Bond Board meeting, Johnny Nelms, the bail industry member of the Board, makes the claim that the Pretrial Services Agency is taking and holding collateral (a claim that has never been substantiated). The Attorney General has previously issued an opinion that argues against such practices by personal bond offices (Harris County Bail Bond Board, 1994:25-35).

Taking advantage of the concern and confusion among some of those in attendance, NABIC representative Jerry Watson portrays the PTSA as "an entity that competes so significantly with [the bail insurance industry] on an uneven playing field" that the industry's ability to survive in Harris County is in jeopardy. In a statement to one board member who defended the use of personal bonds, District Judge William Harmon, Watson said, ". . . if you really knew that more than one out of every four [defendants released on personal bonds] are never coming back to court . . . I think you would be more reluctant than you are today to grant a [PTSA release] request" (1994:26)

By the meeting's end, a number of members were expressing questions about the PTSA operation. One board member asked "If I say that something's going wrong [in the PTSA] who do I go to to correct it?" (1994:30)

Item 5 of the manifesto (urge a review of the effectiveness, value, and track record of PTSA), is fulfilled. While not the Commissioners Court, the Bail Bond Board is not without political potency. By confusing the issues regarding PTSA performance, the bond agents were at least able to further isolate the agency, and perhaps get more demands for answers flowing in from a wide range of sources.

Where did Watson get his "one out of every four" figure? While the Harris County PTSA failure to appear rate held to about 8 percent, a figure of 20 percent was reported by the National Pretrial Reporting Program (NPRP) on a national sample of pretrial release, including commercial bonds.

June 11, 1994
In a newspaper article, Gerald Monks claims that "anyone can find a friend or family member to pay the bail to spring a loved one from the county lockup." Clearly defining his notion of a "criminal indigent," Monks describes such a person as a penniless defendant without resources who can find no one, "not even his own mother," willing to bail him out. According to the article, Monks believes no one should post bail for a criminal indigent (Greene, 1994).

Note the similarity of Monk's claim and the assertion of George Will some 30 years earlier. Will (Goldfarb, 1965:119-123) claimed that there is no such thing as a "good risk indigent." In Greene's June 11, 1994 news article, shown above, Gerald Monks coined the term "criminal indigent" to reflect a similar sentiment. Both of these terms serve a common purpose of justifying bond agents for ignoring these defendants. It does not merely excuse their neglect, it actually makes the bond agents the responsible ones for refusing to do business with them.

June 13, 1994
A variant of the full-page "You paid for it" ad from June 7, 1994 runs in the *Houston Chronicle*. Based on the same time period as the previous advertisement, this ad evinces blatant inflation of the release figures presented previously and contains an addition error that increases the release count by nearly 700.

June 15, 1994
In a seeming attempt to distance NABIC from Gerald Monks and the "ads run by various social and political interest groups," Jerry Watson, in his role as the Chairman of the NABIC Legislative Committee, again writes to Administrative Judge Miron Love.

Portraying NABIC as a bystander and the PTSA as a competitor, Watson observes that, "from what we have been able to review, it seems that a controversy is now 'full blown,' and it focuses on" the charges for which defendants are being released on personal bonds and the comparative failure-to-appear rates for personal bond and financial release. "It [has not] been our objective to become embroiled in controversy. But, clearly, we find ourselves now being attacked by Harris County Pretrial Release. Apparently, it was seen as a ploy for getting attention off of self[sic] by pointing to another target."

"What we want, and all we want, is a continued opportunity to earn a living for ourselves by doing good work in the criminal justice system. Pretrial release threatens this . . . Our firm belief is that we can do a much better job than our competitor if given the chance, and all at absolutely no cost to the taxpayer. Perhaps an impartial review of the systems—theirs and ours—by an outside party, an unbiased party, would let the courts and local government officials know, once and for all, exactly how the public's interest and safety are best served" (J. Watson, letter, June 15, 1994).

Item #8 (keep the issue alive), is being met. Watson makes two observations that are quite telling. First, Watson makes a reference to the National Pretrial Reporting Program, where a sample of national data is compiled. Harris County's contribution to the national data was about

165 of the study's total of 51,002 cases (Austin, 1995:3). From the national study, Watson was convinced that the PTSA was lying. This is notwithstanding the fact that, one year earlier, Cuvelier and Potts (1993) completed a study that corroborated the agency figures. Second, Watson appears to think that the agency was conducting an attack on the bail industry. The PTSA had maintained a relatively stable 16 percent share of the bonds written in the county. There is no evidence to suggest an increase in the proportion of non-financial release or an attack on the bail industry by the PTSA, but the number of registered bond agents in Harris County rose faster than the increase in bond volume. Perhaps most telling is the third excerpt, where the "continued opportunity to earn a living" is raised. Was the PTSA threatening their livelihood or were bond agents feeling the pressure of competition within their own industry?

June 17, 1994
State Representative Talmadge Heflin writes to the Harris County Commissioners.

"Recent media attention on the policies and practices of the Harris County Pretrial Release Agency prompts this letter expressing my concern. If the published material is correct, and I believe it is, we have a serious problem on our hands. My understanding is that about 25% of the perpetrators of crimes released under taxpayer funded bonds fail to appear for trial. We should not be casual when it comes to protecting the honest, law abiding citizens we represent. It appears that an independent auditis in order to determine the failure to appear rate of accused criminals released on taxpayer funded bonds by the Pretrial Release Agency" (T. Heflin, letter, June 17, 1994).

Heflin expresses a realistic concern. Once information finds its way into the media, it takes on a kind of reality that cannot be ignored, regardless of its validity. The "published material" is assumed to be from the NPRP, but characterizing the Harris County failure-to-appear rate as "25 percent" suggests that he did not read the report for himself. Had he read the report, the figure would have been 20 percent. The stated level likely came from Watson's May 15 statement at the bail board meeting or directly from Watson himself. Under oath, Watson disclosed that he had actively and financially supported Heflin's campaign and encouraged other bond agents to do the same. This may have given Watson a direct line of communication with Heflin. Item #7 (support this "encouragement to examine" by personal contacts), of the manifesto is being played out here.

June 17, 1994

Jerry Watson, in his role as Chairman of the NABIC Legislative Committee, writes the Harris County Commissioners.

Watson tells the commissioners that his organization does not oppose release through pretrial services agencies "as it was intended to operate. On the one hand, Watson affirms that "a non-serious, non-multiple offender who is financially indigent should not be housed at long duration in the Harris County jail[s] at taxpayer expense." On the other hand, "neither should the . . . taxpayer[s] finance the release of all types of offenders when they have the ability to secure their own release." Watson notes that "pretrial release in Harris County has deserted its original worthwhile purpose and has set itself up, quite intentionally, as the competitor of our insurance companies. Of course, we are forced to resist that." Watson then again calls for an outside review of the PTSA, focusing on the "types of offenders" being released and the PTSA's failure-to-appear rate (J. Watson, letter, June 17, 1994).

June 24, 1994

Commissioner Fonteno writes the PTSA.

"I recently received a letter from State Representative Talmadge Heflin expressing his concern over recent media attention on the policies and practices of the Pre-Trial Release Agency. I, too, am concerned. Please provide me with a report on the failure to appear rate of accused criminals released on taxpayer funded bonds by the Agency" (J. Fonteno, letter, June 24, 1994).

June 27, 1994

Charles Noble, PTSA Director, responds to Commissioner Fonteno.

Noble indicates to Fonteno that the available data, whether at the national or local level, do not support bail industry claims, and that Heflin was either "misled or misinformed regarding . . . the 25% FTA rate." He attaches a copy of a letter from D. Alan Henry, PSRC Director, to Heflin, in which Henry attempts to clarify misconceptions about the limitations and meaning of NPRP data. Noble also expresses his support for an independent study of comparative FTA and rearrest rates for all forms of release (D. Henry, letter, 1994; C. Noble, letter, 1994).

Notice the shift in the language. In his June 24th communication, Fonteno is referring to Pretrial Bonds as ""taxpayer funded bonds," language picked up directly from the letters and advertisements from the bail insurance industry. While this may be coincidental, we have never heard pretrial bonds referenced this way outside of the references by the commercial bail industry. Apparently manifesto item #4 (meet and 'educate' public officials) had been achieved.

June 27, 1994

Jerry Watson, in his role as NABIC Counsel (on NABIC Legislative Committee letterhead), writes to judges in Harris County.

Watson complains that even as Noble and his staff are citing low agency failure-to-appear to the judges, "Pretrial Release's National Director [a position that does not exist] has just published their 'admitted' FTA for felonies. He observes, without benefit of supporting data, that "obviously, misdemeanor [figures] would be much higher." Again, without reference to supporting data, Watson notes that "[the bail industry's] FTA rate, on the other hand, *must* be quite low [underline in original]. Otherwise, we would go out of business. . . . We have been trying for a long time to get pretrial services to get 'open' about their true FTA. Frankly, we believe that a good, independent review in Harris County would show that it is even worse . . ." (J. Watson, letter, June 27, 1994).

Watson was referring to the Pretrial Services Resource Center, in Washington DC and a communication from D. Alan Henry, PSRC Director, reflecting on the NPRP conducted by the Department of Justice. It would appear that Watson either does not have a clear idea of how pretrial is structured, or is attempting to confuse issues. Nevertheless, the issue is being kept alive (manifesto item #8).

July 7, 1994

Four bail insurance companies—International Fidelity, Allegheny Mutual Casualty, American Bonding, and National American—file a lawsuit in federal district court against Charles Noble and Carol Oeller, individually and in their capacities as director and assistant director, respectively, of the *Harris County Pretrial Services Agency* (Plaintiff's Original Complaint in International Fidelity, *et al. v. Noble, et al.*)

In the facts of the case, the plaintiffs allege that the defendants and/or their subordinates:

- misrepresented the personal bond FTA rate as 7 percent, when the true rate was in excess of 20 percent;

- refused access to records that would verify the true FTA rate and records that a surety must have before posting a bail bond;

- developed, and offered to make available to other pretrial services programs, a computer program that analyzes the FTA rate by type of offense for persons released on personal bond. The purpose of this program was to "cause the

> release of persons that they know will not return to court if released on personal bond" and thereby deprive "the Plaintiffs of the opportunity to post bail bonds for these persons" (pp. 4-5); and
>
> • held money as collateral in violation of applicable law, and used or applied that collateral improperly for purposes beneficial to the PTSA.
>
> Among other causes of action, the plaintiffs alleged:
>
> • deprivation of equal protection of the law, under Title 42 of the United States Code;
>
> • deprivation of property (the right to earn a living) without due process, under state and federal constitutional provisions; and
>
> • conspiracy to commit mail fraud, wire fraud, and obstruction of justice, under Title 18 of the United States Code, amounting to a violation of the Racketeer Influenced and Corrupt Organizations Act (18 U.S.C. §1961, et seq.).

The first item cites the 20 percent national estimate from the NPRP as the "true rate" for the county. This is taken directly from Jerry Watson's allegations, though Watson was not an actor in the legal proceedings. Refusing access to records is a specious allegation in that Fonteno's request was met in about two weeks, producing a 450-page report on 14,352 bonds. No documented request for information by the bond agents has been uncovered to date. Finally, hardly a month had lapsed between the bail bond board meeting where the allegations of holding collateral were raised and the entry into the suit. There was hardly sufficient time to establish the facts of the claim.

The computer program development poses an interesting item, insomuch as the reference is to a risk-assessment instrument developed and validated in the PTSA the year before (Cuvelier & Potts, 1993). While the characterization of a risk-assessment instrument is quite distorted, even amusing, it may well be that the bond agents knew too well the potential impact of better information. We are now in the era of preventative detention where greater judicial control of defendant populations, and improved information resources could potentially increase the influence and credibility and use of PTSA alternatives to commercial bail.

July 25, 1994
Jerry Watson, as Chairman of the NABIC Legislative Committee, writes to Administrative Judge Miron Love.

Watson sets forth some reasons for the civil action against Noble and Oeller. He notes communications with Harris County judges that identify PTSA representations of lower FTA rates as "a major reason why your courts limit the use of our services." Watson tells Love that he believes (a) the representations are "incorrect"; (b) they were made for the purpose of discouraging the use of surety bail services; and (c) the industry had "requested investigation, to no avail."

Watson, expressing positive results from the filing, observes that:

- "failure-to-appear rate . . . has surfaced as the KEY ISSUE" [emphasis in original];

- Noble has agreed that "the system [that] guarantees the most community safety must be utilized";

- "if there is a problem in how persons are being released pending trial in Harris County, THAT PROBLEM IS NOT CREATED BY, NOR IS IT THE RESPONSIBILITY OF, THE CRIMINAL COURTS" [emphasis in original]; and

- "it is now 'out in the open' . . . that [the PTSA's] intention is to remove our companies from the arena. We will resist that. We have to."

In closing, Watson candidly tells Love that "this is a suit brought by national insurance companies to protect their industry in the private sector" (J. Watson, letter, July 25, 1994).

September 28, 1994
The *Houston Post* ran a feature titled: "Bail Bondsmen offer to pay for study." In this article, Commissioner Fonteno is quoted, speaking for the bondsmen, as offering to pay $30,000 for a study as long as a "Big Eight" accounting firm conducted it. The article further states, "The private bondsmen, in a bid to gain more bail bond business, hope to show that Pretrial Services has a higher failure-to-appear rate than they do with the cash and surety bonds they issue" (Steinbaker & Smith, 1994)

The suit against the director and pretrial agency was withdrawn in 1995 and the PTSA director subsequently counter sued. The counter suit was settled out of court and terms of the settlement are not known.

Have we reached the end of the story? Not quite. With the disappointing resolution of the lawsuits, the bondsmen went back on the offensive in 1996. We see the entrance of a non-profit organization known as STRIKE BACK! Based in Virginia, the organization has been characterized as "Lobbyists for the bail bond industry masquerading as a victim's rights organization" (Kiesling & Corcoran, 1998). In an investigative report, Kiesling and Corcoran quote Rodney Mitchell, the spokesman for STRIKE BACK!, as claiming that the organization had no interest in the private bail industry and was only interested in protecting victim's rights. Yet, they report that the three corporate officers of STRIKE BACK! Have financial interests in a number of bail firms nationwide. STRIKE BACK! was founded by a grant from the National Association of Bail Insurance Companies, a national organization of bail bond agents (Kiesling & Corcoran, 1998).

As of the March, 29, 1998 press date of their news article, Kiesling and Corcoran identify STRIKE BACK!'s president John T. Whitlock as (1) the president of Underwriter's Surety Inc., a bail bond corporation listed in 13 states, (2) owner of Allied Bonding Agency of Houston, (3) president of Surety Associates Inc. of New Orleans, (4) president of USI Agency Inc. of Reno, (5) president of USI Agency of Indianapolis, and (6) owner of USI Bail Bonds of Los Angeles.

Kiesling and Corcoran (1998), also identified STRIKE BACK!'s vice president and treasurer as having bail industry connections. Vice President Brian Nairin is identified as (1) the owner of Associated Bond and Insurance Inc., of Pasadena (2) the president of the National Association of Bail Insurance Companies of Pasadena, (3) the president of the Nevada incorporation of STRIKE BACK! and (4) the president and registered agent of the National Association of Bail Insurance Companies. Treasurer Jefferey Shonka is identified as the vice president and director of Allwest General Bail Bond Agency, Inc. of Salt Lake City.

March 11, 1996
STRIKE BACK!, in time for budget hearing that may affect PTSA funding, writes to a range of Harris County officials. Their attached literature clearly reflects a working partnership between STRIKE BACK! And the ALEC. It also includes a copy of a January 21, 1996 letter written to STRIKE BACK! Executive Director Gary Barrett by Kathy Peavy Bailey, sister of Tony Dixon's victim:

"I, along with my family, am a victim of the Harris County Pretrial Services Agency. On Sunday, May 15,1994, my sister, Dr. Elizabeth Ann Peavy, was murdered during a carjacking at 4:00 p.m. Her murderer, Tony Dixon, was released on a pretrial release bond in Harris County in November of the previous year.

Every day, I consider that as a taxpayer in Harris County, I helped pay for the bond of my sister's murderer. What if he had not been released? Perhaps my sister, a dentist known for her Christian beliefs and actions, would still be alive today. Perhaps my sister, who spent Friday evenings rocking babies to sleep at a home for abused and HIV infected children, could still be with those babies. Perhaps my sister Beth, who had no children of her own, would be married now with children. Because of Tony Dixon and the Harris County Pretrial Release Agency, we will never know.

I will do whatever I can in the hope that no other person or family will have to bear the devastation that is caused by a known violent criminal released with our taxpayer money" (Barrett, 1996:2).

While we deeply regret the loss suffered by Dr. Peavy's loved ones, and we certainly want the good she represented to be her legacy, we cannot help but notice that this letter was sent to STRIKE BACK! *two years* following Dr. Peavy's murder and Tony Dixon has become a "known violent criminal." STRIKE BACK! has given this letter wide circulation, along with the standard litany of high costs and low performance of pretrial agencies.

March 27, 1996
Still anticipating budget hearings, Gary Barrett writes to members of the Harris County District Attorney's Office.

"As a follow-up to my previous letters, I have obtained the data regarding this taxpayer funded program[the PTSA] for December, 1995, and January, 1996. . . . According to [PTSA] records, they released 868 serious offenders in December, 1995, and 901 serious offenders in January, 1996. If this rate were to continue then approximately 10,614 serious offenders will be released at little or no cost to themselves." Barrett urges the recipients to call their county commissioners (G. Barrett, letter, March 27, 1996).

April 18, 1996
Barrett sends a similar letter to the county judge and commissioners, urging them "to help protect the citizens of Harris County by eliminating the funding of this dangerous program" (G. Barrett, letter, April 18, 1996).

Barrett apparently was unable to distinguish the difference between "bonds written" and "defendants under supervision," as his figures for the three months show the total number of defendants being supervised. With an average of a 90-day wait between release and case termination, for example, a defendant will appear in three monthly reports as being under supervision, but represents only one bond. Was this an honest mistake, or a calculated attempt to disseminate misleading information?

While one cannot be totally sure, it seems inconceivable that someone so close to the bonding business could unknowingly fall into such an error.

May 29, 1996
From NABIC President John T. Whitlock to judges in Harris County.

Showing PTSA reports from December, 1995, January, and February 1996, there was a total of 289 pretrial releases (in a county that processes upward of 50,000 criminal cases per year).

Whitlock charges that:

1. "The Harris County Pretrial Services Agency sees us as their 'competitor.'"

2. ". . . gets the 'pick' of who it will take out, leaving our industry with only the poorer appearance risks."

3. "The Agency is unable to outperform the private sector in getting its charges back to Court."

4. "The Agency costs . . . taxpayers . . . FOUR MILLION DOLLARS PER YEAR . . . we actually generate revenue for the county of over TWO MILLION DOLLARS annually."

5. "PERSONS OUT ON PERSONAL RECOGNIZANCE BONDS ARE MUCH MORE APT TO COMMIT ANOTHER CRIME than are persons on secured release bond."

Whitlock concludes by expressing "hopes that you might consider using the private sector more. We felt that if you were aware of not only the local economic benefits, but of the public safety interests as well, perhaps it would make a difference in how Defendants in your Court are released, pending trial." (J. Whitlock, letter, May 29, 1996).

Once again, we see the same type of misleading statements as used in 1994. While the agency records are accurately portrayed, there is offered no evidence to back up any of the other claims made in this document. In fact, a study conducted by the NCCD (Austin, 1995:6) affirmed the agency's defendant-based failure-to-appear rates to be 7.0 percent, with surety releasees failing at a rate of 8.9 percent. In terms of risk scores, using the PTSA's risk-assessment instrument, the average surety release score was 3.4 and the average PTSA release was 4.0 out of an 8-point range, with the low score reflecting the higher risk. In sum, there is little to no empirical evidence to support Whitlock's claims. That may not be an issue, however, as the purpose of this correspondence is to maintain the propaganda flow (manifesto item #8).

June 10, 1996
Jerry Watson writes to the judges of Harris County.

"On May 28, 1996 we sent you a letter reporting the referenced releases through your court for each of the months of last December, January and February, respectively. Since our letter we have received calls from Harris County Judges wanting to know how we came up with those numbers. Actually, the answer is very simple: we just took the numbers from the monthly reports as filed in the clerk's office by the Harris County pretrial agency. . . . We then simply 'tallied' the numbers of cases shown in each month's report for each court listed. This is how we came up with the month-by-month release statistics for your court. And then we sent you that data to you in our May 28, 1996 letter. . . . Some judges had authorized only a very small number of pretrial agency releases, and several had permitted none at all. For those, we sent no May 28, 1996 report letter, as we saw no point in doing so. Nevertheless, we are now providing all judges with a copy of the activity reports for the months of December, January and February" (J. Watson, letter, June 10, 1996).

A change of tactics! This letter thinly veils a threat to any sitting judge, that his or her court statistics could become public information in a most slanted and defamatory means possible. This has got to be unsettling. It is not the veracity of the information that is at issue, but the way that information is framed that could be devastating to a judge at re-election time. One can be assured that the failures to appear for pretrial release will not be compared to comparable figures on surety bonds. Thus, we see an attempt by the bail industry at statistical hostage-taking.

September 7, 1996
"A Harris County state district judge said he will recommend next week that Commissioners Court abolish the county's Pretrial Services Agency and turn most of the program over to private bail-bonding companies. . . . [The agency] has long been criticized for using tax-payer money to arrange bonds that might otherwise be set up through commercial bonding agencies. . . . Pretrial Services now spends as much as $2.5 million annually just to gather information, a figure [Administrative Judge David West] said commercial agencies could virtually eliminate. . . . [Jerry] Watson said a private contractor probably would not need to interview defendants being booked into jail or provide criminal histories. Instead, he said, that would still be left up to Harris County because most of that information already is readily available when a defendant is booked into jail. . . . Some 8,000 defendants are released each year on Pretrial Services bonds, Watson said. Of those bonds, [Watson] said he believes at least half could probably afford to pay their own bonds" (Stinebaker & Smith, 1996).

This news story certainly underscores the theory that if you say something loud enough and often enough, it can become a fact. Two years of constant bombardment by unsubstantiated claims yields the "fact" that the agency has "long been criticized." Further, the information that Watson suggests is "readily available" is available because the data are collected by the pretrial staff. If information for decisionmaking is to be collected, this expense would have to be shifted to some other governmental agency, thus displacing costs rather than eliminating them. The count of 8,000 defendants is clearly wrong, even by the PTSA records NABIC president John Whitlock cited on May 29, 1996. Showing under 300 released in a three-month period, an increase of 700 percent would be necessary to reach Watson's figure of 8,000 releases per year. Again, we see that information is wielded like a club to confuse and co-opt public opinion.

September 13, 1996
Jerry Watson writes to the judges of Harris County

Watson unveils a plan to privatize certain functions of Harris County PTSA—the "Indigent Release Program." Under this plan, Harris county would be invoiced $100 per defendant released through this plan, not to be submitted until the defendant's case is disposed. In the event of a failure-to-appear, the private contractor forfeits the $100 fee (J. Watson, letter, September 13, 1996).

What could be sweeter? The private contractor risks nothing, collects or contributes nothing, but simply signs the bonds on cases that he or she deems "indigent." If a person does not qualify, what better time to set a commercial bail contract in front of the defendant! This plan is little more than corporate welfare at public expense, which would place all released defendants in the hands of an industry that has a poorer track record for failures than the PTSA they would seek to replace.

The proposal also does not recognize the *Alberti v. Sheriff of Harris County* (1975) stipulations regarding the interview of all defendants book into the jail. There is no provision for an information gathering function. This backward step in information gathering is clearly antithetical to the movements in public interest toward preventative detention and other forms of risk management. Without information, the decision-making process cannot focus effectively on the public interest, and the bail decision remains an economic one. Additionally, no mechanism was proposed to monitor whether commercial bondsman were adequately fulfilling their obligations.

Aftermath

At this point, the record goes silent. The pretrial agency has continued to function in the two and one-half years since this last entry. The bondsman have not scored a total victory, but to date, the number of pretrial bonds under Pretrial Agency supervision has yet to reach its 1994 levels (Harris County Pretrial Services Agency, 1994, 1995, 1996, 1997, 1998).

Is this just one isolated example? And if not, doesn't the apparent failure of the commercial bond industry to bring down the Harris County PTSA suggest that their national strategy is a failure? Not exactly, consider the following observation of Dade County, Florida:

> By the end of 1994, the news had not improved . . . since the 1991 court study, the state of the pretrial release function in Dade County has worsened in many important respects. The pretrial services agency shows signs of "forgetting" its mission, disappearing as a key agency, or, sadly, becoming altogether irrelevant . . . [P]retrial services in Dade County appear to have been unable even to respond to criticisms and lobbying efforts orchestrated by organized bail bondsmen, the traditional adversaries of bail reform and pretrial services initiatives. That the entreaties of bail bondsmen could be seriously considered by the judicial leaders—if, in fact, they have been a symptom of a judicial environment that has failed to move forward . . . (Goldkamp et al., 1995:300-301).

Perhaps this excerpt can provide a sense of what has been happening in Dade County.

Miami Review April 26, 1993
"The issue got the attention of court and county officials after a push by the Dade County Bail Bond Association, which engaged a lobbyist and began compiling statistics on pretrial release in early March. . . . Members of the Bail Bond Association . . . proposed a 72-hour waiting period before jailed defendants could be accepted into the [pretrial] program . . . [The bondsmen] suspect many defendants would find a way to post bond . . . rather than spend 72 hours in jail. . . . But Russell Buckhalt, who runs the program . . . says the program's no-show rate is closer to 7 or 8 percent. 'I think that their [bondsmen] motives are strictly financial'" (Dunnigan, 1993).

This certainly has an all-too-familiar ring to it. The manifesto is alive and functioning outside of Harris County.

The Commercial Bail Industry and Pretrial Services Agency Conflict in Perspective

Tracing the historical development we can see four general presumptions underlying the implementation of pretrial release. As the focus of these and other presumptions evolve, so also must change the practices and procedures of pretrial release. The four pretrial release presumptions we cover include: responsibility, innocence, equal protection, and dangerousness.

The presumption of responsibility. Bail is presumed to enforce responsible behavior on the part of the accused in assuring his or her appearance in court. Responsible behavior may come from directly influencing the accused to appear in court, or it may come indirectly, by passing consequences to the surety, if an accused does not appear in court. The Federal Bail Reform Act of 1984 (18 USC §3142(e)), authorized pretrial detention for public safety, and thus expanded responsibility to include the defendant's behavior on the street while awaiting trial.

Who is made responsible for the accused changes as we move from the English system, to the American Bail system and PTSA release systems. Responsibility under the English system often fell on the family, who would have property that could be forfeited if the accused was not brought to court. Under the American bail system, responsibility would fall onto the surety, who would have to produce the accused or pay a forfeiture to the court. This financial risk opened the door to the use of bounty hunters to forcibly return defendants to court when necessary and financially prudent. Under government sponsored release programs, the decision to release falls to the judge, who in turn, becomes responsible for the defendant's actions on the street. This responsibility may dampen judicial enthusiasm for pretrial release in some cases, but certainly underscores the need for more defendant information and oversight on behalf of the court, as provided by pretrial services.

Gerald Monks' letter of May 17, 1994 clearly underscores the attribution of responsibility for defendant behavior released through the court back on the judges' shoulders. It also clearly bears a threat to make the supporters of PTSA "pay the price," suggesting political ramifications. Jerry Watson's letter of June 10, 1996 shows a more subtle communication of this same message, by letting the judges know that their use of PTSA was being monitored and had the potential to become publicized.

The presumption of innocence. The concept that persons accused of crimes are 'innocent until proven guilty' is fundamental to due process in the administration of justice in the United States (Goldkamp et al., 1995:3). As such, detaining a defendant before trial without proper cause may be construed as punishment without a finding of guilt, so there is great pressure on the system to grant release before trial. The court can take measures to make pretrial release possible by alternatives to secured bail or lowering the bail amount.

The Federal Bail Reform Act of 1984 (18 USC §3142(e)) and cases such as *United States v. Salerno,* have established that preventive detention is justifiable in the interests of public safety. This weakens the presumption of innocence as a rationale for release by forcing judges to balance public safety considerations against release. Losing the ability to base release decisions simply on principles of law, judges need more and better information on which to rationalize their decisions.

The presumption of equal protection. While equal protection under the law is not in itself "presumed," but rather a well-grounded principle, its application to pretrial release has undergone changes over time. In previously cited cases (*Williams v. Illinois* (1970), *Tate v. Short* (1971), we see that equal protection issues challenge using detention when financial remedies are not possible due to indigence. *Alberti v. Sheriff of Harris County* (1975) directly addressed the Harris County PTSA mission as an equal protection issue by mandating that *all* defendants be given consideration for a pretrial bond, not just those who could not afford a commercial bond.

The emerging definition of equal protection in pretrial release underscores a significant shift in legal thinking. Whereas, the presumption that indigents represent a body of undeserving poor, we see the emergence of an awareness that poverty is not a condition brought on solely by the lack of industriousness. The presumption of equal protection becomes the first point in social policy that the commercial bail industry is not prepared to satisfy.

In the business of making a profit, those without money have nothing to trade for services rendered. It is not a criticism of a private sector business if it chooses to not pursue unprofitable markets. However, attempting to justify the industry by maligning the poor as "high risks" or "criminally indigent," is simply hypocritical. Structured for profit and not loss, the bond industry simply left the unprofitable (indigent) defendants to the government.

Leaving the indigent defendants to the government let the genie out of the bottle. With the government taking up the needs of the indigent defendants in matters of pretrial release, under the principle of equal protection, these services cannot arbitrarily exclude defendants from consideration solely because they can afford to pay for a commercial bond. Now the bond industry must "compete" with a government infrastructure that will claim some share of the markets over which they had previously had exclusive control.

The presumption of dangerousness. Around 1970, we begin to see the formation of preventive detention laws, which culminated in the passage of the Federal Bail Reform Act of 1984 (18 USC §3142(e)). Through this Act, we see official recognition of community protection added to the function of pretrial release. The Act authorizes four possible courses of action: (1) release the defendant on recognizance or unsecured appearance bond, (2) release the defendant to a condition or combination of conditions, (3) temporarily detain the defendant, or (4) detain the defendant. While the conditions and procedures on which a decision is based are too detailed for treatment here, the Act anticipates a substantial volume of valid information upon which preventive detention decisions are to be based. We have seen that the primary function of PTSAs is to gather information for court decisionmaking, thus, the need for the government function is affirmed.

In a critical examination of pretrial detention, Klein (1997:281) suggests that ". . . the enhancement of pretrial services is paramount to the successful renovation of the pretrial detention system . . . a separate, well-funded, well-organized pretrial services office (PTSO) is ideal." Klein's comments underscore how the changing basis of pretrial decision making is changing the role and function of pretrial release mechanisms. As this occurs, the viability of the bond agent role may be slipping vis-à-vis pretrial services offices. Goldkamp, et al. (1995) further illustrate the shifting role as decision guidelines play an increasing role in balancing the issues of personal liberty and community safety.

Again, the bail industry cannot address the information-gathering function. Information gathering is not a function they are structured to perform and there would not likely be any profit in it, especially if the data did not support their vested interests. The bond industry generally downplays the importance of this role, and has even suggested that the county's information system has the information that the PTSA would collect. This claim apparently overlooks the fact that much of the information in question is entered into the information system by the pretrial interview process the first place.

What makes public/private interaction somewhat different in certain criminal justice issues is the degree to which the drive for profit translates into manipulation of public policy. Gilbert (1996a:13) asserts that the proper role of government in a civil society should "punish offenders according to objective laws; maintain sovereignty through the control of public policy; and protect public interest." The incursion of private interests in the administration of justice "adds profit as a new powerful motive . . . [in which] . . . economic rationality and corporate survival supplant public interest as the dominant standard of success (Gilbert, 1996a:17).

The degree to which private interests may affect public policy depends upon the extent to which private interests penetrate the functions of justice administration, which may range from ancillary services to essential functions (Gilbert, 1996b:66-67). Beyond penetration by virtue of their *assigned* a role, we see bail agents applying political leverage through direct contact with public officials and disseminating propaganda through the media to influence policymaking. The anti-pretrial services agency campaign may be construed to be an attempt to undermine governmental sovereignty of the administration of justice. Having been a long-term player in the pretrial bond game, the bond agents have taken a position that they have a right to profit, and that issues of the public interest must be subjugated to these "higher values."

So how might this analysis inform us as to the future of privatization in other areas of criminal justice? It is widely known that it is the nature of a bureaucracy to persist and grow. Kolderie (1986) warns of "creeping privatization," in which the private sector expands its function and influence in public policy decisionmaking. Beyond assuming operational roles in the decision-making process, however, the bail industry response has taught us that direct pressure on public officials and leveraging public opinion may also be expected, in the name of public interest, of course.

On Whose Field Are We Playing?

In the case of Harris County, we have seen the commercial bail industry attack government functioning as if it were a business, with bond agents even identifying TSA as a "competitor." Yet, we have seen the application of political pressure to force policy changes. The relentless attack by the commercial bond industry was sustained largely because, as a government agency, the PTSA could not counter attack. The commercial bail representatives could say whatever they wanted to the public or to the actors in the justice system with impunity.

As Judge Barr (letter, June 14, 1994) observed:

> Of great concern is the willingness of the various assailants to use both public fear and fear of political reprisal as a vehicle for the pursuit of profit and the reduction of matters of due process and equal protection to a myopic perspective of the 'business side' of criminal justice. The debate is clearly moving away from what is best for the public to what is best for private industry.

Self-interest is the primary concern for any commercial enterprise, what is best for the public is the primary concern of government. We should neither be surprised or dismayed if private industry acts in self-interest, even to the point of attempting to influence public policy formation through public fear, political manipulation, and libelous claims. That is the nature of the beast. The question in need of an answer is how close we will allow the beast to get to the jugular of public interest.

The campaign against the Harris County PTSA could not have been conducted as it was, had the agency possessed the legal alternatives of the private sector. Had Jerry Watson attacked a private entity as he did the PTSA, he certainly would have been called to account for his utterances, perhaps answering to libel charges.

Regarding the commercial bail industry charges against the Harris County PTSA, Judge Jim Barr (letter, June 14, 1994) writes:

> Management principles suggest that the truth, as best it may be determined from verifiable evidence, is the best response to these attacks. If the evidence refutes the claims, the critics may be forced into silence or to reformulate their arguments at a higher level. If the critics are supported by the evidence, then it is incumbent upon the judiciary to take remedial action. In either case, the judiciary will be best served by sound research and full disclosure on the subject.

The experiences with the commercial bond industry in Harris County would certainly call into question the wisdom of opening up traditionally public functions to the private sector. But *if* the door is opened to the private sector, we must at least establish a common set of ground rules. Without the ability to confront and silence accusers with evidence, profit-seeking combatants can engage in guerrilla warfare, where allegations, no matter how absurd and unfounded, will eventually take on the guise of truth simply for having been said loud enough and often enough.

The Enduring Role of Commercial Bail

In the final analysis we have to ask, how is it that the commercial bail industry has been so enduring despite the criticisms leveled at the practice of bail. Technically, there is nothing a bail agent does that a PTSA could not do.

Political aspirations have sold the public on the fear of crime and cost containment to such a point that we are saddled with the need to protect decisionmakers from political repercussions when something goes wrong. It is somewhat ironic, that due to neglect of the impoverished defendant, the bail industry forced the government's hand in creating a release mechanism that has now become a kind of competition with private industry for all defendants.

Public sentiment on pretrial release has definitely regulated its use. There is usually a conservative screening process to select those who appear to pose minimal risk. But, taking part in a decision-making process makes one responsible for the outcome of each individual decision. There is no concept of "calculated risk" in these issues.

As a result, the presence of the bail industry provides a perfect cover. The judge sets bail, and the release decision is simply one of a private transaction between the defendant and bail agent. In the face of adverse publicity, the judge can take refuge behind the constitutional right (against excessive bail) and the fact that the judicial decision is not directly involved in the bail transaction.

General Implications for Conflict between Private and Public Sectors in Criminal Justice

Mintzberg (1989) makes observations regarding diversified organizations that are appropriate to discussions of privatization in government. Regardless of whether policy decisions are made by a public or a private organization, a balance must be struck between the social and economic consequences of those decisions. The pursuit of socially responsible goals generally requires some diminution of concern for the economic consequences of that pursuit, and vice versa.

When organizations are established, whether as private or public organisms, they originate from real or perceived need and seek survival and growth. In the public sector, organizations survive and grow because of a continued social need for the organization, or because the organization is authorized to redirect its services to meet a different social need. If the original need is satisfied and no other need arises, sunset legislation and related mechanisms ably facilitate the dissolution of governmental bodies. By contrast, origin, survival and growth, and dissolution of private sector organizations arise from economic determinations. They originate to meet an existing need, or to create a need and meet it, for profit. They are "bottom line" decisions.

The commercial bail industry originated to meet the needs of jailed persons who desired release until trial, but liberty itself, from the defendant's point of view, is an invariant product. Its workmanship is hardly at issue, and, after release, purchasers are rarely interested in quality customer service. Thus, it would seem that the survival and growth of any individual bail agent's business is dependent upon his or her ability to limit exposure to risk of defendant flight.

Unfortunately, market forces appear to work against limiting exposure. Foremost among these is competition that keeps prices low, generally around 10 percent of the bail amount. Given a finite pool of customers, low prices drive: (a) the need to limit overhead, including staff to supervise defendants, and (b) the need to increase exposure to risk either by increasing the number or face amount of bail bonds written, or both.

Under these circumstances, the establishment of a pretrial services agency that makes possible non-financial release alternatives diminishes the pool of bail customers, reduces reliance on the bail industry to meet criminal justice system needs, and exacerbates the extant market pressures on the local bail industry. Unable to adapt its product to a changed environment, the bail industry can do little for its survival but take all necessary measures to change the environment to create a need for what the bail industry has to offer. In Harris County, the industry's response to its perception of sagging profits was to follow a plan that portrayed the PTSA as a taxpayer-funded organization offering free bail bonds to serious offenders.

In the years since the bail industry suit was filed in Harris County, there has been an increase in the number of surety-bailed defendants ordered under PTSA supervision. Often, the courts will initiate the supervision, but occasionally a bail agent, seeking to insure his risk at no cost, will ask for it. This function never came under bail industry fire, even though it apparently began around 1991 and its use has flourished. It was embraced by the former PTSA director and by bail insurance industry representatives and attracted the attention of judges. At this writing, those defendants in Harris County under this supervision hybrid far outnumber those under non-financial release and supervision (e.g., those released directly through PTSA).

It is reasonable to question whether hybrid supervision is a surprising success or whether it is just a corporate welfare program that offers nothing of value to the public. For example, bail industry claims in recent years touted its ability to provide public safety at no cost to the taxpayers. It claimed that defendants should not receive bail or other pretrial services at little or no cost. It claimed that pretrial services agencies provided inadequate supervision and had high rates of failure.

Because hybrid supervision does not differ from non-financial supervision, it offers no cost savings to the public over non-financial release and supervision. It does, however, benefit the bail industry by offering supervision alternatives rarely available through a bail agent, and bail agents will ask for hybrid supervision if they feel a defendant's risk of flight warrants the additional supervision. At this writing, the Harris County PTSA has no statutory authority to charge for its hybrid supervision services, except for fees associated with electronic monitoring or drug screening that are passed on to all defendants. Although this means operating at a sustained loss, the PTSA is meeting a social need that the courts have placed above economic concerns. In contrast to Kolderie's (1986) notion of "creeping privatization," this hybrid supervision may represent "creeping publicization"—a gradual expansion of public function that progressively returns public policy influence to the public realm.

What about the bail industry's negative remarks about pretrial services agencies? It seems that concern for taxpayers' money, allegations of ineffective supervision by PTSA, and claims about high PTSA failure rates evaporate in the presence of profits. With their survival not at risk and their right to profit assured, the bail industry has embraced the hybrid supervision provided by the Harris County PTSA.

We must look beyond bail to other points of contact between the private sector and the criminal justice system and consider carefully the questions raised by the experiences with perhaps the oldest private sector criminal justice service areas. Is the bail industry unique among private service providers in its use of political leverage, public scare tactics, and misinformation? As other private services become increasingly invested in the administration of justice, will they not also seek to protect themselves against shifts in the public interest? In the name of public safety, will they not also seek to mold criminal justice policy in ways that assure their own right to profit?

Part IV   Methodological Issues and Epilogue

12

Private Adult Prisons: What Do We Really Know and Why Don't We Know More?

Scott D. Camp and Gerald G. Gaes
*Office of Research and Evaluation,
Federal Bureau of Prisons*

Proponents of privatization repeatedly make two claims that are of keen, pragmatic interest to policymakers: private contractors can operate prisons more efficiently than can government bureaucracies and can provide equal or better services to inmates. In other words, proponents assert that for less money, government agencies can purchase prison services of equal or greater quality by turning the care of inmates over to private contractors.

With a rapidly expanding prison population in the United States and a tighter squeeze on tax dollars, claims that private contractors can provide higher quality services at lower costs are quite attractive to responsible policymakers. In 1985, there were 487,593 persons in state and federal prisons (Gilliard & Beck, 1998:2). By June 1997, the State and federal prison population was 1,158,763. This growth in the U.S. prisoner "market" has generated optimistic expectations among private entrepreneurs that they can capitalize on this increase and gain a substantial market share of it. Clearly, even if the market share for private companies remained a fixed proportion, the growth in the market itself might ensure future private prison prosperity.

This chapter involves two parts. In the first section, we criticize the general approach evaluators have used to compare public and private prisons, and we suggest some alternative strategies. We find fault with the prison privatization research because it often fails to address, in a systematic way, why public and private prisons should differ in their effectiveness. For the most part, proponents of privatization make global, unsubstantiated, speculative claims that are rarely addressed with concrete evidence. While our discussion focuses exclusively on methodological problems found in evaluations of private prisons, the methodological concerns apply equally well to other areas of the criminal justice system where privatization is common, such as the increasing use of private security firms. In the second section, we lay the groundwork for a testable theory of the similarities and differences in ways that public and private sector prisons are managed.

Why Prior Evaluations Have Been Inadequate

Is there supporting evidence for the claims of lower cost and superior quality put forth by proponents of prison privatization? While there is at present a small but growing body of empirical evidence on cost and quality issues, almost none of it has been peer reviewed. The General Accounting Office (GAO) (1996) published a review of cost and quality evaluations conducted between 1991 and 1996, and it identified five studies that empirically compared actual operations of at least one public and one private prison. These were state-sponsored studies in California (Sechrest & Shichor, 1994), Tennessee (Tennessee Select Oversight Committee on Corrections, 1995), and Texas (Texas Sunset Advisory Commission, 1991); a comparison of a federal prison for females and a private New Mexico prison for females (Logan, 1991); and a review of facilities in Tennessee, Louisiana, and Washington (Thomas, Gookin, Keating, Whitener, Williams, Crane & Broom, 1996). Since the GAO review, two major evaluations of private prisons have been released, one of privatization experiences in Louisiana (Archambeault & Deis, 1996a) and another on privatization in Arizona (Thomas, 1997). A third study that appeared since the GAO review (Lanza-Kaduce, Parker & Thomas, 1999) compared the recidivism of Florida inmates released from prisons operated by the Florida Department of Corrections to that of inmates released from two privately operated prisons, one by Corrections Corporation of America and the other by Wackenhut Corrections Corporation. These three new studies, along with an older one conducted by Hatry and his colleagues for the Urban Institute (Hatry, Brounstein & Levinson, 1994; Urban Institute, 1989) on prisons in Kentucky and Massachusetts, as well as those identified by GAO, have been reviewed by researchers at the Bureau of Prisons (Gaes, Camp, & Saylor, 1998). Generally, the authors of the cost and quality evaluations have reported that private prisons provided quality services at reduced costs. In contrast, GAO cautioned that the methodological limitations of the studies they reviewed made it difficult to generalize the results (General Accounting Office, 1996). The Bureau of Prisons' researchers as well as McDonald (1990; 1992) also concluded that it is difficult to generalize the results.

The methodology of the GAO review has been criticized (Harding, 1997:109; Logan, 1996; Thomas, 1996b). Rather than discuss in detail the methodological strengths and weaknesses of the GAO review, it is sufficient for our purposes to note that the cost and quality evaluations of private prisons, as well as the GAO review, have a common short-coming. They did not identify or statistically control for variables that influence the outcome measures, particularly in analyses that were conducted on measures of quality of prison performance.

For example, researchers often compare inmate misconduct rates for private and public prisons. However, in none of the studies of which we are aware has there been an attempt to control for structural factors that may influence misconduct rates. These factors would include staff-to-inmate ratios, custody technologies, and policies that lead to deliberate or unintended differences in reporting of misconduct incidents. In fact, there have been only weak attempts to control for individual differences, such as age or race of the inmates, so essential to explaining misconduct rates. For example, in the Tennessee evaluation, arguably one of the better comparisons of public and private prisons, there were wide discrepancies in the average age and racial composition of inmates among the three comparison prisons (two public and one private). If a fair and thorough comparison is to be made, it is necessary to control as rigorously as possible for other factors that influence prison outcome measures in addition to indicators of management performance. That is, it is necessary to develop models of the variables that influence cost and quality measures and to measure their effects instead of simply assuming that institutions differ only in performance.

The paucity of empirical evaluations of privatization is not surprising. Private adult prisons have only recently made a resurgence in the United States after use in the nineteenth century (Durham, 1994a,b), and evaluation research is time-consuming, difficult, and costly. Also, Harding (1997) noted that with rare exceptions, requirements for rigorous evaluations are not written into the contracts for prisons. One exception to this situation, is language in the legislation which authorized the Federal Bureau of Prisons to privatize the Taft, California facility, mandating an empirical evaluation: ". . . the Committee directs the Bureau of Prisons to undertake a 5-year prison privatization demonstration project involving the two Taft facilities. A demonstration project is needed to give the administration and Congress an opportunity to monitor safety and operational concerns. . . ." (Senate Conference Report 104-863:791, accompanying HR 3610, Public Law 104-208). To meet the specifications of this legislation, research requirements were incorporated into the original statement of work that was used to solicit requests for proposals to operate Taft (Federal Bureau of Prisons, 1997). Also, a number of states that are heavily involved in privatization, including Florida, Texas, Tennessee, and Arizona, have contract stipulations that require some demonstration that the private contractors provide lower cost and/or superior quality in comparison to the state-operated prisons. However, these requirements have not been met by rigorous research evaluations.

The General Strategy Employed in Existing Evaluations

Generally speaking, very little attention has been given to developing detailed and interrelated propositions about how private prisons operate differently from public ones. Inattention to this basic task is evident in prior research. Most existing comparisons of private and public prisons have relied upon "laundry lists" of readily available items in the official data of correctional agencies. Researchers have determined which institutions fared "better" or "worse" on such measures so that they could report whether the private or public facilities "won" on more of the data items.

There are several problems with the "laundry list" approach. First, insufficient attention has been paid to demonstrating whether some of the measures examined are more objective or important in tracking or predicting specified processes or outcomes. For example, comparing institutions on the respective proportions of staff expressing job satisfaction only makes sense if (1) job satisfaction is related to an organizational performance measure such as productivity and if (2) levels of job satisfaction are influenced by managerial practices. However, the theoretical relevance of job satisfaction and sources of variability in measures of it (and other variables) have not often been elaborated in the existing evaluations.

In the studies by Logan (1991, 1992) and other researchers, the methodological assumption usually has been that differences in staff job satisfaction, or in the number of inmates with recorded misconduct arise almost entirely from differences in management practices between the respective institutions. However, this is a highly dubious assumption. For example, in work done by Camp and colleagues (Camp, Saylor & Harer, 1997; Camp, Saylor & Wright, 1999), it was shown that a scale of staff ratings of commitment to the institution can be extremely misleading unless appropriate control variables are included. Although he labeled it job satisfaction, Logan (1991, 1992) used this same commitment scale in his study of a women's prison in New Mexico. In their work, Camp and his colleagues ranked 80 prisons based on their raw, unadjusted scores on the commitment scale. The highest rated institution was given a rank of 1. The researchers then adjusted the ratings by introducing appropriate controls for characteristics of the staff, such as age, racial composition, and tenure. The institutions were then ranked based on the adjusted ratings. As an example of how different the unadjusted and adjusted rankings were, one institution achieved an unadjusted ranking of 59th and an adjusted ranking of 8th out of the 80 prisons. Clearly, by failing to account and statistically control for characteristics of staff on survey items, misleading results and inaccurate conclusions can follow.

This problem also arises with objective indicators (e.g., inmate misconduct) and policy compliance measures (e.g., audits of institution practices). Researchers such as Archambeault and Deis (1996a) and Thomas (1997) have compared public and private prisons on such indicators without paying adequate attention to the possible variation in characteristics of staff, inmates, and institutions. Archambeault and Deis used three institutions with the same architectural footprint, activated at about the same time, and having the same physical security. Charles Thomas chose comparison institutions having the same degree of physical security. While these are important dimensions to control, there can be considerable variation among prisons on dozens of other important dimensions even when the institutions all have the same security level. *Prior research has either ignored potential confounding differences among comparison institutions or has made limited, ineffective attempts to control for these differences.*

The second problem with the laundry-list approach is that it gives insufficient attention to delineating the actual or hypothesized factors or processes that produced more favorable cost and quality outcomes in private prisons. Logan (1991) has developed the clearest classification of the features of good prisons. He used this scheme to guide his comparison of female facilities in New Mexico and the federal system. However, he failed to identify the actual mechanisms that might enable private prisons to operate with greater efficiency or provide higher quality services. In most of the literature in favor of privatization, there are emphatic but vague references to "market pressures" that force efficiencies in private companies, but little or no detail is offered as to how these market pressures actually translate into real differences between private and public prisons (for a typical review, see Moore, 1998:16-18).

Charles Thomas (1997), for example, noted that the public sector designed and built the three prisons used in the evaluation of privatization in Tennessee (Tennessee Select Oversight Committee on Corrections 1995). He claimed that "much of the opportunity the private management firms would otherwise have had to provide cost savings does not exist when facilities are designed and constructed by government agencies" (Thomas, 1997:46). We are unaware of any breakthrough in the design of prisons that was not a result of input from public sector correctional experts in conjunction with public and private sector architects and private sector builders and suppliers. We are puzzled as to why designs that improve prison efficiencies, whether developed by the public or private sector, cannot then be used by everyone for future prison construction. The clear presumption of such commentary is that it is only the private sector that is interested in these efficiencies.

Toward a Theory of the Differences Between Publicly and Privately Operated Prisons

Missing from research comparing public and private prisons and essays arguing the pros and cons of privatization is a theory that will guide an explicit assessment of the practices that distinguish the two sectors and produce efficiency and quality differences. Articulating the underlying hypothetical processes will allow us to design better evaluations of quality and operational efficiency and to assess whether practices can be altered to provide better quality and/or greater operational efficiencies in public sector prisons. Given that public prisons still account for more than 95 percent of the prison beds in the United States, the potential for cost savings and value gains is greatest there.

At the most general level, proponents of privatization argue that the normal operation of a free market insures that only service providers who provide a quality product at a competitive market price will survive. Those companies that do not provide quality services and/or do not offer a competitive price will drop from the market. Proponents of privatization portray government agencies that run prisons as being more "labor intensive than what one finds in private corporations" (Thomas, 1997:38). They assert that the workers filling the positions in government agencies "are not known for their dedication and zeal" (Champion, 1996:v). Champion himself is not necessarily advocating this view toward civil servants. He is simply reporting that this view has both advocates and a long history.

Proponents of privatization invoke classic economic theory and argue that a free market introduces discipline and efficiency through the mechanisms of supply and demand. This is, of course, an idealized, hypothetical market operating in the long run. However, if we are to advance beyond the level of rhetorical appeal, then it is necessary to specify exactly how the specific prison market operates to produce these gains, in the long and the short term. Unfortunately, few proponents of privatization provide specific theoretical or practical arguments about how the market operates to discipline the organizational performance of private sector providers of prison services, though there are hints scattered throughout the literature. In the discussion that follows, we draw out those theoretical arguments for critical examination. We do not investigate the competitiveness of the private adult corrections market. We simply assume that there is competition in the market even though Corrections Corporation of America and Wackenhut Corrections Corporation control approximately 70 percent of the worldwide market.

As is probably obvious even to casual observers, bureaucrats and bureaucracy are often blamed for the alleged inefficiencies of government agencies. This claim, though, is much too broad and vague. If government bureaucracies operate less efficiently than private sector ones, is it due to the different goals pursued by public and private bureaucracies or to differences in the operating efficiencies of the respective bureaucracies? In fact, the goals of public and private correctional organizations are different. The first and foremost goal of a private prison or the corporation running it is to generate a profit for shareholders or owners of the company. (This discussion generally assumes that the private organizations are for-profit. The major players in the private adult corrections market are all for-profit.) However, profits most directly benefit the owners/stockholders of the company and the profit goal is not necessarily or automatically a primary one for many of the managers and workers. Organizations are composed of individuals and groups who have their own vested interests and agendas. Simply assuming that managers and workers in private firms always put profits before their other interests is a far too simplistic and naive understanding of human nature and the nature of organizations.

Casile (1994) is one of the few analysts to bring an organizational viewpoint to the topic of privatization. Drawing upon a rich tradition in organizational research, in particular the institutional (Meyer & Rowan, 1977) and resource dependence (Pfeffer, 1982; Pfeffer & Salancik, 1978) perspectives, she developed specific propositions about how power is distributed in private firms that take over functions formerly performed by the public sector. Her focus was wider than simply prison privatization, but her points apply equally well. Casile argued that privatization shifts power in prisons away from members of those groups who are either part of or interact with the prison, such as correctional officer unions, legislators, and other special interest groups, and places control of the administration of the prison more directly in the hands of shareholders. As a result, the private organization can place less emphasis upon, and direct much fewer resources toward, certain functions than can their public sector counterparts.

Casile (1994) noted that power in private entities is shifted under normal circumstances away from workers, and especially from the labor unions that typically represent public sector workers. This can be a strong incentive to consider privatization, according to Casile (1994:2), if the existing relationship between management and the public sector labor unions is strained. In the case where labor relations are rigidly locked in place, as they were in England (James, Bottomley, Liebling & Clare, 1997) and Australia (Harding, 1997), there is more potential to generate cost reductions and labor efficiencies. However, actual or threatened privatization and the corresponding competition it generates also provides public managers with additional leverage over public workers and unions, as we note later in reference to public workers and potholes in Indianapolis.

It appears from the literature that proponents of prison privatization have four propositions in mind when they speak of greater labor efficiencies. All four reflect a shift in power away from line-level staff. First, proponents imply, or directly state, that many correctional workers in the public sector are overcompensated through a combination of direct pay and fringe benefits (Thomas, 1997:38). Doctor Crants, the ex-chief executive officer of Corrections Corporation of America, was explicit on this point: "Efficient labor is precluded in public facilities in several states by unionized labor. Union contracts tend to increase wage costs and promote unjustified job security" (Crants, 1991:53). In addition to excessive direct labor costs, privatization proponents often argue that indirect labor costs are also too high in the public sector. They often propose that the expensive benefits packages of union and government workers be replaced with less costly schemes such as the one used by Corrections Corporation of America. At that firm, workers "benefit from participation in a stock ownership program" (Crants, 1991:54).

Second, advocates such as Crants (1991) assert that private managers have greater flexibility in assigning staff. He claimed that managers in private firms have the flexibility to assign labor where it is needed. "Using temporary labor from the worker pool, private managers can dramatically reduce overtime expenses and can increase and decrease staffing to match demand" (Crants, 1991:53-54). This flexibility presumably pays off because managers in private firms do not have to resort to overtime pay as often as do managers in public firms to cover staffing needs. Thomas and his colleagues (Thomas et al., 1996) found this to be the case in their review of private operations in Louisiana and Tennessee.

Third, proponents assert that private managers can use technology more effectively to augment the efficiency of existing labor, and as a result, less human labor is required per unit of output. Although this claim is often voiced, we are unaware of any persuasive argument as to why private contractors can utilize technology while public prison operators cannot. Ad hoc claims typically heard at privatization conferences allude to the benefits of increased use of electronic surveillance equipment and other design features. But, while The Office of Program Policy Analysis and Government Accountability (1998), in reviewing the operations of two private facilities in Florida, did note that the private prisons used a more compact prison design and a greater use of cameras in the housing areas than did the typical public prison, there appears to be no fundamental barriers to the use of these same features in public institutions.

A fourth assumption is that private managers are better able to create a disciplined, motivated, and productive workforce and that there are several benefits to having such a productive workforce. Private prison managers allege that they employ more extensive screening to ensure that the proper type of individual is hired. In addition to selecting motivated employees with good work habits and skills, private prison operators hope to reduce staff turnover by screening out workers likely to voluntarily leave prison employment well before retirement and workers likely to be dismissed for cause (misconduct or poor performance). Then, too, private prison managers claim that improved training protects their employees from being placed in situations that are beyond their capabilities. The expectation is that well-trained workers will be motivated to superior performance, and they will be better protected from stress and burn-out.

Private managers also assert that they are more free to promote on the basis of merit instead of seniority or political considerations. In turn, they claim that they can develop a work environment where the sense of fair play leads to strong employee commitment to the goals of the organization. This commitment and morale are believed to help reduce negative organizational outcomes such as turnover and the irresponsible use of sick leave. Reducing sick leave is important because overtime must often be paid to employees to cover mandatory posts that are temporarily vacated by a "sick" worker. Corrections Corporation of America even increases the incentive to restrict the use of sick leave by paying employees bonuses for unused sick time (Crants, 1991:54).

In addition to the savings from the efficient use of labor, Crants identified another major advantage that managers of private prisons have over their counterparts in public institutions (see also Thomas, 1997:38-39): namely, a comparative edge in purchasing supplies. Quite simply, he claimed that the bureaucratic purchasing regulations of government agencies limit their flexibility in purchasing needed goods and services. It should be noted, though, that many bureaucratic purchasing restrictions in government agencies arose to limit opportunities for favoritism and to promote social goals (such as stimulating opportunities for minority-owned businesses or supporting drug-free work environments). Whatever the political acceptability of these purposes, the restrictions clearly add overhead to government purchasing practices.

Private managers, on the other hand, can often sidestep such bureaucratic regulations and purchase goods and services at spot prices. In fact, Crants (1991:54-55) argued that given the cumbersome nature of regulations, there is often a tendency for public managers to maintain expensive inventories of goods. However, even if these claims are correct, the potential savings from purchasing costs are modest since labor costs account for about 70 percent of the total operating costs over the life of a prison (Crants, 1991:53; Thomas et al., 1996:15). Crants (1991) also reviewed issues related to financing and constructing prisons, but that is not our focus.

Critique of the Claimed Superiority of Private Operations

Privatization proponents express a good deal of confidence about the superiority of management practices and performance in the private sector. They state that cost savings, at least, are almost guaranteed by turning prison operations over to the private sector. For example, Thomas (1997:38) recently noted that ". . . a reasonable person ought to be surprised only if he or she encountered a contracting initiative that failed to yield at least some cost savings. Simple economic logic suggests that the real question is how great the cost savings of contracting are likely to be rather than whether there will be any cost savings."

Proponents of privatization focus almost exclusively on costs, with much less being said about the promotion of innovations designed to fundamentally alter the way a prison program or service is provided so as to better perform such tasks as rehabilitation. Standing in stark contrast is the delivery of medical services in prisons. There, privatization proponents can clearly point to innovations that they believe will produce cost savings while maintaining or even improving quality. For example, in an ongoing evaluation of the contracting of medical services at the Federal Corrections Complex in Beaumont, Texas, the contractor, University of Texas Medical Branch (UTMB), plans to reduce costs by substituting emergency medical technicians and registered nurses for more expensive medical doctors and physician's assistants to deal with routine medical concerns. Similarly, the contractor has employed a method of distributing medicine that does not require a licensed pharmacist to be on-site at the prison (as is the case in other federal prisons). The contractors also use tele-medicine to reduce the cost of transporting prisoners and to minimize the amount of time medical consultants must spend traveling back and forth from the UTMB hospital to the prison. Whether or not this contract will ultimately produce cost savings and preserve or improve the quality of care provided to inmates is unknown as yet. But, unlike most of the claims in the literature extolling the benefits of privatization, in this case, proposed cost-saving innovations are clearly and precisely delineated.

The savings associated with innovations in delivery of medical services are not typically mentioned by privatization proponents, but there is new evidence that these may comprise a major portion of the cost savings associated with turning an entire prison over to the private sector.

In a study commissioned by the National Institute of Corrections and included as Appendix 1 in the recent Abt report on privatization (McDonald, Fournier, Russell-Einhorn & Crawford, 1998), Nelson re-analyzed cost data for the Tennessee and Louisiana evaluations (Nelson, 1998). Those two cost studies are often pointed to as among the best such investigations, in part because the facilities compared within each state were built at about the same time with the same general designs. *Nelson found that the operational expenses for running two public prisons and one private prison in Tennessee were virtually identical when medical costs were excluded.* However, Tennessee taxpayers actually did save money because the private facility had substantially lower medical costs on a per inmate basis. It is also possible that the private prisons may have produced lower overhead costs (Nelson, 1998:9). In the case of the Louisiana data, Nelson found that the difference in operating costs between the two private prisons and the one public prison for the fiscal year 1995-1996 was probably in the range of 5 percent or less rather than the 12 percent reported by Archambeault and Deis (1996a); however, because of the lack of specificity in the line item expenditures, it was not possible to determine precisely where the savings accrued.

Generally speaking, some fairly sketchy observations have been presented about where cost savings can be generated, but regarding quality, much less has been said, and it appears that private vendors are usually not practicing new ways of doing things. Instead, private vendors seem to see their task as one of refining processes already represented in the best practices of well-operated public systems.

If advocates of private prisons are convinced that contractors restructure their operations to maximize performance quality, it is surprising that there are so few attempts to document how private vendors actually do this. Archambeault and Deis (1996a) argued that the management approach in the CCA-operated facility in Louisiana was more team-oriented and egalitarian than that of Wackenhut and the public institution they evaluated. They concluded that this approach produced a better run facility. While their analysis of quality performance measures was flawed (Gaes et al., 1998), their study at least attempted to show how an innovative management approach may have improved prison operations.

Better designed studies of prison privatization may demonstrate private sector advantages in some areas of prison operations and public sector advantages in others. To capitalize on the best practices of each sector, we believe that work must proceed on two fronts. Efforts must be made to determine whether the hypothesized differences between public and private sector prison operations are immutable or variable. In other words, can the best practices of one sector be adopted by the other? We also need to understand what types of evaluation strategies would allow us to more directly answer the more general questions about the sources of the supposed differences.

Immutable or Variable Differences?

Missing from discussions of the advantages of private prisons is an explanation of why public correctional agencies cannot adopt flexible labor practices and streamlined purchasing procedures. In fact, it is possible that well-run public agencies already follow some of the practices that the private sector has adopted. Public agencies, just as private companies, are faced with cost constraints, and efficiency is not solely a concern of private companies. It is tempting to overstate the pressures for efficiency in private companies, just as it is easy to overestimate waste in public agencies. Proponents of privatization, for example, state that public sector agencies never go out of business, i.e., they are immune to the pressures of the market. However, with the introduction of privatization into corrections, this claim is no longer true. While no publicly operated prison system has yet gone out of existence, it is not inconceivable that a public sector prison system could be entirely privatized. In fact, Corrections Corporation of America has on at least two occasions proposed to take over the entire Tennessee prison system, and the Governor of Tennessee announced in 1998 his support for privatization of up to 70 percent of the Tennessee prisons (Bates, 1998a). Also, while no state system has "failed," it could be argued that the District of Columbia prison system failed. Primarily because of a budget deal, all adult D.C. prison inmates will be turned over to the custody of the Federal Bureau of Prisons. One-half of the D.C. inmates will be placed in private correctional facilities by the year 2002.

We maintain that differences between the operations of public and private prisons are matters of degree, not of kind, that follow from the power held by different interest groups. We do not deny the disciplinary power of the market in the long-run, but we also note that the market can (and has) been subverted in the short-run in both the public and private sectors.

Prison privatization has brought indirect, but nonetheless real, market pressures to bear upon the public sector. However, while it is true that there may be restraints in the public sector that can be circumvented by turning prison operations over to the private sector, the potential advantages of the private sector are not necessarily fixed. Some of the workplace issues facing publicly operated prisons are beginning to affect the operations of privately operated prisons. Wage demands, higher expectations of government oversight staff, and other pressures seem to be increasing the costs of private contracts. At the same time, competition seems to be decreasing the costs of government operations. There has already been movement toward convergence of public-sector and private-sector costs (Thomas et al., 1996).

To date, private sector prison managers in the United States operate with an almost entirely non-union workforce. Does this provide potential advantages for private-sector managers in holding down labor costs? It would seem to, but again we argue that there are pressures that push these sectors toward comparability in public- and private-sector wages. For example, in the public sector, especially the federal sector, several measures have been enacted that have helped control labor costs. There has been an extensive effort by the Clinton administration to reduce the number of federal employees and improve the efficiency of government (National Performance Review, 1993). Even in the few instances where there has been continued growth in the federal sector, there have been simultaneous reductions in certain types of positions, especially procurement and administrative ones. Additionally, there are experimental programs that provide managers with increased flexibility to reward good performance and keep poor performers from receiving automatic pay increases (Vice President Gore's National Partnership for Reinventing Government, 1999).

Private-sector managers also have restrictions imposed on their flexibility to hold down labor costs because they must compete for good workers, run quality prisons, and abide by contractual stipulations. For example, when contracting with the federal government, a contractor is held to wage rates (at least for key positions) that are set by the Service Contract Act of 1965. The U.S. Department of Labor sets wage rates that are based on prevailing practices in the local labor market, and these wage rates have to be used by the contractor.

There are also public sector constraints. In many circumstances, public sector managers are bound by more workplace restrictions such as those that limit their ability to reward workers, reduce their flexibility in assigning workers to jobs outside of their position descriptions, and constrain their decisionmaking in hiring and firing workers. These restrictions have been built into the structure of the work relationship in the form of rules, policies, and contracts and exist largely because there are better organized interest groups representing public-sector workers both at the workplace (unions) and in the political arenas (unions, other pro-labor interest groups, and legislators). At a broader level than workplace relationships, Stolz (1997; see also chapter in this text) outlined the potential changes in who participates at the level of public policymaking when prisons are privatized (see also Shichor, 1999). Stolz also relied upon an interest group perspective and noted (Stolz, 1997:102) that: "The changes are not just changes in who participates but in the stakes and goals, the tools and techniques of influence, the access and decision points, and the dynamics of the process of corrections policymaking." Stolz pointed out that privatization fundamentally realigns the existing structure of interest group politics that surrounds the running of prisons. In particular, elected officials have less direct control over the operations of private prisons than they do over public prisons. Nonetheless, if the private sector currently enjoys advantages

that limit the influence of competing interest groups, they are advantages of degree. The power of managers to structure work relationships in private firms is never absolute, and public agency managers are
not powerless to redesign or "re-engineer," as it is now fashionable to say,
their work setting.

An illustration of the ability to restructure the work relationships of
public employees when faced with competition from the private sector
is provided by the case study of filling potholes in Indianapolis (Kaplan,
1996a; Kaplan, 1996b). With the election in the early 1990s of a Republican mayor who favored privatizing services to improve the efficiency
of government, city workers were forced into the position of rethinking
the way they filled potholes. By coming under the threat of losing their
jobs to the private sector, public workers were forced into the difficult
position of rethinking costs and restructuring the way they did business.
By more efficiently utilizing manpower (for example, by eliminating
many supervisory, patronage positions and reducing crew sizes from
eight to four union workers), materials, and capital assets, the workers
were able to bid on and win those projects that they identified as falling
within their area of comparative advantage.

What Differences Should We Seek?

The discussion so far has focused on two primary problems in existing evaluations of prison privatization efforts. First, existing evaluations
have not been technical and comprehensive; rather, simple comparisons
of public and private institutions have been made. The differences
observed and reported could have been caused by performance differences, but they could also have been caused by a host of unaccounted for
factors. Second, and equally important, existing evaluations have not
asked all of the right types of questions. In particular, there has been little attempt to analyze where the innovations in the use of labor or purchasing practices exist, or if they exist, in the private sector. This second
shortcoming, we have argued, is due primarily to a lack of theory about
why private sector firms should be able to perform better. We have proposed the beginning of such a theory. Privatization often shifts power
among the competing interest groups involved in operating a prison, and
this shift in power may provide an advantage to the owners/managers
who are more likely to give priority to operating prisons efficiently.

What is needed is a coupling of a more organizational or even business practice type of analysis with rigorous assessments of public and
private performance outputs. We find a starting point in the work of
Charles Logan (1990; 1991; 1992). Logan classified performance outputs
in relation to the goals he argued prison systems ought to pursue. However, Logan stopped short of conceptualizing the antecedents and intermediate processes that determine if and when a prison will perform suc-

cessfully. These "black box" processes must be articulated if we are to have a thorough understanding of why prisons are more or less successful in providing services to inmates and protecting public safety. What we are calling for is nothing short of a comprehensive theory of prison performance coupled with a theory of interest group participation in setting prison goals. This must occur before we can make sense of the comparison between public and private prisons.

With a model or conceptualization of prison performance, we can make sense of answers to the fundamental questions which document how public and private prisons use labor and how they purchase goods and services. Although we believe a comprehensive theory of prison performance may take some time to develop, we can approach the problem in incremental steps. Prison services are organized around relatively discrete components. For example, there are inmate programs, medical care, and inmate and staff safety to mention a few. We can analyze these components separately and ask how they can be delivered more efficiently and assess which innovations produce the greatest gains. This approach allows us to systematically evaluate prison performance, compare prisons on key performance outputs, and incorporate analyses of innovation and efficiency.

Conclusions

In answer to the question "what do we really know?" we have to admit, not as much as we would like. This is generally the case when policy and social science intersect. In the case of private prisons, though, the lack of knowledge is aggravated by the fact that we have not been asking all of the right questions.

Despite this seemingly pessimistic overview of the state of knowledge, there are some very important things that we have already learned. We have some evidence from Australia and the United Kingdom that privatization has brought competition to the public sector, and this has improved the overall operations of the prison systems in these countries (both public and private). In particular, in England, privatization has brought the use of standards to the operations of public prisons where previously there had been resistance from top management to their use (Vagg, 1994:307). There is not as much evidence that similar system-wide changes have occurred in the United States, but there are hints that the competition created by private prisons has improved the cost performance of some prison systems.

There are many advantages to articulating the theoretical reasons why public and private prisons approach prison operations differently. The best practices of each approach may be used to improve operations throughout entire prison systems. The entire discipline of corrections might improve if we move beyond slogans and speculation and clearly delineate *if*, *how*, and *why* private prisons improve performance and efficiency. Understanding the differences also makes the public policy choices clearer. Assuming that private contractors can generate cost savings, and these cost savings are achieved by reducing the wages and/or benefits of line staff, by structuring purchasing practices so that they are unencumbered by such "guidelines" as Federal Acquisitions Restrictions (FAR), and by dramatically restructuring prison medical care delivery, does it make sense for government to support such practices? The answers to these types of policy questions depend in part upon philosophical or political notions about the proper role of government, what we earlier referred to as normative issues. But we hope we have demonstrated that the policy choices also depend upon empirical issues. Issues such as whether savings in direct labor costs are offset by higher rates of turnover and corresponding training and recruitment costs, or whether higher-paid medical staff can be replaced with lower-paid medical workers while maintaining the quality of medical services? It is the latter types of issues that better designed and conducted research evaluations can address.

13   Epilogue

David Shichor
California State University,
San Bernardino

In the Anglo-American cultural tradition, the participation of private entities, both business and nonprofit, in the planning, establishment and operation of public programs is accepted (Preston & Post, 1975), and often encouraged. This tradition prevails in various aspects of public policy concerning business activities, social services, and criminal justice as well. This closing segment of the book presents a short review of some of the factors that facilitated the recent increase in the involvement of private for-profit companies in the operation of the criminal justice system.

Private sector involvement in criminal justice has deep roots in the history of western societies, especially in those with Anglo-Saxon cultural and legal heritage. Private entrepreneurs and private companies were involved in managing and operating jails, workhouses, prisons, and police forces for a long time. Private attorneys acted as prosecutors in some of the American colonies and states. Bails were posted by friends or relatives of the accused long before professional bondsmen took over and institutionalized this practice. Also, many community-based diversion, substance abuse and other kinds of treatment programs are managed or operated by for-profit private companies. In some jurisdictions pre-sentence reports prepared by private individuals or firms are used at sentencing. Also, electronic monitoring of intermediate punishments, such as house arrest, is often contracted out to private companies. Referring to the contemporary situation in criminal justice, Benson (1996:3) pointed out that: "[v]irtually everything governments do, including police, security, jails, prisons, and court-related services, is being contracted out somewhere in the United States."

Historically, private involvement in criminal justice indicated that the monarch, and later the state, does not have unlimited power to enforce the law and to punish offenders. In a sense, the Magna Carta, signed in 1215 in England, provided an opening for others than the king to participate in ruling the country. In the Middle Ages, this document provided a degree of participation in the governing to the nobility, and curbed the absolute power of the King. It also set a precedent and allowed a wider level of participation than before of individuals other than the king in the management of various state functions. Thus, this tradition limited the legitimate authority of the state to enforce the law and exclusively operate the criminal justice system.

The participation of the private sector in the management and operation of various components of the criminal justice system brings up questions concerning the general concept of the state, its functions, responsibilities, and authority. The criminal justice system is established for the purpose of enforcement of the laws that are created by a legislative body representing the state. There is a strong opinion that posits that the very raison d'etre of government is the provision of legal order (van den Haag, 1975). This function includes and focuses on the exercise of formal social control.

On the theoretical level the general idea of "social contract" has deep roots in Western culture. Barker (1962), in his introduction to the essays of Locke, Hume, and Rousseau focusing on the political and social aspects of this concept, traced the historical development of the idea of social contract back to the days of Plato in the fourth century B.C. This concept appeared in the writings of Saint Thomas Aquinas in the Middle Ages, but reached its most developed conceptualization during the Enlightenment period in the seventeenth and eighteen centuries in Western Europe. This view of the emergence of the state, its nature, and functions has strongly influenced American culture. According to this perspective, members of society gave up some of their individual rights and political power to the state for the sake of securing order. Locke (1692/1955) suggested that, in spite of this delegation of authority to the state by the people, the ultimate power still resides with the individuals who make up society. This concept of the state leads to the conclusion that if the state does not satisfactorily fulfill the task of protecting the members of society, they have the right and the power to dissolve the state (Carnoy, 1984). Accordingly, "Sovereign power . . . remains ultimately with the people" (Held, 1984:39).

Thus the classical-liberal tradition viewed authority as bedded in the consent of citizens. The emergence of a strong state signaled the centralization of power. It usurped the authority to maintain a monopoly over the use of legitimate coercive power. However, the monopoly over coercive authority was delegated to the state by citizens who retain the ultimate power. This perspective of the state has probably become more widespread in the United States than in the countries of continental Europe because Europeans inherited a strong central authority from the *ancient regime* (Shils, 1997:131). In America there is a general feeling of mistrust of the government, and as Shils pointed out, nearly everyone in the United States at one time or other, was opposed to the authority of the state. Therefore, the state is accorded only a limited function whereby: "[I]ts only concern is to regulate the conflicts among the different groups with their different conceptions of the good life" (Spragens, 1986:39). To a somewhat lesser degree, the ambivalence toward the state also can be found in other societies with an Anglo-Saxon cultural and political heritage. For example, it has been pointed out that the political culture in Britain "is thought to inhabit neutral ground in liberal democracy, even-handedly balancing the interests of a plurality of competing institutions and groups" (Abercombie, Hill & Turner, 1980:136-137).

This sociopolitical perspective led to the libertarian concept of the "minimal state" (see Nozick, 1974). Privatization of government services, including criminal justice, is related to the ideal of the minimal state. The libertarian view challenges the widely held validity of criminal law that considers crime as an act against society. According to this perspective "the notion that punishing criminals is the exclusive prerogative of the state appears to be an invention of the state" (Logan, 1990:240). If this approach is followed to the extreme, victims would be the only ones who would have the right to pursue offenders, to apprehend them, and to determine their punishment. Logan (1990:244) summarized this view by claiming that: "Only the victim has a right to restitution and may use force against the offender for this and only this, purpose." Thus the minimal state concept claims all rights to be individual and views the state as an artificial construct having no legitimate authority by itself but only rights transferred to it by individual citizens. This view opens the door for the active participation of private entities in the criminal justice process.

Following this tradition one of the major questions will be: "How much of the legitimate coercive power could or should be delegated to private parties?" In other words, where should the line be drawn between government powers that can and those that cannot be delegated? This question is similar to the one asked by Michael Gilbert in this volume in the chapter titled "How Much Is Too Much Privatization in Criminal Justice?" This issue relates to both the external and the internal security of the state. For example, the U.S. armed forces have contracts with numerous private companies not only for the delivery of supplies, weapons, ammunition, and other equipment, but also for various services. However, the critical question is whether the commanding of military forces should be contracted to private firms even if they could run them in a cheaper and in a more flexible manner. This example is somewhat parallel to the private operation of the component agencies of the criminal justice system. As a reminder, according to the classical-liberal doctrine the sovereign (in this case the state) has the authority and obligation to maintain peace at home and protect the citizens against enemies from abroad (Hobbes, 1651/1969). The fact is, that the issues arising from the privatization of criminal justice are dramatically different from the privatization of other services usually provided by the government such as garbage collection, public transportation, maintenance of public buildings, and mail delivery (see DiIulio, 1988; Starr, 1987). Criminal justice personnel are often involved, literally, in life and death decisions such as the use of deadly force, or making quasi-judicial decisions that could effect one's personal liberty. For example, disciplinary measures in prisons could lengthen the time an offender is confined. As Foucault (1977:177) noted in the prison "disciplinary power . . . is everywhere and always alert." These issues are amplified by the fact that the private companies involved in the provision of criminal justice services are strongly focused on profit-making. Some of them are traded on the stock exchanges and are under constant pressure to produce monetary gains for their investors. They are clearly expansion-oriented like corporations in any other branch of the economy, and the question is how much they can and will influence criminal justice policies not necessarily for the benefit of the public good, but for the purpose of increasing their own financial gains. It may be a considerable problem when "a divergence of duty and interest" for an individual or a company exists (Gentry, 1986:355; Ogle, 1999). There is a concern, as several scholars suggested, that private companies may be more interested to do well for themselves than to good for society (e.g., Robbins, 1986; Gentry, 1986, Ogle, 1999). As it was shown in some of the chapters in this volume, politicians who have a major impact on legislation involving criminal justice policies, may also have strong financial interests in some of the private corporations. This conflict of interest, coupled with recent indications of possible co-optation of some academic researchers who conduct evaluations of performance and operation in privatized correctional facilities (see Geis, Mobley & Shichor, 1999), should raise the level of apprehension concerning private involvement in criminal justice among policymakers.

In addition, other issues relating to privatization should be addressed. These issues include, among others, equity in providing services, quality of personnel and adequate training in private policing and the use of deadly force by private officers. One of the critical and sensitive issues is whether some neighborhoods, or entire areas of a city, can afford hiring a private police-security force, while less affluent areas cannot. Limiting police services to more affluent areas will perpetuate and even exacerbate social class, racial, and ethnic differences. This would increase the vulnerability of the poorer neighborhoods to crime and increase their risk of victimization. Nigel South (1988) who conducted a detailed study on private police and security in Britain examined the differential impact of such organizations on communities. He states that:

> Private security is not in the business to serve the general public good; it is in business to serve the needs of its paying clients. It clearly does make a contribution to, for example, crime prevention in some respects, although how much this is offset by a displacement effect, which means those less able to pay for additional security become more heavily victimized, is unknown but probably significant (South, 1988:152).

There is also the issue of accountability. In their study of shoplifters and private corporate police Davis, Lundman, and Martinez (1991:407) found that "(p)ublic systems of justice are either the targets of routine research or publicly accountable actors," on the other hand "[p]rivate justice systems are neither." While public records are open for review, private institutions can prevent or make it very hard to access their records. Moyle (1995:55) in his study of Borallon Correctional Centre in Australia, operated by the Corrections Corporation of Australia, found that "the inaccessibility of contractual arrangements due to CCA's claims to 'commercial confidentiality', inhibits effective evaluation of Borallon's performance." Thus, in the private facility documents were considered private business secrets and were not open for review. This policy of keeping proprietary secrets closed to monitors may hinder contract monitoring and the attribution of accountability to private firms.

It seems quite feasible that private involvement in the operation of criminal justice systems in industrialized countries, especially anglophone countries, will continue to exist and even expand (see Harding, 1998). As seen, there is a general sociopolitical climate coupled with historical tradition that presents a fertile ground for private sector participation in the keeping of peace, maintaining order, and punishment of those who violate the law. In America, this public atmosphere was rekindled and flourished during the Reagan administration in the 1980s. President Reagan appointed a special Commission on Privatization looking into the feasibility of privatizing various government services. The Commission's report was published in 1988. In the preface of the report, the Commission Chair David F. Liwones (1988:VII) stated that:

> The American people have often complained of the intrusiveness of federal programs, of inadequate performance, and excessive expenditures. In light of these public concerns, government should consider turning to the creative talents and ingenuity in the private sector to provide, wherever possible and appropriate, better answers to present and future challenges.

This statement revealed a general negative attitude toward the public sector. In American society, government is generally considered to be ineffective, wasteful, lacking imagination, and discouraging of innovation and personal initiative. This public attitude is reflected in everyday life and often in the media. One of the manifestations of this view of the public sector is that government is the butt of innumerable jokes heard about lousy services and lazy, ineffective, uninspired, and at times outrightly stupid public employees.

Thus, in the American cultural tradition there is a strong mistrust in the government (Bellah, Madsen, Sullivan, Swidler & Tipton, 1985). However, there are also contradictions in this tradition. The laissez-faire market and minimal-state ideology, prevalent during the Reagan administration in the United States and was the Thatcher administration in the United Kingdom, led to major cutbacks in government social programs such as health and welfare. However, in social control the conservative agenda extended and strengthened the reach of law and criminal justice. This trend was reflected during the 1980s and 1990s, for example, in campaigns against pornography and reproductive choice, in legislation and implementation of mandatory punishments, in longer prison sentences, and in the war on drugs that reached even into other countries (e.g., Colombia, Peru, Mexico, and Panama). Paradoxically, the advocates of curtailment of the state's coercive power used more intrusive government practices to assist them in implementing crime control policies that were consistent with their sociopolitical and economic agenda. Similarly, the most fervent supporters of cost cutting in social programs advocated large spending programs for crime control.

Another important reason for the increasing trend toward privatization in criminal justice is economic. Politicians are attracted to privatization mainly because of the promise of reduced public costs of contracting the provision of public services to private companies. From the perspective of the private corporations, the availability of large public budgets dedicated to criminal justice operations is attractive. Private companies, from various business areas, have found that criminal justice markets can be lucrative. For example, since 1996 there has been an Annual Privatizing Correctional Facilities conference organized by the World Research Group in which representatives from private correctional companies, brokerages, investment firms, financial institutions, insurance companies and government agencies are urged to participate. The advertising brochure of the 2nd Annual conference (1997) was marketed by using the slogan: "maximize returns by investing in this $1 billion a year industry." A year later a similar slogan suggested: "penetrate the $2 billion market for privatized correctional facilities." In the 1999 advertising brochure, the slogan on the first page read: "Grow Profits and Maximize Investment Opportunities in this Explosive Industry" (World Research Group, 1997; 1998; 1999). Also, the various sessions of these conferences focus on the business aspects of correctional privatization. The profit potential can be surmised from the size of the correctional budgets. In California alone, the 1999 annual prison budget was $4.7 billion (Morain, 1999). Because of the large budgets allocated to criminal justice it will remain a highly attractive market for private companies and they will continue their attempts to increase their share of this potentially lucrative market.

The continued growth of privatization benefits from the negative image of the public sector as bloated, inefficient, and ineffective. Some scholars argue that the criminal justice system has the characteristics of a "loosely coupled system." In this kind of system: "(1) organizational elements... are only loosely linked to one another; (2) rules are often violated; (3) decisions often go unimplemented, or if implemented have uncertain consequences; and (4) techniques are often subverted or rendered so vague as to provide little coordination" (Hagan, 1994:144). In addition to the negative image of the criminal justice system in general, several individual components of this system carry a negative public image and reputation. For example, police departments have often been cited for brutality and corruption. Some recent examples include a New York case in which a black immigrant was sodomized by police officers; the killing of a young black women in Riverside, California by four policemen, and scores of other unspeakable acts. The situation is not better in corrections. The news about inmate "gladiator games" arranged by guards in Corcoran prison in California, was reported and became known all over the country. Several inmates were shot in the same prison by the guards, and some of them died. The California Department of Corrections was accused of stonewalling the investigation of the brutal treatment of prisoners. There have been a host of other cases in which criminal justice agencies and their personnel acted in ways seen as reproachful by large segments of the general public.

According to Logan and Rausch (1985) there is another reason for the negative image and inefficiency of public organizations. This is related to the way that they are financed. The private sector is committed to the free market system that promises to provide maximum satisfaction at a minimum cost. On the other hand, according to their critics, public organizations are monopolistic, their size and budget are not dependent on their performance, thus they do not have strong incentives to improve the quality of their services or reduce expenses. Therefore, the best way to ensure free competition and achieve good performance is to reduce government intrusion into the economic marketplace (Logan & Rausch, 1985). This comparison reveals a generally positive view of the private sector, and privatization advocates use it to advance their cause.

A related source pressing for greater extent of privatization of government services, including criminal justice functions, is the general trend toward "load-shedding." Its main focus is to ease the system's "overload." This is part of a wider trend that aims at reducing the "social role and responsibility" of government (Kamerman & Kahn, 1989:256). While the literature on load-shedding is usually concerned with the role of the federal government (see, Bendick, 1989; Kamerman & Kahn, 1989), it is relevant for state and county governments as well. This policy "may either be symbolic (that is, arising from a desire to hide the level of government expenses through subcontracting) or substantive with the intention of devolving administration to independent bodies" (Rein, 1989:52). In general, governmental load-shedding may include various forms of private involvement in the delivery of social services such as welfare or medicare. This usually means reduction both in the quantity and quality of these services. Load-shedding tends to increase bifurcation in criminal justice by dislodging the "soft bits," such as status offenses and victimless crimes, from the criminal justice system and the concentration of the "hard end," on crimes that were defined as "dangerous " (Cohen, 1985). Government agencies dealing with the soft end became dependent on, and supported by "the selection procedures, discretion, financing, and back-up authority" of the criminal justice system (Cohen, 1985 p. 138). Such strategies as decarceration (Scull, 1977), diversion, and dispute resolution reflect the "bifurcation principle," by which soft-end offenders are diverted out of the system and hard-core offenders are targeted for more severe penalties by public agencies (Cohen, 1985). Often the handling of soft-end offenders is contracted out to private companies who operate various community-based treatment programs.

The growing trend of bifurcation in some respects is in contradiction with the concept of the minimal-state. First, the financing, classification, selection of offenders, and back-up authority for the offenders diverted from the system remain in the hands of government. Second, bifurcation usually leads to "net widening," so that more people are handled by criminal justice related programs than before. Without the existence of these programs many of the participants would not have been involved with the justice system at all. Thus, the formal control of the state is expanded, rather than reduced. In this way, the movement toward a minimal state is thwarted by the load-shedding in criminal justice.

Bifurcation is intriguing because it was initially pursued when the main goal of social control was rehabilitation rather than punishment of offenders. At that time, the justifications for pursuing this policy were that it was a more humane way to deal with offenders who committed relatively minor crimes, that it furthered the treatment of offenders, and that it mitigated their labeling. The adoption and extension of bifurcation policies have also expanded the opportunities for private-sector involvement in the criminal justice process, because many programs aimed at offenders at the soft-end of this process such as diversion, counseling, drug rehabilitation, and electronic monitoring were contracted out to private companies. In fact, private contractors are often favored to operate these programs rather than programs aimed at more serious criminals, because of the lower liability involved with handling soft-end criminals, and the greater potential for positive results with less serious offenders. There may also be more profit in diversion programs that involve counseling and individual treatment than in the operation of custodial institutions, because higher fees can be charged for professional treatment than for custody.

There is an often-heard concern regarding the ability of government agencies to be flexible in establishing and enforcing performance standards for private contractors. The effectiveness of enforcement of these standards might depend on the government's capacity to take over privatized services in the case of contractors' bankruptcy, contract violations, poor performance or when the contractor asks to terminate the contract for any legitimate reason. Despite formal and informal pressures to expand private sector involvement in delivery of government services, including criminal justice, there is a risk that continuous reliance on private companies for public services may lead to the: "giving up of capacity for government to operate in some areas. Soon it lacks yardsticks and alternatives, and can be at the mercy of contract agencies, unable to enforce expectations" (Kamerman & Kahn, 1989:263).

According to the relatively new "reinventing government" movement, government should "steer" rather than "row," direct rather than operate, but there are doubts that criminal justice agencies will adapt to this role easily (Osborne & Gaebler, 1993). Privatization advocates, for obvious reasons, support this trend. However, it is somewhat ingenious to suggest that the very same government agencies that are criticized for being wasteful and ineffective will become very alert, resourceful, and effective in directing, overseeing, and monitoring private operations in the criminal justice system. Concern has been voiced by some about long-run developments, because budgetary constraints may limit the ability of government agencies to monitor contract compliance effectively, and to take over privatized criminal justice functions when needed (see, for example, Shichor, 1995).

In spite of the privatization advocates' credo that there is no limit to the type of government functions that can be delegated to private parties (see, Logan, 1990), there are still persistent questions about whether certain public services should be delegated to the private sector. Schiflett and Zey (1990), in their organizational analysis, compared "private product-producing organizations" (PPOs), which are privately held and have a tangible product, and "public service organizations" (PSOs), which are government agencies providing public service. At the end of their analysis, the authors concluded that due to the differing organizational characteristics, "attempts to privatize PSOs by applying business models . . . will be ineffective" (Schiflett & Zey, 1990:580). The differences in organizational characteristics between public agencies and private for-profit companies include their goal orientation. This point is important because the goal orientation is considered to be the most defining element of an organization (Etzioni, 1964; Parsons, 1951; Selznick, 1948). While the primary goal of PPOs is profit-making, the PSOs were established to serve the public. This fundamental difference, regardless of the actual performance of organizations, is so basic that it must be taken seriously when privatization in the criminal justice system is considered (Ogle, 1999).

It is important to recognize that at the pragmatic level the participation of private companies in fulfilling some criminal justice functions heralded the break-up of the monopoly of public agencies over formal social control. This development may spur these agencies and their personnel to become more efficient, to be more cost effective, to provide better services, and to improve their public image. However, the main question as was poignantly put by Michael Gilbert in this volume and was noted earlier in this epilogue, will remain: "How much is too much privatization in criminal justice?"

Finally, a few words considering future developments are in order. As was mentioned earlier, it seems that privatization in criminal justice will continue and grow in the foreseeable future. There is so much money involved in social control that private industry would be reluctant to relinquish the opportunity to have "a piece of the pie." The English-American historical and cultural heritage supports the involvement of private interests in the provision of public services, private companies entering into the criminal justice market have political connections, and the politicians, government officials, and the general public accept favorably the promises of cost savings made by the private companies. The question seems to be not whether this trend will continue, but how much of the social control and the coercive power of the government will be delegated to the private for-profit sector.

References

Abercombie, N., Hill, S. & Turner, B.S. (1980). *The Dominant Ideology Thesis.* London, UK: George Allen & Unwin.

Adolfo Alvarez, Sr. v. Mona Hoyle, Pete Espinosa, Veronica Valle Otero and Juanita Trevino, Cause No. 92-04-00148-CVF, 1992.

Alberti, et al. v. Sheriff of Harris County, et al., 406 F. Supp. 649 (1975).

Aldrich, M. (1998, September 19). "Firm's Imported Inmates Endanger Tenn, Lawmaker Says." *The Commercial Appeal*, p. A-11.

Allen, H.E. & Simonsen, C.E. (1998). *Corrections in America: An Introduction* (8th ed.). Upper Saddle River, NJ: Prentice Hall, Inc.

Allied-Bruce Terminix Cos. v. Dobson, 513 U.S. 265 (1995).

Alvarez, A. (1998, July 23). *Personal Interview: Adolfo Alvarez, County Commissioner— Precinct No. 3.* Pearsall, TX.

American Correctional Association (1989). *Standards for Small Jail Facilities.* Lanham, MD: American Correctional Association.

American Correctional Association (1991). *Standards for Adult Local Detention Facilities* (3rd ed.). Lanham, MD: American Correctional Association.

American Jail Association (1997a). *Minutes of AJA Executive Committee Meeting, September 24, 1997.* Hagerstown, MD: American Jail Association.

American Jail Association (1997b). *Minutes of AJA Board of Directors Meeting, November 1, 1997.* Hagerstown, MD: American Jail Association.

American Jail Association (1999a). *1999 Product/Service/Resource Directory.* Hagerstown, MD: American Jail Association.

American Jail Association (1999b). *Who's Who in Jail Management.* Hagerstown, MD: American Jail Association.

Amnesty International (1998). *Amnesty International's Recommendations to the United States Government to Address Human Rights Violations in the USA* [Online: //www.amnesty.org/ailib/aipub/1998/ 25104698.html as of March 4, 1999]. London, UK: Amnesty International Secretariat.

Appleby, L. (1997). "Privatization: Government Abandons its Citizens." *National Lawyers Guild Practitioner, 54*, 65-81.

Apsler, R. (1994). "Is Drug Abuse Treatment Effective?" *American Enterprise, 5*(2), 46-54.

Archambeault, W.G. & Deis, D.R. (1996a). *Cost Effectiveness Comparisons of Private Versus Public Prisons in Louisiana: A Comprehensive Analysis of Allen, Avoyelles, and Winn Correctional Centers.* Baton Rouge, LA: Louisiana State University.

Archambeault, W.G. & Deis, D.R. (1996b, December 10). *Executive Summary—Cost Effectiveness Comparisons of Private Versus Public Prisonsin Louisiana: Comprehensive Analysis of Allen, Avoyelles, and Winn Correctional Centers, Phase I* [Online: //www.ucc.uconn.edu/~wwwsoci/exsumla.html as of January 7, 1999]. Baton Rouge, LA: School of Business, Louisiana State University.

Ares, C., Rankin, A. & Sturz, H. (1963). "The Manhattan Bail Project: An Interim Report on the Use of Pre-Trial Parole." *New York University Law Review, 39*, 67-95.

Armitage, G. (1932). *The History of the Bow Street Runners, 1729-1829.* London, UK: Wishart and Co.

Asin, S. (1996, November 21). "'Predator' Who Killed His Ex-Girlfriend Receives Life." *Houston Chronicle*, Section A, p. 30.

Associated Press (1985, July 4) "Prison Damage Set at $11 Million." *New York Times*, p. A9.

Associated Press (1998a, March 11). "Panel Gives Opinion of Privatized Prisons in Tennessee." *The Commercial Appeal*, p. A-12.

Associated Press (1998b, April 8). "Privatization Issue Losing Momentum." *The Commercial Appeal*, p. B-2.

Associated Press (1998c, September 6). "Mother of Dead Inmate Among CCA's Growing List of Critics." *Regional News, AM Cycle.* [Online: Lexis-Nexis Academic Universe, //web.lexis-nexis.com as of September 29, 1999]

Associated Press (1999, May 18). "Prison Realty Stock Plummets Amid Increased Jail Costs." *Regional News, AM Cycle.* [Online: Lexis-Nexis Academic Universe, //web.lexis-nexis.com as of September 29, 1999].

Associated Press (2000, March 31). "Govt. Seeks Intervention at Prison." *New York Times*. [Online: The New York Times on the Web, //www.nytimes.com/aponline/a/AP-Juvenile-Prison.html as of March 31, 20000].

Aucher, R. (1997, December 12). "Activists Cow to Defeat Prison Privatization." *Executive Intelligence Review, 29*, 61-64.

Austin, J. (1995). *Analysis of Harris County Pretrial Releases Failure to Appear Rates.* San Francisco, CA: National Council on Crime and Delinquency.

Aydin, A.H. (1996). "Private Voluntary Policing Service in Turkey." *Security Journal, 7*(2), 129-133.

Ayers, E.L. (1984). *Vengeance and Justice: Crime and Punishment in the 19th-Century American South.* New York, NY: Oxford University Press.

Bail USA, Inc. (No Date). *Methods of Exposing the Fraud of Pre-Release.* Greenville, PA: Bail USA, Inc.

Bailey, R.W. (1987). "Uses and Misuses of Privatization." In S.H. Hanke (ed.) *Prospects for Privatization*, New York, NY: The Academy of Political Science.

Ball, L.D. (1981). "The People as Law Enforcers: The 'Posse Comitatus' in New Mexico and Arizona Territories." *Quarterly of the National Outlaw and Lawman Association, 4*, 2-22.

Barak-Erez, D. (1995). "A State Action Doctrine for an Age of Privatization." *Syracuse Law Review, 45*, 1169-1193 [Online: Lexis-Nexis Academic Universe, //web.lexis-nexis.com as of October 10, 1998]

Bardwell, S.K. (1996, August 10). "Local Private Jail Begins Moving Oregon Inmates." *Houston Chronicle*, p. A-1.

Bardwell, S., Makeig, J., Liebrum, J., Milling, T. & Johnson, S. (1994, May 18). "Youth Held in Dentist's Murder: Mentally Impaired 17-year-old 'Wanted the Car.'" *Houston Chronicle*, p. A-1.

Barker, E. (1962). "Introduction." In E. Baker (ed.) *Social Contract*, pp. vii-xliv. New York, NY: Oxford University Press.

Barrett, G. (ed.) (1996, February). *The STRIKE BACK! Alert*. (Available from STRIKE BACK!, 655 15th Street, N.W., Suite 300, Washington, DC, 20005).

Bates, E. (1998a). "Prisons for Profit." *The Nation, 266*, 5.

Bates, E. (1998b). "Over the Next 5 Years Analysts Expect the Private Share of The Prison 'Market' to More Than Double." *The Nation*, 11.

Bates, E. (1999). "Prisons for Profit." In K. Haas & G.P. Alpert (eds.) *The Dilemmas of Corrections: Contemporary Readings (4th ed)*. Prospect Heights, IL: Waveland.

Bayley, D.H. (1985). *Patterns of Policing: A Comparative International Analysis*. Newark, NJ: Rutgers, The State University of New Jersey.

Bayley, D.H. (1994). *Police for the Future*. New York, NY: Oxford University.

Bayley, D.H. & Shearing, C.D. (1996). "The Future of Policing." *Law & Society Review, 30*, 585-606.

Becker, R. (1997). "The Privatization of Prisons." In J.M. Pollack (ed.) *Prisons Today and Tomorrow*. Gaithersburg, MD: Aspen Publishers.

Becker, T.M. (1974). "The Place of Private Police in Society." *Social Problems, 21*(3), 438-452.

Beeley, A. (1927). *The Bail System in Chicago*. Chicago, IL: The University of Chicago Press.

Behar, R. (1992, March 9). "Thugs in Uniform." *Time*, pp. 44-47.

Bellah, R.N., Madsen, R., Sullivan, W.M., Swidler, A. & Tipton, S.M. (1985). *Habits of the Heart: Individualism and Commitment in American Life*. New York, NY: Harper & Row.

Bendick, M., Jr. (1989). "Privatizing the Delivery of Social Welfare Services: An Idea to Be Taken Seriously." In S.B. Kamerman & A.J. Kahn (eds.) *Privatization and the Welfare State*. Princeton, NJ: Princeton University Press.

Benson, B.L. (1990). *The Enterprise of Law: Justice Without the State*. San Francisco, CA: Pacific Research Institute for Public Policy.

Benson, B.L. (1996). *Privatization in Criminal Justice.* Oakland, CA: The Independent Institute.

Benyon, J. (1994). "Policing the European Union: The Changing Basis of Cooperation on Law Enforcement." *International Affairs, 70,* 497-517.

Benyon, J. (1996). "The Politics of Police Co-Operation in the European Union." *International Journal of the Sociology of Law, 24,* 353-379.

Berk, R. & Rossi, P. (1977). *Prison Reform and the Elites.* Cambridge, MA: Ballinger.

Berk, R., Brackman, H. & Lesser, S. (1977). *A Measure of Justice.* New York, NY: Academic Press.

Berrones, H. (1998, July 22). *Personal Interview: Humberto Berrones, County Commissioner—Precinct No. 4.* Pearsall, TX.

Beyerlein, T. (1998, August 13). "Senator: Prison Company Lied," *Dayton Daily News,* 1B.

Billy, G. (1999). *Personal Telephone Communication with Licking County, Ohio Sheriff Gerry Billy, March 10, 1999.*

Bittner, E. (1970). *The Function of Police in Modern Society.* Washington, DC: U.S. Government Printing Office.

Blackstone, E. & Hakim, S. (1996). "Crying Wolf with Public Safety." *American City and County, 8,* 54.

Blackwell et al. v. Harris County, Texas, 909 S.W.2d 135 (Tex.App.-Houston [14th Dist.] 1995).

Blum v. Yaretsky, 457 U.S. 991 (1982).

Blumberg, P.I. (1971). "Corporate Responsibility and the Employee's Duty of Loyalty and Obedience." *Oklahoma Law Review, 24,* 279-318.

Bohm, R.M. & Haley, K.N. (1999). *Introduction to Criminal Justice* (2nd ed.). New York, NY: Glencoe/McGraw-Hill.

Bomer, E. (1999, May 26). *Certificate of Non-Existence: Regarding Governmental Construction Company.* Austin, TX: State of Texas, Office of the Secretary of State, Corporations Section.

Boostrom, R.L. & Draper, C.A. (1992). "Community Policing, Problem-Oriented Policing, Police-Citizen Coproduction of Public Safety, and the Privatization of Crime Control." In G.W. Bowman, Hakim & P. Seidenstat (eds.) *Privatizing the United States Justice System: Police, Adjudication, and Corrections Services from the Private Sector.* Jefferson, NC: McFarland.

Borg-Warner Security Corporation (1998). *Borg-Warner Security Corporation 10-K405 Filing for 1997 (3/30/98)* [Online: //www.freeedgar.com/oem/ccbn1/ViewF...=0& CompanyName=BORG+ WARNER+ SECURITY+CO as of February 21, 1999]. Kirkland, WA: Partes Corporation.

Bowden, T. (1977). "Who's Guarding the Guards?" *Political Quarterly, 48,* 347-353.

Boyd v. United States, 116 U.S. 616 (1886).

Bradford, C.A. & Simonsen, C.E. (1998). "The Need for Cooperative Efforts Between Private Security and Public Law Enforcement in the Prevention, Investigation, and Prosecution of Fraud-Related Criminal Activity." *Security Journal, 10*(3), 161-168.

Braun, M.A. & Lee, D.J. (1971). "Private Police Forces: Legal Powers and Limitations." *University of Chicago Law Review, 38*, 555-582.

Brennan, D.T. (1975). *The Other Police.* Cleveland, OH: Administration of Justice Committee.

Briggs, J., Harrison, C., McInnis, A. & Vincent, D. (1996). *Crime and Punishment in England: An Introductory History.* New York, NY: St. Martin's Press.

Brodeur, P. (1985). *Outrageous Misconduct: The Asbestos Industry on Trial.* New York, NY: Pantheon Books.

Brooks, D. (1989). *Texas Practice Series: County and Special District Law (Vol. 35, section 5.11).* St. Paul, MN: West Publishing, p. 148.

Brown, R.M. (1975). *Strain of Violence: Historical Studies of American Violence and Vigilantism.* New York, NY: Oxford University Press.

Brundage, W.F. (1993). *Lynching in the New South: Georgia and Virginia, 1880-1930.* Urbana, IL: University of Illinois Press.

Buerger, M.E. & Mazerolle, L.G. (1998). "Third-Party Policing: A Theoretical Analysis of an Emerging Trend." *Justice Quarterly, 15*, 301-327.

Bunch, B. (1996a, spring). "Current Practices and Issues in Capital Budgeting and Reporting." *Public Budgeting & Finance*, 7-25.

Bunch, B. (1996b, winter). "The Evolution of Lease-Purchase Guidelines in the State of Texas. *Public Budgeting & Finance*, 114-124.

Burdeau v. McDowell, 256 U.S. 465 (1921).

Bureau of Justice Statistics (1998). *Census of State and Local Law Enforcement Agencies, 1996.* Washington, DC: United States Department of Justice.

Bureau of Justice Statistics (1999). *Correctional Populations in the United States, 1998.* Washington, DC: United States Department of Justice.

Burkholder, E.A. (1993). "Confidentiality and the Courts: Protecting the Right to Privacy." *Judicature, 76*, 311-313.

Burris, C. (1996, March 27). *Personal Interview: Carl Burris, Frio County Sheriff 1992-Present.* Pearsall, TX.

Burrows, Q. (1997). "Scowl Because You're on Candid Camera: Privacy and Video Surveillance." *Valparaiso University Law Review, 31*, 1079-1139.

Burton v. Wilmington Parking Authority, 365 U.S. 715 (1961).

Butterfield, F. (2000a, March 16). "Privately Run Juvenile Prison in Louisiana Is Attacked for Abuse of 6 Inmates." *New York Times.* [Online: The New York Times on the Web, //www.nytimes.com/00/03/16/news/national/la-prison-juvenile.html as of March 16, 2000].

Butterfield, F. (2000b, March 31). "Justice Department Sues to Alter Conditions at a Prison." *New York Times.* [Online: the New York Times on the Web, //www.nytimes.com/00/03/31/news/national/juvenile-prison.html as of March 31, 2000].

Button, M. (1998). "Beyond the Public Gaze—The Exclusion of Private Investigations from the British Debate Over Regulating Private Security." *International Journal of the Sociology of Law, 26*, 1-16.

Caffuzzi, M. (1995). "Private Police and Personal Privacy: Who's Guarding the Guards?" *New York Law School Law Review, 40,* 225-250.

Calavita, K. & Pontell, H.N. (1991). "'Other People's Money' Revisited: Collective Embezzlement in the Savings and Loan and Insurance Industries." *Social Problems, 38*(1), 94-102.

Calder, J.D. (1974, November). "Policing and Securing the Campus: The Need for Complementary Organizations." *Police Chief,* pp. 60-64.

Calder, J.D. (1980). "The Security-Criminal Justice Connection: Toward Elimination of Separate-But-Equal Status." *Journal of Security Administration, 3*(2), 25-52.

Calder, J.D. (1985). "Industrial Guards in the Nineteenth and Twentieth Centuries: The Mean Years." *Journal of Security Administration, 8*(2), 11-20.

Calder, J.D. (1992). "Factory Security in World War II: A Fifty Year Celebration of the Auxiliary Military Police." An unpublished paper presented at the Academy of Criminal Justice Sciences, Pittsburgh, PA.

Calder, J.D. (1993). *Origins and Development of Federal Crime Control Policy: Herbert Hoover's Initiatives.* Westport, CT: Praeger.

Calder, J.D. & Mattson, G.A. (1990). "Privatizing Justice Agencies: The Due Process Dilemma of At-Will Employees." *Government Union Review, 11*(4), 32-50.

Camp, G.M. & Camp, C.G. (1997). *The Corrections Yearbook, 1997: Adult Corrections.* South Salem, NY: Criminal Justice Institute.

Camp, S.D., Saylor, W.G. & Harer, M.D. (1997). "Aggregating Individual-Level Evaluations of the Organizational Social Climate: A Multilevel Investigation of the Work Environment at the Federal Bureau of Prisons." *Justice Quarterly, 14*(4), 739-761.

Camp, S.D., Saylor, W.G. & Wright, K.N. (1999). "Creating Performance Measures from Survey Data: A Practical Discussion." *Corrections Management Quarterly, 3*(1), 71-80.

Carbonneau, T.E. (1989). *Alternative Dispute Resolution: Melting the Lances and Dismounting the Steeds.* Urbana, IL: University of Illinois Press.

Carbonneau, T.E. (1996). "Arbitral Justice: The Demise of Due Process in American Law." *Tulane Law Review, 70,* 1945-1967.

Carleton, M.T. (1971). *Politics and Punishment: The History of the Louisiana State Penal System.* Baton Rouge, LA: Louisiana State University Press.

Carnoy, M. (1984). *The State and Political Theory.* Princeton, NJ: Princeton University Press.

Carr, F. (1996). "The New Security Politics in Europe." *International Journal of the Sociology of Law, 24*(4), 381-398.

Casanova, J.E. (1992, Sept. 3). "Jail Employees Organize Protest." *Frio-Nueces Current, 98*(36), p. 1

Casarez, N.B. (1995). "Furthering the Accountability Principle in Privatized Federal Corrections: The Need for Access to Private Prison Records." *University of Michigan Journal of Law, 28,* 249-304 [Online: Lexis-Nexis Academic Universe, //web.lexis-nexis.com as of October 6, 1998].

Casey, C.S. (1996). *A Case Study of the Privatization and Subsequent Government Takeover of the Monroe County Florida Sheriff's Office Detention facilities.* Alexandria, VA: National Sheriffs' Association.

Casey, C.S. (1997, Jan./Feb.). "How the Private Corrections Firms Really Cut Costs: A Case Comparison of a Public Versus Private Retirement Plan." *American Jails*, pp. 43-46.

Casile, M. (1994). "The New Boss: How Privatization Changes the Strategy and Structure of Formerly Public Organizations." Unpublished paper.

Cayer, N.J. & Weschler, L.F. (1988). *Public Administration: Social Change and Adaptive Management.* New York, NY: St. Martin's Press.

Chaiken, J., Greenwood, P. & Petersilia, J. (1977). "The Criminal Investigation Process: A Summary Report." *Policy Analysis, 3*(2), 187-217.

Chaires, R.H. & Lentz, S.A. (1996). "Some Legal Considerations in Prison Privatization." In G.L. Mays & T. Gray (eds.) *Privatization and the Provision of Correctional Services: Context and Consequences.* Cincinnati, OH: Anderson Publishing Co.

Chamberlin, J. (1998). "Bounty Hunters: Can the Criminal Justice System Live Without Them?" *University of Illinois Law Review*, 1175. (LEXIS, Lawrev, Bail).

Champion, D.J. (1996). "Foreword." In G.L. Mays & T. Gray (eds.) *Privatization and the Provision of Correctional Services: Context and Consequences.* Cincinnati, OH: Anderson Publishing Co.

Champion, D.J. (1990). *Corrections in the United States: A Contemporary Perspective.* Englewood Cliffs, NJ: Regents/Prentice Hall, Inc.

Charry, R. (1999, June 13). "Locked Out on the Prison Decision." *The Washington Post*, p. B-08.

Cherniack, M. (1986). *The Hawk's Nest Incident: America's Worst Industrial Disaster.* New Haven, CT: Yale University Press.

Chesteen, R.D. (1998). "The Tennessee Prison System: A Study of Evolving Public Policy in State Corrections." In J. Vile & M. Byrnes (eds.) *Tennessee Government and Politics: Democracy in the Volunteer State.* Westport, CT: Greenwood Press.

Christie, N. (1995). *Crime Control as Industry* (2nd ed.). London, UK: Routledge.

Clark, J. (ed.) (1993, October). *Pretrial Reporter.* (Available from the Pretrial Services Resource Center, 1325 G Street N.W., Suite 770, Washington, DC, 20005).

Clark, J.L. (1998). *Report to the Attorney General: Inspection and Review of the Northeast Ohio Correctional Center.* Washington, DC: Office of the Corrections Trustee (November 25).

Cobb, R. & Elder, C.D. (1972). *Participation in American Politics: The Dynamics of Agenda-Building.* Boston, MA: Allyn & Bacon, Inc.

Cobb, R., Keith-Ross, J. & M.H. Ross (1976). "Agenda Building as a Comparative Political Process." *American Political Science Review, 70*, 126-138.

Cochran, T.C. & Miller, W. (1961). *The Age of Enterprise: A Social History of Industrial America.* New York, NY: Harper & Row.

Cody, W.J.M. &. Bennett, A.D. (1987). "The Privatization of Correctional Institutions: The Tennessee Experience." *Vanderbilt Law Journal, 40*, 829-849.

Cohen, S. (1985). *Visions of Social Control.* Cambridge, UK: Polity.

Colletti, J.L. (1996). "Why Not Hire Civilian Commanders?" *FBI Law Enforcement Bulletin, 65*(10), 8-11.

Collins, W.C. (1999). *Personal Telephone Conversation with William C. Collins of the Correctional Law Reporter.*

Colvin, M. (1997). *Penitentiaries, Reformatories, and Chain Gangs: Social Theory and the History of Punishment in Nineteenth-Century America.* New York, NY: St. Martin's Press.

Conley, J.A. (1980). "Prisons, Production, and Profit: Reconsidering the Importance of Prison Industries." *Journal of Social History, 14*(2), 257-276.

Conlon, S.B. (1993). "Confidentiality and the Courts: Preserving Judicial Discretion." *Judicature, 76,* 304-313.

Consolidated Financial Resources Incorporated (1985, April 30). *Articles of Incorporation of Consolidated Financial Resources Incorporated.* Austin, TX: Office of the Secretary of State of Texas, Corporations Section.

Consolidated Financial Resources Incorporated (1987, Sept. 1). *Lease-Purchase Agreement: Frio County, Texas.* Greenville, TX: Consolidated Financial Resources Incorporated.

Consolidated Financial Resources Incorporated (1988, June 1). *Lease-Purchase Agreement: Frio County, Texas.* Greenville, TX: Consolidated Financial Resources Incorporated.

Consolidated Financial Resources Incorporated (1991, May 2). *Statement of Change of Registered Office or Registered Agent or Both by a Profit Corporation (signed by Tom Shirey).* Austin, TX: Office of the Secretary of State of Texas, Corporations Section.

Consolidated Financial Resources Incorporated (1994, April 19). *Lease-Purchase Agreement: Frio County, Texas.* Greenville, TX: Consolidated Financial Resources Incorporated.

Cornell Corrections, Inc. (1997). *Cornell Corrections 1997 Annual Report.* Houston, TX: Cornell Corrections, Inc.

Cornell Corrections, Inc. (1998). "Private Sector Corrections: The Promise of the Future." *The Cornell Papers, 1,* 12-13.

Corrections Corporation of America. (1985, Fall). *The Private Line, 3.*

Corrections Corporation of America (1993). *Corrections Corporation of America—1992 Annual Report.* Nashville, TN: Corrections Corporation of America.

Corrections Corporation of America (1994). *Corrections Corporation of America 1994 Annual Report.* Nashville, TN: Corrections Corporation of America.

Corrections Corporation of America (1997). "To our Shareholders: Letter by Doctor R. Crants, CEO." In Corrections Corporation of America, *1996 Annual report* [Online: //www.correctionscorp.com/letter.html as of January 7, 1999]. Nashville, TN: Corrections Corporation of America.

Corrections Corporation of America (1998a). *Corrections Corporation of America—1997 Annual Report.* Nashville, TN: Corrections Corporation of America.

Corrections Corporation of America. (1998b). "To Our Shareholders: Letter by Doctor R. Crants, CEO." In Corrections Corporation of America, *1997 Annual Report* [Online: //www.correctionscorp.com/letter97.html as of January 7, 1999]. Nashville, TN: Corrections Corporation of America.

Corrections Corporation of America (1998c). *Press Release: CCA Co-Founder Doctor R. Crants named 1998 National Entrepreneur of the Year* [Online: //www.corrections corp.com/archive11_15.html as of March 3, 1999]. Nashville, TN: Corrections Corporation of America.

Corrections Corporation of America (1998d). *Proxy Statement.* Washington, DC: Securities and Exchange Commission.

Corrections Corporation of America (1999a). *CCA: Brief History* [Online: //www. correctionscorp.com/ history.html as of January 7, 1999]. Nashville, TN: Corrections Corporation of America.

Corrections Corporation of America (1999b). *CCA: Investor FAQ* [Online: //www. correctionscorp.com/ faq.html as of January 7, 1999]. Nashville, TN: Corrections Corporation of America.

Corrections Professional (1997, May 23). "South Carolina Ends CCA Contract, Learns Slow Approach Needed." *LRP Publications, 2.*

Couch, S.R. (1981). "Selling and Reclaiming State Sovereignty: The Case of the Coal and Iron Police." *Insurgent Sociologist, 10*(4), 85-91.

Cox, N.R. (1988). *Frio County Jail: Technical Assistance Report—NIC T.A. 88-J1311.* San Antonio, TX: N.R. Cox Associates, Inc.

Cox, N.R. & Osterhoff, W.E. (1991). "Managing the Crisis in Local Corrections: A Public-Private Partnership Approach. In J.A. Thompson & G.L. Mays (eds.) *American Jails: Public Policy Issues.* Chicago, IL: Nelson-Hall Publishers.

Crants, D.R. (1991). "Private Prison Management: A Study in Economic Efficiency." *Journal of Contemporary Criminal Justice, 7*(1), 49-59.

Cubriel, G. (1996, Feb. 14). *Personal Interview: Gloria Cubriel—Former County Jail Administrator Under Sheriff Del Toro.* Pearsall, TX.

Cubriel, G. (1999, April 7). *Telephone Interview: Regarding Actions of Out Going County Judge Williams and County Clerk Hoyle During the Period Between the March 1994 Primary and the January 1, 1995 installation of Judge Garcia's Administration.* Pearsall, TX: Office of the Frio County Clerk.

Cullen, F.T., Maakestad, W.J. & Cavender, G. (1987). *Corporate Crime Under Attack: The Ford Pinto Case and Beyond.* Cincinnati, OH: Anderson Publishing Co.

Culp, R.F. (1998). "Privatization of Juvenile Correctional Facilities in the US: A Comparison of Conditions of Confinement in Private and Government Operated Programs." *Security Journal, 11*(2,3), 289-301.

Cunningham, W.C. & Taylor, T.M. (1985). *The Hallcrest Report: Private Security and Police in America.* Portland, OR: Chancellor.

Cunningham, W.C., Strauchs, J.J. & Van Meter, C.W. (1990). *The Hallcrest Report II: Private Security Trends 1970-2000.* Stoneham, MA: Butterworth-Heinemann.

Currie, E. (1985). *Confronting Crime: An American Challenge.* New York, NY: Pantheon Books.

Cuvelier, S. & Potts, D. (1993). *The Bail Classification Profile Project—Harris County, Texas: Final Report.* State Justice Institute: Alexandria, VA.

Dahl, R. (1961). *Who Governs.* New Haven, CT: Yale University Press.

Daniel, P. (1972). "We Are Going to Do Away with These Boys. . . ." *American Heritage,* 308-315.

Daniel, P. (1975). "The Tennessee Convict War." *Tennessee Historical Quarterly, 34,* 273-292.

Daniels, M.R. (1997). *Terminating Public Programs: An American Political Paradox.* Armonk, NY: M.E. Sharpe.

Dannin, E.J. (1998, February). "Labor and Employment Law Developments in Privatization—1997." *Labor Law Journal,* 834-843.

Dart, R.C. (1992). "Police Privatization Ventures as Strategies to Maintain and Enhance Public Safety." In G.W. Bowman, S. Hakim & P. Seidenstat (eds.) *Privatizing the United States Justice System: Police, Adjudication, and Corrections Services from the Private Sector.* Jefferson, NC: McFarland.

Davis, M.G., Lundman, R.J. & Martinez, R. (1991). "Private Corporate Justice: Store Police, Shoplifters, and Civil Recovery." *Social Problems, 38*(3), 395-411.

de Tocqueville, A. (1969). *Democracy in America* (G. Lawrence, Trans.). New York, NY: Anchor Books.

de Waard, Jap (1993). "The Private Security Sector in Fifteen European Countries: Size, Rules, and Legislation." *Security Journal, 4*(2), 58-63.

Del Toro, G. (1996, April 15). *Personal Interview: Gabriel Del Toro—Former County Sheriff (1989-1992).* Pearsall, TX.

DeNinno, D.L. (1980). "Private Searches and Seizures: An Application of the Public Function Theory." *George Washington Law Review, 48,* 433-455.

DiIulio, J., Jr. (1988). "What Is Wrong with Private Prisons?" *The Public Interest, 92,* 66-83.

DiIulio, J. (1993) "The Duty to Govern: A Critical Perspective on the Private Management of Prisons and Jails." In R.C. Monk (ed.) *Taking Sides: Clashing Views on Controversial Issues in Crime and Criminology.* Guilford, CT: Dushkin Publishing Company.

Doggett, L. & Mucchetti, M.J. (1991). "Public Access to Public Courts: Discouraging Secrecy in the Public Interest." *Texas Law Review, 69,* 643-689.

Donahue, J. (1989). *The Privatization Decision: Public Ends, Private Means.* New York, NY: Basic Books.

Donizer, S.R. (ed.) (1996). *The Real War on Crime: The Report of the National Criminal Justice Commission.* New York, NY: Harper Perennial Library.

Dove Development Corporation (1988, May 2). *Articles of Incorporation of Dove Development Corporation.* Austin, TX: Office of the Secretary of State of Texas, Corporations Section.

Dove Development Corporation (1992, Sept. 8). *Assumed Name Certificate for Dove Development Corporation to Conduct Business as Frio Detention Management.* Austin, TX: Office of the Secretary of State of Texas, Corporations Section.

Dove Development Corporation (1993, April 23). *Assumed Name Certificate for Dove Development Corporation*. Austin, TX: Office of the Secretary of State of Texas, Corporations Section.

Dove Development Corporation (1994, April 28). *Invoice to County Judge Sid J. Williams for Emergency Inmate Housing—Start up Date 4/14/94 (First Draw—$699,999.60)*. Greenville, TX: Dove Development Corporation.

Downs, G. (1976). *Bureaucracy, Innovation, and Public Policy*. Lexington, MA: D.C. Heath.

Dralla, G.G., Honig, D.B., Port, D.P., Power, S.H. & Simmons, S.A. (1975). "Who's Watching the Watchman? The Regulation, or Non-Regulation, of America's Largest Law Enforcement Institution, the Private Police." *Golden Gate University Law Review*, 5, 433-483.

Draper, H. (1978). *Private Police*. Harmondsworth, UK: Penguin.

Drobney, J.A. (1994). "Where Palm and Pine are Blowing: Convict Labor in the North Florida Turpentine Industry, 1877-1923." *Florida Historical Quarterly*, 72,(4), 411-434.

Drobney, J.A. (1998). *Lumbermen and Log Sawyers: Life, Labor, and Culture in the North Florida Timber Industry, 1830-1930*. Macon, GA: Mercer University Press.

Dunnigan, P. (1993, April 28). "Court No-Shows Prompt Study." *Miami Review*, p. 1.

Durham, A.M. (1988). "The Justice Model in Historical Context: Early Law, the Emergence of Science, and the Rise of Incarceration." *Journal of Criminal Justice*, 16, 331-346.

Durham, A.M. (1989a). "Managing the Costs of Modern Corrections: Implications of Nineteenth-Century Privatized Prison-Labor Programs." *Journal of Criminal Justice*, 17, 441-455.

Durham, A.M. (1989b). "Rehabilitation and Correctional Privatization: Observations on the 19th Century Experience and Implications for Modern Corrections." *Federal Probation*, 52, 43-52.

Durham, A.M. (1989c). "Origins of Interest in the Privatization of Punishment: The Nineteenth and Twentieth Century American Experience." *Criminology*, 27, 107-139.

Durham, A.M. (1994a). *Crisis and Reform: Current Issues in American Punishment*. New York, NY: Little, Brown and Company.

Durham, A.M. (1994b). "The Future of Correctional Privatization: Lessons from the Past." In G.W. Bowman, S. Hakim & P. Seidenstat (eds.) *Privatizing Correctional Institutions*. New Brunswick, NJ: Transaction Books.

"Early Data in SA Provider Study Reveal Struggle for Survival." (1996). *Mental Health Weekly*, 6(37), 8-9.

Edwards, H.T. (1986). "Alternative Dispute Resolution: Panacea or Anathema?" *Harvard Law Review*, 99, 668-684.

Ericson, R. (1995). "The Division of Expert Knowledge in Policing and Security." *British Journal of Sociology*, 45(2), 149-175.

Ethridge, P.A. & Liebowitz, S.W. (1994, May/June). "The Attitudes of Sheriffs in Texas Toward Privatization of County Jails." *American Jails*, 55-60.

Ethridge, P.A. & Marquart, J.W. (1993). "Private Prisons in Texas: The New Penology for Profit." *Justice Quarterly, 10*(1), 29-48.

Etzioni, A. (1964). *Modern Organizations*. Englewood-Cliffs, NJ: Prentice Hall.

Euller, S. (1980). "Private Security and the Exclusionary Rule." *Harvard Civil Rights-Civil Liberties Law Review, 15*, 649-684.

Evancho, M. (1997, March/April). "Jails . . . and the Vendors Who Serve Them." *American Jails*, pp. 57-60.

Ewick, P. (1993). "Corporate Cures: The Commodification of Social Control." *Studies in Law, Politics, and Society, 13*, 137-157.

Fabelo, T. (1995a, October). "More Incarceration as the Newest Entitlement Program in Texas." *Bulletin from the Executive Director: State of Texas, Criminal Justice Policy Council, 18.*

Fabelo, T. (1995b). *Testing the Case for More Incarceration in Texas: The Record So Far.* Austin, TX: Criminal Justice Policy Council, State of Texas.

Fair, H. (1992a, Aug. 27). "Jail Management Changes to Save Taxpayers Money." *Frio-Nueces Current, 98*(35), p. 1.

Fair, H. (1992b, Sept. 3). "Employees Retain Jobs." *Frio-Nueces Current, 98*(36), 1.

Fairchild, E. S. (1981). "Interest Groups in the Criminal Justice Process." *Journal of Criminal Justice, 9*, 181-194.

Falkin, G.P., Wexler, H.K. & Lipton, D.S. (1992). *Drugs and Jail Inmates, 1989.* Washington, DC: U.S. Department of Justice.

Farris, L.S. (1998). "Private Jails in Oklahoma: An Unconstitutional Delegation of Legislative Authority." *Tulsa Law Journal, 33*, 959-977.

Federal Bureau of Prisons (1997). *Taft Correctional Institution Statement of Work.* Washington, DC: Federal Bureau of Prisons.

Feigenbaum, H.B. (1998). *Shrinking the State: The Political Underpinnings of Privatization.* New York, NY: Cambridge University Press.

Felson, M. (1994). *Crime & Everyday Life: Insights and Implications for Society.* Thousand Oaks, CA: Pine Forge Press.

Felson, M. (1998). *Crime & Everyday life: Insight and Implications for Society,* (2nd ed.). Thousand Oaks, CA: Pine Forge Press.

Ferrar, R. (1997, June 8), "Prison Privatization Bill Leads List of Bills That Failed to Pass." *Knoxville News-Sentinel*, p. A-4.

Field, G. (1992). "Oregon Prison Drug Treatment Programs." In C.G. Leukefeld & F.M. Tims (eds.) *Drug Abuse Treatment in Prisons and Jails: NIDA Research Monograph 118*. Washington, DC: National Institute on Drug Abuse, U.S. Government Printing Office.

Fierce, M. C. (1994). *Slavery Revisited: Blacks and the Southern Convict Lease System, 1865-1933.* New York, NY: Africana Studies Research Center.

FIND/SVP (1999a). *The Corrections Market: Table of Contents* [Online: //www.findsvp. com/ tocs/LA431.HTM as of January 7, 1999]. New York, NY: FIND/SVP, Inc.

FIND/SVP (1999b). *Market Looks: The U.S. Private Prison Management Market* [Online: //www.findsvp.com/tocs/ML0167.HTM as of February 18, 1999]. New York, NY: FIND/SVP, Inc.

FIND/SVP (1999c). *Market Looks: The U.S. Corrections Foodservice Market* [Online: //www.findsvp.com/tocs/ML0121.HTM as of February 18, 1999]. New York, NY: FIND/SVP, Inc.

FIND/SVP (1999d). *Market Looks: The U.S. Corrections Telecommunications Market* [Online: //www.findsvp.com/tocs/ML0166.HTM as of February 18, 1999]. New York, NY: FIND/SVP, Inc.

FIND/SVP (1999e). *Market Looks: The U.S. Corrections Healthcare Service Market* [Online: //www.findsvp.com/tocs/ML0166.HTM as of February 18, 1999]. New York, NY: FIND/SVP, Inc.

Fiss, O.M. (1984). "Against Settlement." *Yale Law Journal, 93*, 1073-1090.

Fitzgerald, R. (1988). *When Government Goes Private: Successful Alternatives to Public Services.* New York, NY: Universe Books.

Fixler, P.E. & Poole, R.E. (1988). "Can Police Services Be Privatized?" *Annals of the American Academy of Political and Social Science, 498*, 108-118.

Flagg Brothers, Inc. v. Brooks, 436 U.S. 149 (1978).

Flanagan, T.J. (1996). "Public Opinion on Crime and Justice: History, Development, and Trends." In T.J. Flanagan & D.R. Longmire (eds.) *Americans View Crime and Justice: A National Public Opinion Survey*. Thousand Oaks, CA: Sage.

Flaum, D. (1999, June 9). "CCA's Parent Faces 8 Shareholder Lawsuits." *The Commercial Appeal*, p. C2.

Flores, M. (1994). "Frio County Approves Temporary Prison Beds." *San Antonio Express News*, p. 4A.

Foley, D.E., Mota, C., Post, D.E. & Lozano, I. (1988). *From Peones to Politicos: Class and Ethnicity in a South Texas Town—1990-1987*. Austin, TX: University of Texas Press.

Folz, D.H. & Scheb, J.M. II (1989). "Prisons, Profits, and Politics: The Tennessee Privatization Experiment." *Judicature, 73* (2), 98-102.

Foucault, M. (1977). *Discipline and Punish: The Birth of the Prison.* New York, NY: Random House.

Freedman, D.J. & Stenning, P.C. (1977). *Private Security, Police, and the Law in Canada.* Toronto, CN: Centre of Criminology, University of Toronto.

Freeman, M. (1992). "Contracting Out: The Most Viable Solution. In G.W. Bowman, S. Hakim & P. Seidenstat (eds.) *Privatizing the United States Justice System: Police, Adjudication, and Corrections Services from the Private Sector.* Jefferson, NC: McFarland.

Friedman, J., Hakim, S. & Spiegel, U. (1987). "The Effects of Community Size on the Mix of Private and Public Use of Security Services. *Journal of Urban Economics, 22*, 230-241.

Friedman, L.M. (1993). *Crime and Punishment in American History.* New York, NY: Basic Books.

Friedrichs, D.O. (1996). *Trusted Criminals: White Collar Crime in Contemporary Society.* Belmont, CA: Wadsworth Publishing Company.

Frio County (1994a, April 19). *Resolution—Re: Use of County powers of Eminent Domain to Condemn and Claim Property to Allow Expansion of the Main Jail.* Pearsall, TX: Office of Frio County Clerk.

Frio County (1994b, June 13). *Resolution—Re: Authorization for Dove Development Corporation to Construct Housing for 96 prisoners in Frio County and 240 Prisoners in the City of Crystal City.* Pearsall, TX: Office of Frio County Clerk.

Frio County (undated). *Williams & Crystal City Unit II: History.* Pearsall, TX: Office of the Frio County Clerk.

Frio County Commissioners Court (1989a). *Minutes of the Commissioners Court Meeting—January 31, 1989: Lease Rate Set at $30/Bed/Day for Washington, DC Inmates.* Pearsall, TX: Office of the Frio County Clerk.

Frio County Commissioners Court (1989b). *Minutes of the Commissioners Court Meeting—March 13, 1989: All Bids for Fencing Around the Jail Rejected.* Pearsall, TX: Office of the Frio County Clerk.

Frio County Commissioners Court (1989c). *Minutes of the Commissioners Court Meeting—April 10, 1989: Sheriff's Request for Fencing Around the Jail Tabled.* Pearsall, TX: Office of the Frio County Clerk.

Frio County Commissioners Court (1989d). *Minutes of the Commissioners Court Meeting—May 8, 1989: Sheriff's Request for Fencing and Other Security Items Denied.* Pearsall, TX: Office of the Frio County Clerk.

Frio County Commissioners Court (1989e). *Minutes of the Commissioners Court Meeting—July 25, 1989: Commissioners Court Orders Jailers Scheduled for 171 Hours of Work in a 28-Day Period.* Pearsall, TX: Office of the Frio County Clerk.

Frio County Commissioners Court (1989f). *Minutes of the Commissioners Court Meeting—July 25, 1989: Use of Compensatory Time to Pay County Employees for Work Hours in Excess of 40-Hours per Week.* Pearsall, TX: Office of the Frio County Clerk.

Frio County Commissioners Court (1989g). *Minutes of the Commissioners Court Meeting—September 14, 1989: CFRI Proposes the Use of Private Contractor to Operate the New County Jail.* Pearsall, TX: Office of the Frio County Clerk.

Frio County Commissioners Court (1989h). *Minutes of the Commissioners Court Meeting—October 24, 1989: Presentation by Mr. Ron Champion Regarding the Wackenhut Corrections Corporation Proposal to Privatize the New Jail.* Pearsall, TX: Office of the Frio County Clerk.

Frio County Commissioners Court (1991a). *Minutes of the Commissioners Court Meeting—August 26, 1991: Vote to Use the "Sheriff's House" for Additional Office Space.* Pearsall, TX: Office of the Frio County Clerk.

Frio County Commissioners Court (1991b). *Minutes of the Commissioners Court Meeting—December 23, 1991: Sheriff Del Toro Ordered Out of the "Sheriff's House."* Pearsall, TX: Office of the Frio County Clerk.

Frio County Commissioners Court (1992a). *Minutes of the Commissioners Court Meeting—August 24, 1992: Approved Privatization with Frio Detention Management to Provide Inmate Management Services (vote 3-2).* Pearsall, TX: Office of the Frio County Clerk.

Frio County Commissioners Court (1992b). *Minutes of the Commissioners Court Meeting—August 27, 1992: Approved Privatization with Frio Detention Management to Provide Inmate Management Services (vote 4-1).* Pearsall, TX: Office of the Frio County Clerk.

Frio County Commissioners Court (1992c). *Minutes of the Commissioners Court Meeting—October 19, 1992: CFRI/DDC Propose a New Detention Facility Project in Frio County.* Pearsall, TX: Office of the Frio County Clerk.

Frio County Commissioners Court (1994a). *Minutes of the Commissioners Court Meeting—March 14, 1994: CFRI/DDC Propose a 130 Bed Expansion of the Main Jail.* Pearsall, TX: Office of the Frio County Clerk.

Frio County Commissioners Court (1994b). *Minutes of the Commissioners Court Meeting—April 11, 1994: Increase the Size of the Main Jail Expansion to the Range of 150-200.* Pearsall, TX: Office of the Frio County Clerk.

Frio County Commissioners Court (1994c). *Minutes of the Commissioners Court Meeting—April 19, 1994: Emergency Meeting to Pass a Resolution to Authorize Dove Development Corporation to Construct and Obtain Financing for a Temporary Detention Facility.* Pearsall, TX: Office of the Frio County Clerk.

Frio County Commissioners Court (1994d). *Minutes of the Commissioners Court Meeting—June 2, 1994: Approval of a Resolution Approving Agreements Between Frio County and Dove Development Company for Temporary Detention Facility Operation and Management.* Pearsall, TX: Office of the Frio County Clerk.

Frio County Commissioners Court (1995a). *Minutes of the Commissioners Court Meeting—January 9, 1995: Motion That Dove Development Corporation Provide Information Regarding Expenditures in Construction of the Frio County Detention Facility as in Commissioner Espinosa's Letter to Tom Shirey on December 2, 1994 due by January 23, 1995.* Pearsall, TX: Office of the Frio County Clerk.

Frio County Commissioners Court (1995b). *Minutes of the Commissioners Court Meeting—January 23, 1995: James W. Smith, County Attorney Speaks for Don Greiner, DDC About Notification That the State Will Progressively Remove State Inmates As New State Prison Beds Become Operational.* Pearsall, TX: Office of the Frio County Clerk.

Frio County Commissioners Court (1995c). *Minutes of the Commissioners Court Meeting—January 30, 1995: Mr. Don Greiner of DDC Informed Requests That the Court Approve a One Year Contract with the State of Colorado to House Inmates at $40 per Day.* Pearsall, TX: Office of the Frio County Clerk.

Frio County Commissioners Court (1995d). *Minutes of the Commissioners Court Meeting—January 23, 1995: Commissioner J.M. Lindsey Asked If the New Administration Was Going to Produce Verbatim Minutes of Commissioners Court Meetings.* Pearsall, TX: Office of the Frio County Clerk.

Frio County Commissioners Court (1995e). *Minutes of the Commissioners Court Meeting—May 8, 1995: Commissioner Lindsey Objects to Verbatim Transcript as the Minutes of Commissioners Court Meetings.* Pearsall, TX: Office of the Frio County Clerk.

Frio County Commissioners Court (1995f). *Minutes of the Commissioners Court Meeting—January 23, 1995: Investigation of Missing Computers and Computer Parts from the County Judge's Office.* Pearsall, TX: Office of the Frio County Clerk.

Frio County Commissioners Court (1995g). *Minutes of the Commissioners Court Meeting—May 8, 1995: Motion to Approve the Utah Contract is Discussed and Rejected.* Pearsall, TX: Office of the Frio County Clerk.

Frio County Commissioners Court (1995h). *Minutes of the Commissioners Court Meeting—April 10, 1995: Discussion by Mr. Bleecker Morse Concerning the Underfunding of the Sheriff's Prisoner Care Budget and DDC's Request for "Moratorium" from Payment of Its Debts to the County.* Pearsall, TX: Office of the Frio County Clerk.

Frio County Commissioners Court (1995i). *Minutes of the Commissioners Court Meeting—February 13, 1995: Briefing by County Auditor Mary Hornbostel Concerning Under Budgeting for Prisoner Care.* Pearsall, TX: Office of the Frio County Clerk.

Frio County Commissioners Court (1995j). *Minutes of the Commissioners Court Meeting—March 31, 1995: Sheriff Burris Presents His Assessment of the Prisoner Care Budget Crisis in the Sheriff Office and Makes Recommendations.* Pearsall, TX: Office of the Frio County Clerk.

Frio County Commissioners Court (1995k). *Minutes of the Commissioners Court Meeting—May 8, 1995: Judge Garcia Confronts Tom Shirey Over the Attempt to Coerce Him to Informally Approve the Utah Contact.* Pearsall, TX: Office of the Frio County Clerk.

Frio County Commissioners Court (1995l). *Minutes of the Commissioners Court Meeting—May 8, 1995: Ad Hoc Committee Presentation Recommends That All New Agreements, Amendments and Contracts with Dove Development Corporation Be Tabled Until It Is Determined That Current Agreements, Amendments and Contracts Did Not Violate the Open Meetings Act.* Pearsall, TX: Office of the Frio County Clerk.

Frio County Commissioners Court (1995m). *Minutes of the Commissioners Court Meeting—May 8, 1995: Commissioner Lindsey Confronts Sheriff Burris Over His Intent to Resume Public Operation of the Jail and the High Cost of Resuming Public Operations.* Pearsall, TX: Office of the Frio County Clerk.

Fritschler, A. Lee. & Hoefler, J.M. (1996). *Smoking and Politics: Policy Making in the Federal Bureaucracy* (5th ed.). Englewood Cliffs, NJ: Prentice Hall.

Gaes, G.G., Camp, S.D. & Saylor, W.G. (1998). "Appendix 2: Comparing the Quality of Publicly and Privately Operated Prisons: A Review." In D. McDonald, E. Fournier, M. Russell-Einhorn & S. Crawford (eds.) *Private Prisons in the United States: An Assessment of Current Practice.* Boston, MA: Abt Associates Inc.

Gagel, L. M. (1995). "Stealthy Encroachments Upon the Fourth Amendment: Constitutional Constraints and Their Applicability to the Long Arm of Ohio's Private Security Forces." *University of Cincinnati Law Review, 63*, 1807-1850.

Gain, M. (1989). "The Bail Reform Act of 1984 and *United States v. Salerno*: Too Easy to Believe." *Case Western Reserve Law Review, 39*, 1371. (LEXIS, Lawrev, Bail).

Galanter, M. (1974). "Why the 'Haves' Come Out Ahead: Speculations on the Limits of Legal Change." *Law and Society Review 9*, 95-160.

Gallagher, J. (1998, Jan./Feb.). "Second Opinion: How a Private Firm Can Help Counties Improve Correctional Health Care." *American Jails*, pp. 65-67.

Garcia, C.A. (1999a, May 24). *Telephone Interview: Regarding Itemization of Purchases from the 1994 Loan for $1,000,000 to DDC Using Frio County Ad Valorem Taxes as Collateral.* Pearsall, TX: Office of the Frio County Judge.

Garcia, C.A. (1999b, May 26). *Telephone Interview: Regarding Actions of Out Going County Judge Williams and County Clerk Hoyle During the Period Between the March 1994 Primary and the January 1, 1995 Installation of Judge Garcia's Administration.* Pearsall, TX: Office of the Frio County Judge.

Garcia, C.A. (1999c, May 27). *Telephone Interview: Regarding Judge Garcia's Management Style for Dealing with Local Politics and Voting Patterns on the Commissioners Court 1994-1996.* Pearsall, TX: Office of the Frio County Judge.

Garcia, C.A. (1999d, May 27). *Telephone Interview: Regarding His Strategy of Guarding Absentee Ballots at the Courthouse During the 30 Days Leading Up to the Primary Election.* Pearsall, TX: Office of the Frio County Judge.

Gardner, G. (1987). "The Emergence of the New York State Prison System: A Critique of the Rusche-Kirchheimer Model." *Crime and Social Justice, 29,* 88-109.

Geis, G., Mobley, A. & Shichor, D. (1999). "Private Prisons, Criminological Research, and Conflict of Interest: A Case Study." *Crime & Delinquency, 45*(3), 372-388.

Gemignani, R.J. (1992). "The Public Sector's Responsibilities in Privatizing Court-Related and Correctional Services." In G.W Bowman, S. Hakim & P. Seidenstat (eds.) *Privatizing the United States Justice System: Police, Adjudication, and Corrections Services from the Private Sector.* Jefferson, NC: McFarland and Company.

General Accounting Office (1986, August). *Private and Public Prisons—Studies Comparing Operational Cost and the Quality of Services.* Washington, DC: GAO.

General Accounting Office (1996). *Private & Public Prisons. Report to Subcommittee on Crime, Committee on Judiciary, House of Representatives.* Washington, DC.

Gentry, J.T. (1986). "The Panopticon Revisited: The Problem of Monitoring Private Prisons." *Yale Law Journal, 96,* 333-375.

George, B. & Button, M. (1995). "The Case for Regulation." *International Journal of Risk, Security and Crime Prevention, 1,* 53-57.

George, B. & Button, M. (1998). "Too Little Too Late? An Assessment of Recent Proposals for the Private Security Industry in the UK." *Security Journal, 10,* 1-7.

Ghezzi, S.G. (1983). "A Private Network of Social Control: Insurance Investigation Units." *Social Problems, 30*(5), 521-531.

Giese, W. (1991, October). "Unappetizing Suggestions for Tasty Stock Profits: Or, How to Clean Up with Grubby-Sounding Companies." *Kiplinger's Personal Finance Magazine,* p. 73-76.

Giever, D. (1997). "Jails." In J.M. Pollock (ed.) *Prisons Today and Tomorrow.* Gaithersburg, MD: Aspen Publishers.

Gilbert, M. (1996a). "Private Confinement and the Role of Government in a Civil Society." In G.L Mays & T. Gray (eds.) *Privatization and the Provision of Correctional Services: Context and Consequences.* Cincinnati, OH: Anderson Publishing Co.

Gilbert, M. (1996b). "Making Privatization Decisions Without Getting Burned: A Guide for Understanding the Risks." In G.L Mays & T. Gray (eds.) *Privatization and the Provision of Correctional Services: Context and Consequences.* Cincinnati, OH: Anderson Publishing Co.

Gilbert, M.J. (1997, April/May). "Correctional Privatization: Understanding—and Reducing—the Risks." *Corrections Managers' Report*, pp. 3-4, 11-12.

Gilbert, M.J. (1999). *Personal Telephone Communications with Richard Kiekbusch, January-July, 1999.*

Gildemeister, G.A. (1987). *Prison Labor Convict Competition with Free Workers in Industrializing America, 1840-1890.* New York, NY: Garland.

Gill, M. & Hart, J. (1997). "Exploring Investigative Policing: A Study of Private Detectives in Britain." *British Journal of Criminology, 37*(4), 549-567.

Gillette, C.P. & Stephan, P.B. (1998). "Constitutional Limitations on Privatization." *American Journal of Comparative Law, 46*, 481-503 [Online: Lexis-Nexis Academic Universe, //web.lexis-nexis.com as of September 29, 1998].

Gilliard, D.K. & Beck, A.J. (1998). *Prison and Jail Inmates at Midyear 1997 (Bureau of Justice Statistics Bulletin NCJ 167247).* Washington, DC: Office of Justice Programs.

Gilmer v. Interstate/Johnson Lane Corp., 500 U.S. 20 (1991).

Gilmour, R.S. & Jensen, L.S. (1998). "Reinventing Government Accountability: Public Functions, Privatization and the Meaning of State Action." *Public Administration Review, 58*(3), 247-258.

Gladstone, M. & Arax, M. (1999, February 2). "State to Form Special Unit to Probe Prisons Guards." *Los Angeles Times*, A1, A3.

Globe Newspaper Co. v. Superior Court, 457 U.S. 596 (1982).

Godec, P.D. (1987). "Public Liability for Privately Employed Security Personnel." *Municipal Attorney, 28*, 1-4.

Goldfarb, R. (1965). *Ransom: A Critique of the American Bail System.* New York, NY: Harper & Row.

Goldkamp, J., Gottfredson, M., Jones, P. & Weiland, D. (1995). *Personal Liberty and Community Safety: Pretrial Release in the Criminal Court.* New York, NY: Plenum Press.

Goldstein, J. (1992). *The Intelligible Constitution: The Supreme Court's Obligation to Maintain the Constitution as Something We the People Can Understand.* New York, NY: Oxford University Press.

Golsby, M. (1998). "Formalizing Co-Operation in Crime Prevention: Police and Security Sectors Working Together." *Security Journal, 10*(2), 121-129.

Government Construction Company, Inc. (1996, Nov. 12). *Assumed Name Certificate (Company DBA as Dove Correction Services Company).* Austin, TX: Office of the Secretary of State of Texas, Corporations Section.

Gray, T. (1998, November 10). "What Happens When State Loses Its Locks on Prisons: Transfer of Prison Control to Private Corporations." *Raleigh News and Observer*, pp. 1, 12.

Green, J.A. (1990). *English Sheriffs to 1154.* London, UK: HMSO.

Greenberg, D. (1976). *Crime and Law Enforcement in the Colony of New York 1691-1776.* Ithaca, NY: Cornell University.

Greene, A. (1994, June 11). "Bondsman Hopes to Kill Agency That Helps Free Poor Defendants." *Houston Chronicle,* A-34.

Greenwald, C. (1977). *Group Power: Lobbying and Public Policy.* New York, NY: Praeger.

Hafen, L. (1961). *Western America.* Englewood Cliffs, NJ: Prentice Hall.

Hagan, J. (1994). *Crime and Disrepute.* Thousand Oaks, CA: Pine Forge.

Hair, R.A. (1979). "Private Security and Police Relations." In J.T. O'Brien & M. Marcus (eds.) *Crime and Justice in America: Critical Issues for the Future."* New York, NY: Pergamon.

Haley, M.W. (1999). *Personal Telephone Communication with Michael W. Haley, Commissioner, Alabama Department of Corrections, March 26, 1999.*

Halford, S. (1998, May/June). "National Regional Jail Survey." *American Jails,* pp. 45-49.

Hallet, M. & D. Palumbo (1993). *U.S. Criminal Justice Interest Groups: Institutional Profiles.* Westport: CT: Greenwood Press.

Hallett, M.A. (1997). *Statement on the Proposal to Privatize Tennessee Prisons.* Nashville, TN: Tennessee State Employees Association.

Hallihan, J.T. (1997, August 17). "Private Prisons Go Public with Bang." *New Orleans Times Picayune,* p. A26.

Hallihan, J.T. (1998, December 31). "Private Prisons Not Saving: Strapped Company Closing Three in Texas." *New Orleans Times Picayune,* A10.

Hamilton, A., Jay, J. & Madison, J. (1787). *The Federalist.* New York, NY: Modern Library College Editions.

Hammack, L. (1995, February 26). "Profit Behind Bars." *Roanoke Times and World News,* p. Gl.

Hammurabi (1903). *The Oldest Code of Laws in the World* (translation by C.H.W. Johns). Edinburgh: T. & T. Clark.

Hancock, L. (1998, December). "Contractualism, Privatisation and Justice: Citizenship, the State and Managing Risk." *Australian Journal of Public Administration, 57*(4), 118-127.

Handsley, E. (1997). "Suits Against the Police for Failure to Protect Victims of Violent Crime: A Feminist Perspective in the Use of Dichotomies." *Anglo-American Law Review, 26*(1), 37-81.

Haney, C. & Zimbardo, P. (1998). "The Past and Future of United States Prison Policy." *American Psychologist, 73,* 709-725.

Harding, R.W. (1997). *Private Prisons and Public Accountability.* New Brunswick, NJ: Transaction.

Harding, R.W. (1998). "Private Prisons." In M. Tonry (ed.) *The Handbook of Crime & Punishment.* New York, NY: Oxford University Press.

Hare, F.H., Gilbert, J.L. & ReMine, W.H. (1988). *Confidentiality Orders.* New York, NY: Wiley Law Publications.

Harris County Bail Bond Board (1994, June 8). *Transcript of Proceedings.* Houston, TX: Harris County Bail Bond Board.

Harris County Pretrial Services Agency (1994). *1994 Annual Report*. Houston, TX: Harris County Pretrial Services Agency.

Harris County Pretrial Services Agency (1995). *1995 Annual Report*. Houston, TX: Harris County Pretrial Services Agency.

Harris County Pretrial Services Agency (1996). *1996 Annual Report*. Houston, TX: Harris County Pretrial Services Agency.

Harris County Pretrial Services Agency (1997). *1997 Annual Report*. Houston, TX: Harris County Pretrial Services Agency.

Harris County Pretrial Services Agency (1998). *1998 Annual Report*. Houston, TX: Harris County Pretrial Services Agency.

Hartmann, S. (1998a, December 2). "Shareholders Give CCA Their Approval for Merger." *The Tennessean*, p. B7.

Hartmann, S. (1998b, August 2), "A Private Solution; Governments Put Corrections in Companies' Hands Despite Problems." *The Tennessean*, p. E-1.

Harvey, A.J. (1996). "Building an Organizational Foundation for the Future." *FBI Law Enforcement Bulletin, 65*(11), 12-17.

Hatry, H.P., Brounstein, P.J. & Levinson, R.B. (1994). "Comparison of Privately and Publically Operated Corrections Facilities in Kentucky and Massachusetts." In G.W. Bowman, S. Hakim & P. Seidenstat (eds.) *Privatizing Correctional Institutions.* New Brunswick, NJ: Transaction Books.

Hawk, K. (1995, June 8) *Testimony Before the House Subcommittee on Crime, Committee on the Judiciary*. Washington, DC: Federal Document Clearing House.

Hawkins, D.F. (1983). "State Versus County: Prison Policy and Conflicts of Interest in North Carolina." *Criminal Justice History, 4*, 91-128.

Hazard, G.C. & Scott, P.D. (1988). "The Public Nature of Private Adjudication." *Yale Law and Policy Review, 6*, 42-60.

Heide, K.M. (1999). *Young Killers: The Challenge of Juvenile Homicide.* Thousand Oaks, CA: Sage Publications.

Heitzeg, N.A. (1996). *Deviance: Rulemakers and Rulebreakers.* Minneapolis/St.Paul, MN West Publishing Company.

Held, D. (1984). "Central Perspectives on the Modern State." In G. McLennan, D. Held, & S. Hall (eds.) *The Idea of the Modern State.* Milton Keynes, UK: Open University Press.

Henry, G.A. (1993). "Editorial." *The Pretrial Reporter*, 19(5).

Hershey, R.D. (1999, Dec. 28). "The Markets: Prison Realty Trust, Once a High-Flying REIT, Is Plagued by a Bad Market and Management Woes." *New York Times,* p. C-6 [Online: Lexis-Nexis Academic Universe, //web.lexis-nexis.com as of March 31, 2000].

Hesseling, R.B.P. (1995). "Functional Surveillance in The Netherlands: Exemplary Projects." *Security Journal, 6*(1), 21-25.

Ho, W. (1997). "Discovery in Commercial Arbitration Proceedings." *Houston Law Review, 34*, 199-228.

Hobbes, T. (1969). *Leviathan*. New York, NY: Washington Square Press. (Original work published in 1651).

Hofstader, R. (1944). *Social Darwinism in American Thought.* Boston, MA: Beacon Press.

Honorio Gonzales and Rudy Alvarez vs. Humberto Berrones, Ernesto Berrones, Anita Canales and Mona Hoyle, Cause No. F86-10-02834, (1986).

Hoogenboom, B. (1991). "Grey Policing: A Theoretical Framework." *Policing and Society, 2,* 17-30.

Hoover, T. (1999). "Glantz Seeks 30% Budget Increase for Department." *Tulsa World*, pp. A11-A12.

Hornbostel, M. (1996, March 13). *Personal Interview: Mary Hornbostal—Frio County Auditor.* Pearsall, TX: Office of the Frio County Auditor.

Hou, C. & Sheu, C.J. (1994). "A Study of the Determinants of Participation in a Private Security System Among Taiwanese Enterprises." *Police Studies, 17*(1), 13-23.

Hougen, H.R. (1977). "The Impact of Politics and Prison Industry on the General Management of the Kansas State Penitentiary, 1883-1900." *Kansas Historical Quarterly, 43*(3), 297-318.

Houston, J. (1995). *Correctional Management: Functions, Skills, and Systems.* Chicago, IL: Nelson-Hall Publishers.

Howe, H.M. (1998). "Global Order and the Privatization of Security." *Fletcher Forum of World Affairs, 22,* 1-9.

Howson, G. (1970). *Thief-Taker General: The Rise and Fall of Jonathan Wild.* New York, NY: St. Martin's Press.

Hubbard, R.L. (1992). "Evaluation and Treatment Outcome." In J.H. Lowinson, P. Ruiz, R.B. Millman & J.G. Langrod (eds.) *Substance Abuse: A Comprehensive Textbook*, pp. 599-611. Baltimore, MD: Williams & Wilkins.

Huberman, L. (1937). *The Labor Spy Racket.* New York, NY: Modern Age Books.

Hudgens v. NLRB, 424 U.S. 507 (1976).

Hui-Wen, K. & Png, I.P.L. (1994). "Private Security: Deterrent or Diversion?" *International Review of Law and Economics, 14,* 87-101.

Humphrey, T. (1997, April 18). "Labor, State Employees at Odds Over Prison Privatization Plan." *Knoxville News-Sentinel*, p. A-1.

Humphrey, T. (1998, May 24), "Legislature Listens Where Money Talks; Lobbyists' Track Records Tied to Fatness of Purses." *Knoxville News Sentinel*, p. A-1.

Hunzeker, D. (1991, November). "Private Cells, Public Prisons." *State Legislatures*, 24-27.

Inciardi, J.A., Martin, S. S., Lockwood, D., Hooper, R.M. & Wald, B.M. (1992). "Obstacles to the Implementation and Evaluation of Drug Treatment Programs in Corrections Settings: Reviewing the Delaware KEY Experience." In C.G. Leukefeld & F.M. Tims (eds.) *Drug Abuse Treatment in Prisons and Jails: NIDA Research Monograph 118.* Washington, DC: National Institute on Drug Abuse, U.S. Government Printing Office.

"Industrial Policing and Espionage" (1939). *Harvard Law Review, 52,* 793-804.

Ingalls, R.P. (1988). *Urban Vigilantes in the New South—Tampa, 1882-1936.* Knoxville, TN: University of Tennessee Press.

Ingley, S.J. (1997, June/July). "Why Association Membership Makes Sense for Corrections Professionals." *Corrections Managers' Report*, pp. 8, 16.

Ingley, S.J. (1999). *Personal Telephone Communication with Stephen J. Ingley, Executive Director, American Jail Association, March 8, 1999.*

Institute of Local Self-Government (1974). *Private Security and the Public Interest.* Berkeley, CA: Author.

Institute of Local Self-Government (1977). *Alternatives to Traditional Public Safety Delivery Systems: Civilians in Public Safety Services.* Berkeley, CA: Author.

Ireland, R.M. (1995). "Privately Funded Prosecution of Crime in the Nineteenth-Century United States." *American Journal of Legal History, 39*(1), 43-58.

Irwin, J. & Austin, J. (1997). *It's About Time: America's Imprisonment Binge* (2nd ed.). Belmont, CA: Wadsworth Publishing Company.

Isikoff, M. (1991, November 19). "Inmate Who Claimed to Be Quayle's Drug Dealer Presses Rights Case." *Washington Post*, A3.

Jackson v. Metropolitan Edison, 419 U.S. 35 (1974).

Jacobson, J.S. (1995). "The Model Campus Police Jurisdiction Act: Toward Broader Jurisdiction For University Police." *Columbia Journal of Law and Social Problems, 29*(1), 39-83.

Jaffe, G. & Brooks, R. (1998, August 5). "Violence at Prison Run by Corrections Corp. Irks Youngstown, Ohio." *Wall Street Journal*, Al, A8.

James, A. Bottomley, A.K., Liebling, A. & Clare, E. (1997). *Privatizing Prisons: Rhetoric and Reality*. London, UK: Sage.

Janus, M. (1989). Privatizing Corrections: Symbolic and Policy Issues." *The Bureaucrat, 18*(1), 32-36.

Janus, M. (1993). "Bars on the Iron Tiangle: Public Policy Issues in the Privatization of Corrections." In G.H. Bowman, S. Hakim & P. Seidenstadt (eds.) *Privatizing Correctional Institutions*. New Brunswick, NJ: Transaction Books.

Johnson, D.R. (1981). *American Law Enforcement: A History.* St. Louis, MO: Forum.

Johnson, H.A. (1988). *History of Criminal Justice.* Cincinnati, OH: Anderson Publishing Co.

Johnson, R. & Toch, H. (eds.) (1982). *The Pains of Imprisonment.* Beverly Hills, CA: Sage.

Johnston, D.C. (1998). "Merger of Prison Operation into Reit Sends Both Stocks Down." *New York Times*, (April 21), D3.

Johnston, L. (1992a). *The Rebirth of Private Policing.* London, UK: Routledge.

Johnston, L. (1992b). "Regulating Private Security." *International Journal of Sociology of Law, 20*, 1-16.

Johnston, L. (1993). "Privatisation and Protection: Spatial and Sectoral Ideologies in British Policing and Crime Prevention." *Modern Law Review, 56*(6), 771-792.

Jones, R.P. (1998a, November 11). "State Now Admits Private Prison Abuse." *Milwaukee Journal Sentinel*, p. 1.

Jones, R.P. (1998b, November 12). "Legislators to Visit Private Prison." *Milwaukee Journal Sentinel*, p. l.

Jones, T. & Newburn, T. (1995). "How Big Is Private Security?" *Policing and Society, 5*, 221-230.

Josi, D. & Sechrest, D.K. (1998a). "Treatment Versus Security: Adversarial Relationship Between Treatment Facilitators and Correctional Officers." *Journal of Offender Rehabilitation, 23*(1/2), 167-184.

Josi, D. & Sechrest, D.K. (1998b). *The Changing Career of the Correctional Officer: Policy Implications for the 21st Century.* Oxford, UK: Butterworth-Heinemann.

Juceam, D.J. (1997). "Recent Developments—Privatizing Section 1983 Immunity: The Prison Guard's Dilemma After *Richardson v. McKnight*, 117 S. Ct. 2100 (1997)." *Harvard Journal of Law & Public Policy, 21*(1), 251-272.

Kakalik, J. & Wildhorn, S. (1971). *Private Police in the United States: Volumes 1-5.* Santa Monica, CA: Rand.

Kakalik, J. & Wildhorn, S. (1977*). The Private Police: Security and Danger.* New York, NY: Crane, Russak.

Kamerman, S.B. & Kahn, A.J. (eds.) (1989). *Privatization and the Welfare State.* Princeton, NJ: Princeton University Press.

Kaplan, R.S. (1996a). *Indianapolis: Activity-Based Costing of City Services (Vol. 9-196-115).* Boston, MA: Harvard Business School.

Kaplan, R.S. (1996b). *Indianapolis: Activity-Based Costing of City Services (Vol. 9-196-117).* Boston, MA: Harvard Business School.

Katsampes, P., Pogrebin, N. & Winkler, G.M. (1998). "Reinventing County Corrections." *Corrections Management Quarterly, 2*(2), 70-75.

Kelling, G.L., Pate, T., Dieckman, D. & Brown, C.E. (1974). *The Kansas City Preventive Patrol Experiment.* Washington, DC: The Police Foundation.

Kennedy, D.B. (1995). "A Synopsis of Private Security in the United States." *Security Journal, 6*(2), 101-105.

Kennedy, S. (1994). *Commercial Surety Bail: Assessing Its Role in the Pretrial Release and Detention Decision.* Washington, DC: Pretrial Services Resource Center.

Kent, C.A. (ed.) (1987). *Entrepreneurship and the Privatizing of Government.* New York, NY: Quorum Books.

Kentucky Corrections Cabinet, Office of Corrections Training (1985, September). *Changing Faces, Common Walls: History of Corrections in Kentucky.* Louisville, KY: Kentucky Corrections Cabinet.

Kerle, K.E. (1998). *American Jails: Looking to the Future.* Boston, MA: Butterworth-Heinemann.

Kerle, K.E. (1999, March 15). *Personal Telephone Communication with Dr. Kenneth E. Kerle, Managing Editor of American Jails, AJA's Bimonthly Magazine.*

Keve, P.W. (1986). *The History of Corrections in Virginia.* Charlottesville, VA: University of Virginia Press.

Keve, P.W. (1991). *Prisons and the American Conscience: A History of U.S. Federal Corrections.* Carbondale, IL: Southern Illinois University Press.

Key, V.O. (1964). *Politics, Parties, and Pressure Groups* (5th ed.). New York, NY: Thomas Y. Crowell.

Kiekbusch, R.G. (1998, Summer). "Some Random Thoughts on the American Jail and Public Misconceptions About It." *Key Issues*, pp. 2-4.

Kiekbusch, R.G. (1999, Dec./Jan.). "Why and How Sheriffs Must Lead Corrections into the 21st Century." *Corrections Managers' Report*, pp. 3-4, 11.

Kiesling, M. & Corcoran, K. (1998, March 29). "Lobbyists Pose as Reformers: Bail Bond Group's Officers Would Benefit from Millions in New Business if System Goes Private." *The Times* (Munster, IN). Retrieved June 1, 1999 from NewsBank NewsFile online database (Record No. 002980D56C96A0B3413B5).

Kilburn, J.C. & Shrum, W. (1998). "Private Collective Protection in Urban Areas." *Urban Affairs Review, 33*(6), 790-812.

Kim, A.S. (1994). "Rent-a-Judges and the Cost of Selling Justice." *Duke Law Journal, 44*, 166-199.

Kleck, G. (1988). "Crime Control Through the Private Use of Armed Force." *Social Problems, 35*(1), 1-21.

Klein, D. (1997). "The Pretrial Detention 'Crisis': The Causes and the Cure." Washington University Journal of *Urban and Contemporary Law, 52*, 281. (LEXIS, Lawrev, Bail).

Klockars, C.B. (1985). *The Idea of Police.* Beverly Hills, CA: Sage.

Kolderie, T. (1986). "Two Different Concepts of Privatization." *Public Administration Review, 46*(July/August), 285-291.

Kotz, N. (1988). *Wild Blue Yonder: Money, Politics and the B1-Bomber.* Princeton, NJ: Princeton University Press.

Kovach, K.K. (1994). *Mediation: Principles and Practice.* St. Paul, MN: West Publishing.

Kritsiotis, D. (1998). "Mercenaries and the Privatization of Warfare." *Fletcher Forum of World Affairs, 22*, 11-25.

Kronstein, H. (1944). "Business Arbitration-Instrument of Private Government." *Yale Law Journal, 54*, 36-69.

Kronstein, H. (1963). "Arbitration is Power." *New York University Law Review, 38*, 661-700.

Krotoszynski, R.J. (1995). "Back to the Briarpatch: An Argument in Favor of Constitutional Meta-Analysis in State Action Determinations." *Michigan Law Review, 94*(2), 302-347.

Kyle, J. (1998). "The Privatization Debate Continues: Tennessee's Experience Highlights Scope of Controversy Over Private Prisons." *Corrections Today, 60*(5), 88.

Lampkin, L. (1991). "Does Crime Pay? AFSCME Reviews the Record on the Privatization of Prisons." *Journal of Contemporary Criminal Justice, 7*(1), 41-48.

Landes, W.M. & Posner, R.A. (1979). "Adjudication as a Private Good." *Journal of Legal Studies, 8*, 235-284.

Langworthy, R.H. & Travis, L.P. (1999). *Policing in America: A Balance of Forces* (2nd ed.). Upper Saddle River, NJ: Prentice Hall.

Lanza-Kadduce, L., Parker, K.F. & Thomas, C.W. (1999). "A Comparative Recidivism Analysis of Releasees from Private and Public Prisons." *Crime & Delinquency, 45*, 28-47.

Lauriault, R. N. (1989). "From Can't to Can't: The North Florida Turpentine Camp, 1900-1950." *Florida Historical Quarterly, 67*(3), 310-328.

Lavrakas, P.J. & Herz, E.J. (1982). "Citizen Participation in Neighborhood Crime Prevention." *Criminology, 20*, 479-498.

Ledbetter, C.R. (1993). "The Long Struggle to End Convict Leasing in Arkansas." *Arkansas Historical Quarterly, 52*(1), 1-27.

Lee, M. (1995). "Across the Public-Private Divide? Private Policing, Grey Intelligence and Civil Actions in Local Drugs Control." *European Journal of Crime, Criminal Law and Criminal Justice, 3*(4), 381-394.

Lee, R.E. (1985). "The American Courts as Public Goods: Who Should Pay the Costs of Litigation?" *Catholic University Law Review, 34*, 267-276.

Leo, R.A. (1996). "Police Scholarship for the Future: Resisting the Pull of the Policy Audience." *Law & Society Review, 30*, 865-879.

Leukefeld, C.G. & Tims, F.R. (1992). *Drug Abuse Treatment in Prisons and Jails: NIDA Research Monograph 118*. Washington, DC: U.S. Department of Health and Human Services, Public Health Service, Alcohol, Drug Abuse, and Mental Health Administration.

Leukefeld, C.G. & Tims, F.R. (1993). "Drug Abuse Treatment in Prisons and Jails." *Journal of Substance Abuse Treatment, 10*(1), 77-84.

Lilly, J.R. & Knepper, P. (1993). "The Corrections-Commercial Complex." *Crime & Delinquency, 39*(2), 150-166.

Lindblom, C.E. (1977). *Politics and Markets: The World's Political-Economic Systems.* New York, NY: Basic Books, Inc.

Lindblom, C.E. (1979). "Still Muddling, Not Yet Through." *Public Administration Review, 39*, 517-524.

Linowes, D.F. (1988). *Privatization: Toward More Effective Government.* Chicago, IL: University of Illinois Press.

Lipson, M. (1988). "Private Security: A Retrospective." *Annals of the American Academy of Political and Social Science, 498*, 11-22.

Litkovitz, A.L. (1995). "The Advantages of Using a 'Rent-A-Judge' System in Ohio." *Ohio State Journal on Dispute Resolution, 10*, 491-506.

Little Hoover Commission (1998, January). "Beyond Bars: Correctional Reforms to Lower Prison Costs and Reduce Crime." Sacramento, CA: Little Hoover Commission.

Livingston, D. (1997) "Police Discretion and the Quality of Life in Public Places: Courts, Communities, and the New Policing." *Columbia Law Review, 97*(3), 551-672.

Loader, I. (1997a). "Private Security and the Demand for Protection in Contemporary Britain." *Policing & Society, 7*(3), 143-162.

Loader, I. (1997b). "Thinking Normatively About Private Security." *Journal of Law and Society, 24*(3), 377-394.

Local Government Code (1995). *Vernon's Texas Codes Annotated, 1995 Cumulative Annual Pocket Part, Section 351.102.*

Locke, J. (1955). *On Civil Government.* Chicago, IL: Henry Reguery. (Original work published 1692).

Locker, R. (1997a, May 23). "Prison Bill Won't See Action by End of This Session; Privatization Foes Cheer Decision." *The Commercial Appeal,* p. B-1.

Locker, R. (1997b, May 25). "Personal, Political, Business Ties Bind CCA, State." *The Commercial Appeal,* p. B-3.

Locker, R. (1997c, April 23). "Firm Hoping to Run Private Prisons Writing Bill Creating Them." *The Commercial Appeal,* p. A-1.

Locker, R. (1997d, May 23). "Prison Bill Won't See Action by The End of This Session; Privatization Foes Cheer Decision." *The Commercial Appeal,* p. B-1.

Locker, R. (1998, April 15). "Vote-Starved Prison Bill Dies; Workers Cheer but Tenn Privatization May Revive in '99." *The Commercial Appeal,* p. A-1.

Logan, C. & B.W. McGriff (1989). *Comparing Costs of Public and Private Prisons.* Washington, DC: National Institute of Justice.

Logan, C.H. (1990). *Private Prisons: Cons and Pros.* New York, NY: Oxford University Press.

Logan, C.H. (1991). *Well Kept: Comparing Quality of Confinement in a Public and a Private Prison.* Washington, DC: National Institute of Justice.

Logan, C.H. (1992). "Well Kept: Comparing Quality of Confinement in Private and Public Prisons." *The Journal of Criminal Law and Criminology, 83*(3), 577-613.

Logan, C.H. (1996). *Open Letter to Representative Bill McCollum.* [Available: http://www.ucc.uconn.edu/~wwwsoci/gaochl.html.]

Logan, CH. & McGriff, B.W. (1989). *Comparing Costs of Public and Private Prisons: A Case Study, 216 NIJ Reports* Washington, DC: National Institute of Justice.

Logan, C.H. & Rausch, S.P. (1985). "Punish and Profit: The Emergence of Private Enterprise Prisons." *Justice Quarterly, 2,* 303-318.

Lowi, T. (1971). *The Politics of Disorder.* New York, NY: Basic Books.

Luban, D. (1995). "Settlements and the Erosion of the Public Realm." *Georgetown Law Journal, 83,* 2619-2662.

Lucken, K. (1997). "Privatizing Discretion: 'Rehabilitating Treatment' Treatment in Community Corrections." *Crime & Delinquency, 43*(3), 243-260.

Lustig v. United States, 338 U.S. 78 (1949).

Lutrin, C.E. & Settle, A.K. (1992). *American Public Administration: Concepts and Cases* (4th ed.). St. Paul, MN: West Publishing Company.

Lyman, M.D. (1999). *The Police: An Introduction.* Upper Saddle River, NJ: Prentice Hall.

Maffly, B. (1996, Feb. 4). "Utahans Bolting Texas Lockups." *The Salt Lake Tribune,* pp. B1, B4.

Maghan, J. (1998). "Cell Out: Renting Out the Responsibility for the Criminally Confined." In J. Kamerman (ed.) *Negotiating Responsibility in the Criminal Justice System.* Carbondale, IL: Southern Illinois University Press.

Maguire, K. & Pastore, A. (1996). *Sourcebook of Criminal Justice Statistics—1995.* Washington, DC: U.S. Department of Justice, Office of Justice Programs, Bureau of Justice Statistics.

Maguire, K. & Pastore, A. (1998). *Sourcebook of Criminal Justice Statistics—1997.* Washington, DC: U.S. Department of Justice, Office of Justice Programs, Bureau of Justice Statistics.

Mancini, M.J. (1996). *One Dies, Get Another: Convict Leasing in the American South, 1866-1928.* Columbia, SC: University of South Carolina Press.

Marcus, R. (1995, February 26). "Ventures During Public Service Multiplied Net Worth by 10." *Washington Post*, p. A19.

Marcus, R.L. (1991). "Evidence and Procedure for the Future: The Discovery Confidentiality Controversy." *University of Illinois Law Review,* 457-506.

Marion, N. (1995). *A Primer in the Politics of Criminal Justice.* Albany, NY: Harrow and Heston, Publishers.

Markos, P.A. & Grierson, S. (1998). "A Case Study of a Private Correctional Substance Abuse Treatment Program." *Guidance and Counseling, Spring 13*(3), 40-43.

Marsh v. Alabama, 326 U.S. 501 (1946).

Martin, J.B. (1954). *Break Down the Walls.* New York, NY: Ballantine.

Martin, S.J. & Ekland-Olson, S. (1987). *Texas Prisons: The Walls Came Tumbling Down.* Austin, TX: Texas Monthly Press.

Marx, G.T. & Archer, D. (1976). "Community Policing Patrols and Vigilantism." In H.J. Rosenbaum & P.C. Sederberg (eds.) *Vigilante Politics.* University Park, PA: University of Pennsylvania.

Marx, G.T. (1987). "The Interweaving of Public and Private Police in Undercover Work." In C.D. Shearing & P.C. Stenning (eds.) *Private Policing.* Newbury Park, CA: Sage.

Mays, G.L. (1996). "Correctional Privatization: Defining the Issues and Searching for Answers." In G.L. Mays & T. Gray (eds.) *Privatization and the Provision of Correctional Services: Context and Consequences.* Cincinnati, OH: Anderson Publishing Co.

Mays, G.L. & Gray, T. (eds.) (1996). *Privatization and the Provision of Correctional Services: Context and Consequences.* Cincinnati, OH: Anderson Publishing Co.

Mays, G.L. & Thompson, J.A. (1991). "The Political and Organizational Context of American Jails." In J.A. Thompson & G.L. Mays (eds.) *American Jails: Public Policy Issues.* Chicago, IL: Nelson-Hall Publishers.

Mays, G.L. & Winfree, L.T. (1998). *Contemporary Corrections.* Belmont, CA: Wadsworth Publishing Company.

Mays, S. L. (1995). "Privatization of Municipal Services: Contagion in the Body Politic." *Duquesne Law Review, 34*, 41-70.

McCrie, R.D. (1988). "The Development of the U.S. Security Industry." *Annals of the American Academy of Political and Social Science, 498*, 23-34.

McDonald, D.C. (1990). "The Cost of Operating Public and Private Correctional Facilities." In D.C. McDonald (ed.) *Private Prisons and Public Interests.* New Brunswick, NJ: Rutgers University Press.

McDonald, D.C. (1992). "Private Penal Institutions." In M. Tonry (ed.) *Crime and Justice: An Annual Review of Research (Vol. 16)*. Chicago, IL: University of Chicago Press.

McDonald, D.C., Fournier, E., Russell-Einhorn, M. & Crawford, S. (1998). *Private Prisons in the United States: An Assessment of Current Practices*. Cambridge, MA: Abt Associates.

McGrath, R.D. (1972). *Gunfighters, Highwaymen and Vigilantes: Violence on the Frontier*. Berkeley, CA: University of California Press.

Meachum, L. (1998). *Resident Substance Abuse Treatment Programs for State Prisoners; Answers to Frequently Asked Questions*. U.S. Department of Justice, Office of Justice Programs, Corrections Program Office.

Meranze, M. (1996). *Laboratories of Virtue: Punishment, Revolution, and Authority in Philadelphia, 1760-1835*. Chapel Hill, NC: University of North Carolina Press.

Merryman, J.H. (1985). *The Civil Law Tradition*. Stanford, CA: Stanford University Press.

Messner, S.F. & Rosenfeld, R. (1997). *Crime and the American Dream* (2nd ed.). Belmont, CA: Wadsworth Publishing Company.

Meyer, J.W. & Rowan, B. (1977). "Institutionalized Organizations: Formal Structure as Myth and Ceremony." *American Journal of Sociology, 83*, 340-363.

Miller, A.R. (1991). "Confidentiality, Protective Orders, and Public Access to the Courts." *Harvard Law Review, 105*, 427-502.

Miller, K. (1999, December 27). "Prison Company Getting New Money, Management, Structure." *Associated Press State & Local Wire* [Online: Lexis-Nexis Academic Universe, //web.lexis-nexis.com as of March 31, 2000].

Miller, W.R. (1992). "The Effectiveness of Treatment for Substance Abuse: Reasons for Optimism." *Journal of Substance Abuse Treatment, 9*(2), 93-103.

Mimlitch, S. (1994, May 5). *Letter to Judge Williams from Sue Mimlitch, Contract Administrator, Consolidated Financial Resources, Inc., Re: Lease purchase agreement dated as of April 19, 1994 by and Between Frio County as Lessee and Consolidated Financial Resources, Inc., as Lessor, for the Acquisition of Furniture, Fixtures, and Equipment for the Jail Expansions*. Greenville, TX: Consolidated Financial Resources, Inc.

Mintz, M. (1985). *At Any Cost: Corporate Greed, Women, and the Dalkon Shield*. New York, NY: Pantheon Books.

Mintzberg, H. (1989). *Mintzberg on Management: Inside Our Strange World of Organizations*. New York, NY: Free Press.

Mitsubishi Motors Corporation v. Soler Chrysler-Plymouth, Inc., 473 U.S. 614 (1985).

Monas, S. (1961). *The Third Section: Police and Society in Russia Under Nicholas I*. Cambridge, MA: Harvard University Press.

Moore, A.T. (1998). *Private Prisons: Quality Corrections at Lower Cost*. Los Angeles, CA: Reason Public Policy Institute.

Morain (1999, July 13). "Private Prison Has Everything But Prisoners." *Los Angeles Times*, pp. A1, A19.

Morgan, D.R. & England, R.E. (1988). "The Two Faces of Privatization." *Public Administration Review, 48*(6), 979-987.

Morley, H.N. & Fong, R.S. (1995). "Can We All Get Along? A Study of Why Strained Relations Continue to Exist Between Sworn Law Enforcement and Private Security." *Security Journal, 6*(2), 85-92.

Morn, F.T. (1982). *The Eye That Never Sleeps: A History of the Pinkerton National Detective Agency.* Bloomington, IN: Indiana University Press.

Morris, W.A. (1927). *The Medieval Sheriff to 1300.* New York, NY: Manchester University Press.

Morse, B. (1996). *Personal Interview: Bleecker Morse—Chair, Ad Hoc Committee Appointed by the Commissioners Court to Make Recommendations on Managing the Jail Related Financial Crisis with Dove Development Corporation.* Pearsall, TX.

Moyle, P.D. (1995. "Private Prison Research in Queensland, Australia: A Case Study of Borallon Coreectional Centre, 1991." *British Journal of Criminology, 35*(1), 34-62.

Mullen, R., Ratelle, J., Abraham, E. & Boyle, J. (1996, August). "California Program Reduces Recidivism and Saves Tax Dollars." *Corrections Today*, pp. 118-123.

Mullen, R., Schuettinger, M., Arbiter, N. & Conn, D. (1997). "Reducing Recidivism: Amity Foundation of California and the California Department of Corrections Demonstrate How to Do It." In C. Whitman, J. Zimmerman & T. Miller (eds.) *Frontiers of Justice: Volume II.* Biddle Publishing Company.

Mumola, C.J. (1999). *Substance Abuse and Treatment, State and Federal Prisoners, 1997: Special Report.* Washington, DC: U.S. Department of Justice, Bureau of Justice Statistics.

Murray, C. (1995). "The Case Against Regulation." *International Journal of Risk, Security and Crime Prevention, 1*, 59-62.

Myers, M.A. (1998). *Race, Labor & Punishment in the New South.* Columbus, OH: Ohio State University Press.

Nader, R., Green, M. & Seligman, J. (1976). *Taming the Giant Corporation.* New York, NY: W.W. Norton & Company, Inc.

Nalla, M. & Newman, G. (1990). *A Primer in Private Security.* New York, NY: Harrow and Heston.

National Advisory Commission on Criminal Justice Standards and Goals (1976). *Private security: Report of the Task Force on Private Security.* Washington, DC: Government Printing Office.

National Association of Counties (1999). *Personal Telephone Communication with NACO Staff Member, May 14, 1999.*

National Center for Policy Analysis (1996a). *NCPA Crime—Executive Summary* [Online: //www.ncpa.org/studies.s181/s181a.html as of January 6, 1999]. Dallas, TX: Author.

National Center for Policy Analysis (1996b). *NCPA Crime—Bounty Hunting: Making the Bail System Work* [Online: //www.ncpa.org/studies/s181/s181g.html as of January 6, 1999]. Dallas, TX: Author.

National Center for Policy Analysis (1996c). *NCPA Crime—Privatizing the Probation and Parole Systems* [Online: //www.ncpa.org/studies/s181/181m.html as of January 6, 1999]. Dallas, TX: Author.

National Center for Policy Analysis (1996d). *NCPA Crime—Privatizing the Prosecution of Criminals* [Online: //www.ncpa.org/studies/s181/s181l.html as of January 6, 1999]. Dallas, TX: Author.

National Center for Policy Analysis (1996e). *NCPA Crime—Private Sector Law Enforcement* [Online: //www.ncpa.org/studies/s181/s181e.html as of January 6, 1999]. Dallas, TX: Author.

National Center for Policy Analysis (1996f). *NCPA Crime—Potential Abuses Under Private Sector Law Enforcement* [Online: //www.ncpa.org/studies/s181/s181j.html as of January 6, 1999]. Dallas, TX: Author.

National Institute of Corrections (1996). *Planning of New Institutions Workshop: Life Cycle Costing (Curriculum Materials as of Nov. 18-22, 1996)*. Longmont, CO: National Institute of Corrections.

National Institute of Justice (1987). *Issues in Contracting for the Private Operation of Prisons and Jails*. Washington, DC: U.S. Department of Justice.

National Performance Review (1993). *Creating Government That Works Better and Costs Less*. Washington, DC: Government Printing Office.

National Sheriffs' Association (1998). *Annual Sheriffs' Directory*. Alexandria, VA: National Sheriffs' Association.

National Sheriffs' Association (1999a). *Personal Telephone Communication with NSA Staff Member, March 15, 1999*.

National Sheriffs' Association (1999b). *Personal Telephone Communication with NSA Staff Member, May 14, 1999*.

Nelson, J. (1998). "Appendix 1: Comparing Public and Private Prison Costs." In D. McDonald, E. Fournier, M. Russell-Einhorn & S. Crawford (eds.) *Private Prisons in the United States: An Assessment of Current Practice*. Boston, MA: Abt Associates Inc.

Nemeth, C.P. (1995). *Private Security and the Law* (2nd. ed.). Cincinnati, OH: Anderson Publishing Co.

Newton, J. (1998, June 2). "County to Consider Addict Treatment Reforms." *Los Angeles Times*, p. B8.

Newton, W.F. & Swenson, D.G. (1984). "Adjudication by Privately Compensated Judges in Texas." *Baylor Law Review, 36*, 813-853.

Nozick, R. (1974). *Anarchy, State and Utopia*. New York, NY: Basic Books.

Nuzum, M. (1998). "The Commercialization of Justice: Public Good or Private Greed?" *The Critical Criminologist, 8*(3), 1, 5-8.

Office of Program Policy Analysis and Government Accountability (1995, November). *Review of Correctional Privatization (Report No. 95-12)*. State of Florida: The Florida Legislature.

Office of Program Policy Analysis and Government Accountability (1997a, March). *Information Brief Comparing Costs of Public and Private Prisons (Report No. 96-69)*. State of Florida: The Florida Legislature.

Office of Program Policy Analysis and Government Accountability (1997b, September). *Follow-Up Report on the Review of Correctional Privatization (Report No. 97-06)*. State of Florida: The Florida Legislature.

Office of Program Policy Analysis and Government Accountability (1998). *Review of Bay Correctional Facility and Moore Haven Correctional Facility (97-68)*. Tallahassee, FL: Office of Program Policy and Government Accountability.

Office of the Corrections Trustee of the District of Columbia (1998 November 25). *Report to the Attorney General: Inspection and Review of the Northeast Ohio Correctional Center, Washington, DC*. Washington, DC: Author.

Ogle, R.S. (1999). "Prison Privatization: An Environmental Catch-22." *Justice Quarterly, 16*(3), 579-600.

Ohlin, L.E. (1960). "Conflicting Interests in Correctional Objectives." In *Theoretical Studies in Social Organization of Prisons*. New York, NY: Social Science Research Council.

O'Leary, D. (1994). "Reflections on Police Privatization." *FBI Law Enforcement Bulletin, 9*, 21-25.

Oliver, W.M. (1998). *Community-Oriented Policing: A Systemic Approach to Policing*. Upper Saddle River, NJ: Prentice Hall.

Operations and Management Agreement (1992, Sept. 1). *County Jail and Detention Facility Operation and Management Agreement*. Pearsall, TX: Office of the Frio County Clerk.

Operations and Management Agreement (1995, Dec. 22). *Amendments to the County Jail and Detention Facility Operations and Management Agreement*. Pearsall, TX: Office of the Frio County Clerk.

Osborne, D. & Gaebler, T. (1992). *Reinventing Government*. Reading, MA: Addison-Wesley.

Ostrow, R. (1992, December 4). "Federal Prison Chief Expected to Resign Soon Due to Illness." *Los Angeles Times*, p. A39.

O'Toole, M. (1997). *Jails and Prisons: The Numbers Say They Are More Different Than Generally Assumed*. Presentation at the annual meeting, Academy of Criminal Justice Sciences, Louisville, Kentucky.

"Overcrowded County Jails to Get Emergency Help from State" (1994, April 15). *Legislative Newsletter, 4*(2), 1 (a publication of the Texas Association of Counties).

Palmer, H.S. (1976). "Sticky Fingers, Deep Pockets, and the Long Arm of the Law: Illegal Searches of Shoplifers by Private Merchant Security Personnel." *Oregon Law Review, 55*(2), 279-290.

Palumbo, D. (1994). *Public Policy in America: Government in Action*. New York, NY: Harcourt Brace

Pancake, D. (1983). "Cooperation Between Police Departments and Private Security." *Police Chief, 50*(6), 34-36.

Parenti, C. (1997). "I Hunt Men." *The Progressive, 61*(1), pp. 21-23.

Parsons, T. (1951). *The Social System*. New York, NY: Free Press.

Patterson, S.C., Davidson, R.H. & Ripley, R.B. (1979). *A More Perfect Union*. Belmont, CA: Dorsey Press.

Pennell, R. (1995). "State Power in the Chronically Weak State: Spanish Coastguards as Pirates, 1814-50." *European History Quarterly, 25*(3), 353-379.

People v. Zelinski, (594 P.2d 1000) (Cal. 1979).

Perry v. Thomas, 482 U.S. 483 (1987).

Peters, E.M. (1995). "Prison Before the Prison: The Ancient and Medieval Worlds." In N. Morris & D.J. Rothman (eds.) *Oxford History of the Prison: The Practice of Punishment in Western Society.* New York, NY: Oxford University Press.

Pfeffer, J. (1982). *Organizations and Organization Theory.* Marshfield, MA: Pitman.

Pfeffer, J. & Salancik, G.R. (1978). *The External Control of Organizations: A Resource Dependence Perspective.* New York, NY: Harper and Row.

Pfeifer, S. (1999, April 20). "Patient Gives Tearful Testimony." *Orange County Register*, p. A6.

Pisciotta, A.W. (1994). *Benevolent Repression: Social Control and the American Reformatory-Prison Movement.* New York, NY: New York University Press.

Pivar, D.J. (1973). *Purity Crusade: Sexual Morality and Social Control, 1868-1900.* Westport, CT: Greenwood Press.

Platt, A. (1969). *The Child Savers.* Chicago, IL: University of Chicago Press.

Posner, R.A. (1985). *The Federal Courts: Crisis and Reform.* Cambridge, MA: Harvard University Press.

Potts, D. (ed.) (1995, March). "A Bail Industry Guide for Dismantling Pretrial Services Programs." *NAPSA News* (The Newsletter of the National Association of Pretrial Services Agencies).

PR Newswire (1999a, January 4). "PZN Finalizes Merger with CCA." *PR Newswire Association*, p. 1.

PR Newswire (1999b, June 3). "Wolf Popper LLP Accuses Prison Realty Trust Inc. of Securities Violations." *PR Newswire Association*, pp. 1-2.

Prassel, F.R. (1972). *The Western Peace Officer: A Legacy of Law and Order.* Norman, OK: University of Oklahoma.

Prenzler, T., Draper, R. & Harrison, A. (1996). "The Case for Non-Police Private Security." *Journal of Security Administration, 19*(1), 16-33.

President's Commission on Law Enforcement and the Administration of Justice (1967). *The Challenge of Crime in a Free Society.* Washington, DC: U.S. Government Printing Office.

President's Commission on Privatization (1988). *Privatization: Toward More Effective Government.* Washington, DC: Government Printing Office.

Press-Enterprise Co. v. Superior Court, 478 U.S. 1 (1986).

Preston, L.E. & Post, J.E. (1975). *Private Management and Public Policy.* Englewood Cliffs, NJ: Prentice Hall.

Pringle, P. (1958). *The Thief Takers.* London, UK: Museum Press.

Prison Realty Trust (1997, July 15). *Prospectus: 18,500,000 Shares.* Nashville, TN: Author.

Private Security (1997, October). *Jane's Intelligence Review, Special Report No. 15*, pp. 19-21.

Procunier v. Navarette, 434 U.S. 555, 561-562 (1978).

Public/Private Construction, Inc. (1994, April 14). *Articles of Incorporation of Public/Private Construction, Inc.* Austin, TX: Office of the Secretary of State of Texas, Corporations Section.

Public/Private Construction, Inc. (1994, May 6). *Articles of Amendment to the Articles of Incorporation (Corporate Name Changed to Government Construction Company, Inc.).* Austin, TX: Office of the Secretary of State of Texas, Corporations Section.

Punch, M. (1996). *Dirty Business: Exploring Corporate Misconduct.* Thousand Oaks, CA: Sage Publications.

Pyatt, R.A. (1999, June 14). "Pyatt on Business: Let's Try Not to Dance to This Jail House Rock." *Washington Post*, p. F-04.

Quinney, R. (1977). *Class, State, and Crime.* New York, NY: David McKay Company.

Radzinowicz, L. (1956). *A History of English Criminal Law and its Administration from 1750; Vol. III: The Clash Between Private Initiative and the Public Interest in the Enforcement of the Law.* London, UK: Stevens and Sons.

Ratliff, W.L. (1997). "The Due Process Failure of America's Prison Privatization Statutes." *Seton Hall Legislative Journal, 21*, 371-425 [Online: Lexis-Nexis Academic Universe, //web.lexis-nexis.com as of October 5, 1998].

Rawson, H. & Miner, M. (1986). *The New International Dictionary of Quotations.* New York, NY: A Mentor Book, New American Library.

Ray, J. (1998). "Contracting out Corrections (Letter to the Editor)." *Washington Post*, (April 3), p. A-20.

Redmon, J. (1999, June 15). "Zoning Board Nixes SW Jail: Fears it Would Shackle Growth. *The Washington Times*.

Reed, C.J. (1993). "Confidentiality and the Courts: Secrecy's Threat to Public Safety." *Judicature, 76*, 308-310.

Rein, M. (1989). "The Social Structure of Institutions: Neither Public nor Private." In S.B. Kamerman & A.J. Kahn (eds.) *Privatization and the Welfare State.* Princeton, NJ: Princeton University Press.

Reiss, A.J. (1988). *Private Employment of Public Police.* Washington, DC: Government Printing Office.

Rendell-Baker v. Kohn, 457 U.S. 830 (1982).

Research & Policy Committee (1982). *Public-Private Partnership, An Opportunity for Urban Communities.* New York, NY: Committee for Economic Development.

Resnik, J. (1982). "Managerial Judges." *Harvard Law Review, 96*, 374-448.

Resnik, J. (1986). "Failing Faith: Adjudicatory Procedure in Decline." *University of Chicago Law Review, 53*, 494-560.

Richardson, et al. v. McKnight, 117 S. Ct. 2100 (1997).

Richardson, J. (1974). "Urban Police in the United States." Port Washington, NY: Kennikat Press.

Richardson, N.C. (1997). "Is There a Current Incarceration Crisis in the Black Community? An Analysis of the Link Between Confinement, Capital, and Racism in the United States." *New England Journal on Criminal and Civil Confinement, 23*, [Online: Lexis-Nexis Academic Universe, //web.lexis-nexis.com as of October 6, 1998].

Richmond Newspapers, Inc. v. Virginia, 448 U.S. 555 (1980).

Rishikoff, H. & Wohl, A. (1996). "Private Communities or Public Governments: 'The State Will Make the Call.'" *Valparaiso University Law Review, 30,* 509-548.

Robbins, I.P. (1986, September). "Privatization of Corrections: Defining the Issues." *Federal Probation, 50,* 24-30.

Roberts, G. (1996, Feb. 2). *Personal Interview: Grady Roberts—Attorney at Law.* Pearsall, TX.

Rodriguez, M. (1993, July 8). "Justice Must Prevail." *Frio-Nueces Current,* p. 7.

Rose-Ackerman, S. (1992). *Rethinking the Progressive Agenda: The Reform of the American Regulatory State.* New York, NY: The Free Press.

Rosoff, S.M., Pontell, H.N. & Tillman, R. (1998). *Profit Without Honor: White-Collar Crime and the Looting of America.* Upper Saddle River, NJ: Prentice Hall.

Rothman, D.J. (1971). *The Discovery of the Asylum: Social Order and Disorder in the New Republic.* Boston, MA: Little, Brown.

Rubel, C. (1995). "No Larger Captive Market Than This One." *Marketing News, 29,* pp. 1, 7.

Russell-Einhorn, M. (1998). "Appendix 3: Legal Issues Relevant to Private Prisons." In D. McDonald, E. Fournier, M. Russell-Einhorn & S. Crawford, *Private Prisons in the United States: An Assessment of Current Practices* (National Institute of Corrections Cooperative Agreement #98K38GIG5). Cambridge, MA: Abt Associates, Inc.

Rützel, S. (1995). "Snitching for the Common Good: In Search of a Response to the Legal Problems Posed by Environmental Whistleblowing." *Temple Environmental Law and Technology Journal, 14,* 1-53.

Ryan, M. (1997). "Review: The State of Our Prisons." *British Journal of Criminology, 37,* 300.

Ryan, M. & Ward, T. (1980). *Privatization and the Penal System: The American Experience and the Debate in Britain.* Milton Keynes, UK: Open University Press.

Sabatino, J.M. (1997). "Privatization and Punitives: Should Government Contractors Share the Sovereign's Immunity from Exemplary Damages?" *Ohio State Law Journal, 58,* 175-239 [Online: Lexis-Nexis Academic Universe, //web.lexis-nexis.com as of October 16, 1998].

Sanders, B. (1996, Feb. 7). *Personal Interview: Benny Sanders—Former Frio County Sheriff (1965-1989).* Pearsall, TX.

Sarre, R. (1998). "Accountability and the Private Sector: Putting Accountability of Private Security Under the Spotlight." *Security Journal, 10*(2), 97-102.

Savas, E.S. (1987). *Privatization: The Key to Better Government.* Chatham, NJ: Chatham House Publishers.

Sawyer, B.N. (1996). *Getting a Better Picture: A Profile of the American Jail Association 1994 Directory of Jails.* Odessa, TX: University of Texas–Permian Basin.

Schaffer, R.G. (1996). "The Public Interest in Private Party Immunity: Extending Qualified Immunity from 42 U.S.C. § 1983 to Private Prisons." *Duke Law Journal,* 45:1049-1087.

Schiflett, K.L. & Zey, M. (1990). "Comparison of Characteristics of Private Product Producing Organizations and Public Service Organizations." *Sociological Quarterly, 31*, pp. 563-583.

Schiraldi, V. (1994). *The Undue Influence of California's Prison Guards Unions: California's Correctional-Industrial Complex—In Brief.* San Francisco, CA: Center on Juvenile and Criminal Justice.

Schlosser, E. (1998, December). "The Prison Industrial Complex." *The Atlantic Monthly, 282*(6), pp. 51-77.

Schmalleger, F. (1999). *Criminal Justice Today: An Introductory Text for the 21st Century* (5th ed.). Upper Saddle River, NJ: Prentice Hall, Inc.

Schneider, A.L. (1986). "Coproduction of Public and Private Safety: An Analysis of Bystander Intervention, 'Protective Neighboring,' and Person Protection." *Western Political Science Quarterly, 12*, 611-630.

Schuck, P.H. (1986). *Agent Orange on Trial: Mass Toxic Disasters in the Courts.* Cambridge, MA: Harvard University Press.

Schwartz, D.S. (1997). "Enforcing Small Print to Protect Big Business: Employee and Consumer Rights Claims in an Age of Compelled Arbitration." *Wisconsin Law Review, 1997*, 33-132.

Schwartz, M. (1994, September 28). "Bail Bondsmen Offer to Pay for Study." *Houston Post*, p. A-27.

Schydlower, M. & Anglin, T.R. (1995). "Financing of Substance Abuse Treatment for Children and Adolescents: Statement of the Committee on Child Health Financing and Committee on Substance, American Academy of Pediatrics." *Pediatrics, 95*(2), 308-311.

Scott, T.M. & McPherson, M. (1971). "The Development of the Private Sector of the Criminal Justice System." *Law & Society Review, 5*, 267-288.

Scull, A.T. (1977). *Decarceration: Community Treatment and the Deviant—A Radical View.* Englewood Cliffs, NJ: Prentice Hall.

Seattle Times Co. v. Rhinehart, 467 U.S. 20 (1984).

Sechrest, D.K. & Shichor, D. (1993). "Corrections Goes Public and Private in California." *Federal Probation, 57*, 3-8.

Sechrest, D.K. & Shichor, D. (1994). *Final Report: Exploratory Study of California's Community Correctional Facilities.* Parole and Community Services Division, California Department of Corrections.

Sechrest, D.K. & Shichor, D. (1996). "Comparing Public and Private Correctional Facilities in California: An Exploratory Study." In G.L. Mays & T. Gray (eds.) *Privatization and the Provision of Correctional Services: Context and Consequences.* Cincinnati, OH: Anderson Publishing Co.

Select Oversight Committee on Corrections (1995). *Comparative Evaluation of Privately-Managed Corrections Corporation of America Prison (South Central Correctional Center) and State-Managed Prototypical Prisons (Northeast Correctional Center, Northwest Correctional Center).* Nashville, TN: Tennessee Select Oversight Committee on Corrections (February, 1995).

Selznick, P. (1948). "Foundations of the Theory of Organizations." *American Sociological Review, 13*, 25-35.

Shalloo, J.P. (1929). "The Private Police of Pennsylvania." *Annals of the American Academy of Political and Social Science, 146*, 55-62.

Shalloo, J.P. (1933). *Private Police with Special Reference to Pennsylvania (Monograph 1)*. Philadelphia, PA: American Academy of Political and Social Science.

Shapiro, D.J. (1990). "Private Judging in the State of New York: A Critical Introduction." *Columbia Journal of Law and Social Problems, 23*, 275-315.

Shearing, C.D. (1992). "The Relation Between Public and Private Policing." In M. Tonry & N. Morris (eds.) *Crime and Justice: An Annual Review of Research*. Chicago, IL: University of Chicago.

Shearing, C.D. & Addario, S. (1985a). "Police Perceptions of Private Security." *Canadian Police College Journal, 9*(2), 127-153.

Shearing, C.D. & Addario, S. (1985b). "Public Perceptions of Private Security." *Canadian Police College Journal 9*(3), 225-253.

Shearing, C.D. & Stenning, P.C. (1980). "The Quiet Revolution: The Nature, Development and General Legal Implications of Private Security in Canada." *Criminal Law Quarterly, 22*, 220-248.

Shearing, C.D. & Stenning, P.C. (1981). "Modern Private Security: its Growth and Implications." In M. Tonry & N. Norris (eds.) *Crime and Justice: An Annual Review of Research*. Chicago, IL: University of Chicago.

Shearing, C.D. & Stenning, P.C. (1983). "Private Security: Implications for Social Control." *Social Problems, 30*, 493-506.

Shearing, C.D. & Stenning, P.C. (eds.) (1987). *Private Policing*. Newbury Park, CA: Sage.

Shenk, J.W. (1995). "The Perils of Privatization." *Washington Monthly, 27*(5), pp. 16-24.

Sher, A. (1997). "Talks on Prison Privatization Go Behind Closed Hotel Doors." *The Nashville Banner*, p. A-1.

Shichor, D. (1993). "The Corporate Context of Private Corrections." *Crime, Law and Social Change, 20*, 113-138.

Shichor, D. (1995). *Punishment for Profit: Private Prisons/Public Concerns*. Thousand Oaks, CA: Sage.

Shichor, D. (1999). "Privatizing Correctional Institutions: An Organizational Perspective." *The Prison Journal, 79*(2), 226-249.

Shichor, D. & Sechrest, D. (1995). "Quick Fixes in Corrections: Reconsidering Private and Public For-Profit Facilities." *The Prison Journal, 4*, 457-478.

Shils, E. (1997). *The Virtue of Civility: Selected Essays on Liberalism, Tradition, and Civil Society*. Indianapolis, IN: Liberty Fund.

Shlapentokh, V. (1996). "Russia: Privatization and Illegalization of Social and Political Life." *Washington Quarterly, 19*(1), 65-85.

Shofner, J.H. (1981a). "Forced Labor in the Florida Forests, 1880-1950." *Journal of Forest History, 25*(1), 14-25.

Shofner, J.H. (1981b). "The Legacy of Racial Slavery: Free Enterprise and Forced Labor in Florida in the 1940s." *Journal of Southern History, 47*(3), 411-426.

Shofner, J.H. (1981c). "Postscript to the Martin Tabert Case: Peonage as Usual in the Florida Turpentine Camps." *Florida Historical Quarterly, 60*(2), 161-173.

Silverman, I.J. & Vega, M. (1996). *Corrections: A Comprehensive View.* Minneapolis/ St.Paul, MN: West Publishing Company.

Skerrett, J. (1998, April 21). "Corrections Corp. Firm Joins with Affiliate in REIT Bid." *Chicago Tribune*, p. 2A.

Smith, B.A. (1989). "Female Admissions and Paroles from the Western House of Refuge in the 1880s: An Historical Example of Community Corrections." *Journal of Research in Crime and Delinquency, 26*(1), 36-66.

Smith, B. (1933). *Rural Crime Control.* New York, NY: Columbia University Institute of Public Administration.

Smith, J.W. (1994, April 28). *Letter to Consolidated Financial Resources, Inc.: Re: Municipal Lease-Purchase Agreement Dated as of April 19, 1994.* Pearsall, TX: Office of the Frio County Attorney.

Smith, J.W. (1995, Feb. 16). *Letter to Mr. Tom Shirey, President, Dove Development Corporation: Re: Mr. Shirey's Response to Commissioner Espinosa's Letter of December 2, 1994.* Pearsall, TX: Office of the Frio County Attorney.

Smith, J.W. (1999a, May 24). *Telephone Interview: Regarding Itemization of Purchases from the 1994 Loan for $1,000,000 to DDC Using Frio County Ad Valorem Taxes as Collateral.* Pearsall, TX: Office of the Frio County Attorney.

Smith, J.W. (1999b, May 26). *Telephone interview: Regarding the April 19, 1994 resolution for eminent domain to obtain fee simple title to land adjacent to the Frio County Jail to accommodate the jail expansion.* Pearsall, TX: Office of the Frio County Attorney.

Smith, J.W. (undated). *Work Product Notes of County Attorney J.W. Smith: Summary of the Contracts and Amendments with Dove Development Corporation.* Pearsall, TX: Office of the Frio County Attorney.

South, N. (1983). "The Corruption of Commercial Justice: The Case of the Private Security Sector." In M. Clarke (ed.) *Corruption: Causes, Consequences and Control.* London, UK: Francis Pinter.

South, N. (1984). "Private Security, the Division of Policing Labor and the Commercial Compromise of the State." In S. Spitzer & A. Scull (eds.) *Research in Law, Deviance and Social Control.* Greenwich, CT: JAI.

South, N. (1988). *Policing for Profit: The Private Security Sector.* London, UK: Sage.

South, N. (1994). "Privatizing Policing in the European Market: Some Issues for Theory, Policy and Research." *European Sociological Review, 10*, 219-233.

Southland Corp. v. Keating, 465 U.S. 1 (1984).

Spitzer, S. & Scull, A. (1977). "Privatization and Capitalist Development: The Case of the Private Police." *Social Problems, 25*, 18-29.

Spragens, T.A. (1986). "Reconstructing Liberal Theory: Reason and Liberal Culture." In A.J. Damico (ed.) *Liberals on Liberalism.* Totowa, NJ: Rowman & Littlefield.

Staples, W.G. (1990). "In the Interest of the State: Production Politics in the Nineteenth Century Prison." *Sociological Perspectives, 33*(3), 375-395.

Starr, P. (1988). "The Meaning of Privatization." *Yale Law and Policy Review, 6,* 6-41.

Starr, P. (1987). "The Limits of Privatization." *Proceedings of the Academy of Political Sciences, 3*(3), 124-137.

State ex rel. Taylor v. Halleck, et al., 98-CO-50.

Stead, P.J. (1983). *The Police of France.* New York, NY: MacMillan.

Steinberg, A. (1984). "From Private Prosecution to Plea Bargaining: Criminal Prosecution, the District Attorney, and American Legal History." *Crime & Delinquency, 30*(4), 568-593.

Steinberg, A. (1989). *The Transformation of Criminal Justice in Philadelphia, 1800-1880.* Charlotte, NC: University of North Carolina Press.

Stenning, P. & Shearing, C. (1979). "Private Security and Private Justice." *British Journal of Law and Society, 6,* 261-271.

Sterk, S.E. (1981). "Enforceability of Agreements to Arbitrate: An Examination of the Public Policy Defense." *Cardozo Law Review, 2,* 481-543.

Stern, G.M. (1976). *The Buffalo Creek Disaster: The Story of the Survivors' Unprecedented Lawsuit.* New York, NY: Random House.

Stern, V. (1998). *A Sin Against the Future: Imprisonment in the World.* Boston, MA: Northeastern University Press.

Stewart, J. (1985). "Public Safety and Private Policing." *Public Administration Review, 45*(11), 758-765.

Stewart, J. (1996). "The Next Eden—The Movement Into Gated Communities Is Not About Escape. It's About Building Neighborhoods." *California Lawyer, 16,* 38-45.

Stinebaker, J. & Smith, M. (1996, September 7). "Shutdown of Pretrial Unit Sought: State Judge Favors Private Bail Firms." *Houston Chronicle,* p. A-1.

Stipanowich, T.J. (1997). "Punitive Damages and the Consumerization of Arbitration." *Northwestern University Law Review, 92,* 1-68.

Stolz, B. (1975). "The Massachusetts Department of Youth Services 1969-1973: A Study of How Policy Change Within an Agency Is Affected by Its External Political Environment." Unpublished doctoral dissertation, Brandeis University, Waltham, MA.

Stolz, B. (1978). "Prisons as Political Institutions: What Are the Implications for Prison Ministry?" In *Proceedings of the American Correctional Association,* 11-20.

Stolz, B. (1984a). "Decarceration in Massachusetts: A Study of Disjointed Incrementalism." *Criminal Justice Review, 9*(2), 53-62.

Stolz, B. (1984b). "Interest Groups and Criminal Law: The Case of Federal Criminal Code Revision." *Crime & Delinquency, 30*(1), 91-106.

Stolz, B. (1985). "Congress and Criminal Justice Policy Making: The Impact of Interest Groups and Symbolic Politics." *Journal of Criminal Justice, 13*(4), 307-319.

Stolz, B. (1997). "Privatizing Corrections: Changing the Corrections Policy-Making Subgovernment." *The Prison Journal, 77*(1), 92-111.

Struckhoff, D.R. (1994). *The American Sheriff.* Joliet, IL: Justice Research Institute.

Sullivan, H.J. (1987). "Privatization of Public Services: A Growing Threat to Constitutional Rights." *Public Administration Review, 47*(6), 461-467.

Sunstein, C.R. (1990). *After the Rights Revolution: Reconceiving the Regulatory State.* Cambridge, MA: Harvard University Press.

Swope, C. (1998, October). "The Inmate Bazaar." *Congressional Quarterly DBA Governing Magazine*, p. 18.

Sykes, G. (1957). *The Society of Captives.* Princeton, NJ: Princeton University Press.

Takacs, G. (1994). "Tyranny on the Streets: Connecticut's Need for the Regulation of Bounty Hunters." *QLR, 14*(3), 479-527.

Tate v. Short, 401 U.S. 395 (1971)

Tatge, M. (1998a, July 17). "Judge to Rule on Youngstown Prison Security Issue." *Cleveland Plain Dealer*, p. 5B.

Tatge, M. (1998b, August 18). "More CCA Prison Assaults Revealed." *Cleveland Plain Dealer*, p. 5B.

Tatge, M. (1998c, September 2). "Transferred Inmates Attack New Mexico Guards." *Cleveland Plain Dealer*, p. 4B.

Taylor, W.B. (1993). *Brokered Justice: Race, Politics, and Mississippi Prisons, 1798-1992.* Columbus, OH: Ohio State University Press.

Teeters, N.K. (1955). *The Cradle of the American Penitentiary: The Walnut Street Jail at Philadelphia 1773-1835.* Philadelphia, PA: Pennsylvania Prison Society.

Tennessee Select Oversight Committee on Corrections (1995). *Comparative Evaluation of Privately-Managed Corrections Corporation of America Prison (South Central Correctional Center) and State-Managed Prototypical Prisons (Northeast Correctional Center, Northwest Correctional Center)—Executive Summary.* Nashville, TN: Author.

Tewksbury, R.A. (1997). *Introduction to Corrections* (3rd ed.). New York, NY: Glencoe/McGraw-Hill.

Texas Commission on Jail Standards (1999, May 1). *Jail Population Report.* Austin, TX: Author.

Texas Commission on Jail Standards (1999). *Texas County Jail Population, February 1, 1999.* Austin, TX: Author.

Texas Department of Criminal Justice (1992, Sept. 4). *Inmate Housing Payment Agreement with Frio County.* Austin, TX: Author.

Texas Department of Criminal Justice (1994, April 22). *State of Texas Purchase Voucher #94012658: Re: Temporary Housing Agreement, Lump Sum Payment for Housing and Care of 336 Inmates from 6-1-94 thru 8-31-94 at $3,969.25/Bed ($1,333,332.00).* Austin, TX: State of Texas.

Texas Sunset Advisory Commission (1991a). *Information Report on Contracts for Correction Facilities and Services: Recommendations to the Governor of Texas and Member of the Seventy-Second Legislature—Final report.* Austin, TX: Author.

Texas Sunset Advisory Commission (1991b). *Information Report on Contracts and Correctional Facilities and Services, Recommendations to the Governor of Texas and Members of the Seventy-Second Legislature.* Austin, TX: Texas Sunset Advisory Commission.

Theoharis, A.G. & Cox, J.S. (1988). *The Boss: J. Edgar Hoover and the Great American Inquisition.* Philadelphia, PA: Temple University Press.

Thomas, C.W. (1995). *Correctional Privatization: The Issues and the Evidence.* Toronto, CN: The Fraser Institute.

Thomas, C.W. (1996a). *Correctional Privatization: The Issues and the Evidence.* Vancouver, British Columbia, CN: The Fraser Institute.

Thomas, C.W. (1996b). *Open Letter to Representative Bill McCollum.* [Online: http://www.ucc.uconn.edu/~wwwsoci/gaocwt.htmlInternet].

Thomas, C.W. (1996c). *Testimony Regarding Correctional Privatization.* Subcommittee on Crime, House Committee on the Judiciary. Washington, DC.

Thomas, C.W. (1997). *Comparing the Cost and Performance of Public and Private Prisons in Arizona.* Center for Studies in Criminology & Law, University of Florida (for the Arizona Department of Corrections).

Thomas, C.W. & Bolinger, D. (1997). *Private Adult Correctional Facility Census: A December 31, 1997 Statistical Profile* [Online: //web.crim.ufl.edu/pcp/census/11th.html as of November 27, 1998]. Private Corrections Project, University of Florida.

Thomas, C.W. & Bolinger, D. (1999a). *Private Adult Correctional Facility Census: A "Real Time" Statistical Profile* [Online: //web.crim.ufl.edu/pcp/census/1999/Market.html as of January 29, 1999]. Private Corrections Project, University of Florida.

Thomas, C.W. & Bolinger, D. (1999b). *Private Adult Correctional Facility Census: Private Prisons/Alternative Programs* [Online: http://web.crim.ufl.edu/pcp/census/1999/cns-1altpro.html]. Private Corrections Project, University of Florida.

Thomas, R.C., Gookin, K., Keating, B., Whitener, V., Williams, R.M., Crane, R. & Broom, C. (1996). *Department of Corrections Privatization Feasibility Study (96-2).* Legislative Budget Committee, State of Washington.

Thompson, C. (1998, December 5). "D.C. Prisoner Transfer Faulted." *Washington Post,* p. B1.

Thompson, J. (1996, November 6). "Texas Faces Problem with Private Prisons: Inmates Sent from Other States Can Evade Law." *Dallas Morning News,* p. 19A.

Tolchin, M. (1985, November 29). "Private Guards Get New Role in Public Law Enforcement." *New York Times,* p. D27.

Traub, S.H. (1988). "Rewards, Bounty Hunting, and Criminal Justice in the West: 1865-1900." *Western Historical Quarterly, 19*(3), 287-301.

Trevino, R. (1992, Nov. 25). *Exhibit D: Statement by Roger Trevino in Adolfo Alvarez, Sr. v. Mona Hoyle, et al., Cause No. 92-00148-CVF, 1992.*

Turnbull, L. (1998, July 27). "Breakout Spurs Talk of Prison Closing." *Columbus Dispatch,* pp. 1A, 2A.

Turner, A. (1996, August 23). "Feds to Review Handling or Riot at Texas Prison." *Houston Chronicle,* p. A33.

U.S. Congress, Senate (1939). *Committee on Education and Labor. Private Police Systems, Report No. 6, Part 2. 76th Congress, 1st Session.* Washington, DC: U.S. Government Printing Office.

U.S. Department of Health and Human Services (1995). *Overview of the National Drug and Alcoholism Treatment Unit Survey (NDATUS): 1993 and 1980-1992.* Washington, DC: U.S. Department of Health and Human Services.

United Press International (1985, April 12). "McWherter Sells Stock in CCA, Honey Alexander Undecided." *Regional News, AM Cycle.*

United States v. Francoeur, 547 F.2d 891 (5th Cir.), *cert. denied*, 431 U.S. 932 (1977).

United States v. Salerno, 481 U.S. 739 (1987).

Urban Institute (1989). *Comparison of Privately and Publicly Operated Correctional Facilities in Kentucky and Massachusetts.* Washington, DC: U.S. Department of Justice, National Institute of Justice.

Usher, J.A. (1992). "Privatization in Criminal Justice: One Perspective in Southern California." In G.W. Bowman, S. Hakim & P. Seidenstat (eds.) *Privatizing the United States Justice System: Police, Adjudication, and Corrections Services from the Private Sector.* Jefferson, NC: McFarland.

Vagg, J. (1994). *Prison Systems: A Comparative Study of Accountability in England, France, Germany, and the Netherlands.* New York, NY: Oxford.

Van den Berg, E.M.C. (1995). "Crime Prevention on Industrial Sites: Security Through Public-Private Partnerships." *Security Journal, 6*(1), 27-35.

van den Haag, E. (1975). *Punishing Criminals.* New York, NY: Basic Books.

Van Vugt, M. (1997). Concerns About the Privatization of Public Goods: A Social Dilemma Analysis. *Social Psychology Quarterly, 60*(4), 355-367.

Vara, R. (1995, July 22). "Healing the Heart: Prayer Vigils Held to Mourn Violence Victims." *Houston Chronicle*, Religion Section, p. 1.

Vardalis, J.J. (1992). "Privatization of Public Police: Houston, Texas." *Security Journal, 3*(4), 210-214.

Vice President Gore's National Partnership for Reinventing Government (1999). *Electronic Town Hall Wall.* [Available: http://www.npr.gov].

Vickers, T. (1999). *Insider Trading.* Quicken.com.

Wackenhut Corporation (1998). *Wackenhut Corporation Form 10-K405 12/28/97— Security an Exchange Commission* [Online: //www.sec.gov/Archives/edgar/data/102030/0000950144-98-002859.t as of February 20, 1999]. Palm Beach Gardens, FL: Wackenhut Corporation.

Wade, P. (1997a, April 30). "Senators Attend Prison-Bill Briefing Closed to Public." *The Commercial Appeal*, p. A-1.

Wade, P. (1997b, April 20). "Insider Job? Secrecy Clouds Prison Privatization." *The Commercial Appeal*, p. A-6).

Wade, P. (1997c, May 17, 1997). "Kyle Tries to Soothe Privatizing Skeptics; Foes Fear Prison Concept Detrimental to Safety, Society." *The Commerical Appeal*, p. B-1.

Wade, P. (1997d, October 24). "Lawmakers Uneasy on Provision for Prisons." *The Commercial Appeal*, p. B-1.

Wade, P. (1997e, November 6). "Sundquist Hits Wall in Prison Power Try; Lawmakers Seek Voice in Privatization Move." *The Commercial Appeal*, p. B-1.

Wade, P. (1998a, September 2). "Bill to Privatize Prisons Falls on Hard Times." *The Commercial Appeal*, p. B-1.

Wade, P. (1998b, September 24), "Sundquist Slows Privatized Prison Rush," *The Commercial Appeal*, p. B-1.

Waldman, M. (1990). *Who Robbed America? A Citizens Guide to the Savings & Loan Scandal.* New York, NY: Random House.

Waldrum, J. (1996, March 4). *Personal Interview: Joan Waldrum—Former Frio County Auditor 1986-1991.* Pearsall, TX.

Walker, D.B. & Richards, M. (1996). "A Service Under Change: Current Issues in Policing in England and Wales." *Police Studies, 19*(1), 53-73.

Walker, D.R. (1988). *Penology for Profit: A History of the Texas Prison System, 1867-1912.* College Station, TX: Texas A&M Press.

Walker, S. (1980). *Popular Justice: A History of American Criminal Justice.* New York, NY: Oxford University Press.

Walker, S. (1998a). *Popular Justice: A History of American Criminal Justice (2nd ed.).* New York, NY: Oxford University Press.

Walker, S. (1998b). *Sense and Nonsense About Crime and Drugs: A Policy Guide* (4th ed.). Belmont, CA: West/Wadsworth Publishing Company.

Walker, S., Spohn, C. & DeLone, M. (1996). *The Color of Justice: Race, Ethnicity and Crime in America.* Belmont, CA: Wadsworth Publishing Company.

Walsh, W.F. & Donovan, E.J. (1989). "Private Security and Community Policing: Evaluation and Comment." *Journal of Criminal Justice, 17*(3), 187-197.

Walsh, W.F., Donovan, E.J. & McNicholas, J.F. (1992). "The Starrett Protective Service: Private Policing in an Urban Community." In G.W. Bowman, S. Hakim & P. Seidenstat (eds.) *Privatizing the United States Justice System: Police, Adjudication, and Corrections Services from the Private Sector.* Jefferson, NC: McFarland.

Ward, G. (1999, June 16). "Change at Top for CCA: Appointment Comes Amid Money Worries." *The Tennessean*, pp. E1, E6.

Ward, R.D. & Rogers, W.W. (1987). *Convicts, Coal, and the Banner Mine Tragedy.* Tuscaloosa, AL: University of Alabama Press.

Ware, S.J. (1994). "Punitive Damages in Arbitration: Contracting Out of Government's Role in Punishment and Preemption of State Law." *Fordham Law Review, 63*, 529-572.

Ware, S.J. (1999). "Default Rules from Mandatory Rules: Privatizing Law Through Arbitration." *Minnesota Law Review, 83*, 703-754.

Warren, B. (1998, October 22). "Prison Official Fired as Escape Probe Continues." *The Tennessean*, p. A1.

Watson, E.M., Stone, A.R. & DeLuca, J. (1998). *Strategies for Community Policing.* Upper Saddle River, NJ: Prentice Hall.

Watson, J. (1995, March 29). *Testimony Given Before the Texas House of Representatives, Criminal Jurisprudence Subcommittee Regarding House Bill 1396.* Austin, TX: Texas Legislative Reference Library.

Weeks v. United States, 232 U.S. 383 (1914).

Weinstein, B.S. (1997). "In Defense of Jeffrey Wigand: A First Amendment Challenge to the Enforcement of Employee Confidentiality Agreements Against Whistleblowers." *South Carolina Law Review, 49,* 129-165.

Weinstein, J.B. (1996). "Some Benefits and Risks of Privatization of Justice Through ADR." *Ohio State Journal on Dispute Resolution, 11,* 241-295.

Weiss, R.P. (1978, Spring/Summer). "The Emergence and Transformation of Private Detective Industrial Policing in the United States, 1850-1940." *Crime and Social Justice,* (2), 35-48.

Weiss, R.P. (1981). "The Private Detective Agency in the Development of Policing Forms In The Rural and Frontier United States." *Insurgent Sociologist, 10*(4), 7-21.

Welle, E.A. (1996). "Public Service—Opting Out of Public Provision: Constraints and Policy Considerations." *Denver University Law Review, 73,* 1221-1235.

West, P. (1998a, January 17). "Prison Bill Highlights." *The Commercial Appeal,* p. A-1.

West, P. (1998b, April 1). "Plan to Privatize Prisons Faces Tough Time in Senate." *The Commercial Appeal,* p. A-7.

West, P. (200, March 31). "Prison Company Reports $53 Million Loss, Has Doubts About its Future." *The Associated Press State & Local Wire* [Online: Lexis-Nexis Academic Universe, //web.lexis-nexis.com as of March 31, 2000].

Wexler, H.K., Falkin, G.P., Lipton, D.S. & Rosenblum, A.B. (1992). "Outcome Evaluation of a Prisons Therapeutic Community for Substance Abuse Treatment." In C.G. Leukefeld & F.M. Tims (eds.) *Drug Abuse Treatment in Prisons and Jails.* Washington, DC: National Institute on Drug Abuse, U.S. Government Printing Office.

Wice, P. (1984). *Freedom for Sale: A National Study of Pretrial Release.* Lexington, MA: Lexington Books.

Wicker, T. (1975). *A Time to Die.* New York, NY: Quadrangle/New York Times Book Co.

Wilko v. Swan, 346 U.S. 427 (1953).

Williams v. Illinois, 399 U.S. 235 (1970).

Williams, S. (1992, October 14). *Personal Interview: Sid Williams—Frio County Judge.* Pearsall, TX: Office of the County Judge.

Williams, S. (1994, April 22). *Letter to Mr. Milton Mallory, Texas Department of Criminal Justice Authorizing Officers of Dove Development Corporation to Pick Up the Check for Jail Construction.* Pearsall, TX: Office of the County Judge.

Wilson, J. (1998, October 16). "CCA Firm Celebrates Growth at Silverdale Anniversary Event." *Chattanooga News Free-Press,* p. A-4.

Windham, T.R. (1992). "A Police Chief's View of Privatization of the Criminal Justice System." In G.W. Bowman, S. Hakim & P. Seidenstat (eds.) *Privatizing the United States Justice System: Police, Adjudication, and Corrections Services from the Private Sector.* Jefferson, NC: McFarland.

Wolfe, A. (1989). *Whose Keeper? Social Science and Moral Obligation.* Los Angeles, CA: University of California Press.

Woods, D. (1995, November 27). *Letter from Warden Darrell Woods, Frio Detention Division to Tom Shirey, President/Treasurer, Dove Development Corporation.* Pearsall, TX: Dove Development Corporation.

Woods, D. (1996, Feb. 4). *Personal Interview: Darrell Woods, Warden, Frio Detention Division 1994-1996.* Pearsall, TX: Dove Development Corporation.

Woods, D. (1998, July 21). *Personal Interview: Darrell Woods, Former Warden, Frio Detention Division 1994-1996.* Pleasanton TX.

World Research Group (1997). *2nd Annual Privatizing Correctional Facilities.* New York, NY. World Research Group.

World Research Group (1998). *3rd Annual Privatizing Correctional Facilities.* New York, NY: World Research Group.

World Research Group (1999). *4th Annual Privatizing Correctional Facilities.* New York, NY: World Research Group.

Wright, G.C. (1990). *Racial Violence in Kentucky, 1865-1940: Lynchings, Mob Rule, and "Legal Lynchings."* Baton Rouge, LA: Louisiana State University Press.

Wyatt v. Cole, 504 U.S. 158 (1992).

Yergin, D. & Stanislaw, J. (1998). *The Commanding Heights: The Battle Between Government and the Marketplace That Is Remaking the Modern World.* New York, NY: Simon & Schuster.

Zarate, J.C. (1998). "The Emergence of a New Dog of War: Private International Security Companies, International Law, and the New World Disorder." *Stanford Journal of International Law, 34*(1), 75-162.

Zedlewski, E.W. (1992). "Private Security and Controlling Crime." In G.W. Bowman, S. Hakim & P. Seidenstat (eds.) *Privatizing the United States Justice System: Police, Adjudication, and Corrections Services from the Private Sector.* Jefferson, NC: McFarland.

Ziegenhagen, E.A. & Brosnan, D. (1991). "Citizen Orientations Toward State and Non-State Policing." *Law & Policy, 13*(3), 245-257.

Ziff, H.L. (1967). "Seizures by Private Parties: Exclusion in Criminal Cases." *Stanford Law Review, 19*(3), 608-618.

Zimring, F.E. & Hawkins, G. (1997). *Crime Is Not the Problem: Lethal Violence in America.* New York, NY: Oxford University Press.

Zupan, L.L. (1991). *Jails: Reform and the New Generation Philosophy.* Cincinnati, OH: Anderson Publishing Co.

Index

Biographical Sketches

Volume Editors

David Shichor is Professor Emeritus of Criminal Justice at California State University, San Bernardino. He received his undergraduate degree from the Hebrew University in Jerusalem in Sociology and History. His Ph.D. is in Sociology from the University of Southern California. He has conducted research on juvenile institutions, restorative justice, victimology, punishment, crime among the elderly, investment fraud, and prison privatization. He is the author of *Punishment for Profit: Private Prisons/Public Concerns*, and has co-authored three other books. He has published more than 20 chapters in various books. His latest articles appeared in *Crime & Delinquency; The Prison Journal; The Howard Journal of Criminal Justice; Juvenile and Family Court Journal; Women and Criminal Justice; Crime, Law and Social Change;* and *Federal Probation.* He has two additional co-edited books forthcoming.

Michael J. Gilbert is Associate Professor of Criminal Justice at The University of Texas at San Antonio. His research interests focus on adult corrections, correctional privatization, juvenile delinquency, violence, white-collar crime, and organization crime. He has published articles in *Public Productivity Review; Public Personnel Management; Criminal Justice Review;* and *Crime, Law and Social Change,* and has edited books. He also has more than 20 years of experience in corrections as a manager, trainer, consultant, and researcher. He was an adjunct instructor at the National Academy of Corrections between 1980 and 1989. He continues to serve as a consultant to the National Institute of Corrections. He is a past president of the International Association of Correc-

371

tional Training Personnel. He holds a Doctor of Public Administration degree from Arizona State University (1990).

Contributing Authors

James D. Calder, Ph.D. is Associate Professor of Criminal Justice at The University of Texas at San Antonio. His teaching and research specialties include private and government security; legal issues in security management; American criminal justice history; and intelligence and national security. He has published several articles on these topics in *Security Journal; Journal of Criminal Justice; Crime, Law and Social Change;* and *Journal of Contemporary Criminal Justice*. A forthcoming essay on robbery will appear in the *Encyclopedia of Criminology and Deviant Behavior*. His most recent book appeared in 1999, *Intelligence, Espionage and Related Topics: An Annotated Bibliography of Serial Journal and Magazine Scholarship, 1844-1998*. A previous book, *The Origins and Development of Federal Crime Control Policy: Herbert Hoover's Initiatives*, discussed national crime prevention policies. He is working on a history of private police in wartime American industrial factories.

Scott D. Camp moved to the Office of Research and Evaluation at the Federal Bureau of Prisons as a Social Science Research Analyst after completing a Ph.D. in Sociology at The Pennsylvania State University. He is the author of *Worker Response to Plant Closings: Steelworkers in Johnstown and Youngstown* (Garland 1995). Much of his current research focuses on using survey data collected from inmates and staff to compare prisons. His research has appeared in *The Prison Journal, Justice Quarterly*, and *Corrections Management Quarterly*. Dr. Camp and his colleague Dr. Gerald G. Gaes have produced several reports on private prisons, and their latest work, *Private Prisons in the United States, 1999: An Assessment of Growth, Performance, Custody Standards, and Training Requirements* (March 2000), was prepared in response to a request from the Appropriations Committee of the House of Representatives of the U.S. Congress.

Steven J. Cuvelier has served as a population projection specialist for the Ohio Department of Rehabilitation and Corrections and as a senior research associate for the National Council on Crime and Delinquency. He received his doctorate in sociology and minor in public administration from Ohio State University in 1988 and is presently an associate professor of criminal justice at Sam Houston State University. His research for the past eight years has centered on inmate classification and pretrial release issues. However, his more recent work has focused on the correctional-industrial complex and the reinvention of probation. The long-term goal of his academic research is to develop decision support technology using criminal justice applications for fuzzy neural networks, adaptive classification systems, and fuzzy geo-informational systems.

Gerry Gaes received a Ph.D. in Social Psychology from the State University of New York at Albany in 1980. He joined the Bureau of Prisons in 1980 and has worked in the Office of Research from 1980 to the present. From 1985-1987, he was assigned to the United States Sentencing Commission to develop a population projection micro-simulation to assess the implications of the U.S. Sentencing Guidelines. He has served as Chief of the Office of Research since 1988. His most recent chapters focus on prison rehabilitation programs. These works are *"Adult Correctional Treatment"* in *Prisons, Crime and Justice: A Review of Research*, edited by Michael Tonry and Joan Petersilia and *"Correctional Treatment"* in *The Handbook of Crime and Punishment*, edited by Michael Tonry. His current research interests include prison privatization, evaluation methodology, inmate gangs, inmate classification, criminal justice simulations, prison crowding, prison violence, and the effectiveness of prison program interventions on post-release outcomes.

Gilbert Geis is Professor Emeritus, Department of Criminology, Law and Society, University of California, Irvine. He is a former president of the American Society of Criminology and recipient of its Edwin H. Sutherland award for research. His recent books are: *A Trial of Witches: A Seventeenth Century Witchcraft Trials* with Ivan Bunn (London: Routledge, 1997), and *Crimes of the Century: From Leopold and Loeb to O.J. Simpson* with Leigh Bienen (Boston: Northeastern University Press).

Michael J. Gilbert—*see* **Volume Editors** *section above*

Michael A. Hallett, Ph.D., is Associate Professor of Criminal Justice at the University of North Florida in Jacksonville. Dr. Hallett has testified before three state legislatures on issues related to prison privatization, including Tennessee's experience with Corrections Corporation of America. He has worked as a consultant for such organizations as the Tennessee Supreme Court, American Judicature Society, and the National Center for State Courts. He is currently completing a study of outcomes in judicial elections across the American South.

Richard G. Kiekbusch, Ph.D., is an Assistant Professor of Criminology at The University of Texas–Permian Basin, where he directs the master's degree program in Criminal Justice Administration. He holds a BA, MA, and a Ph.D., all in Sociology, from the University of Notre Dame. Dr. Kiekbusch has more than 20 years of experience in correctional administration—including work in juvenile corrections, jail administration, and private corrections. He is active in a number of professional associations, and was president of the American Jail Association in 1992-93. He has provided expert witness and other consulting services in the area of correctional management. He is a contributing editor for *Corrections Managers' Report* and serves on the editorial boards of several other practitioner publications and scholarly journals.

J. Frank Lee, Ph.D., is Professor and Chair of the Department of Criminal Justice at Middle Tennessee State University. He also serves as Chairman of the Board of Control of the Tennessee Corrections Institute. Dr. Lee also serves as a member of the Tennessee Bureau of Investigations Statistical Analysis Advisory Board.

Alan Mobley is a Ph.D. candidate in the Department of Criminology, Law and Society at the University of California, Irvine. His research interests include prisons, the sociology of law, and peacemaking.

Frank T. Morn holds an undergraduate degree and a master's degree from Brigham Young University in ancient history. He earned a Doctorate from the University of Chicago in Law and Social History. Has written several books which include: *"The Eye That Never Sleeps": A History of the Pinkerton Detective Agency*; and *Academic Politics and The History of Criminal Justice Education*; and *Foundations of Criminal Investigation*. Also in progress is *A Puritan in Babylon: Robert McClaughry and the Criminal Justice Profession in the Late Nineteenth Century*. He has taught in China, Russia, and Puerto Rico. Currently he is professor of criminal justice sciences at Illinois State University.

Dennis W. Potts is a doctoral student attending the George J. Beto Criminal Justice Center at Sam Houston State University. Mr. Potts has worked in the criminal justice system since 1981, serving in various capacities in law enforcement, community corrections, and, for the past decade, in pretrial services delivery. In addition, Mr. Potts serves as an adjunct sociology instructor with Our Lady of the Lake University's Houston Weekend Program.

Matthew A. Robby is a Research Assistant in the Criminal Justice Department of California State University, San Bernardino. For the past three years, he has worked on evaluation projects involving victim/offender reconciliation, at-risk youth in alternative schools, offenders in substance abuse treatment programs in corrections and in drug courts. He is currently a Research Assistant for the evaluation of the San Bernardino County Mentally Ill Offender Crime Reduction Program. He received a B.A. degree in Criminal Justice and a B.A. degree in Social

Sciences from California State University, San Bernardino. In June of 2000, he received an M.A. degree in Criminal Justice from California State University, San Bernardino.

Steve Russell served as a trial judge in Texas courts for 17 years, and has been taking judicial assignments as a former judge for five years. He is currently Assistant Professor of Criminal Justice at The University of Texas at San Antonio. In addition to judicial policy issues, he has published on white-collar crime, domestic violence, and American Indian justice policy. He is the Immediate Past President of the Texas Indian Bar Association.

Dale K. Sechrest is a Professor of Criminal Justice at California State University, San Bernardino, where he has taught since 1990. Prior to this, he taught in Florida and worked on national commissions on correctional manpower and standards and accreditation. He completed a study of methadone programs at the Center for Criminal Justice, Harvard Law School, and directed community-based research projects in Santa Clara County, California. He has served as a Deputy Chief Probation Officer. Publications include articles on privatization in corrections, drug programs, diversion, community corrections, and white-collar crime. He has published the following books *Jail Management and Liability Issues* (1989), *Three Strikes and You're Out: Vengeance as Public Policy* (1996), and *The Changing Career of the Correctional Officer* (1998). He earned a Doctorate in Criminology from the University of California at Berkeley in 1974.

David Shichor—*see* **Volume Editors** *section above*

Beverly A. Smith received a B.A. in history and English from Ashland College, now Ashland University, and both an M.A. and a Ph.D. in nineteenth-century history from Miami University. Before coming to the Department of Criminal Justice Sciences at Illinois State University in 1983, she held visiting positions at the University of Cincinnati, Western Michigan University, and the State University of New York at Albany. At SUNY-Albany she also completed a two-year post-doctoral fellowship from NIMH in the Graduate School of Criminal Justice. A full professor at Illinois State since 1990, she has participated in two interdisciplinary NEH summer seminars. She has published in Ireland, England, Canada, and Germany, as well as the United States, on nineteenth-century prisons, murder in rural areas, jail populations, female criminality, and links between popular culture and crime.

Barbara A. Stolz is a political scientist/criminologist. She has held positions in academia and in government. As a Fulbright scholar, she taught American politics at Yaroslavl State University in Russia. Her primary research interest is criminal justice policymaking. She has published articles on the role of symbolic politics, interest groups, and sub-governments in determining U.S. criminal justice policies regarding capital punishment, juvenile delinquency, drug control, corrections, and domestic violence. In addition, she has written about symbolic politics and the law-abiding in Russia. She has also published a book titled *Still Struggling: America's Low-Income Women Confronting the 1980s*. Currently, she is a senior evaluator engaged in research on criminal justice issues.